# Small and Expanding Businesses: Getting the Tax Right

Kerri O'Connell

Published by
Chartered Accountants Ireland
Chartered Accountants House
47–49 Pearse Street
Dublin 2
www.charteredaccountants.ie



Source legislation and other official material is reproduced from Irish Government sources further to the European Communities (Re-Use of Public Sector Information) Regulations 2005 (S.I. No. 279 of 2005) as amended.

The author and the publisher acknowledge that the extracts from *Special Condition 3* of the Contract for Sale (© Law Society of Ireland) are reproduced in Chapter 3 with the approval of the Law Society of Ireland, subject to the caveat that they are extracts only and that before any transaction is embarked upon, proper legal advice should be obtained by reference to the entirety of the current Law Society Clauses.



ISBN: 978-1-910374-72-6

Typeset by Datapage
Printed by CPI Group (UK) Ltd, Croydon, CR0 4YY

FSC
www.fsc.org
MIX
Paper from responsible sources
FSC® C013604

*"Small business isn't for the faint of heart. It's for the brave, the patient and the persistent. It's for the overcomer."*

*This book is dedicated to all overcomers.*

# Contents

# Introduction

This book is intended as a roadmap of the tax issues typically encountered by small and expanding businesses in Ireland, signposting the tax implications of a variety of business decisions and providing general guidance. It is written in an informal and accessible style, with a minimum of jargon, to ensure that the tax concepts can be clearly understood.

The book is aimed at the smart business owner, often sourcing ad hoc tax information from many sources and wondering how it could impact *their* business. It is also aimed at accountants and lawyers, who must know enough to understand the possible tax implications of various business decisions/transactions and to also know when to call in the tax specialists. This book is also aimed at the student, certainly of tax but also of finance and entrepreneurship, who needs an understanding of the tax environment in which Irish business operates.

The focus is on four main tax heads:

- payroll taxes,
- VAT,
- income tax on business profits earned by a sole trader or partnership, and
- corporation tax on business profits earned by a company,

as these are the taxes that affect most Irish businesses. While other taxes are briefly mentioned to illustrate certain points, they are beyond the scope of this book.

## Overview of the Book

The opening chapters are aimed at the new business, looking at the tax implications of business structures (**Chapter 1**) and financing the business (**Chapter 2**). These chapters give an overview of the tax issues involved and are intended to enable the business owner and their advisors understand the tax implications of choosing a certain business structure and funding mix. **Chapter 3** (Acquiring or Letting a Business Premises) focuses mainly on the often-vexed question of the VAT implications of securing business premises and the responsibilities taken on by a business owner that buys or leases property subject to VAT.

**Chapters 4** and **5**, which focus on VAT and payroll taxes, are certainly aimed at the new business but are also required reading for existing businesses, as the implications of getting these taxes wrong can be so significant. Included in **Chapter 4** is our 'VAT 101' concept, which provides a fundamental framework for understanding how VAT works. Also reviewed in this chapter are the VAT implications of purchasing goods or services from abroad. **Chapter 5** looks at the *employed vs self-employed* debate, highlighting recent focus by the Revenue Commissioners on this issue, as well as the income tax, USC and PRSI implications of being a director or shareholder of a 'close company'. This chapter also sets out some opportunities to reduce payroll taxes.

A subject close to all business owners' hearts, **Chapter 6** is titled Keeping Taxes on Profits Down and includes a review of valuable capital allowances, the corporation tax exemption for start-up companies and close company surcharges. The focus of **Chapter 7**, Managing Tax Payments and Returns, is timing, both in relation to keeping tax payments and returns up-to-date, and highlighting how the timing rules of the tax code can legitimately be used to delay tax payments and improve a business's cash flow. This chapter also sets out what happens when a business is repeatedly late with tax payments and returns, and the sanctions available to Revenue.

Though dreaded by many business owners, Revenue audits are a part of business life and taking a co-operative approach is the best way of getting through the process as quickly as possible. **Chapter 8** (Dealing with a Revenue Audit) brings the reader through the process and highlights the types of issues often encountered in small and medium Irish businesses. Also set out in this chapter are a review of other types of Revenue interventions, as well as a section on how to deal proactively with errors in the tax returns.

**Chapters 9** and **10** are more likely to be of use to an expanding business, as they focus on the potential structure and external investment required to provide a springboard for the next stage of development. **Chapter 9** (Business Structures for Expansion) sets out an overview of the process of incorporating a sole trade or partnership business, as well as some tax issues involved in the creation of a group structure and the introduction of key employees as shareholders. The Employment and Investment Incentive Scheme (EIIS), the successor to BES is reviewed in **Chapter 10**, which highlights why having the right external advisors is key to the success of these schemes.

The well-established R&D Tax Credit and the new 'Knowledge Development Box' regimes are reviewed in **Chapter 11**. This chapter provides sufficient information for a business owner to assess whether *their* business can avail of these regimes so they know whether it is worth their while pursuing these incentives with their external advisors.

Finally, **Chapters 12** and **13** look at the process of internationalising an Irish business. **Chapter 12** (VAT and Personal Tax Issues arising from International Sales) reviews the implications where an Irish business supplies goods or services abroad, and sends staff abroad on short- or long-term stays. By contrast, **Chapter 13** (Establishing a Foreign Presence) gives a flavour of the likely tax issues arising when the Irish business sets up a branch, subsidiary company, etc. in another country.

## Overview of the Case Studies

Many of the tax issues explained in this book are illustrated with worked examples. Reviewing endless new profiles in order to understand examples can be tedious and time-consuming, so this book uses just three **case-study businesses** for almost all examples. Based on the author's experience of a variety of small and medium-sized businesses in Ireland, the case-studies do not refer to any specific real-life businesses and any perceived similarities with a real-life business are purely coincidental.

The development of the case-study businesses and the tax implications of some of the decisions they make are interspersed throughout the book. In order to apply current tax law and Revenue practice, the timing of developments in the case studies is necessarily compressed. The three case-study businesses are introduced below.

### Four Blue Ducks

Married couple, Jim and Cathy McLachlan, open a new café called Four Blue Ducks on 2 March 2014. The café is located in a converted coach house and stables in a forest park in County Meath. After redundancy and some time on social welfare, former electrician Jim decided to change tack and completed a year-long SOLAS food catering course. Cathy had previously worked as a baker; she took voluntary redundancy from her job at the end of 2013 and invested most of her redundancy payment into the café. The couple both work full-time in the business while their children are looked after by au pairs.

The café initially serves light lunches, salads, patisseries and good coffee. All food, including the café's popular jams and preserves, is prepared on the premises and is also available for take away. Within the first year of trading, the café secures a wine licence. Jim and Cathy are surprised and delighted to note that the volume of take-away sales has completely exceeded all expectations.

### Tigim Language Learning Ltd

Two college friends, accountant Aoife O'Byrne and language teacher Sarah Gaynor, who are NUI Galway graduates, meet for their usual Christmas drinks in December 2008 and realise that they are both looking for a new challenge. Sarah has developed an innovative language-teaching method, in which Aoife sees a lot of potential. Meanwhile, Aoife is looking for a business opportunity into which she can invest her years of experience as a financial controller and also her savings. When they discuss the idea of starting a new language-teaching business with their friend, Jamie Ring, an experienced marketer, they realise that Sarah's new language-teaching methods could work on an online platform, which could open up the business to international customers.

Fired up by the possibilities, the three friends agree to start a new Galway-based business, with an initial focus on classroom-based teaching and a plan to develop an online product. The business opens its doors on 1 November 2009.

### Neally Engineering Ltd

Experienced production engineering duo Danielle and Martin Neally, who are brother and sister, spot a gap in the market for manufacturing certain metal products/tools for the aviation industry. From a family of entrepreneurs and with many years of manufacturing experience working for large multinational companies under their belts, Danielle and Martin decide to set up their own business. In addition to the aviation industry niche that they have identified, the duo are also interested in the development of plastic tools for other industries.

Because of their stellar careers to date, Danielle and Martin have plenty of interested potential customers and manage to convert that interest and their experience into significant bank financing. This allows them to purchase a factory in Navan, County Meath and the equipment they need to get started. Manufacturing commences in July 2013.

## Context and Timing

Readers will know that tax law and Revenue practice are subject to constant change and update. This book is up-to-date to 30 June 2016, which means that the relevant provisions of Finance Act 2015 are included, as well as Revenue's known practice to 30 June 2016.

Business readers may identify with some aspects of a case-study business. This does not mean, however, that the approach taken by the case-study business is therefore suitable for the reader's business. As always, professional advice that is specific and tailored to the business should be secured. It follows, of course, that no responsibility for any loss arising to any person or entity as a result of any material in this book will be accepted by the authors or publisher. Readers are advised to take appropriate legal, accounting and tax advice in relation to all matters discussed in this book.

**Kerri O'Connell**, FCA, AITI, TEP
30 June 2016

# Acknowledgements

To the publishing team at Chartered Accountants Ireland, especially Michael Diviney and Liam Boyle, many thanks for your guidance and support. And to my fellow Chartered Accountants Ireland authors, Kieran McCarthy and Mark Doyle, thank you for your encouragement.

I am very grateful to colleagues and friends who gave me most useful input into some specific chapters of the book: Liz Lyne, Sandra Chambers, Richard Cowley, Gabrielle Dillon, Orla Trappe, Randal Doherty and Kieran McCarthy. Thanks also to Julian Michael, Julie Herlihy, Daisy Downes and Emma Farrell, for their general advice and encouragement.

Heartfelt thanks to my mentors in business (and in life!): George Reddin, Paul Hamill-Spence and, most especially, Pat O'Connell.

To the Mornington Singers choir and their marvellous director Dr Orla Flanagan, thanks for the creative inspiration, music-making and general craic.

To my wonderful family, Rory, Nora and Cillian and most especially my parents, Lottie and Pat O'Connell, thank you for your unyielding support throughout my life.

To Kevin, for all your patience and loving care, and for 'keeping the show on the road'. Thank you.

And to Aoibhín, thank you for being my new source of inspiration!

CHAPTER 1

# BUSINESS STRUCTURES AND THEIR TAX IMPLICATIONS



For an entrepreneur with an idea and business plans on turnover, cash flow and resources, one of the big questions is: what structure should be used?

When considering a new business, many people assume that it is standard practice to set up a company or companies, but this is not necessarily the case. This chapter will look at the business structures typically used by small and medium enterprises (SMEs) and briefly consider the tax implications of each structure. We will also review the upsides and downsides of each structure and then look at our three case study businesses (see **Introduction**) to see what structure is chosen and why.

## 1.1 Structures for New Businesses

The vast majority of new businesses will operate through one of the following structures, at least in the start-up phase:

- sole trade
- partnership
- limited company.

It is worth noting that the decision to choose a certain structure at the outset does not mean that the business must use that structure forever

FIGURE 1.1: GETTING THE BUSINESS STRUCTURE RIGHT

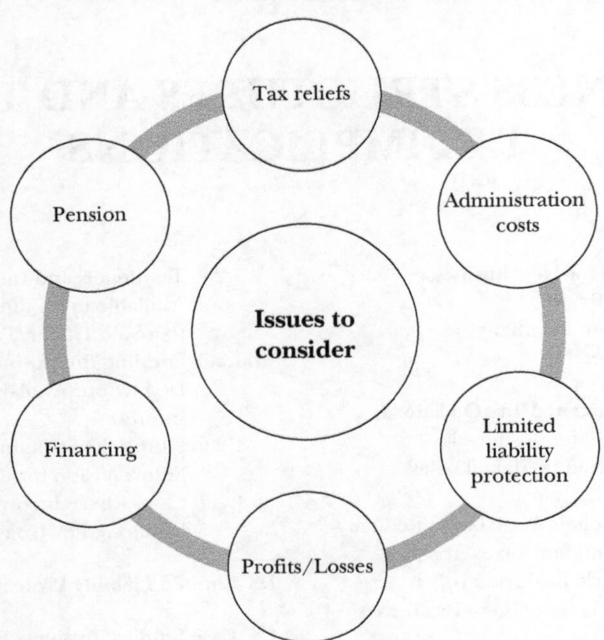


after. It is entirely possible to make changes after trading commences and, in fact, many businesses do exactly that, i.e. they start with the minimum structure required for their business and later review that structure. In **Chapter 9** we will look at some of the possibilities open to expanding businesses in this regard.

### *1.1.1 Sole Trade*

A 'sole trade' is a business owned directly by one person, known as the 'sole trader'. As the sole trader owns the business, she pays income tax, PRSI and USC on all business profits as they are generated. Depending on the sole trader's total amount of business profits, from 1 January 2016 the total percentage of income taxes and charges applicable to these profits could be as high as 55%. This assumes the top rate for all income taxes and charges, i.e. 40% income tax, 11% USC and 4% PRSI.

Often the 'knee-jerk' reaction to hearing this potential 55% total rate is to say: "Well, if a company only pays 12.5% tax, then of course I need to set up a company." We must be careful here, however, and consider that the actual (or effective) rate of income taxes and charges payable by a sole trader will depend on the amount of the taxable business profits earned.

To illustrate this point, we can compare the estimated income taxes and charges payable by a sole trader who generates €60,000 of taxable business profits with one who generates €110,000 of taxable business profits in a trading year.

### Example 1.1: Headline Tax Rates vs Effective Tax Rates

| | € | € |
|---|---|---|
| **Taxable business profits** | 60,000 | 110,000 |
| *Income Tax* | | |
| Income tax at 20% on first €33,800 | 6,760 | 6,760 |
| Income tax at 40% on balance | 10,480 | 30,480 |
| *PRSI* | | |
| PRSI at 4% on €60,000/€110,000 | 2,400 | 4,400 |
| *Universal Social Charge* | | |
| First €12,012 at 1% | 120 | 120 |
| Next €6,656 at 3% | 200 | 200 |
| Next €51,376 at 5.5% | 2,273* | 2,826 |
| Next €29,956 at 8% | – | 2,396 |
| Balance at 11% | – | 1,100 |
| Less: personal tax credit | (1,650) | (1,650) |
| Less: earned income credit | (550) | (550) |
| Total income taxes and charges | 20,033 | 46,082 |
| *Effective rate:* $\frac{\textit{Total liabilities}}{\textit{Taxable profits}}$ | *33.4%* | *41.9%* |

* Calculated as [€60,000 – €12,012 – €6,656] = balance €41,332 × 5.5 %.

(***Note:*** the above example assumes that the sole trader is single, has no other income source, is entitled to the personal tax credit of €1,650 and the new (in 2016) earned income credit of €550, and is less than 70 years of age with no medical card.)

**Example 1.1** highlights that the effective tax rate, i.e. the actual rate that applies in the specific circumstances of the sole trader, will always differ from the headline rate. It must not be forgotten that the examples used of taxable figures of €60,000 and €110,000 are *taxable profit* figures and, of course, there is a world of difference between sales figures and profit figures.

### 1.1.2 Limited Company

A limited company is treated as a separate legal entity that is distinct from its shareholders. The assets, liabilities and obligations of a company generally belong to the company itself and do not impact on the shareholders directly. This means that the company itself is the taxpayer and is subject to corporation tax on its profits.

There are a number of types of companies, including public limited companies (listed on stock exchanges), companies limited by guarantee (these tend to be used by charities, for example) and unlimited companies. The most typical company type used by start-up businesses, however, is a private company limited by shares, which, under the Companies Act 2014, will typically have the word(s) 'Limited' or 'Designated Activity Company' in the company name.[1] As the most popular form of trading company will continue to be a private company limited by shares, we will refer to these companies only throughout this book.

The corporation tax rate for trading profits is 12.5% and there is also a 25% corporation tax rate that applies to non-trading profits, e.g. rental profits or deposit interest income. Note also that some companies – known as 'close companies' – may be subject to additional corporation tax in the form of 'close company surcharges', where profits are retained by the company. These surcharges can push the effective tax rates on trading profits to 19%, and on non-trading profits as high as 40%. (We will look at these surcharges in **Chapter 6**.)

While a potential 12.5% corporation tax rate for trading profits is very attractive, it must be remembered that the after-tax profits remain in the company. This contrasts with the position of a sole trader, who has likely paid higher income tax rates and charges on her business profits, but who holds these after-tax profits directly herself. If a company shareholder wishes to obtain the company's after-tax profits, then another layer of tax will have to be paid by her in order to do so.

Generally, there are three ways for company shareholders to take the profits out of the company:

- the shareholder receives a salary from the company;
- the shareholder receives a dividend from the company;
- the company is liquidated.

[1] As set out in Part 16 of the Companies Act 2014 (CA 2014), a designated activity company (DAC) is defined as a private company limited by shares, with the capacity to do only those acts or things set out in its constitution.

### 1.1.2.1 *The Shareholder Receives a Salary from the Company*

The payment of salary will be subject to payroll withholding taxes (PAYE income tax, PRSI and USC), which can run to a maximum rate of 52%[2] (though see the comments above in relation to *effective* rates). The other tax implication of the payment of salary is that the company will get a deduction against taxable profits for the salary paid.

If the shareholder decides to take all of the taxable profits as salary, then no corporation tax will arise. This is because the company gets a tax deduction for the salary amount, leaving it with no taxable profits on which to pay corporation tax. The following example illustrates this principle.

EXAMPLE 1.2: TAKING TAXABLE PROFITS BY WAY OF SALARY

| | € | € |
|---|---|---|
| Business profits (before salary deduction) | 60,000 | 110,000 |
| Salary equal to business profits | (60,000) | (110,000) |
| Profits subject to corporation tax | NIL | NIL |

In this situation, the business profits will 'flow through' the company and be subject to full payroll taxes (PAYE income tax, PRSI and USC) at the usual rates. It should be noted that in the examples above there are no actual tax liabilities at the first level (i.e. the company) because all of the business profits have been taken as salary. Of course if some of these trading profits were left in the company, then corporation tax at 12.5% would arise on the balance left behind.

Where the shareholder owns/controls at least 50% of the company shares, then the amount of income taxes and charges on that shareholder's salary will usually be *exactly the same* as set out above for the sole trader, i.e. €20,033 on a salary of €60,000 and €46,082 on a salary of €110,000. The significance of this 50% test is that where the shareholder owns/controls less than this quantity of shares, then the company may have an employer's PRSI liability in relation to salary paid to the shareholder. In effect, the tax position would be slightly worse when compared to the taxation of the sole trader. (For more on this aspect, see **Chapter 5**.)

### 1.1.2.2 *The Shareholder Receives a Dividend from the Company*

From the company's perspective, the significant tax difference between salary and a dividend is that the company will not get a deduction against

[2] The eagle-eyed reader will have spotted that the maximum rate noted here is 52% and not the 55% rate mentioned earlier. This is not an error. Where a sole trader generates trading profits exceeding €100,000, a higher USC rate of 11% applies to the excess over €100,000. For taxpayers in receipt of a salary greater than €100,000, the USC rate applicable to the excess over €100,000 is 8%.

taxable profits for payment of the dividend. This means that there will be two layers of taxation: corporation tax to be paid by the company (first layer) and then income taxes and charges to be paid by the shareholder (second layer) on the dividend paid out of the company's after-tax profits.

(***Note:*** in general, a dividend will also be subject to withholding tax, known as 'dividend withholding tax', which is of a different type to the payroll withholding taxes that apply to salary. Dividend withholding tax is currently set at the rate of 20%. As an Irish tax-resident shareholder should receive a credit for this withholding tax in her personal tax return, it will not impact the total tax liabilities arising and will not be highlighted separately here.)

### Example 1.3: Taking Taxable Profits by Way of Dividend

| | | € | | € |
|---|---|---|---|---|
| Taxable trading profits | | 60,000 | | 110,000 |
| **First Layer of Tax on Trading Profits** | | | | |
| *Corporation Tax (CT)* | | | | |
| CT at 12.5% on profits | **A.** | (7,500) | **A.** | (13,750) |
| After-tax amounts available to pay dividend | | 52,500 | | 96,250 |
| **Second Layer of Tax on Dividends (assuming maximum dividend of €52,500/€96,250)** | | | | |
| *Income Tax* | | | | |
| Income tax at 20% on first €33,800 | | 6,760 | | 6,760 |
| Income tax at 40% on balance | | 7,480 | | 24,980 |
| *PRSI* | | | | |
| PRSI at 4% | | 2,100 | | 3,850 |
| *Universal Social Charge* | | | | |
| First €12,012 at 1% | | 120 | | 120 |
| Next €6,656 at 3% | | 200 | | 200 |
| Next €51,376 at 5.5% | | 1,861* | | 2,826 |
| Next €29,956 at 8% | | – | | 2,096** |
| Balance at 11% | | – | | – |
| Less: personal tax credit | | (1,650) | | (1,650) |
| Less: earned income credit | | (550) | | (550) |
| Total income taxes and charges | **B.** | 16,321 | **B.** | 38,632 |

| | | € | | € |
|---|---|---|---|---|
| All tax liabilities | **A. + B.** | 23,821 | **A. + B.** | 52,382 |
| *Effective rate:* *Total liabilities / Taxable profits* | | *39.7%* | | *47.6%* |

* Calculated as [€52,500 – €12,012 – €6,656] = balance €33,832 × 5.5%.
** Calculated as [€96,250 – €12,012 – €6,656 – €51,376] = balance €26,206 × 8%.

(***Note:*** as with **Example 1.1**, the above calculations assume that the sole trader is single, has no other income source, is entitled to the personal tax credit of €1,650 and the earned income credit of €550, and is less than 70 years of age with no medical card. Also, it is assumed that the company has sufficient 'distributable reserves' to declare the full amount of after-tax profits as dividends. The concept of 'distributable reserves' is set out in the Companies Act 2014, and is outside the scope of this book.)

It is clear from the above examples that the same total tax liabilities will arise for a sole trader and a shareholder who owns/controls at least 50% of the company shares and takes all of the company profits by way of salary. By contrast, the 50% shareholder who takes all the company profits by way of dividend will generate higher tax costs overall, as a corporation tax liability will arise along with income tax, PRSI and USC.

### *1.1.2.3 The Company is Liquidated*

Liquidation is a drastic step as it means that the company will cease to exist. While this *is* a method for the shareholder to take the after-tax business profits out of the company, it is *not* an action that can be carried out on an annual basis. Of course, it would always be possible for a shareholder to liquidate one company and then start another company, but there is specific anti-avoidance legislation to stop taxpayers doing this purely to take advantage of lower tax rates.

Consider the situation, however, where the business has come to the end of its natural life or the shareholder wishes to retire and close the company down. The tax implications are somewhat like the situation where a shareholder takes either some salary or a dividend from the company, in that there are two layers of taxation. However, in the case of liquidation, the second layer of tax will be capital gains tax, as opposed to income taxes and charges. This is because the liquidation is treated as a 'capital' event, being the cessation of the company shares.

Using the same taxable business profit figures of €60,000 and €110,000 as above, and assuming that no salary or dividend is taken before liquidation and that the company has no other accumulated profits/losses, the calculations would be as follows:

### Example 1.4: Taking Taxable Profits by Way of Liquidation

| | | € | | € |
|---|---|---|---|---|
| Taxable trading profits | | 60,000 | | 110,000 |
| **First Layer of Tax on Trading Profits** | | | | |
| *Corporation Tax (CT)* | | | | |
| CT at 12.5% on profits | **A.** | (7,500) | **A.** | (13,750) |
| After-tax amounts available for liquidation | | 52,500 | | 96,250 |
| **Second Layer of Tax on Liquidation** | | | | |
| *Capital Gains Tax (CGT)* | | | | |
| CGT at 33% on liquidation proceeds* | **B.** | 17,325 | **B.** | 31,763 |
| All tax liabilities | **A. + B.** | 24,825 | **A. + B.** | 45,513 |
| *Effective rate:* $\frac{\textit{Total liabilities}}{\textit{Taxable profits}}$ | | *41.4%* | | *41.4%* |

* Excluding the nominal value of the company's shares and any other allowable CGT deductions.

When we compare the tax implications of the three different scenarios – salary, dividend and liquidation – we can see that the use of salary payments produces the lowest overall total tax liabilities. Also, in the specific circumstances of the examples set out above, where the 50% shareholder takes all of the company business profits by way of salary, then the tax liabilities arising are equal to those payable by the sole trader.

### *1.1.2.4 Borrowing from the Company*

We have set out above the three 'obvious' ways for a shareholder to access the company's after-tax funds. What might be regarded as a fourth method of accessing company funds, albeit a temporary one, is a company loan to a shareholder/director of the company.

While it is possible for a shareholder/director to take a loan from the company, this will attract tax consequences in the form of the payroll taxes that apply to this 'free use of money' (a taxable benefit-in-kind). Assuming the loan is not used for buying or refurbishing the individual's home, this benefit is calculated at an annual rate of 13.5% of the loan balance, e.g. €6,750 of taxable benefit-in-kind on a loan of €50,000. There are additional tax implications where the company is a 'close company', i.e. a company that is owned by five or fewer individuals, or a company that is controlled by its directors. We will look at the area of close companies in **Chapters 5** and **6** but for now we can say that a very large proportion of Irish companies would be classified as 'close companies' and this is the usual status of SMEs and start-up businesses.

In addition to these tax implications, there is a specific company law prohibition on the value of directors' loans exceeding 10% of the company's 'relevant assets'.[3]

So, why use a company at all? The answer is because what we have set out above is just part of the story and there are plenty of other considerations, both tax and non-tax, when looking at business structures. We will review some of these in **Section 1.2** below.

### *1.1.3 Partnership*

A partnership is a rather strange construct. It arises where two or more partners come together to carry out a business venture but the partnership itself is not treated as a separate legal entity. This means that the assets, liabilities and obligations of the partnership attach to the individual partners personally. From a tax perspective, the best way to think of it is that two (or more) partners come together to form one sole trade-type business. It is also possible for companies to be members of a partnership; for example, a partnership of three, which includes two individuals and a company.

As it is not a separate legal entity, the partnership itself is not subject to tax on partnership profits. Instead, partnership accounts are prepared and the profits or losses are divided between the partners, usually according to their share of the partnership. For example, if a partnership of three individuals earns business profits of €60,000 and the partnership agreement calls for a three-way split of profits, then each partner will include €20,000 of business profits in their income tax return and pay income taxes and charges as appropriate to their own circumstances.

It is not necessary to set out examples here of the income taxes and charges that arise on partnership profits in the tax return of each individual partner as, in general, these will be calculated in the same way as the tax liabilities arising on business profits of a sole trader.

## 1.2 The Fundamental Tax Questions

In this section we look at some of the other tax issues that should be considered by the new business owner(s) before deciding on the most suitable structure.

[3] Sections 239 and 240 CA 2014.

The first step is to ask the following questions, some of which really require the entrepreneur(s) to think about how the business is expected to operate in the first, say, three or four years:

- Is the business expected to make losses in the early years? (And, of course, if losses are expected, the obvious non-tax question is: what is the plan for funding these losses?) (See **Section 1.2.1** below.)
- If the business is expected to make profits in the early years, are there any tax reliefs available to reduce, or even eliminate, taxes arising on those business profits? (See **Section 1.2.2**.)
- If the business is expected to make profits in the early years, will the owner need all of the after-tax profits to finance her own living expenses, etc.? If not, what will the extra profits be used for? (See **Section 1.2.3**.)
- Are there tax reliefs or incentives that the business hopes to rely upon and that are available to a company but not to a sole trader/ partnership? (See **Section 1.2.4**.)
- How will the business be funded? If there is to be loan financing, will the entity/person taking out the loan be in a position to claim a tax deduction for the loan interest payable? (See **Section 1.2.5**.)
- How long does the owner intend to have the business? Is it intended to be held for the long term, or developed and then sold on in the medium term? Is it intended to introduce other senior managers into the business, and could they ultimately own some of the business? (See **Section 1.2.6**.)
- Is the business dealing with any external parties that will insist on the business being operated through a company that produces audited financial statements? Is incorporation specifically disallowed for the intended business activity? (See **Section 1.2.7** below.)

Even though it is not a tax question, this last question is included because it highlights the fact that the new business owner(s) may have no choice as to business structure.

These questions will now be examined individually.

### *1.2.1 Where the Business is Expected to Make Losses in its Early Years*

If losses, or a mixture of losses and profits, are expected in the early years of the business, then the owner will want to make maximum use of these losses by offsetting them against other taxable income/profits arising. There are two main considerations here:

(a) If the owner has other sources of personal income (e.g. rental profits, dividends or employment income) that will be subject to income taxes and charges, then losses of the trading business may be used to reduce the liabilities arising on this other income if the business is operated as a sole trade or partnership. The reason for this is that the same person generates the taxable personal income and the business loss (or a share of the business loss, in the case of a partnership), so the loss can be used to reduce the person's taxable income. This assumes that the person is active in the business. However, if the business has been incorporated, i.e. it is being operated by a company, then ownership of the trading loss is with the company while the other taxable income is owned by the company shareholder, so the other taxable personal income cannot be reduced by the trading loss. Unused trading losses generated by the company can be carried forward for offset (i.e. to 'shelter') against future company trading profits.

It is, of course, much more tax efficient to offset a trading loss against taxable income subject to income taxes and charges (at a potential rate of 55%) as opposed to against future trading profits of a company (at a rate of 12.5%).

(b) If the results for the first few years are expected to be inconsistent, perhaps generating a profit one year and a loss the next year, then it is important to be aware of the different tax rules that apply to the use of unused trading losses by individuals (sole trade or individual partner) and by a company. These rules cover the situation where a trading loss has been generated in a specific tax year but there is insufficient other taxable income to offset the loss against. In this case, the trading loss not used in that specific tax year is not lost.

An individual taxpayer can use this trading loss in subsequent tax years to reduce taxable business profits arising in those years. She can continue to 'carry' this loss forward until it has been used up. A company that generates a trading loss has more flexibility, however, as the company can also use the loss to reduce the *previous* tax year's trading profits.[4] Assuming a corporation tax liability has already been paid on the previous tax year's taxable profits, this could then generate a tax refund for the company. A brief example will illustrate the point.

### Example 1.5: Using a Trading Loss to Generate a Tax Refund

Lisa has drafted a very comprehensive business plan and she projects the following results for the first three years of business:

| | € |
|---|---|
| Year ended 31 December 2013 | €10,000 profit |
| Year ended 31 December 2014 | €15,000 loss |
| Year ended 31 December 2015 | Break-even (no profit/loss) |

[4] Section 396(2) of the Taxes Consolidation Act 1997 (TCA 1997).

If Lisa operated her business through a company, then the company could re-open the 2013 corporation tax return and offset the 2014 €15,000 loss against the 2013 profit of €10,000. This would generate a refund of €1,250 corporation tax for 2013 (being €10,000 × 12.5%). The 2014 loss is €5,000 greater than the 2013 profit and the tax rules limit the offset of the loss to the amount of the profit, meaning that there would be an unused loss of €5,000 still available. No profit arises in 2015, so this trading loss would be carried forward and could be used for offset against trading profits arising in 2016, etc.

The position would be different, however, if Lisa had decided not to incorporate and instead operated as a sole trader for these first three years. Lisa would pay income taxes and charges – the rates would depend on her personal circumstances – on her 2013 business profits. The 2014 loss could not be offset against the 2013 business profits, so the income taxes and charges already paid on the 2013 profits would stand. The 2014 €15,000 loss could be carried forward and offset against trading profits arising in 2016, etc.

### 1.2.2 *Tax Reliefs Available to Reduce or Eliminate Taxes Arising on Early Business Profits*

#### 1.2.2.1 *Start Your Own Business Relief*

Start your own business (SYOB) relief is a tax relief that may be claimed by a long-term unemployed person who starts a new business.[5] It is specifically available only where the business is unincorporated, i.e. it is a sole trade. The tax relief operates by providing an exemption from income tax for business profits for two years, up to a maximum of €40,000 per 12 months of trading. (***Note:*** the exemption relates to income tax only; there is no exemption from PRSI or USC.)

As we have noted above, an individual's effective tax rate will depend on their personal circumstances and so too will the amount of actual tax savings generated by this tax relief. Set out below are examples of the tax savings that would arise for 12 months of trading profits where the taxpayer is single, has no other sources of income, is entitled to the personal tax credit and the earned income credit, and is less than 70 years of age with no medical card. Also, we assume that the business commenced on 1 January of a year within the 'qualifying period' (see definition below).

[5] Section 472AA TCA 1997.

### Example 1.6: Tax Savings Generated by SYOB Tax Relief

| | € | € |
|---|---|---|
| Business profits | 30,000 | 60,000 |
| Less: SYOB tax relief | (30,000) | (40,000) |
| Taxable business profits | NIL | 20,000 |
| | | |
| *Income Tax* | | |
| Income tax at 20% on first €33,800 | – | 4,000 |
| Income tax at 40% on balance | – | – |
| *PRSI* | | |
| PRSI at 4% on €30,000/€60,000 | 1,200 | 2,400 |
| *Universal Social Charge* | | |
| First €12,012 at 1% | 120 | 120 |
| Next €6,656 at 3% | 200 | 200 |
| Balance at 5.5% | 623 | 2,273 |
| Less: personal tax credit | – | (1,650) |
| Less: earned income credit | – | (550) |
| Total income taxes and charges | 2,143 | 6,793 |

If SYOB relief was not available, then the sole trader who earned €30,000 of business profits would have had a net income tax liability of €3,800 (i.e. €6,000 less credits of €2,200). The sole trader who earned €60,000 of business profits has saved €13,240 of tax because she could claim this relief.

(***Note:*** the personal tax credit and earned income credit are only available to reduce income tax liabilities; as no income tax liability arises for the sole trader who earned €30,000 of business profits, they are excluded from the calculations.)

The specific conditions that must be met in order for the relief to apply include:

- Specific to business owner:
  - The business owner must have been unemployed for a period of at least 12 months and in receipt of certain Department of Social Protection (DSP) benefits. Time spent participating in approved training schemes, employment placements or work experience count as a period of 'unemployment' for these purposes.
- Specific to business:
  - The business must commence during the period 25 October 2013 to 31 December 2016; this is known as the 'qualifying period'.

- It must be unincorporated, i.e. the business must be operated as a sole trade.
- The business must be a new business and not just 'new' to the taxpayer, i.e. the business cannot have been bought, gifted or inherited.

The maximum income tax relief that may be claimed for the first 24 months of trading is an exemption for €80,000 of business profits. This means that if an individual set up two businesses and both she and the two businesses met all of the conditions set out above, the total amount of business profits that she could shelter for both businesses would still be €80,000. For more information on this tax relief, see the Revenue website.[6]

#### *1.2.2.2 Corporation Tax Exemption for Start-up Companies*

An exemption from corporation tax, with the potential to generate total tax savings of around €120,000, may apply to companies that commence in the period 1 January 2009 to 31 December 2018.[7] This is because the exemption can be used to shelter up to around €320,000 of corporate business profits in each year of the first three years of trading (around €960,000 in total). If the company is loss-making in the early years, it may also be possible to carry forward this tax relief until profits arise.

We will look at the details of this tax relief in **Chapter 6**, but for the purposes of assessing the right structure at the start-up phase of business, we will focus on two key points here. The first issue to note is that the exemption is *not* available to the following companies:

(a) companies involved in dealing in or developing land, or in exploration and extraction of natural resources;

(b) 'service companies', as defined by the rules on close companies.

While we have already noted that we will look at the area of close companies in later chapters, broadly speaking a 'service company' is a close company that is involved in one of the following activities:

- carries on a profession or provides professional services; or
- exercises an office or employment, e.g. the company itself provides directorship services; or
- provides services or facilities to professional service providers or businesses who exercise an office or employment.[8]

Examples of service companies include companies that provide services in: accountancy, auditing, engineering, architecture, veterinary, management consultancy, financial services, auctioneer/estate agent services and actuarial services.

[6] See www.revenue.ie/en/tax/it/reliefs/own-business-scheme/index.html (accessed May 2016.)

[7] Section 486C TCA 1997, as amended by section 30 of the Finance Act 2015 (FA 2015).

[8] Section 441 TCA 1997.

The other significant point to note here is that while the corporation tax exemption is available for a new company that meets the various conditions, it will not be available in the situation where the business is started as a sole trade and is later incorporated. We will look at this option in **Chapter 9**, but for now it is enough to note that the exemption will not arise where a new company 'succeeds' to a business carried on by another person. This means that if the new business would be entitled to the corporation tax exemption and it is likely that the business owner expects to use a company in the future, it may be better to consider operating the business through a company right from the start.

### 1.2.3 Tax-efficient Use of Business Profits

We have seen in **Section 1.1.2.1** that where the business owner intends to take all of a company's after-tax profits as salary, then, from a tax perspective, there is little merit in using a company to operate the business and the business may be better operated as a sole trade or partnership.

Assume, however, that the business owner does not intend to use all of the after-tax profits to fund their lifestyle and is happy to leave a portion of those profits in the business (what we can refer to as 'surplus profits'). There may be a number of reasons for this; for example, the business owner may wish to reinvest these surplus profits into expanding the business, paying down business debt or making pension contributions for the benefit of the business owner.

To the extent that the business owner wishes to reinvest surplus profits or retain them for paying down business debt, it makes tax sense for the business to be operated through a company. We know that a sole trader will pay income taxes and charges (at her effective tax rates, which could be as high as 55% in total) on all business profits *as they arise.* If the sole trader has other personal income and has, say, surplus profits of €100,000 in her business, she could have a personal tax liability as high as €55,000 on those profits, leaving only €45,000 of after-tax profits available for reinvestment in the business. However, in the case of a company whose business profits are subject to tax at 12.5%, then, excluding the effect of any potential close company surcharges (which we will review in **Chapter 6**), the company generating €100,000 of profits could have €87,500 of after-tax profits available for reinvestment.

Another significant option here is pension provision for the business owner. If the business owner intends to use a large part of the 'surplus profits' for making pension provision for her retirement, then operating the business through a company, and having the company make pension contributions into a company pension scheme for the benefit of the business owner, is the most tax-efficient way of doing so. There are two reasons for this:

- In general, an employer pension contribution is not treated as a taxable 'benefit-in-kind' to the employee and is, therefore, not subject to PAYE income tax, PRSI and USC.

- If the business owner were to contribute to a personal pension scheme herself, there are specific limits as to the maximum pension contributions that can attract tax relief. These limits are expressed as a percentage of the individual's 'net relevant earnings', subject to a maximum earnings figure of €115,000, and are dependent on the individual's age (see table below).[9]

| Age of Individual | Maximum Percentage of Earnings of €115,000 | Maximum Contribution that Attracts Tax Relief |
|---|---|---|
| Less than 30 years | 15% | €17,250 |
| Between 30 and 39 | 20% | €23,000 |
| Between 40 and 49 | 25% | €28,750 |
| Between 50 and 54 | 30% | €34,500 |
| Between 55 and 59 | 35% | €40,250 |
| 60 and over | 40% | €46,000 |

This means, for example, that an individual aged 42 who makes pension contributions into her personal pension scheme may claim tax relief on up to a maximum of €28,750 of contributions.

There are no equivalent limits on the tax relief available on *employer* contributions to a company pension scheme. Note that in order to avoid any tax penalty, the current maximum value for an individual's pension scheme is €2 million (although an individual may have a Revenue-approved higher value pension scheme in certain circumstances). It is this upper-value limit on the shareholder's/director's pension scheme, along with the extent of the company's resources, that will determine what level of pension contributions the company may make on behalf of the shareholder/director.

### *1.2.4 Tax Reliefs and Incentives Available to a Company but Not to a Sole Trader/Partnership*

There are a number of tax reliefs and incentives designed to encourage business expansion, but some of these are only available to companies. If a business carries out activities that makes it potentially eligible for these tax reliefs and the owner expects that the business will apply for these reliefs, then it makes sense to consider incorporating the business right from the start.

These tax reliefs and incentives include:

- **Research & Development (R&D) Credit** This can operate by providing tax relief or even a cash refund to a 'qualifying company', and

[9] Part 30 TCA 1997.

potentially its 'key employees', for monies spent by the company on R&D activities. These R&D activities must be operated by a company in order for the relief to apply. We will look at R&D credits more closely in **Chapter 11**.

- **Knowledge Development Box** This new regime was introduced by Finance Act 2015 and operates to apply a lower rate of 6.25% corporation tax to profits from 'qualifying assets' earned by an Irish company carrying on a 'specified trade'. Some commentary on this new regime is also included in **Chapter 11**.
- **Accelerated capital allowances for certain types of equipment** Capital allowances of 100% may be available where a company buys new energy-efficient equipment for the purposes of its trade. These accelerated allowances are detailed in **Chapter 6**.
- **Capital allowances for expenditure incurred by a company in producing or acquiring 'intangible assets' for the purposes of its trade** These will also be detailed in **Chapter 6**.

### *1.2.5 Funding the Business and Tax Deductions Available on Loan Interest*

In **Chapter 2**, we will look more generally at the tax implications of how a business may be financed. Here we will focus on two types of finance: bank financing and private equity financing.

Private equity financing involves an individual, or a group of individuals, lending personal cash to the business in return for shares and potential access to the business profits. There are two main tax incentives that operate to encourage private equity investment in business, and both of these are available only where the business is incorporated:

- **The Startup Refunds for Entrepreneurs (SURE) Scheme** Where certain conditions are met, a full-time employee or full-time director of a new company that is carrying out 'relevant trading activities' may get an income tax deduction for the value of the amount of shares he subscribes for (purchases) in that new company. This income tax deduction may be available for up to six years preceding the year in which the shares are purchased and can generate a tax refund for the investor. More details on this scheme are set out in **Chapter 2**.
- **The Employment and Investment Incentive Scheme (EIIS)** This scheme provides a tax deduction of up to 40% for investors purchasing shares in an unconnected company that is carrying on 'relevant trading activities'. Details of this tax relief are set out in **Chapter 10**.

Securing bank loans may be more difficult for start-up businesses, but it is possible, especially where the business owner has a good track record in that industry. For the individual or entity drawing down the loan, the key question from a tax perspective will be whether a tax deduction for the interest payable on the loan will be available to reduce taxable profits. In other words, if there is an annual bank interest charge of €8,000 on a €100,000 bank loan, will the taxable profit figure be reduced by that €8,000 charge?

If bank loans can be secured, the first question is: who the bank will lend to? If the bank is happy to lend *either* to the individual behind the business or to a company incorporated by that individual to operate the business, then the question of 'interest deduction' is relatively straightforward. If the business is a sole trade, then the sole trader should draw the loan personally and the interest charge will reduce taxable profits for the sole trader. Conversely, if the business is incorporated, then the company should draw the loan and it is the company profits that will be reduced by the amount of the interest charge.

The problem arises where the business is incorporated (or is a partnership) and the bank will only lend to the business owner on a personal basis. If a company shareholder borrows from the bank in a personal capacity and then lends the bank loan monies to the company, then, in broad terms, the shareholder will not be in a position to use the interest charge arising on the bank loan to reduce her taxable income. The situation is slightly better in the case of an individual who borrows from a bank and then lends the bank loan monies to a partnership. We will look at this question of bank financing further in **Chapter 2**; for now it is worth noting that if the figures are significant enough, the question of the 'interest deduction' on bank financing may well drive the business structure.

### *1.2.6 Fitting the Structure to the Future Vision for the Business*

At the outset, we asked the following questions with regard to the owner 's/founder's vision for the future of the business:

- How long does the owner expect to hold the business?
- Is it intended to be held for the long term, or developed and then sold on in the medium term?
- Will other senior managers be introduced into the business and could they ultimately own some of the business?

For some new businesses, these questions may seem to add more complexity than is really necessary at the outset. However, many entrepreneurs have a definite long-term vision as to where they see their business going and will want to have a structure fitting with that vision right from the start.

Generally, incorporation of a business will allow much more flexibility if it is expected that additional owners will be introduced in the future. This expectation could be driven by future personal or business succession plans with family members or key business managers, or by a desire to incentivise key employees by giving them a 'share of the action'. If the business is initially operated as a sole trade, it is entirely possible to facilitate the introduction of additional business owners later by incorporating the sole trade and then transferring shares. We will look at various potential changes to business structure in **Chapter 9**, including the incorporation of a sole trade. A key point to note, however, is that the transfer of shares in a business that is already valuable usually triggers tax liabilities. These taxes may be reduced or avoided altogether if the intended additional business owners receive their shares in the start-up phase.

Another vision that the entrepreneur may have is to develop her business in the medium term, sell it on and then reinvest the sales proceeds into further business ventures. In general, the most tax-efficient way of doing this is by having the original business operated by a company. But an entrepreneur with this vision may want to consider setting up more than one company and instead establish a group structure, comprising say a holding company (owned by her) that has one or more subsidiary companies. Again, it is possible to convert the original business structure into a group structure once the business has moved beyond the start-up phase (and we will look at this in **Chapter 9**), but for some entrepreneurs, establishing a group structure from the outset will be a better decision.

### *1.2.7 Cases where Incorporation is Disallowed or Unavoidable*

Much of the discussion in the previous sections assumes that the business owner can make their own choice as to a suitable business structure, but there are circumstances where this is not the case. So, a business owner must ask:

- Is incorporation specifically disallowed for the intended business activity?
- Is the business dealing with any external parties that will insist on the business being operated through a company that produces audited financial statements?

There are various business activities that may not be operated through a company, not by reason of tax legislation but because the legislation and/or the body governing that business activity prohibits it. Examples include the activities of medical practitioners, solicitors and Friendly Societies. An entrepreneur would be wise to confirm that such a prohibition does not apply before wasting time on options that may not be available.

It is often the case that where a bank is providing any significant level of loan financing for a business, it will insist on the business producing full financial statements on an annual basis. This may mean that the business must be operated through a company. The reason that the bank may insist on this is that it will take comfort from the fact that, in order to produce full financial statements, the business accounts must be prepared by an accountant who is generally obliged to highlight any serious deficiency in those accounts. As the levels of bank loan financing rise, the bank may demand the production of 'audited financial statements', even where an audit is not required by company law. This is because audited financial statements will have been more thoroughly reviewed, so the bank may place more reliance upon them.

Often, general industry practice will dictate that a business is operated through a company, and a new entrant into that industry who attempts to operate as a sole trade or partnership would have no credibility with suppliers or customers.

## 1.3 Limited Liability Protection

The considerations set out at **Section 1.2.7** above highlight the fact that tax is not the only issue to consider when looking at business structure, and in many cases it will not be the driving factor.

A very significant non-tax issue for business owners is the question of 'limited liability protection' or, more specifically, the protection available to business owners when they operate their business through a limited company. A limited company is treated as a separate legal entity so that, generally, whatever happens within the company will remain within the company.[10] This means that if, for example, the company's business fails and there are unpaid creditors, these creditors are entitled to look to the company's assets to satisfy their debts, but are not entitled to look through the company to its shareholders' assets for satisfaction. Limited liability protection can be subject to qualification. An example of this is where a bank provides a loan to a company that is personally guaranteed by the company shareholders; if the company fails without having repaid the loan, then the bank is entitled to pursue the shareholders' assets in satisfaction.

However, the personal assets of the *directors* of a company (who may or may not be shareholders of the company) may be available to satisfy claims of the company's creditors if the directors are found to have engaged in 'reckless trading' or 'fraudulent trading', including trading when the company is 'insolvent'. (The company law rules relating to 'reckless trading' and 'fraudulent trading' are set out in the Companies Act 2014, and are outside the scope of this book.)

For some entrepreneurs, the limited liability protection provided by a company is such an overriding issue that tax considerations are almost irrelevant in deciding the business structure. It is important to be aware, however, that taking on the role of company director (as many shareholders do) attracts numerous obligations, the breach of which can expose the directors to significant penalties, personal financial exposure or even, in the most serious cases, imprisonment. The security provided by limited liability protection does not, therefore, come without a cost. The additional accounts/financial statements and returns required by a company, in contrast to a sole trade/partnership, will also trigger additional professional fees.

While it is not possible to secure the benefit of limited liability protection when operating as a sole trader, it may be possible to structure a

[10] While the most common form of private company is a limited company, it is possible to operate a business through an unlimited company. As the name suggests, an unlimited company will not have the benefit of 'limited liability protection'. Throughout this book, any reference to 'company' will refer to a private limited company.

partnership in such a way that this protection can effectively be secured. This involves the creation of a 'limited partnership' as opposed to an unlimited partnership, which is the more usual type and the one described above. A limited partnership may have a number of limited partners whose potential loss is capped at the value of their contribution to the partnership, but it must have at least one general partner who has unlimited exposure to partnership liabilities/losses.

## 1.4 Case Studies: Business Structure

Like all entrepreneurs, the owners of each of the case study businesses set out in the **Introduction** had to make their own decisions on business structure. The following sets out what business structure they chose, and why.

### FOUR BLUE DUCKS – SOLE TRADE

When it came to discussing business structure, Jim and Cathy's first instincts were to keep it simple; and they were not keen on paying for what they saw as the expensive cost of keeping a company. They also knew that, for the first few years, any and all profits made by the business were going to be needed by them to keep their family and home ticking over. Jim and Cathy had little expectation of employing many staff in the early years and fully expected to be doing the majority of the work themselves.

When they sat down with their tax advisor, Maeve, Jim and Cathy told her that they wanted to open up their business together and asked about the idea of a partnership. Before she would make a recommendation, however, Maeve wanted to know about their background and experience. She discovered that Jim had been unemployed for more than 12 months and met all of the other conditions attaching to start your own business relief, so she advised that the business be operated as a sole trade by Jim, and that the structure could be revisited later.

### TIGIM LANGUAGE LEARNING LTD – COMPANY

When Aoife and Sarah were initially discussing setting up a language education business, they assumed that the classroom-based language classes would represent most of their income and that any online business would be supplementary to this. However, their friend Jamie could see the potential of developing the online business right from the start and encouraged them to 'think bigger'. He thought that the online education service could be packaged and sold across Ireland and beyond. If that were the case, then protection of this product would be vital, so he suggested that the business should operate through a company.

Aoife was also enthusiastic about using a company as she had big plans to expand the business and fully expected that additional senior employees would be required to supplement the skills of herself, Jamie and Sarah. Based on her previous experience, Aoife also expected that the ownership pool of the business would have to be extended in the future to keep key employees motivated in expanding the business.

### Neally Engineering Ltd – Company

For Martin and Danielle, the decision on business structure was effectively made for them. Their business would be providing metal products/tools to the aviation industry. They knew that the fallout from a badly produced part could have a catastrophic effect, and so any business of any worth operating in the industry must operate through a company. The owners of such businesses could never expose themselves to unlimited liability.

In addition, the attitude of the bank that had committed itself to providing loan financing to the business was also key. The bank had agreed to extend a loan of €1.1 million for factory purchase and fit-out, and some equipment, as well as providing overdraft facilities of €100,000. It demanded the production of annual audited financial statements as one of the conditions of providing finance.

Chapter 2

# TAX IMPLICATIONS OF FINANCING THE BUSINESS



One of the most crucial aspects of starting a new business, or expanding an existing one, is the finance required. In this chapter we will review a number of different financing options, outlining the tax implications of the various methods as well as some of the commercial issues arising. Most businesses use a number of financing methods, the combination of which will vary, depending on factors such as: the industry in which the business operates; the economic environment; the requirements of management and owners; the business plans; and the maturity of the business.

Financing options fall into three categories:

**LOANS**
- Business/personal
- Interest-free
- Leases
- Invoice discounting
- Crowdfunding

**EQUITY**
- Dividend
- Share disposal and entrepreneur relief
- SURE scheme
- Venture capital
- Crowdfunding

**GRANTS AND DONATIONS**
- State agencies
- Employment subsidies
- Crowdfunding

## 2.1 Loans

### *2.1.1 Tax Deduction from Trading Profits*

While the most obvious source of loan finance is a bank, building society or credit union, other loan sources may include family and friends, 'crowd-funding' and state agencies. In **Appendix I** to this chapter we set out a list of some Irish and EU agencies that provide financial support to start-up, early-stage and expanding SMEs.

The main feature of loan financing is that the loan will be subject to repayment, over a set period of time if it is for a fixed term, or subject to regular renegotiation if it is a rolling loan, and the business must pay a financing (interest) cost. In this quite straightforward situation, the important tax issue is to ensure that the business secures a tax deduction for the interest cost.

In **Chapter 6** we will look at reducing tax liabilities by maximising the value of the tax deductions that a business can take. For now, we will note that the general basis for claiming a tax deduction from trading profits is that the money must have been used "wholly and exclusively... for the purposes of the trade or profession".[1] In general this means that, where a business borrows money and uses the money for the purposes of its business, then a tax deduction will be available for the interest charge arising on the borrowings. Note that the repayment of the loan will not generate a tax deduction; it is only the *cost* of the loan (i.e. the interest charge) that is tax deductible.

Case Study: Tigim Language Learning Ltd

The directors of Tigim Language Learning Ltd consider borrowing €50,000 from a bank over a three-year term at a fixed interest charge of 5% per annum. Excluding the impact of interest compounding, the capital repayment in Year 1 would be €16,667 and the annual interest charge would be approximately €2,500. As long as the loan was used by the company for trading purposes, then a corporation tax deduction of €2,500 per annum would be available. No tax deduction would arise in relation to the €16,667 capital repayment amount.

### *2.1.2 'Interest-free' Loans*

Many small and start-up businesses rely on informal loans from friends and family to get started, and it is often the case that no interest is paid

[1] Section 81 of the Taxes Consolidation Act 1997 (TCA 1997).

on these loans. This means, of course, that the business will not have paid a financing cost and so there can be no tax deduction for such a cost. There is another potential tax implication here, however, which relates to what is called the 'free use of money'. The tax rules in relation to gifts recognise that providing an interest-free loan constitutes a gift and, potentially, a charge to capital acquisitions tax (CAT) may arise. One method of valuing the gift of an interest-free loan is by multiplying the loan value by the best interest rate available on the market if the lender were to put that money on deposit, instead of lending it to the business. There will be a gift between lender and business for every 12-month period (or part of it) that the loan remains outstanding. If the lender ultimately writes off the loan, then there would also be a gift of the full value of the loan, at the time of write-off. An example will illustrate the point.

Case Study: Four Blue Ducks

Jim borrows €8,000 from his mother, Darina, to start his Four Blue Ducks café business. Darina does not charge Jim any interest on the loan. Her initial intention was to leave the loan in the business for a year, but the arrangement continues for a number of years until, ultimately, Darina writes off the loan.

This interest-free loan is regarded as 'free use of money' and it should be assessed to determine if any CAT implications arise. Say that the best interest rate for a one-year deposit of €8,000 is 2%, then the annual gift from Darina to her son would be valued at €160 and this gift would arise for every 12-month period (or part of it) that Jim retains the loan. When Darina writes off the loan, she is regarded as having made a gift of €8,000 to Jim. (***Note:*** based on the CAT tax rules, such gifts may not actually generate CAT liabilities. We will not elaborate further here as this tax is outside the scope of this book.)

If interest is charged on an informal loan from friends or family, then as long as the loan is used by the business for its trade and the interest rate does not exceed a market rate, a tax deduction should be available to the business for this charge. The interest will constitute income for the lender, which may generate income tax liabilities for them.

### *2.1.3 Direct and Indirect Loan Financing*

We have noted above the circumstances in which a business can take a tax deduction for the interest charge it pays on borrowed monies. This situation is quite straightforward when the business is a sole trade and it is the sole trader who borrows the monies. It is also straightforward when a business is operated through a company and it is the company that borrows and uses the monies for the purposes of its business. Both of these types of loans can be regarded as 'direct' loan financing.

The situation gets more complicated in cases of 'indirect' loan financing, as where:

- a partner in a trading partnership borrows monies in their own personal name and then lends these monies to the trading partnership; or
- a company shareholder or director borrows monies in their own personal name and then lends these monies to a trading company.

In both situations the individual borrower is the one who is paying the interest charge, but they are not using the loan for a business they are operating; instead, the business is being operated by a separate entity (a partnership or a company) in which they have a share. *If* the individual is entitled to an income tax deduction for the interest charge they are paying on the loan, then the tax deduction would not be set against the taxable profit of the business but would instead reduce their taxable personal income.

### *2.1.3.1 Personal Bank Loan Lent on to Company*

Previously, where an individual took out a personal bank loan and then lent these monies on to a company, the individual would have been entitled to take an income tax deduction for the bank interest paid, as long as certain conditions were met. Since the end of 2013, this tax deduction is no longer available.[2] An example from one of our case studies will illustrate the current tax implications where an individual takes out a personal bank loan and then lends the proceeds of this loan to a company.

#### Case Study: Tigim Language Learning Ltd

A case in point might be the €50,000 bank loan referred to above in the case of Tigim Language Learning Ltd. If this loan was instead personally borrowed by Sarah, a shareholder and full-time working director of the company, on 5 January 2011, and Sarah then lent the €50,000 to Tigim Language Learning Ltd, Sarah will pay the 5% annual interest charge of €2,500 to the bank, but she will not get a personal income tax deduction for this charge.

If Sarah charges the company interest on her loan, say at the same rate of interest that she is paying to the bank, then she will receive taxable income of €2,500 from the company. This must be included in her income tax return and will be subject to income tax, USC and PRSI, as appropriate. Other tax implications may also arise because Tigim Language Learning Ltd would be classified as a 'close company' for corporation tax purposes.

[2] Section 248 TCA 1997.

For more on the 'close company' rules that may impact on a director's loan to a company, see **Chapter 5**.

### *2.1.3.2 Personal Loan Lent on to Partnership*

The income tax deduction currently available on interest charged to an individual who takes out a personal loan and then lends the monies on to a partnership is also being phased out.[3] No tax deduction is available in relation to new loans taken out after 15 October 2013. However, where a 'new loan' is taken out after 15 October 2013 and it replaces a previously qualifying loan ('old loan'), then interest arising may be eligible for tax relief as long as this 'new loan' does not exceed the value or term of the 'old loan'.

In relation to loans taken out before 15 October 2013 or the 'new loans' described above, a tax deduction will be available where certain conditions are met. These include the requirements that the money is applied for trading purposes and that the individual 'personally acts' in the conduct of the trade or profession of the partnership. This latter requirement would prevent an inactive or 'silent' partner from securing an income tax deduction on the interest charge.[4]

Where the conditions are met, a tax deduction in respect of the interest charge will be available to the individual borrower on a phased basis, as follows:

| Year of Assessment | Percentage Tax Deduction Available |
|---|---|
| 2014 | 75% |
| 2015 | 50% |
| 2016 | 25% |

From 1 January 2017, no further tax deduction will be available.

***Note:*** the phasing out of this tax deduction does not apply to farming partnerships. Interest charged on a loan to an individual borrower who then lends on to a farming partnership may still attract income tax relief, as long as all relevant conditions are met.

As these tax deductions have been, or are being, phased out for all except farming partnerships, it is not tax efficient for an individual to borrow in their personal name and then lend the monies on to a company or partnership in which they have a share. Unfortunately, where commercial lending is restricted, this may be the only practical solution to an SME company's or non-farming partnership's need for loan financing.

[3] Section 253 TCA 1997.
[4] Section 1013 TCA 1997.

### 2.1.4 Leases

A lease is another type of loan, only in this case the asset being lent is not cash but equipment, machinery, motor vehicles, etc. The lease arrangement is basically structured the same way, in that an asset is lent (leased) in return for a financing cost (interest charges, which are factored into the lease payments). From a tax perspective, there are generally two types of lease:

- **Operational leases:** where the asset is leased for a period of time that is shorter than the asset's useful life and the lease payments do not cover the cost of the asset.
- **Finance leases:** where the asset is typically leased for a period similar to its useful life and the lease payments exceed the cost of the asset. A finance lease usually involves payment of the full cost of the leased asset along with the financing cost.

One of the significant tax differences between loans and *finance leases* is that, unlike in the case of a loan, *both* the capital and interest element of finance lease payments may be the subject of a tax deduction.

#### 2.1.4.1 Operational Lease

With an operational lease, the business leasing the asset (known as the 'lessee') pays lease payments for the term of the lease. At the end of the lease, the lessee has not accumulated any rights in the leased asset and the lease ceases. As long as the leased asset is being used by the lessee for the purposes of its trade, then a full tax deduction will be available to the lessee for the operational lease payments.

CASE STUDY: FOUR BLUE DUCKS

All of Four Blue Ducks' catering equipment (fridges, ovens, etc.) are the subject of operational leases. This suited Jim and Cathy very well as it meant that they were not required to finance significant asset purchases in the business's early years.

#### 2.1.4.2 Finance Lease for Plant and Machinery

With a finance lease, the usual arrangement is for the business to lease the asset for a fixed period, usually at least three years, at the end of which time the business may return the asset, purchase the asset or trade it in against another leased asset. The lease payments may be structured as regular recurring payments (e.g. monthly payments), one-off upfront payments or a combination of both. Generally, the timing of the tax deductions for the lease payments should be spread evenly over the lease term, as opposed to being linked to when the lease payments are made. The following example from the Neally case study illustrates how finance lease payments may be spread across the term of the lease.

### Case Study: Neally Engineering Ltd

Neally Engineering Ltd leases some engineering equipment under a finance lease with the following terms:

- Cost of engineering equipment: €40,000
- Upfront payment: €15,000
- Total recurring lease payments, including finance charges, payable over a four-year period: €32,000.

Both the upfront payment and the recurring lease payments should be spread evenly across the four-year term of the lease. This means that a tax deduction of €11,750 per annum (i.e. [€15,000 + €32,000] ÷ 4) for four years may be claimed by the business.

As we can see in the Neally case study above, the total payments to the leasing company equal the cost of the leased asset plus the financing charges. The tax implications of the various possible outcomes at the end of the lease period are set out below.

(a) The lessee returns the asset to the leasing company. In this situation, the leasing company will usually sell the asset for its market value and rebate that market value, less a transaction fee, to the lessee. The lessee must include the rebate in its taxable profits and pay the relevant income tax or corporation tax arising. One way of looking at this is to see the rebate as a 'negative deduction': the tax treatment ensures that the lessee ultimately gets a tax deduction only for the *net* leasing charges it incurs, i.e. leasing payments less rebate.

### Case Study: Neally Engineering Ltd

At the end of the four-year lease term, Neally Engineering Ltd returns the asset to the leasing company, which sells it for €8,000, retains an administration fee of €800 and rebates the net amount of €7,200 to the company. As this rebate of €7,200 represents taxable income for Neally Engineering Ltd, the net tax deductions it claims over the course of the lease will match the total payments to the leasing company, i.e. €11,750 + €11,750 + €11,750 + €11,750 – €7,200 rebate = €39,800.

(b) The business buys the leased asset for its market value at the end of the lease. In this case, the leasing company is still obliged to rebate the asset's market value but will offset the rebate against the payment due from the leasing business for the asset. The lessee must include the rebate in its taxable income for that year of assessment;

however, it now owns an asset that is eligible for capital allowances. We will look at the subject of capital allowances in detail in **Chapter 6** but, for now, note that these allowances are a type of tax deduction on capital assets, spread across a number of years. In the case of plant and equipment, the deduction/allowances are typically spread over eight years.

### Case Study: Neally Engineering Ltd

Let us consider the situation that would arise if Neally Engineering Ltd was to buy the equipment for €8,000 (of which €7,200 represents the market value of the asset and €800 is an administration fee) at the end of the four-year period. This would mean that Neally Engineering Ltd would owe €7,200 to the leasing company to purchase the equipment and the leasing company would owe €7,200 to Neally Engineering Ltd, being the rebate on the equipment. Once these two amounts are offset against each other, the net position is that Neally Engineering Ltd would owe the leasing company the administration fee of €800.

Neally Engineering Ltd would include the rebate value of €7,200 in its taxable income for that year of assessment and also start claiming capital allowances on the equipment in the same year. On the assumption that the capital allowances would be available over an eight-year period, this means that, in that year of assessment, the company would have taxable income of €7,200 less the annual capital allowance of €900. Assuming the company retains the asset and uses it for the purposes of its business, the company could claim the annual capital allowance of €900 for the seven subsequent years of assessment. The company would also get a tax deduction for the €800 administration fee.

(c) The business trades in the leased asset for another leased asset and a new lease commences. In this situation, the market value of the 'old' asset (the rebate) is offset against the 'new' asset and the rebate is treated as an upfront lease payment under the terms of the new lease.

### Case Study: Neally Engineering Ltd

What would the position be if Neally Engineering Ltd were to trade in the equipment, with a market value of €7,200, against a new piece of equipment valued at €50,000 but with total lease payments of €60,000 (including the trade-in value of €7,200) due over another four-year term? In this situation, Neally Engineering Ltd must include the rebate of €7,200 (which has become an upfront payment on the new lease) in its taxable profits in that year of assessment and would secure a tax deduction for all €60,000 worth of lease payments over the four-year term of the new lease.

For more information on the tax implications of finance leases, see the Revenue leaflet IT52, *Taxation Treatment of Finance Leases*, available at www.revenue.ie.

#### 2.1.4.3 Finance Lease for Private Cars

The tax deduction for payments on a private car lease is restricted by reference to the car's $CO_2$ emissions, with lower restrictions applying to cars with lower $CO_2$ emissions. The tax deduction is also restricted by reference to the cost of the car when it was new; this means that the more expensive the car, the more the tax deduction is restricted.

Cars in the Group 1 category of $CO_2$ emissions (in the range 0 to 155g/km of emissions) will be subject to a restricted tax deduction based on the following formula:

$$\text{Lease payments} \times \frac{\text{‘Specified limit’ to value of car (currently €24,000)}}{\text{Lease price of car when new}}$$

Cars in the Group 2 category of $CO_2$ emissions (in the range 156 to 190g/km of emissions) will secure only half of the tax deduction calculated above. Cars with emissions higher than 190g/km will not be eligible for tax deductions for their lease payments.[5] For more information on leases for private cars, see Revenue's *Operational Manual* 11.00.01 – Cars: Capital Allowances and Lease/Hire Payments.[6]

### 2.1.5 Invoice Discounting/Debt Factoring

These terms are often used interchangeably and generally refer to a financing arrangement where a business assigns (sells) trade debts to a finance house, which in turn pays a portion of the value of these debts to the business. These arrangements can take many forms, with various characteristics, such as:

- The business may transfer all of the risk of the debts not being paid to the finance house, or it may retain the risk itself. The debts may be collected by the finance house or by the business, as agent for

[5] Section 380M TCA 1997.

[6] Available at www.revenue.ie/en/about/foi/s16/income-tax-capital-gains-tax-corporation-tax/part-11/11-00-01.pdf (accessed May 2016).

the finance house. In the latter case, this may mean that the business's customers are not aware of the arrangement.
- The finance house may charge fees comprising a percentage of each debt, as well as a variety of other fixed fees, including arrangement fees and facility fees.

These arrangements are a method of using the trade debtor list to generate cash in the more immediate term so as to assist the business's cash flow. As long as these arrangements are made "wholly and exclusively" for the purposes of the trade, then the fees charged by the finance house are generally tax deductible.

## 2.2 Equity

An alternative way of financing a business that is being operated through a company is for the company to issue new shares to the investor in exchange for cash. The reason for the *issue of new shares* is that it is a method of contributing cash into the company. This contrasts with the *purchase of existing shares* from an existing shareholder, which involves the purchaser paying the cash to the existing shareholder, who retains the cash personally.

In general, to own a company share is to own a share in the following rights:
- the right to vote at a meeting of the shareholders;
- the right to receive a share of a declared dividend;
- the right to receive a share of the net assets of the company in a winding-up situation; and
- the right to information about the company.

If a company has the usual type of shares (known as ordinary share capital), then a shareholder who owns 10% of the company shares will own 10% of the voting rights, 10% of the declared dividend rights and 10% of the rights to net company assets on a winding-up.

It is possible to change the company's constitutional documents to have a number of different types of shares (known as 'share classes') holding different rights. For example, a company can have ordinary shares, holding all four rights set out above; and preference shares, which hold only the right to a specified annual dividend. Or a company could have two classes of ordinary shares, one of which holds all of the voting rights, and a second class which holds all of the dividend rights and rights to assets on a winding-up.

Where an external investor agrees to purchase (known as 'subscribing for') newly issued shares in the company, these shares may be of the usual ordinary class or they may be shares specifically issued for the purposes of the investment and with restricted share rights. This latter approach is often used when issuing shares to, say, Irish state agencies or venture capital firms.

A company shareholder can typically secure value from/on her shares in either of two ways:

- receive a dividend on the shares; or
- dispose of some or all of her shares.

### 2.2.1 Dividend on Company Shares

Where a company declares a dividend on a share, then the company usually has an obligation to withhold tax at 20% (known as dividend withholding tax (DWT)) on the dividend and pay this over to Revenue. This obligation to withhold DWT generally applies to dividends paid to individual shareholders, though it may not apply where the shares are held by a company or state agency. In general, the gross amount of the dividend (before deduction of DWT) should be included by the individual shareholder in their income tax return and they should secure a credit for DWT already withheld.

Note that, unlike in the case of the interest charge on a loan used for trading purposes, a company will not secure a tax deduction for dividends paid to its shareholders. A dividend may only be declared if the company has accumulated profits that it is allowed to distribute, by way of dividend, under company law rules. Many SME companies rarely, if ever, declare dividends, as they prefer to retain any accumulated profits in the company for the purposes of the business.

### 2.2.2 Disposal of Company Shares

A straightforward sale of company shares will generally have no tax implications for the company itself, as the transaction merely involves a change in the company register of the ownership of the shares. Money paid for the shares will be paid by the purchasing shareholder to the selling shareholder and will not affect the company's cash position.

The selling shareholder will be treated as carrying out a 'capital transaction' from a tax perspective, meaning that any gains or losses would be subject to the capital gains tax (CGT) rules instead of the rules on income tax. (A full discussion of the operation of CGT is outside the scope of this book, though we do refer to it periodically to highlight certain points.[7])

[7] For full details, see *Capital Gains Tax: A Practitioner's Guide* by Mark Doyle (2nd Edition, Chartered Accountants Ireland).

In general, the capital gain or loss would be calculated by comparing the sale price with the original purchase price (also known as the 'base cost'), less associated expenses of the purchase and sale. If the selling shareholder started (incorporated) the company themselves, then generally their 'base cost' will be their portion of the nominal value of the company's shares on incorporation. The case study extract below illustrates how the capital gain arising on the sale of shares would be calculated.

### Case Study: Tigim Language Learning Ltd

Looking again at Tigim Language Learning Ltd – a company that was incorporated in 2009 with 100 issued ordinary shares of €1 each, owned as follows:

- Aoife – 40 shares of €1 each
- Jamie – 30 shares of €1 each
- Sarah – 30 shares of €1 each.

By 2013, Jamie is getting 'itchy feet' and is considering emigrating to Canada. He discusses this with Aoife and Sarah and agrees that, if he goes, he will sell 15 shares each to Aoife and Sarah, for the sum of €10,000 each. This would generate a 2013 capital gain for Jamie, which would be calculated as follows:

| | € | |
|---|---|---|
| Total proceeds | 20,000 | |
| Less: total base cost | (30) | i.e. 30 shares at €1 each |
| Capital gain | 19,970 | |

This gain would be subject to the 33% rate of CGT in force during 2013, though this tax liability could be reduced if Jamie paid any costs on the purchase or sale of the shares and/or if he is entitled to the CGT annual exemption.

It is worth noting what Aoife and Sarah's base cost position would be if they purchase the shares from Jamie. Aoife would own 55 shares, with a total base cost of €10,040, being €40 on the shares she was issued when the company incorporated in 2009, plus the €10,000 purchase price she would pay Jamie for his 15 shares. Sarah would own 45 shares, with a total base cost of €10,030.

After much discussion, Jamie decides not to leave Ireland or Tigim Language Learning Ltd and instead to focus on development of the company's business in UAE and Qatar.

There are other ways in which a shareholder can dispose of some or all of their shares for cash, including a liquidation of the company and share redemption by the company. Though the detail of these types of transactions is beyond the scope of this book, we can note the following:

- The liquidation of a company effectively involves both the complete cessation of the company's business activities and the dissolution of the company itself. The liquidation results in the company's net assets being returned to its shareholders, in the proportion in which they own ordinary shares in the company, i.e. a 10% ordinary shareholder will receive 10% of the company's net assets. This transaction is generally treated as a 'capital transaction' from a tax perspective, so that any gains or losses arising would be subject to CGT rules.
- On the other hand, the redemption of shares by a company from its shareholder is treated as an 'income receipt', subject to the income tax rules, unless certain conditions are met that allow it to be treated as a capital transaction.

### 2.2.2.1 *Tax Relief for Entrepreneurs*

We have been reviewing the disposal of shares by a shareholder, noting that this is generally treated as a 'capital' transaction and is subject to the CGT rules. Finance Act (No. 2) 2013 introduced a new CGT relief for so-called 'serial' entrepreneurs, being entrepreneurs who start businesses, sell or liquidate them, and then reinvest the net proceeds into new businesses.[8] As the relief reduces the amount of CGT payable, it could be argued that it is a tax relief aimed at improving the financing position of the new business of a 'serial entrepreneur'. We will see, however, that the tax relief introduced in 2013 is limited in scope and could really only be said to improve the financing position of a *third* successive business started by an entrepreneur.

In summary, entrepreneur relief operates as follows:

- On or after 1 January 2010, the entrepreneur disposes of their first business, makes a capital gain and pays CGT, at the normal rates, on this.
- During the period 1 January 2014 to 31 December 2018, the entrepreneur reinvests all of the net proceeds (i.e. after-tax proceeds) from the disposal of the first business in a new business.
- The entrepreneur retains this second business for at least three years, then disposes of it and makes a capital gain. When calculating the CGT liability payable on the disposal of the *second* business, the entrepreneur will secure tax relief that is valued at the *lower* of:
  - the CGT paid on the disposal of the first business; and
  - 50% of the CGT payable on the disposal of the second business.
- Where not all of the net proceeds on the disposal of the first business are invested into the second business, the tax relief available on the disposal of the second business will be reduced proportionately.

[8] Section 597A TCA 1997.

There has been recognition that this tax relief in its original form was overly restrictive and potentially ineffective, given that the tax relief could only arise when the 'serial' entrepreneur had disposed of a second business. A more simplified entrepreneur relief was introduced in Finance Act 2015 (FA 2015), and may be claimed in relation to disposals made from 1 January 2016. Effectively, an entrepreneur who disposes of business assets that they have owned for at least three years will be subject to a reduced CGT rate of 20% on the capital gain generated. The relief is subject to a lifetime limit of €1 million; this means that a business owner could benefit from the reduced 20% CGT rate on more than one disposal of business assets, as long as the €1 million threshold is not breached. Where the €1 million threshold is breached, the lower rate of CGT will apply on the first €1 million of capital gains, with the standard CGT rate applying on the 'excess' over €1 million.[9]

The conditions attached to the FA 2015 relief include the requirements that, where the business assets are shares in a trading company, the entrepreneur must hold at least 5% of the company shares (or 5% of a holding company that owns a trading company) for three of the five years before disposal, and must have been an employee/working director of the company for at least three of those five years before disposal. Where the business being disposed of is an unincorporated business (e.g. a sole trade), the business must also have been owned by the business owner for at least three years before disposal.

This reduced CGT rate will not apply to the disposal of a business that involves the holding of investments or development land, or the letting or development of land.

***Note:*** there are now two forms of entrepreneur relief: the newer FA 2015 relief and the original relief set out in Finance Act (No. 2) 2013. If the 2013 relief produces a better result for the taxpayer, then this relief takes precedence. For more information on entrepreneur relief, see Revenue's *Operational Manual*, 19.06.02A – Capital Gains Tax: Entrepreneur Relief.[10]

Despite improvements, the FA 2015 version of entrepreneur relief is also considered too restrictive and, at the time of writing (June 2016), it appears that further updates are on the horizon. In the *Summer Economic Statement*, issued by the Department of Finance in June 2016, a government commitment was made to "[reduce] the rate of Capital Gains Tax for new start-ups to 10 per cent from 2017".[11] The presumption is that this change would be introduced in Finance Bill 2016.

[9] Section 597AA TCA 1997, as introduced by section 35 FA 2015.

[10] See www.revenue.ie/en/about/foi/s16/income-tax-capital-gains-tax-corporation-tax/part-19/19-06-02a.pdf (accessed May 2016).

[11] See www.budget.gov.ie/Budgets/2017/Documents/SES/Summer-Economic-Statement-2016.pdf (accessed June 2016).

### 2.2.3 Startup Refunds for Entrepreneurs Scheme

The Startup Refunds for Entrepreneurs (SURE) scheme is a form of financing available to companies, but not to sole traders/partnerships, that is structured to allow the investor to secure an income tax deduction for the amount of their investment in the company. It is similar to another type of tax-based financing, the Employment and Investment Incentive Scheme (EIIS), which we will review in **Chapter 10**. Many of the conditions and definitions attaching to the operation of the SURE scheme are the same for the EIIS; for example, the requirements that the company be a 'qualifying company' carrying on either 'relevant trading activities' or research and development activities (see **Chapter 10, Section 10.2.1**).[12]

This scheme is an example of the use of the tax rules to encourage former employees to start their own businesses. The other example we have already seen of this use of tax rules is the Start Your Own Business (SYOB) scheme of tax relief, which we reviewed in **Chapter 1**, **Section 1.2.2.1**. As with the entrepreneur relief outlined in **Section 2.2.2.1** above, the conditions attaching to the operation of the SURE scheme are considered restrictive and only a small number of investors qualify for this tax relief every year.

The tax rules setting out the various conditions that must be met in order to rely on the SURE scheme are quite detailed. Set out below is a brief summary of how the scheme operates.

General Overview of the SURE Scheme

- The SURE scheme is available in respect of shares issued by 31 December 2020.
- Where a 'specified individual' (see definition below) subscribes for 'eligible shares' in a 'qualifying company', they will secure an income tax deduction of the value of their investment. This means that if they invest €50,000 in 'eligible shares', they will get a deduction against taxable income of €50,000. The definition of 'eligible shares' is set out in **Chapter 10, Section 10.2.3**.
- The SURE scheme is available only to full-time employees and directors of a 'qualifying company', that is, a newly incorporated company.
- The scheme is not available to a company whose activities were previously carried on by another person, and to which the company

[12] Sections 488 to 507 TCA 1997, as amended by section 18 FA 2015.

succeeded. This means that, for example, where a sole trader incorporates their business into a new company, the new company will not be eligible for a SURE scheme as the activities of the new company were previously carried on by 'another person', in this case, the sole trader.

- There are a number of company activities that are not eligible for the SURE scheme and these are set out at **Appendix I** to **Chapter 10**.
- The relief is available against income tax only; it will not reduce USC or PRSI liabilities.
- The relief is available either for the tax year in which the shares are issued or it can be taken as a deduction from income for any of the six tax years before that tax year.
- The maximum total deduction against taxable income available is €700,000, with a maximum deduction in the year of share issue and each of the six tax years before that tax year of €100,000 per annum. If the SURE investor elects to claim the deduction for any of the six tax years prior to the tax year in which the shares were issued but the deduction is not fully used up, then the deduction may be used in the tax year in which the shares were issued and any subsequent tax year, up to 31 December 2020.
- The tax relief available under the scheme usually operates in a retrospective manner, i.e. it typically triggers a refund of income tax already paid, as opposed to reducing current and future tax liabilities.
- A SURE investor may make two investments into a 'qualifying company', though the second investment must be made by the end of the second tax year following the tax year in which the first investment was made, i.e. by the end of 2017 where the first investment was made in 2015.
- The SURE scheme monies received must be used by the company either for carrying on 'relevant trading activities' or for research and development activities. Additional to this is the requirement that the money is used to 'contribute directly to the creation or maintenance of employment in the company'. Company management may be required to prove to Revenue that the company meets these requirements.

An example of how the SURE scheme may generate refunds of income tax previously paid by a SURE investor is set out in the following case study extract.

## Case Study: Tigim Language Learning Ltd

Aoife is one of the three shareholders of Tigim Language Learning Ltd and has worked as a financial controller and accountant for a number of years. She had always hoped to start her own business and has been quietly saving for a number of years, waiting for an opportunity to arise. After observing Sarah's new methods of language teaching in a classroom location, Aoife became convinced of the huge potential of bringing these methods online and decided to invest her own personal funds in the new business.

Aoife invested €118,000 in Tigim Language Learning Ltd in March 2011, at which point she was earning €20,000 per annum as a director's salary. Aoife's salary for the six years prior to the 2011 year of investment, her election in relation to the tax years in which the deduction should be offset and the tax refunds she expected to secure were as follows:

| | € | € | € |
|---|---|---|---|
| | **Salary level** | **Deduction applied** | **Tax refund** |
| **2011** | 20,000 | – | – |
| **2010** | 12,000 | – | – |
| **2009** | – | – | – |
| **2008** | 85,000 | – | – |
| **2007** | 90,000 | – | – |
| **2006** | 90,000 | 28,000 | 11,760 |
| **2005** | 90,000 | 90,000 | 28,482 |
| | | 118,000 | 40,242 |

Aoife chose to apply the tax deduction in the years 2005 and 2006 as these were the years in which she was paying income tax at a top rate of 42%. Note that Aoife is a single person and was entitled to the single person and PAYE credits for 2005 and 2006.

Unfortunately, Aoife did not take any professional advice in relation to Tigim Language Learning Ltd's eligibility for the SURE scheme. As the scheme requires the investor to subscribe for their shares before making their claim for tax relief, it was only after she had made her investment that Aoife discovered that Tigim Language Learning Ltd was not eligible for the SURE scheme. This was because the Incentives and Financial Services Branch of Revenue, which reviews whether an investment qualifies for the scheme, determined that the company's activities constituted 'professional services' that were being carried out by a 'close company', one of the list of excluded activities noted in **Appendix I** of **Chapter 10**.

#### *2.2.3.1 'Specified Individual' for the Purposes of the SURE Scheme*

To qualify for the tax relief, a SURE investor must be regarded as a 'specified individual', which means meeting a number of conditions, including:

- Owning at least 15% of the SURE scheme company's ordinary share capital for a period of one year, commencing on either the date the SURE shares are issued or the date when the company began carrying on 'relevant trading activities'.
- Being a full-time employee or a full-time director of the new company for this one-year holding period.
- Retaining the SURE shares for at least four years from the date of issue.
- For each of the three years prior to the tax year *before* the tax year in which the SURE investment is made, the investor's income must have been mainly employment/salary income. (***Note:*** in the Tigim case, as Aoife made her investment in March 2011, the three years that must be looked at in relation to the 'sources of income' condition are tax years 2007, 2008 and 2009. The condition would not need to be met in 2010.)
- On the date of investment in SURE shares and for a period of 12 months up to that date, the SURE investor must not own more than 15% of the ordinary shares, loan capital or voting rights of another company. (***Note:*** there are a couple of specific exceptions to this requirement.)[13]

For more information on the SURE scheme, see Revenue leaflet IT15, *Startup Refunds for Entrepreneurs (SURE).*[14]

### *2.2.4 Introduction of Cash by a Shareholder*

We have seen that, unless a company regularly pays dividends to its shareholders, then the only way in which a shareholder can realise cash from their shareholding is to dispose of some or all of their shares in the company. This requires, at the very least, an available purchaser, or, in the more extreme case, liquidation of the company. Many private companies do not pay regular dividends and an individual shareholder (especially a minority shareholder) may not have the influence to change a company's dividend policy.

This lack of flexibility in relation to the ownership of shares highlights a very important point for an existing/potential shareholder who is considering contributing personal cash to the company. The key question is: should this contribution be made by way of a loan, or should the company

[13] See section 495 TCA 1997.

[14] Available at www.revenue.ie/en/tax/it/leaflets/it15.html (accessed May 2016).

issue new shares to the shareholder in return for their contribution? The practical and tax effects of these alternatives are as follows:

- **Contribution by Way of Loan** The shareholder will be subject to income taxes and charges on any interest charged to the company and the company should secure a tax deduction for that interest charge as long as it uses the loan for trading purposes. Some or all of the loan may be repaid without generating any tax liabilities and the loan will not impact on the shareholding of the shareholder. Note that additional tax implications may arise in relation to interest paid on loans provided by directors of a 'close company' – these are set out in **Chapter 5, Section 5.5.2**.
- **Contribution in Exchange for the Issue of Shares** The shareholder will have increased their percentage shareholding in the company and potentially, therefore, their influence. The shareholder will also be entitled to a bigger share of the company's value. There will be no straightforward way for the shareholder to get this contribution back as it is effectively 'locked into' the shares. In order to realise cash, the shareholder will have to dispose of the shares by one of the methods set out in **Section 2.2** above. Assuming this disposal is treated as a 'capital transaction', the issue price of the shares would be included in any future CGT computation as base cost, therefore reducing any capital gain arising.

### *2.2.5 'Business Angels' and Venture Capital*

'Business angels' are typically private investors, many of them successful entrepreneurs, who are looking to invest in start-up and early-stage businesses with potential. They can be individual contacts of the business owner or individuals/syndicates who invest through a more formal process. In Ireland, the Halo Business Angel Network[15] is a joint initiative between Enterprise Ireland and InterTradeIreland. Business angels operating through this network typically take shares in an SME seeking investment, as well as providing their business skills, experience and credibility to the SME. The amount of investment provided is typically in the range €50,000 to €250,000, though syndicates of business angels may invest a lot more than these figures.

For SMEs with greater growth potential (typically within a timeframe of three to five years), venture capital (VC) firms may be a more suitable type of investor. Investments by VC firms often start at the level of €100,000 to €200,000, but may run into the millions for suitable SMEs. Like business angels, VC firms usually invest by subscribing for shares in the SME. The body representing VC firms in the Republic of Ireland and Northern Ireland is the Irish Venture Capital Association. Their website provides a list of all VC firms operating in Ireland.[16]

[15] See www.hban.org

[16] See www.ivca.ie

## 2.3 Grants and Donations

**Appendix I** to this chapter sets out a number of state agencies that provide grants for start-up, early-stage and expanding SMEs. Examples include:

- A feasibility grant from the Local Enterprise Office, which allows a potential start-up to research market demand for a product or service and examine its sustainability (capped at a value of €15,000).[17]
- A digital voucher, worth €2,500, from the Local Enterprise Office for existing SMEs to support the business e-commerce website, online advertising, 'app' development or digital marketing strategy.[18]
- An internationalisation grant, available through Enterprise Ireland, for established SMEs that are researching business opportunities in international markets.[19]

Unless specifically exempted from tax, the proceeds of a grant will be taxable. The specific tax treatment of a taxable grant will depend on whether it is treated as a *revenue* item, i.e. the grant is used to help the business carry out its trading operations and is included in its profit and loss account, or as a *capital* item. If the grant is treated as capital in nature, perhaps because it assists the business in purchasing a significant piece of plant or equipment, then the grant will not be taken into account when calculating the business's trading profits. Instead, it may reduce the capital allowances (tax depreciation) available to the business on the plant or equipment whose purchase was supported by the grant. We will look at capital allowances in more detail in **Chapter 6**. The case study extract below sets out the differing tax treatments of a grant, depending on whether it is regarded as a *revenue* or *capital* item.

### Case Study: Neally Engineering Ltd

Neally Engineering Ltd received a grant of €20,000 from Enterprise Ireland to research the expansion of their business into Spain. The company's auditors determine that the grant should be treated as a revenue item; this means that the €20,000 received is included in the company's trading profits and taxed at the 12.5% trading corporation tax rate, which could generate a tax bill of €2,500. If the company had instead received a €20,000 grant to assist them in the purchase of machinery, then that grant would reduce the 'original cost' of the new machinery by €20,000. Say the machinery cost €150,000, then its 'original cost' would be reduced to €130,000. As capital allowances available for this machinery are claimed over an eight-year period, the net effect of the grant would be to reduce the annual allowance by €2,500.

[17] See www.localenterprise.ie

[18] *Ibid.*

[19] See www.enterpriseireland.ie

### 2.3.1 Employment Grants

Certain employment grants or recruitment subsidies are specifically exempt from tax.[20] An example of such a grant is the JobsPlus scheme, which took effect on 1 July 2013, and encourages employers to recruit unemployed people. Monthly cash payments are made to 'qualifying employers' who employ 'eligible employees' on a full-time basis, as follows:

- for those unemployed for between 12 and 24 months, a payment of €7,500 over two years; and
- the payment for an individual unemployed for more than 24 months will be €10,000 over two years.

Further information on the operation of this scheme can be found on the Department of Social Protection website.[21]

## 2.4 Crowdfunding

'Crowdfunding' is a relatively new concept in Ireland, though its popularity is increasing in an environment where new and existing SMEs are struggling to access financing from the more traditional sources. Crowdfunding is a market-based method of financing, where a large group of individuals or organisations provide finance for business, creative or personal projects, usually via an online platform. There are typically three models for crowdfunding:

(a) **Lending Model** Individuals lend money to a business, organisation or individual to allow them to carry out a specific, named project and the loan is repaid, along with interest. This is also known as 'peer-to-peer lending' and is the most common form of crowdfunding in Ireland. Services such as Linked Finance and GRID Finance allow investors to 'bid' for loans sought by would-be borrowers for amounts from €3,000 to €100,000, at interest rates in the range of 5% to 15%. These fixed-rate loans typically have a maximum term of 36 months.

    From the perspective of the borrowing business, as long as the loan is being used for trading purposes, it will be treated just like a bank loan and the business will get a tax deduction for the interest charged on the loan. An investor in receipt of this interest income is obliged to include this income in their personal tax return and pay income tax, PRSI and USC, as appropriate.

(b) **Equity Model** Individuals make an investment by subscribing for shares in the investee company. This may entitle the investor to an annual return on their shares, i.e. by way of a dividend, or the investor may access any uplift in the value of the company on their exit, e.g. in the event of sale or liquidation of the company. Examples of

[20] Sections 223 to 226 TCA 1997.

[21] See www.welfare.ie/en/Pages/Jobs-Plus.aspx (accessed June 2016).

equity-based crowdfunding businesses are SeedUps, which connects technology start-ups with equity financing of up to €500,000, and Seedrs, which works with a broad range of companies.

With the equity model, the investor is not being paid interest on a loan; however, the company may have an obligation to pay an annual dividend to the investor. Unless certain exceptions apply, the company will be obliged to deduct DWT at the current rate of 20% from the dividend and pay this over to Revenue. An Irish investor shareholder must include the gross dividend in their personal tax return and pay income tax, PRSI and USC, as appropriate. They will get a credit in the tax return for the DWT already withheld. When the Irish investor shareholder disposes of their shares, if the value exceeds the subscription price for the shares they will have made a capital gain, which is subject to capital gains tax (at the current rate of 33%).

(c) **Donations/Rewards Model** Under this model, individuals contribute monies to an entity/project for benevolent reasons and the only reward, if any, is non-financial. This type of crowdfunding often applies to projects in the arts and creative spheres and, given the typically small individual donation size, does not generally trigger tax implications for either the individual contributor or the entity/project in receipt of the monies. Examples of these types of crowdfunding platforms are Fund it and Kickstarter.

***Note:*** the Central Bank of Ireland has stated that the usual protections available to investors (including those provided by the Deposit Guarantee Scheme and the Investor Compensation Company Limited), and the ability to make complaints to the Financial Services Ombudsman, are not available to investors or contributors to crowdfunding websites. This is because this activity is not regulated by the Central Bank. The Central Bank has also highlighted that crowdfunding carries a higher level of commercial risk than other, more mainstream, ways of making investments.[22]

## Appendix I: Examples of Irish State Agencies and Affiliates/Partners providing Financial and Other Supports to Irish SMEs in Start-up, Early-stage and Expansion Phases

In order to increase awareness of the range of state supports for SMEs, an online guide has been made available through the website of the Local Enterprise Offices.[23] We set out below some examples of Irish state agencies and affiliates/partners that provide these supports, categorised

[22] See www.centralbank.ie/press-area/press-releases/Pages/ConsumerNoticeCrowdfunding.aspx (accessed May 2016).

[23] See www.localenterprise.ie/smeonlinetool/businessdetails.aspx

across three headings: General Business, Industry-specific State Agencies and Public/Private Funds.

### *General Business*

- Enterprise Ireland provides financial support for Irish businesses with *export* sales across a range of companies, including high-potential start-ups, SMEs operating in the manufacturing or internationally traded services markets, large Irish companies and foreign-owned businesses in the food and natural resource sectors that are based in Ireland (see www.enterprise-ireland.com). Enterprise Ireland is currently managing a €175 million seed and venture capital scheme that covers the years 2013 to 2018.
- SME Credit Guarantee Scheme – under this scheme, administered by the Department of Jobs, Enterprise and Innovation (DJEI), the State provides commercial lenders with a 75% guarantee, for which a borrower pays a 2% premium. This is aimed at facilitating lending to SMEs that either have inadequate security or have a novel business model, market, sector or technology that is not readily understood by commercial lenders. Application should be made to participating banks. (For more details see www.djei.ie/en/What-We-Do/Supports-for-SMEs/Access-to-Finance/SME-Credit-Guarantee-Scheme.)
- InterTradeIreland – an all-island organisation, supported by the governments of Ireland and Northern Ireland, which offers practical cross-border business funding, intelligence and contacts (see www.intertradeireland.com).
- Irish Business and Innovation Centres – regional centres, part of an EU-supported network, focused on supporting innovative businesses with high growth potential. The websites of the four regional centres are: www.dublinbic.ie; www.southeastbic.ie; www.corkbic.com; and www.westbic.ie.
- Local Enterprise Offices (previously City & County Enterprise Boards) provide advice, information and support for start-up and expanding businesses (see www.localenterprise.ie).
- Microfinance Ireland – under the auspices of the Local Enterprise Offices, this body provides unsecured business loans to start-up and expanding micro-SMEs, being SMEs with a turnover of less than €2 million and staff numbers of no more than 10 (see www.microfinanceireland.ie).
- ManagementWorks – a training network, supported by the Department of Jobs, Enterprise and Innovation, which provides management training services to SMEs, including advice and mentoring on financing the business (see www.managementworks.ie).

### *Industry-specific State Agencies*

- Bord Iascaigh Mhara helps to develop the Irish seafood industry by providing technical expertise, business support, funding, training and promotion of responsible environmental practice (see www.bim.ie).

- Fáilte Ireland supports the tourism industry by providing a range of practical business supports to help tourism businesses better manage and market their products and services (see www.failteireland.ie).
- Teagasc is the national body providing integrated research, advisory and training services to the agriculture and food industry and rural communities (see www.teagasc.ie).
- Bord Bia supports the growth of the Irish food and horticultural industries (see www.bordbia.ie).
- Údarás na Gaeltachta is the regional authority responsible for the development of the Gaeltacht; it does this by funding and fostering a wide range of enterprise development and job creation initiatives and by supporting strategic language, cultural and community-based activities (see www.udaras.ie).

### *Public/Private Funds*

- Ireland Strategic Investment Fund (ISIF) (formerly National Pension Reserve Fund) has established two SME funds, financed by ISIF and third-party investors, and operated by commercial asset managers:
  - €300 million to €350 million SME Equity Fund, operated by Carlyle Cardinal Ireland (www.cardinalcapitalgroup.com).
  - €450 million Irish Direct Lending Fund, operated by BlueBay Asset Management (www.bluebay.com).
- Strategic Banking Corporation of Ireland – initial funding of €400 million provided by ISIF, Germany's KfW bank and the European Investment Bank is available for SMEs through banks and specialist on-lenders on more favourable terms than usually available (see www.sbci.gov.ie).
- €125 million Development Capital Fund – managed by MML Growth Capital Partners Ireland Limited – funded by Enterprise Ireland, the EU and commercial backers (see www.mmlcapital.ie).

CHAPTER 3

# ACQUIRING OR LETTING A BUSINESS PREMISES



Most businesses require premises of some type and the most important tax issue to be dealt with when acquiring or letting premises is value-added tax (VAT). Our main focus in this chapter will, therefore, be the possible VAT implications of buying or letting a business premises, as well as the VAT implications that may arise on the sub-let of a part of such premises. We will also look at the VAT implications that might arise if significant building works are carried out on the premises after they have been purchased by, or let to, the business.

First, it is important to note that the rules relating to the VAT implications of property transactions changed completely on 1 July 2008. In addition, for properties in existence before 1 July 2008, especially those with leases of at least 10 years' duration that continue to run, a set of transitional VAT rules were introduced. So, there are now two systems of VAT on property rules in operation: the 'new rules' and the 'transitional rules'. In order to avoid confusion, all of the VAT information set out below and the illustrative examples relate to the 'new' VAT on property rules.

As we are looking at the possible VAT implications arising when a business acquires business premises, we are solely focused here on commercial property. The VAT implications arising on residential property transactions, or commercial site sales, are outside the scope of this book.

When buying or letting business premises, the other relevant transaction tax is stamp duty and we will discuss this briefly later in the chapter.

## 3.1 A Fundamental VAT Concept: 'VAT In–VAT Out'

VAT is a tax issue that can easily confuse people and this is especially the case when looking at the VAT implications of property transactions.

Before looking at these, it is helpful to note a fundamental VAT concept that provides a general framework for VAT on trading activities as well as for VAT on property transactions. We will call this concept '**VAT 101**' and it goes as follows:

> **VAT 101**: If a business is entitled to reclaim the VAT charged to it when it purchases goods/services that are to be used in the business, then typically that business charges VAT on the goods/services it supplies to its customers.

Another way of thinking about this is 'VAT in–VAT out', i.e. if the business can reclaim the VAT charged to it on its purchases (VAT in) then it must charge VAT on its supplies (VAT out). Of course, there are exceptions to this, but keeping this 'VAT 101' concept in mind will usually provide a useful starting point for addressing VAT issues.

The reverse of this 'VAT 101' concept is also generally true, i.e. that if a business must charge VAT on the supplies (VAT out) it makes to its customers, then generally it may reclaim the VAT charged to it on its purchases (VAT in). (***Note:*** the purchases must be used by the business for the purposes of its VATable business and must not be categorised as 'non-deductible' items. For more on this aspect, see **Chapter 4, Section 4.2.4**.)

Many people assume that if their business is VAT-registered, then any VAT charged to the business may be reclaimed by it, but this is incorrect. The VAT registration can be used for reclaim purposes *only* on purchases that are used by the business to generate its VATable supplies. In other words, the 'use' to which purchases are put will dictate whether or not VAT charged on those purchases may be reclaimed. In **Chapter 4**, we will look at how the 'VAT 101' concept (VAT in–VAT out) applies to the trading activities of different types of businesses.

### *3.1.1 VAT and Legal Documentation*

In addition to looking at some VAT implications of property purchase, letting, sub-letting and refurbishment works, we will also look at how these different VAT implications may impact on the contract for sale or the lease documentation. In doing so we will be referring to some of the sample

VAT clauses set out in the Standard Contract for Sale templates prepared by the Law Society of Ireland.[1] There are a number of sample VAT clauses set out in the Law Society's Standard Contract for Sale, reflecting the fact that there are numerous possible VAT implications on property transactions; we will highlight only the clauses potentially relevant to the specific examples set out below.

VAT clauses form one of the two main VAT-related requirements in the legal documentation for the sale or letting of a property. The other requirement is the completion of the 'Pre-Contract VAT Enquiries', which are effectively a series of questions designed to establish the exact VAT history of a property. (Again, a comprehensive template for these inquiries has been prepared by the Law Society.) It is best practice that the intending purchaser/tenant of a property secure completed Pre-Contract VAT Enquiries from the vendor/landlord, as these should also clearly set out why the intending vendor/landlord is proposing to handle the VAT issues as they are.

## 3.2 VAT Implications of Leasing a Property

The majority of businesses in the start-up phase will not wish to commit limited resources to buying business premises and will instead lease them for a fixed period. The basic rule in relation to leases is that they are treated as a VAT-exempt supply of services. This means that no VAT charges arise, either on the creation of the lease or on the rental payments. However, there is an 'option to tax' a letting of commercial property so that it becomes a VATable letting.[2] A very significant point to note here is that the 'option to tax' a letting can be exercised at the *sole discretion of the landlord* – the agreement of the tenant is not required.

(***Note:*** the 'option to tax' is not available on a letting between 'connected parties'[3] unless the tenant or occupier is in a position to reclaim at least 90% of input VAT in respect of the letting. This concept of 'partial VAT recovery' is explained in **Chapter 4**.)

Why would a landlord exercise an 'option to tax' an otherwise VAT-exempt lease? The answer goes right back to our so-called 'VAT 101' concept. If the landlord was charged VAT on their acquisition of an interest in the property, whether they bought the property or it was let to them, and the landlord reclaimed that VAT (VAT in), then in order to avoid having to repay that VAT to Revenue, the landlord must put the property to VATable use (VAT out). In the context of the letting of property, this means exercising the 'option to tax' and charging VAT at the standard rate (currently 23%) on all rental invoices/payments.

[1] The author and the publisher acknowledge that the extracts from *Special Condition 3* of the Contract for Sale are reproduced on pp. 57 and 59 with the approval of the Law Society of Ireland, subject to the caveat that they are extracts only and that before any transaction is embarked upon, proper legal advice should be obtained by reference to the entirety of the current Law Society Clauses.

[2] Section 97 of the Value-Added Tax Consolidation Act 2010 (VATCA 2010).

[3] As defined in section 97(3) VATCA 2010.

The VAT rules state that the landlord must formally exercise the option to tax by either:

- including a clause in the lease agreement stating that the option to tax is being exercised and that VAT is being charged on the rent; or
- issuing a document/letter to the tenant notifying them that the option to tax is being exercised and that the rent will be subject to VAT.

In the case study extract below, we see how the landlord's exercise of the option to tax a lease impacts on a VAT-exempt business.

### Case Study: Tigim Language Learning Ltd

We return to our training company, Tigim Language Learning Ltd, which provided VAT-exempt vocational language courses only in the early years of the business. The company started trading in 2009, with the intention of providing this training in classrooms, so they took a lease on fairly sizeable commercial premises, including regular office space and some large open space that could be partitioned into small classrooms. The lease is for an eight-year term, with an annual rental of €15,000. During the course of negotiating the lease, the company's finance director, Aoife, is dismayed to discover that the landlord is not obliged to charge VAT on the rent but that he is opting to do so. Aoife assumes that she must have misunderstood; why would the landlord choose to charge VAT to Tigim Language Learning Ltd when he knows the company is a VAT-exempt business and cannot reclaim the VAT? She speaks to the property agent in the hope of persuading the landlord to change his mind but there is no change in the VAT position and, ultimately, she must accept it. In the meantime, Sarah convinces Aoife that these specific premises are the best option for the company in terms of facilities and their central Galway city location, and that the annual irrecoverable VAT cost of €3,225 is definitely worth paying.

All is not lost for Tigim Language Learning Ltd, however. The business expands rapidly, to such an extent that Sarah, Jamie and Aoife are wondering if their business model is sustainable. After all, the more classes they run, the more premises they need, whether that is on-site or by renting conference rooms, etc., by the hour. The shareholders ultimately decide that moving some of their business online – by delivering their courses online – is the way forward. This process is started in early 2011 and proves to be such a success that by mid-2013 most courses are delivered online and the company no longer needs some of the space its rents.

It is not unusual for businesses to sub-lease a portion of their premises and, of course, this sub-letting will also attract VAT implications. Set out below is an example of how a sub-letting can actually improve the VAT position of a landlord.

### Case Study: Tigim Language Learning Ltd

In September 2013, Tigim Language Learning Ltd becomes a landlord itself when it manages to sub-let part of its classroom space to Dugimar Ltd, which is a VATable business. Aoife secures some specific VAT advice prior to granting this sub-lease and is delighted to discover that there is a way of handling this sub-lease that will allow Tigim Language Learning Ltd to reclaim at least some of the now €3,450 (at the higher rate of 23%) VAT being charged to it by its landlord. The company's tax advisor explains that, just as Tigim's landlord had sole discretion to exercise its option to tax the 2009 head lease, so Tigim Language Learning Ltd now has sole discretion to exercise its option to tax on the sub-lease. If the company chooses to exercise its option, this means that Tigim Language Learning Ltd must register for VAT and charge VAT at 23% on the rental invoices to Dugimar Ltd. Tigim Language Learning Ltd will then be allowed to reclaim a portion of the VAT charged by its landlord on the head lease.

But how can this be the case if Tigim Language Learning Ltd is a VAT-exempt business and so cannot register for VAT? The answer is that there has been a change of use of part of the property. Once Tigim Language Learning Ltd stops using part of the property for exempt supplies (i.e. its own business) and instead uses it for VATable lettings (i.e. rental income on which the option to tax is exercised and VAT is charged), then the company creates an entitlement to reclaim VAT in relation to the part of the property now being used for VATable lettings. In other words, by opting to charge VAT on this sub-let ('VAT out'), Tigim Language Learning Ltd has created an entitlement to reclaim VAT ('VAT in').

As it turns out, exactly 50% of the property is now being sub-let on a VATable basis (because Tigim Language Learning Ltd has exercised its option to tax the sub-lease) for an annual rental of €10,000. The VAT implications of this will be as follows.

Tigim Language Learning Ltd can now reclaim 50% of the annual VAT charge arising on its head lease, i.e. €1,725 (€3,450 ÷ 2), so it still incurs a non-deductible annual VAT charge of €1,725 on its head lease. The company must charge VAT at 23% on the sub-lease, being €2,300 (i.e. €10,000 × 23%) and pay this over to Revenue. As Dugimar Ltd is using the property for its VATable business, it can fully reclaim the VAT charge of €2,300 charged to it by Tigim Language Learning Ltd.

Tigim Language Learning Ltd's experience highlights some important points. First, it is the *use* to which the property is put that either allows the tenant (Tigim Language Learning Ltd) to reclaim VAT arising on the rental invoices/payments or not. This use can change during the course of the lease, thereby also changing the entitlement to reclaim VAT. In addition, the company's experience shows that, for VAT purposes, the same property can be divided into two or more portions, with different VAT implications arising for each portion.

To return to an earlier point, it should *not* be assumed that just because Tigim Language Learning Ltd is now VAT-registered, that it can reclaim VAT on all invoices charged to it. The VAT registration is very specifically granted in respect of the company's VATable lettings only and this means that only VAT charged on invoices relating to that taxable activity may be reclaimed.

## 3.3 A Second Fundamental VAT (on Property) Concept

We noted above that the fundamental concept of 'VAT in–VAT out' (our 'VAT 101' concept) is as relevant to VAT on trading activities as it is to VAT on property transactions.

We look now at a second fundamental VAT concept (what we will call our 'VAT 102' concept) that is specific to property transactions. This is the idea that a **'new' property has a 'VAT life' of 20 years**. What this means is that once a property has been 'developed' or 'completed' (i.e. a new build), then there will be VAT implications for any transactions involving that property for its 20-year VAT life. 'Transactions involving the property' refers to the *use* to which the property is put year on year, i.e. whether the property is used to make VATable supplies or VAT-exempt supplies, or both, in each of the 20 years after 'completion'. Once a building's VAT life has expired, then there will be no further VAT implications, unless the property has been 'refurbished' during this time. We will review the VAT implications of refurbishment at **Section 3.6** below.

This point is so important that it bears repeating: a **'new' property has a 'VAT life' of 20 years.** What this means is that once a property has been 'developed' or 'completed' (i.e. a new build), then there will be VAT implications for any transactions involving that property for its 20-year VAT life.

The owner of a property that is within its VAT life is said to be the owner of a 'capital good', the rules relating to which are known collectively as the 'Capital Goods Scheme' (CGS).[4] A property's 20-year VAT life, therefore, refers to the 20-year adjustment period under the CGS.

[4] Sections 63–64 VATCA 2010.

The rules covering capital goods mean that any *change to the use* of a capital good in a given year (as compared to the previous year) during the 20-year adjustment period/VAT life may trigger VAT implications. These VAT implications are referred to as a 'CGS adjustment'. The other significant consequence of owning a capital good is that its owner is obliged to retain a full year-on-year record (the 'CGS record') of the use to which the property is put during its 20-year VAT life. The owner of the capital good may be obliged to produce that record to Revenue officials (e.g. in the case of a Revenue audit or inquiry) or to a future purchaser/tenant of the property.

So, our '**VAT 102**' concept is as follows:

> All 'newly completed' property has a VAT life of 20 years. This VAT life is the 20-year CGS adjustment period and is subject to the Capital Goods Scheme.

Where a property is within its VAT life, then VAT implications may arise depending on the use to which the property is put. If, say, the property is let soon after completion and 12 years later the letting ceases, then, as the property is still within its VAT life, the VAT implications of the change of use of the property will have to be dealt with. If, instead, the letting ceased after 21 years, then the property's VAT life would have expired and no further VAT implications would arise on the use of the property (assuming there is no refurbishment).

This can be illustrated with dates, as in **Example 3.1** below.

### Example 3.1: Expiry of VAT Life of Newly Developed Property

Construction of new commercial property is completed on 1 September 2013, meaning that the property's VAT life (CGS adjustment period) covers the period 1 September 2013 to 31 August 2033. The property is immediately sold, with VAT charged on the sale. The purchaser lets the property on a 30-year lease, which commences on 1 December 2013, and exercises its 'option to tax' the lease.

**Scenario 1** Lease surrendered in December 2025 – property is within its 20-year VAT life, so VAT implications must be dealt with for a further eight years of use.

**Scenario 2** Lease surrendered in December 2034 – property's VAT life has expired so there will be no further VAT implications arising on the use of this property, as long as the property has not been refurbished.

How does this concept of the 'VAT life' link back to the concept of 'VAT in–VAT out'?

In **Example 3.1** above, the builder reclaimed the VAT charged on all construction costs, professional fees, etc. incurred in building the property.

Because the builder reclaimed the VAT charges (VAT in), he must charge VAT on the sale of the property (VAT out), otherwise he may have to repay all input VAT to Revenue. The purchaser of the property then reclaims the VAT charged on purchase (VAT in), so the purchaser/landlord must charge VAT on the rental invoices (VAT out). If the purchaser/landlord charges VAT on the rental invoices for less than 20 years (Scenario 1), then a significant VAT charge could arise for the landlord on the surrender of the lease (depending on the subsequent use to which the property is put). No such charge would arise if the lease surrender happens after the 20-year VAT life has elapsed (Scenario 2).

## 3.4 VAT Implications of Purchasing a Property

When the purchase of a commercial property is being considered, the first questions that should be asked by the purchaser/agent is whether the property is 'within its VAT life' (this is also known as being 'in the VAT net') and whether the vendor is required to charge VAT on the sale. These two questions may appear to be one and the same, but that is not the case, due to one of the specific rules relating to VAT on property transactions.

This rule states that VAT must be charged on the sale of a developed/ completed property where the property is treated as a 'new' property. Conversely, if the property is treated as an 'old' property, then, on the face of it, the sale is VAT-exempt.

A few definitions will clarify the concepts involved and we will see in **Sections 3.4.1** and **3.4.2** below that the determination of the property as being 'completed', 'developed', 'old' or 'new' will impact on whether or not VAT arises on the sale.

### *3.4.1 'Completed' and 'Developed' Property*

We have referred above to the creation of a capital good where a new property is 'completed'. But commercial properties can be sold in different states of completion, so what does 'completion' mean for VAT purposes? Rather unhelpfully, the VAT rules say that a property is treated as a 'completed' property when the property has reached the stage where it can "effectively be used for the purposes for which it was designed".[5]

The rule of thumb here is to consider whether the property is at the stage that is normally regarded by potential purchasers/property agents as 'completed'. What this means is that, for example, if it is typical in the commercial factory market for that type of property to be sold at 'shell and core' stage with the purchaser being left to carry out internal fit-out, then a newly built factory space completed to the 'shell and core' stage will be treated as 'completed' for VAT purposes.

[5] Section 94 VATCA 2010.

In addition to the general definition above, the VAT rules specifically state that all the utility services (i.e. electricity, water, etc.) must be connected in order for a property to be treated as 'completed'.

The concept of 'development' of an existing property is somewhat easier, as two, more clearly defined, tests apply. As we noted above, a capital good can be created when an existing property is the subject of development works and these works are not treated as a 'minor' development. A 'minor'development is either:

- work that does not, and is not intended to, adapt the property for 'materially altered use'; *or*
- the value of work is less than 25% of the property's sale price, after development (the '25% test').

### Example 3.2: 'Minor' Development Works

If a property's development works are valued at €200,000 and the subsequent property sale price is €1,250,000, then the development works are treated as 'minor' (200/1250 = 16%) and the property would not be regarded as 'developed'. If the development works were valued at €400,000 and the subsequent sale price was €1,250,000, then the works would not be treated as 'minor' (400/1250 = 32%).

Note that the '25% test' is subject to the 'materially altered use' test, meaning that if there is materially altered use, then the 25% test is irrelevant and the property will be treated as 'developed'. An example of a 'materially altered use' is a situation where a property that was once used for commercial purposes subsequently being used for residential purposes.

The case study extract below details a property that has been redeveloped with a 'materially altered use' and the VAT implications of this redevelopment for the property owner.

### Case Study: Neally Engineering Ltd

The property purchased by Neally Engineering Ltd is a classic example of property that has a 'materially altered use'. The property is located outside Navan, County Meath and previously comprised the indoor arena, stables and office space of a highly regarded stud farm. In 2004 the business owner died and her husband later closed down the business with a view to developing the property as it is located beside a main access road to Navan. The relevant planning permission was secured and by September 2007 the property had been developed into a factory and office space. As the use of the property had been 'materially altered' from agricultural use to commercial use, the property was treated as 'developed' and the owner was treated as having created a capital good.

Having registered for VAT and reclaimed all VAT charged on the development works, the owner was keen to ensure VAT was charged on the sale of the property.

### *3.4.2 Distinction Between 'New' and 'Old' Property*

In assessing whether or not VAT will arise on the sale of property, not only must consideration be given to whether the property is treated as 'developed' or 'completed' for VAT purposes, regard must also be had as to whether the property is treated as 'old' or 'new' under the VAT rules.

A property will be treated as 'new' property for a maximum of five years following completion or development ('the five-year rule'). However, if the property is sold within that five-year period to an 'unconnected party',[6] then the property will continue to be treated as 'new' for the first two years of occupation only ('the two-year rule') on a second/subsequent sale. If the property is sold after this two-year occupation, then even if the five-year period has not yet elapsed, the property will not be treated as 'new'.

If neither the five-year rule nor the two-year rule applies, then the property will be treated as 'old' and no VAT may be charged on the sale of the property,[7] i.e. the sale would be VAT-exempt. For a potential purchaser, this seems like a good result. If the purchaser is not in a position to reclaim any VAT charged on the sale (because it makes VAT-exempt supplies like Tigim Language Learning Ltd, for example), then this saves them a significant VAT cost. Even if the purchaser can reclaim the VAT charge, a VAT-exempt sale saves them the cost of financing the payment of the VAT charge to the vendor until such time as the VAT reclaim can be secured from Revenue.

### *3.4.3 Joint 'Option to Tax' the Sale*

Where a property is treated as 'old' for VAT purposes, due to the fact that it does not meet either the five-year rule or the two-year rule set out above, then, without further action, the sale of the property would be VAT-exempt. It is unlikely that the vendor would be happy to sell the building on a VAT-exempt basis, however, due to the operation of the 'VAT 101' concept, i.e. the entitlement to reclaim VAT (VAT in) generally arises if VAT is charged on the supply (VAT out). If the vendor has reclaimed VAT

[6] See section 97(3) VATCA 2010.
[7] Section 94 VATCA 2010.

on acquiring/developing the building (VAT in) but cannot charge VAT on the sale of the building (VAT out), then the vendor must repay all this input VAT to Revenue.

For the vendor, however, all is not lost as there is a specific VAT rule that allows the VATable sale of 'old' property *if the vendor and purchaser both agree to it.* By virtue of a rule that seems to defy natural laws, the 'old' property becomes 'new' again. This is known as a 'joint option to tax' and, if exercised, would allow the vendor to retain the input VAT previously claimed because a VAT charge, at the current reduced VAT rate of 13.5%, would now arise on the sale of the property.[8] (***Note:*** the 'joint option to tax' the sale of a property differs from the 'option to tax' the letting of a property, as the former option requires the agreement of both vendor and purchaser, while the latter option can be exercised unilaterally by the landlord.)

Where no 'joint option to tax' is exercised, the vendor may seek an increased purchase price to compensate them for the fact that they have no entitlement to reclaim, or retain a previous claim of, input VAT on the acquisition/development of the property. The size of the increase is likely to be at least the value of the lost VAT reclaim. In this situation, the relevant VAT clause would include the following wording:

> "In addition to the Purchase Price, the Purchaser shall pay the Vendor the sum of € ________ being the amount for which, as a consequence of the Sale being exempt, the Vendor is liable to account to Revenue under Section 64(6)(b)(i) of the VAT Act [and € ________ being the amount which, as a consequence of the Sale not being taxable, the Vendor is unable to reclaim from Revenue under Section 64(6)(a) of the VAT Act]"[9]

The first part of this clause covers the situation where the vendor has already reclaimed VAT on acquisition/development costs from Revenue and is now obliged to refund these reclaims, while the second part covers the situation where the VAT reclaims have not yet been made.

This specific clause is relevant where the purchaser is a taxable person but chooses not to exercise the 'joint option to tax'. A different version of this clause applies where the purchaser is not a taxable entity for VAT purposes. The case study extract below demonstrates how the sale of a property, which is VAT-exempt on the face of it (because the property is defined as 'old' for VAT purposes), becomes subject to VAT by the exercise of the 'joint option to tax.'

[8] Section 94 VATCA 2010.

[9] Law Society of Ireland, *Special Condition 3*, Clause 3.4.1 (February 2014 Edition). © Law Society of Ireland

### Case Study: Neally Engineering Ltd

We referred above to the County Meath factory and office space purchased by Neally Engineering Ltd. The property was completed in September 2007 and, though in 'turnkey' condition, no purchaser was found for it until Neally Engineering Ltd bought the property in February 2013. At that stage, five years had elapsed since the property was 'developed' and it was regarded as 'old' property for VAT purposes. The initial purchase price being discussed by the property agent was €750,000. When the directors of Neally Engineering Ltd, Martin and Danielle, were told of the property's VAT status, they were delighted, thinking that the company could now avoid having to finance a VAT charge of €101,250 (i.e. €750,000 × 13.5%) for the weeks between paying the VAT charge to the vendor and securing the VAT reclaim from Revenue. They also thought that having a VAT-exempt property would give the company more flexibility in relation to future use of the property. Being ambitious, they had long-term business plans setting out huge growth targets, which they hoped would involve a move to bigger premises in the years ahead.

There was a caveat, however, which changed the potential deal significantly. Due to the fact that the vendor had reclaimed all of the VAT on development costs (estimated at €250,000), the vendor required the purchaser to agree to a 'joint option to tax' the sale; otherwise the sale price would be increased to €1 million. The vendor's rationale was very clear – if the purchaser did not agree to the joint option to tax, then he would be obliged to repay all of the VAT on development costs back to Revenue, so instead he intended to add this amount to the initial purchase price of €750,000. The sale price had been presented in this way – a price of €750,000, which would increase to €1 million if the purchaser would not agree to a joint option to tax – because not every purchaser would do so.

Martin and Danielle agreed to the joint option to tax. This generated a VAT charge of €101,250 on the sale and they wondered how the company would be in a position to fund this VAT charge, albeit on a temporary basis.

### *3.4.4 'Self-account/Reverse Charge' to VAT on a Joint Option to Tax*

There is another VAT rule specific to property transactions that applies where there is a sale of commercial property and the parties have agreed to a joint option to tax, and it does away with the movement of the VAT sales charge in a circular loop. In the normal course, the purchaser would pay the sales VAT to the vendor, who would include this amount in the 'VAT on Sales' box of the vendor's VAT return and pay it over to Revenue.

The purchaser would then include the same VAT amount in the 'VAT on Purchases' box of their VAT return and wait to receive a refund of the amount from Revenue. This entire process could take a number of weeks/ months.

In these specific circumstances, the vendor does not charge VAT to the purchaser; instead, the purchaser 'self-accounts' (or 'reverse charges') a sales VAT charge in their own VAT return and also includes a purchases VAT charge for the same amount in the same VAT return. Effectively, the VAT charge is dealt with by two entries in the purchaser's VAT return. The practical impact of this 'reverse charge' rule on the purchase of property that is subject to the 'joint option to tax' is set out below.

### Case Study: Neally Engineering Ltd

The purchasers of the factory, Neally Engineering Ltd, 'self-account' (or 'reverse charge') the VAT amount of €101,250, meaning that the company includes this amount in the 'VAT on Sales' box of its VAT return and take a deduction for the same amount in the 'VAT on Purchases' box in the same VAT return. This leaves a net position of zero VAT payable and means that the VAT charge of €101,250 does not need to be moved through the chain – purchaser to vendor to Revenue to purchaser.

Where the vendor and purchaser are exercising the joint option to tax the sale of a property, the relevant VAT clause would include the following wording:

> "The Sale of the Subject Property is of a Freehold ( . . . ) Interest in the Subject Property, which is otherwise exempt. The Purchaser is a Taxable Person which status the Purchaser warrants to the Vendor. The joint option to tax the Sale under Section 94(5) or Section 94(7)(b) as appropriate of the VAT Act is hereby exercised by the Vendor and the Purchaser. The Purchaser shall account to Revenue for any VAT arising on the Sale upon a reverse charge basis in accordance with Section 94(6) or Section 94(7)(c) as appropriate of the VAT Act".[10]

(***Note:*** the purchaser must warrant to the vendor that the purchaser is a taxable (i.e. VATable) person. Also, the purchaser accounts to Revenue for the VAT on sale by 'self-accounting' for the VAT amount in their VAT return.)

[10] Law Society of Ireland, *Special Condition 3*, Clause 3.3.1 (February 2014 Edition). © Law Society of Ireland

It is very important to understand that exercising a joint option to tax the sale of a property has much more impact than 'solving' a vendor's VAT input issue and simplifying VAT payment issues at the time of the sale. In fact, the exercise of the option has long-term consequences for the purchased property and its new owners, as we can see in the case study extract below.

### Case Study: Neally Engineering Ltd

The tax advisor to Neally Engineering Ltd was very quick to emphasise to Danielle and Martin that although the VAT issues surrounding the purchase of the property were ultimately dealt with by way of some paperwork, they should not assume that the property was 'out of the VAT net'. In fact, in purchasing a premises under a joint option to tax, the company had purchased a capital good with a VAT life of 20 years. This carries two significant consequences:

1. the company had acquired the obligation to retain a full Capital Goods Scheme record of the property, which is essentially a full VAT analysis of the use to which the property is put, for the next 20 years; and
2. any change to the use of the property during this 20-year period could trigger negative VAT implications.

We will look more closely at the record-keeping required by the Capital Goods Scheme in **Section 3.7**. For now, we look at what may happen if, after the initial purchase of commercial property that is subject to the joint option to tax, some of the property that was initially used for VATable purposes is put to VAT-exempt use, i.e. there is a change of use.

## 3.5 Capital Goods Scheme Adjustment due to 'Change of Property Use'

We have noted that the purchase of property that is subject to VAT on purchase results in the creation of a capital good that has a VAT life of 20 years. Combining our 'VAT 101' and 'VAT 102' concepts, where the purchaser has reclaimed all of the VAT arising on the purchase (VAT in), then the purchaser must use the property for a VATable purpose for the next 20 years (VAT out). If the property is put to VAT-exempt use, or partially exempt use, at any time during that 20-year period, a CGS adjustment will arise, which means that the purchaser must repay to Revenue a portion of the VAT reclaimed at the time of purchase.

### Case Study: Neally Engineering Ltd

In the case of Neally Engineering Ltd, the vendor and purchaser agreed to trigger the joint option to tax, meaning that Neally Engineering Ltd could self-account for the VAT of €101,250 (i.e. include this amount in the 'VAT on Sales' box in its VAT return). The company reclaimed this VAT by including an amount of €101,250 in the 'VAT on Purchases' box of the same VAT return. This €101,250 VAT charge could be the subject of a CGS adjustment, requiring repayment of some or all of it to Revenue during the property's 20-year VAT life.

An example of the impact caused by a change of use of a property that is within its 20-year VAT life is set out below.

### Example 3.3: Change of Use and CGS Adjustments

Consider the case where a company that makes VATable supplies (e.g. production and sale of Thai food) to its customers buys a 'new' property, which is subject to a VAT charge of €67,500 on the purchase. As it is entitled to do, the company reclaims this VAT charge from Revenue. After eight years, the company's first generation of owners retires and the next generation decides to experiment with a new income stream, so the company continues to produce and sell Thai food, but also provides Thai cookery classes for professional chefs. As vocational training is a VAT-exempt activity, the company has begun to use a portion of the property to make VAT-exempt supplies (in this case, say, 30% of the property is being used to make VAT-exempt supplies). The property has gone from being used for 100% VATable supplies to being used for a mix of VATable (70%) and VAT-exempt (30%) supplies. The classes continue for two years, at the end of which time the classes cease and, once again, the company is using the property to make 100% VATable supplies.

According to our 'VAT 102' concept (see above), the company owns a property with a 20-year VAT life. For the first eight years of this, the company is using the property to make VATable supplies (production and sale of food) so the VAT status of the property is undisturbed. For the next two years, the use of the property is changed to a mix of making VATable supplies (production and sale of food) and VAT-exempt supplies (provision of cookery classes), thereby generating a CGS adjustment to the company's VAT return for each of these years. In very broad terms, the adjustment in each year would be calculated as a percentage of one year's VAT element, i.e. as a percentage of €3,375 (€67,500 divided by 20). For the Thai food business, the annual CGS adjustment is estimated at €1,013, being €3,375 × 30%. Once the company activities revert to 100% VATable supplies, CGS adjustments would no longer be required.

### 3.5.1 How a Letting can Constitute a Change of Use

We saw in the previous example that, by adding VAT-exempt activities to its business, the company changed the use to which a portion of its premises was being put. The same issue can also arise where a business making VATable supplies lets (or sub-lets) some of its premises. We have seen that the basic rule in relation to the letting of commercial property is that the lease is treated as a VAT-exempt supply of property, unless the landlord exercises their 'option to tax' this VAT-exempt letting. In order for that option to tax to be effective, however, it must be formalised and VAT must be charged on the rental payments. In the case study extract below, we see how an informal letting of surplus space can constitute a VAT-exempt letting, which can trigger a CGS adjustment for the landlord.

#### Case Study: Neally Engineering Ltd

Let's return to our ambitious brother and sister, Martin and Danielle of Neally Engineering Ltd, whose company bought the Meath factory/office space on 4 February 2013. The company had taken on more space than it required for the start-up phase of the business, so in order to maximise cash flow, Danielle and Martin decided to let a part of the factory to a car repair business for 18 months from March 2013. The company retained a significant portion of the factory and all of the office space, and used this space to generate its VATable supplies.

The total floor area of the premises is 1,058 square metres, 285 square metres of which Neally Engineering Ltd let to the car repair business. As the owner of that business, Tom, is an old friend of Martin's, Neally Engineering Ltd did not put formal lease paperwork in place and did not take any VAT advice on the sub-lease. As a result, the company's auditor only discovered the existence of the sub-lease about 14 months after it had started. He discussed the issue with the company's tax advisor and discovered that the company had to pay a CGS adjustment to Revenue as it did not 'opt to tax' the lease and, in not doing so, had put a portion of the property to VAT-exempt use.

If we apply a straight fraction to the estimated annual VAT element of €5,063* that is the subject of a CGS adjustment, we would get the following estimated annual CGS adjustment:

$$\frac{\text{Let space}}{\text{Total property space}} = \frac{285}{1{,}058} \times €5{,}063 = €1{,}364$$

* Being the total VAT charge arising on purchase of €101,250, divided by 20 years of the property's VAT life.

## 3.6 Refurbishment Works

A final element that we need to consider are the VAT implications arising where either the owner of a property or their tenant carry out 'refurbishment works' on a previously 'completed'/'developed' property. In this situation, the party that carries out these works creates their own capital good, which attracts all the obligations arising under the Capital Goods Scheme for the developers/purchasers of property. The significant difference between the capital good of a completed or developed property and the capital good of 'refurbishment works' is that the latter has a VAT life of 10 years.

So, in a variation on a theme, our **'VAT 102A'** concept is:

> All refurbishment works have a VAT life of 10 years. This VAT life is the 10-year CGS adjustment period and is also subject to the full obligations of the CGS.

First, we should note that 'refurbishment works' are 'development works'. 'Development works' include demolition, extension, alteration or construction works. General property fit-out is not treated as 'refurbishment works'; maintenance and repair work are also excluded from the definition.

### Case Study: Neally Engineering Ltd

Our ambitious engineering duo, Martin and Danielle, decide to expand their product lines by manufacturing silicone plastic components for the life sciences industry. This requires a specialised environment, which they decide should be located on a new mezzanine floor to be built into the existing factory space. The total value of the works is €215,000, which is broken down as follows:

- Creation of new mezzanine floor – €64,000.
- Building a sealed, 'white-room' production facility on this mezzanine floor – €25,500.
- Fit-out of this sealed room with appropriate equipment – €95,000.
- Building small offices for two new production managers – €18,500.
- Fit-out of these offices – €12,000.

As a portion of these works are treated as 'refurbishment works', Neally Engineering Ltd have created a capital good with a VAT life of 10 years. Based on the brief description of the works set out above, the value of this capital good is €108,000, as the fit-out/equipment in the new mezzanine floor is excluded. As the owner of this new 10-year capital good, Neally Engineering Ltd must monitor the use of the mezzanine floor for the following 10 years and make any CGS adjustments that may arise if any of this floor is put to VAT-exempt use during this time. The company must also keep a full CGS record in relation to this capital good.

The refurbishment works started in September 2014, immediately after the sub-lease to the car repair business had ceased, and were completed on 27 February 2015. This means that Neally Engineering Ltd's refurbishment capital good has a 10-year VAT life that runs from 28 February 2015 to 27 February 2025. It should be noted that the company had already acquired a capital good when it purchased the property on 4 February 2013. As this capital good arose on a 'newly completed' property, as per the VAT 102 concept it has a 20-year VAT life that runs from 4 February 2013 to 3 February 2033. The company, therefore, owns two capital goods and must retain full CGS records for each for the duration of their respective lives. Also, if the property is put to VAT-exempt use in the future, then two CGS adjustments may be required.

***Note:*** it is not always the landlord that creates a capital good by carrying out refurbishment works. The tenant of a long lease of, say, 20 years or more, may create a capital good by carrying out refurbishment works on a property. In this situation, it is the tenant that acquires the capital good in the leased property, so, if the tenant wishes to reclaim VAT on the refurbishment works, it is the tenant that has the obligation to put the property to VATable use (or otherwise suffer a CGS adjustment). The tenant is also obliged to keep a CGS record for these works.

## 3.7 Capital Goods Scheme Records

We have referred above to the fact that when a capital good is created, either by developing a new property or carrying out refurbishment works on an existing property, a full CGS record of the property must be retained for the period of the capital good's VAT life. Where a property that is subject to the CGS is to be sold or let, the CGS record will be requested by a potential purchaser or tenant. In addition, under VAT rules, in order to avoid a fixed penalty of €4,000, the owner of a capital good must keep a full CGS record.

In broad terms, the information that will form part of the CGS record includes:

- the amount of VAT charged to the owner of the capital good on the property's purchase, development or refurbishment;
- the amount of VAT charged that *was* deducted/reclaimed after acquisition, development or refurbishment;
- the date on which the CGS adjustment period begins – when the property was acquired will be the date of acquisition; when it was developed/refurbished will be the date of completion of those works;
- the number of years (known as 'intervals') in the adjustment period, i.e. 20 or 10;

- the percentage of VATable use in the first interval period – this could be 100% in the case of a fully VATable use, 0% if the property is put to VAT-exempt use or a percentage in between (in the case of mixed use);
- the amount of VAT that *should* have been deducted/reclaimed after acquisition, development or refurbishment. If this differs from the amount that actually was deducted/reclaimed, this could require an immediate CGS adjustment;
- the percentage of VATable use in all intervals after the first interval;
- any CGS adjustments arising during the life of the capital good; and
- details of the VAT treatment on the sale of the property.

A point to note here is that it is somewhat simplistic to say that an 'interval' is equivalent to a year/12-month period, although it is generally true. This is why the sample CGS adjustments set out at **Section 3.5** above (when Neally Engineering Ltd lets part of its property) are estimated figures and are purely illustrative.

## 3.8 Stamp Duty

While most of this chapter has been taken up with setting out some basic VAT rules in relation to property transactions, it would be remiss not to refer to the other transaction tax – stamp duty – that arises on these transactions.

In addition, other taxes may also be relevant to the purchase, sale, lease or sub-lease of commercial property (including capital gains tax, capital acquisitions tax, income tax or corporation tax), though the application of these taxes to property transactions are outside the scope of this book.

### *3.8.1 Stamp Duty on Commercial Property Purchase*

Where the documentation involved in purchasing a property is 'executed' (the legal term; this is also described as the transaction being 'closed') on or after 7 December 2011, stamp duty at a rate of 2% will apply. This is payable by the purchaser of the commercial property.

A reduced rate of stamp duty (1%) may apply on the transfer of farming land between 'related persons' where that land is being actively farmed on a commercial basis. The transfer must take place before 1 January 2018 to be eligible for this reduced rate. A number of conditions must be met in order for this 'consanguinity relief' to apply.[11]

There is an exemption from stamp duty for the transfer of farmland to a 'young trained farmer'. Where various conditions are met, the exemption will apply if the transfer is made before 31 December 2018.[12]

[11] Section 83B of the Stamp Duty Consolidation Act (SDCA) 1999.

[12] Section 81AA SDCA 1999, as amended by section 63 FA 2015.

### 3.8.2 Stamp Duty on Creation of Commercial Lease

Also payable by the acquirer of the interest in property (in this case, the tenant), the stamp duty rates that typically apply on the creation of a commercial lease are as follows:

- lease for a term not exceeding 35 years, or for an indefinite term – 1% average annual rent;
- lease for a term between 36 years and 100 years – 6% average annual rent;
- lease for a term exceeding 100 years – 12% average annual rent.

Finance Act 2014 introduced an exemption from stamp duty in relation to leases of farmland of a duration between six years and 35 years, where a number of conditions are met.[13] This exemption will be effective from the date of the commencement order to be made by the relevant Government Minister. As at 30 June 2016 this Order had not yet been made.

[13] Section 74 FA 2014.

CHAPTER 4

# GETTING THE VAT TREATMENT RIGHT



Value-added tax (VAT) is a tax that many people find confusing as it appears to have a 'life of its own'. As VAT is a consumer tax, it is generally intended to be a cost to the ultimate consumer of a product (good) or service, which means that businesses involved in the production of that good or service should not themselves suffer VAT costs. VAT should 'flow through' these businesses, such that the role of the business in the VAT system is merely to act as a VAT collection agent on behalf of Revenue.

In **Chapter 3**, Section 3.1 we referred to this 'flow through' concept as 'VAT in–VAT out'. This idea is so fundamental that we called it '**VAT 101**':

> If a business is entitled to reclaim the VAT charged to it when it purchases goods/services that are to be used in the business, then typically that business charges VAT on the goods/services it supplies to its customers.

We also highlighted that the reverse of this VAT 101 concept is also generally true, i.e. that if the business must charge VAT on its supplies to its customers, then generally the business may reclaim the VAT charged to it on its purchases. (***Note:*** our VAT 101 concept is a general rule of thumb and, as usual, there are exceptions!)

Our focus initially in this chapter is on the VAT implications arising for an Irish business that makes all its purchases and sales in Ireland. We will consider the VAT implications arising on foreign purchases by an Irish business in **Section 4.6** below and in **Chapter 12** we will consider the VAT implications arising where an Irish business makes sales abroad.

## 4.1 Sales (Output) VAT

### *4.1.1 Current Rates of Sales VAT in Ireland*

At the time of writing, the following VAT rates apply in Ireland[1]:

- standard rate of 23%;
- reduced rates of 13.5% and 9%;
- flat-rate compensation percentage for farmers of 5.2%;
- livestock rate of 4.8%; and
- zero rate of 0%.

The 13.5% rate generally applies to the supply of certain fuels, building services, repair, cleaning and maintenance and photographic supplies. The 9% reduced rate was introduced on 1 July 2011 and generally applies to tourism and entertainment supplies, restaurant and catering services, hot takeaway food, hairdressing services and supplies of newspapers, magazines and promotional material. The 5.2% rate applies to a special scheme for farmers known as the 'flat-rate addition' (see **Section 4.2.1** below). The 4.8% rate applies to certain agricultural supplies that are outside the 'flat-rate addition' scheme, while the 0% rate applies to supplies of basic unprepared food and drink that are not regarded as 'luxury items', children's clothing and footwear, oral medicines, certain animal feed and fertilisers, plants and seeds used to produce food and printed books.

***Note:*** the standard rate of 23% is the default rate, which means that where no VAT rate is specified in tax law for a particular good or service, then the 23% rate will apply.

There are certain supplies that are exempt from VAT, including some (but not all) medical, educational and financial services, certain property lettings, insurance and reinsurance services, betting and the services of a funeral undertaker.

1 Section 46(1)(d) of the Value-Added Tax Consolidation Act 2010 (VATCA 2010).

We have included these notes on the categories of goods and services that are subject to the various VAT rates to provide a general indication of when the different rates may apply. Detailed lists of the VAT rates applicable to various goods and services are set out in Schedules 1, 2 and 3 of the Value-Added Tax Consolidation Act 2010 (VATCA 2010).[2]

All business owners should be absolutely clear on the relevant VAT rate or rates applicable to their business. If it is unclear which VAT rate applies to certain business activities, it is possible to make a written request to Revenue to clarify the relevant rate. It cannot be over-emphasised just how crucial it is that the correct VAT rates are identified from the beginning of trading, as mistakes on this fundamental aspect could be extremely costly in the future.

A word on the 0% rate: on the face of it, this appears to be a 'non-sense' – how can you have a VAT rate of 0% and why not just treat all goods and services that are subject to the 0% rate as being VAT-exempt? There is a very good reason for this rate, and it goes back to the corollary of our VAT 101 concept: a business that makes VAT-exempt supplies is not generally entitled to reclaim VAT on the purchases it makes to produce those supplies. A business that supplies goods or services at the 0% rate is not treated in the same way as one that supplies VAT-exempt goods or services. As a 0% rate business is charging VAT (albeit at a 0% rate), it will generally have an entitlement to reclaim VAT on its purchases.

We have referred to the various VAT rates that currently apply to the supply of goods and services in Ireland. It is, of course, entirely possible for the same business to make a variety of supplies that attract different VAT rates. From our case studies, Four Blue Ducks, for example, supplies hot prepared food, which is subject to the 9% rate, as well as glasses of wine, which are subject to the standard 23% rate.

### *4.1.2 Multiple/Composite Supplies*

Where a business is making a supply of more than one good or service as part of the same supply, and these supplies are subject to different rates of VAT, then the question must be: what VAT rate should apply? In order to answer this question, we must look at the different elements of the supply and determine if they could be supplied separately, or if one of the elements of the supply is merely an enhancement to another element of the supply.

[2] There is a specific VAT rate search function available on the Revenue website. See www.revenue.ie/en/tax/vat/rates/index.jsp (accessed May 2016).

#### *4.1.2.1 Multiple Supplies*

Where the different elements of the supply could be sold separately, then the VAT rules require that the total purchase price for the entire supply is apportioned over each element and the relevant VAT rate is charged on each element.[3]

### Case Study: Four Blue Ducks

An example is the €12.50 lunch special offered by Four Blue Ducks, which includes a choice of lasagne or curry and a glass of red or white wine. As the hot meal and the glass of wine could be sold separately, this will be treated as two separate supplies that form a 'multiple supply'. In this situation, Jim and Cathy must apportion the €12.50 price between the two elements and then account for VAT at 9% on the hot food element and 23% VAT on the glass of wine. The apportionment could be done, for example, on the basis of the percentage cost of each element.

Say Cathy worked out that the total costs involved in supplying the lunch special are €9.20, of which €1.75 (19% of costs) relate to the wine and €7.45 (81% of costs) relate to the hot meal. She might apportion the €12.50 sale price of the lunch special as follows:

- **Wine**: 19% of sale price is €2.375, which is inclusive of VAT at 23%, so the VAT element is €0.44
- **Food**: 81% of sale price is €10.125, which is inclusive of VAT at 9%, so the VAT element is €0.84
- Total VAT included in sales price is €1.28.

While there are other ways of making this apportionment, as long as the apportionment method makes commercial sense and is supported by documentation, it should be acceptable to Revenue.

#### *4.1.2.2 Composite Supplies*

A different VAT treatment applies where the supply has more than one element but the elements are not capable of being split and sold separately. In that case, one element of the supply will be treated as the 'principal' supply, with the other element(s) of the supply being treated as 'ancillary'. This type of supply is called a 'composite supply'. No apportionment of the sales price is required and instead the VAT rate applicable to the *principal* supply will apply to the entire supply.

[3] Section 47 VATCA 2010.

### Case Study: Tigim Language Learning Ltd

An example of a composite supply arises from the classroom-based language education classes offered by Tigim Language Learning Ltd in the early days of the business. Vocational language education taught by a tutor is a VAT-exempt activity, while the provision of printed examination papers is VATable at 0%. Students of these classes paid one overall fee for the course, including the examination papers. In this case, the printed examination papers are regarded as an ancillary supply to the principal supply of language education. Accordingly, this composite supply would be VAT-exempt in its entirety, which means that VAT may not be reclaimed on all purchases associated with this supply.

### *4.1.3 Two-thirds Rule*

The rules in relation to multiple/composite supplies cover supplies of two or more types of goods, two or more types of services or a combination of goods and services. This last type of supply, a combination of goods and services, is also subject to an additional VAT rule which requires that where the VAT-exclusive cost of the goods exceeds two-thirds of the total sales price, then the entire sale is treated as being a supply of goods, at the relevant VAT rate for those goods.

For more information, see Revenue's VAT leaflet, *Mixed Supplies of Goods and Services.*[4]

## 4.2 VAT Registration and Claiming Input VAT

The very first question that must be answered by the business owners is whether the business is making VAT-exempt supplies or VATable supplies; and if the supplies are VATable, what the appropriate VAT rate is. Where the business is making VATable supplies, then a VAT registration *may* be secured immediately, though there are situations where the business owner has a choice as to VAT registration.

When a business registers for VAT, this registration will be used to file VAT returns that will include VAT charges arising on VATable sales (output VAT) less VAT charges arising on purchases required to generate those sales (input VAT).

[4] Available at www.revenue.ie/en/tax/vat/leaflets/mixed-supplies-goods-services.html (accessed May 2016).

### 4.2.1 When to Register for VAT

Where a business is making VATable supplies, there is no obligation to register for VAT until the following turnover thresholds are exceeded, or expected to be exceeded, in a 12-month period:

- supply of services – turnover of €37,500;
- supply of goods and services where 90% of turnover is generated by supplies of goods – €75,000;
- supply of goods – €75,000;
- supplies of goods at reduced/standard VAT rates where supplies are produced from zero-rated materials – €37,500;
- supplies of immovable goods (i.e. property) – no turnover threshold.

***Note:*** the turnover threshold values set out above are all VAT-exclusive amounts.

An unregistered business does not charge VAT on its sales, but it will suffer the cost of VAT charged to it on its purchases as it cannot reclaim this input VAT. An unregistered business can elect to register for VAT even though the business's relevant turnover threshold may not have been reached. A business that makes VAT-exempt supplies cannot, however, choose to register for VAT in respect of those VAT-exempt supplies.

There are specific VAT rules relating to farmers, which are detailed in Revenue's VAT information leaflet, *Farmers & Intra-EU Transactions.*[5] A 'farmer' is defined in VATCA 2010 as an individual whose supplies consist exclusively of agricultural produce or agricultural services,[6] or an individual whose supplies consist partly of these items and also of other supplies, subject to certain turnover limits. Such an individual is not obliged to register for VAT but may elect to do so. If a farmer does not register for VAT in respect of their farming supplies, then their supplies are subject to the 'flat-rate addition', currently 5.2%. This 5.2% VAT rate is designed to compensate the farmer for VAT charged on purchases, which, in most cases, they are unable to recover.

### 4.2.2 Entitlement to Claim Deduction for VAT Charged on Purchases (Input VAT)

Many people assume that if the business has a VAT registration, then any VAT charged to the business may be reclaimed, but it is worth repeating that this is incorrect. The business owner must review each purchase invoice and determine if that purchase is being used for the purposes of producing the goods and/or services that the business supplies. The relevant section of legislation states that a VATable business may deduct VAT charged on supplies of goods and/or services to it "in so far as the goods

[5] See www.revenue.ie/en/tax/vat/leaflets/farmers.html (accessed June 2016).
[6] Schedule 4 Part I VATCA 2010.

and services are **used** [emphasis added] ... for the purposes of ... taxable supplies or of any of the qualifying activities".[7]

This emphasis on the use to which a business's purchases are put tallies exactly with the VAT on property rules. We saw in **Chapter 3** that the question of whether or not a property owner can claim a VAT deduction in relation to the acquisition of VATable property is dependent on the use to which the property is put. If the property is put to exempt use (e.g. by being used as trading premises by a VAT-exempt business), then there is no entitlement to claim a VAT deduction on the letting/sale of that property. Conversely, a VAT deduction is generally available where the property is put to VATable use.

### *4.2.3 No or Restricted Entitlement to Input VAT due to Use of Purchase or Status of Business*

Two obvious examples of situations where there is no, or restricted, entitlement to reclaim VAT on purchases are:

- Where the purchases are not used for VATable business supplies but are diverted to private use.

CASE STUDY: NEALLY ENGINEERING LTD

Martin, an owner/director of Neally Engineering Ltd, wants to buy a new laptop for his daughter as a birthday present and arranges for his company to buy it. As the laptop is not going to be used for business purposes, the VAT charge arising should not be included in the business's input VAT figure.

(***Note***: if Martin does not reimburse the company for the cost of the laptop, then this would be treated as a taxable benefit-in-kind for Martin and subject to payroll taxes – see **Chapter 5**.)

- Where the purchases are used partly for VATable supplies and partly for VAT-exempt supplies.[8] In this situation, a portion of the VAT charges may be deducted and an appropriate method of assessing the percentage of reclaimable VAT must be used. One potential method is by referring to the percentage of VATable turnover as against the entire turnover of the business. Further information on this apportionment is set out in Revenue's *Value-Added Tax: A Guide to Apportionment of Input Tax* (October 2001).[9]

[7] Section 59(2)(a) VATCA 2010.

[8] Section 61 VATCA 2010.

[9] See www.revenue.ie/en/tax/vat/leaflets/guideapp.pdf

### 4.2.4 No Entitlement to Input VAT due to Nature of Expense

There are also a number of business expenses which, although used in generating VATable business, carry no entitlement to VAT deduction. These include:[10]

1. Food, drink and accommodation expenses incurred by the business and/or its employees. The VAT element of the accommodation charges arising during a 'qualifying conference' will, however, be deductible as long as certain conditions are met.[11]
2. Entertainment expenses incurred by the business and/or its employees.
3. There is a general exclusion in relation to the cost of purchasing passenger motor vehicles, although there are exceptions in certain cases, including stock-in-trade and low carbon emission vehicles. In the latter case, a 20% VAT rebate may be claimed by a VATable business that purchases or hires low carbon emission vehicles where the vehicles are used for at least 60% business purposes.[12]
4. Petrol costs, unless the petrol is regarded as stock-in-trade. VAT on diesel is, however, fully deductible by a VATable business.

In order to reclaim VAT charged to the business, the business must have received a complete and valid VAT invoice or Customs receipt, as appropriate.

### 4.2.5 Special VAT Schemes

There are a number of industry-specific VAT schemes that set out specific rules for charging VAT on supplies and reclaiming input VAT on purchases. These are listed in **Appendix I** to this chapter. We would recommend that any start-up business confirm whether or not its activities are covered by one of these schemes before commencing to trade.

## 4.3 Accounting for VAT: Common Mistakes and Missed Opportunities

### 4.3.1 Basis of Accounting for Sales VAT

In broad terms, there are two methods of accounting for sales VAT: the 'cash receipts' basis and the 'invoice' basis (also known as the 'accruals' basis). The decision as to which basis of accounting for sales VAT is used may have a huge impact on a business's cash flow, so this is an obvious, and fundamental, issue to get right.

[10] Section 60 VATCA 2010.

[11] See Revenue's *Conferences – VAT Deductibility* for further information. Available at www.revenue.ie/en/tax/vat/leaflets/conferences.html.

[12] For more information, see Revenue's *Motor Vehicles – Deduction of VAT on certain cars* available on the Revenue website.

The invoice basis requires that once an invoice has been issued by the business, that the VAT charge included in the invoice must be included in the business's sales VAT figure for that VAT period.

### Case Study: Neally Engineering Ltd

Neally Engineering Ltd accounts for sales VAT on an invoice basis and issues an invoice on 15 April. As the company files bi-monthly VAT returns, then the sales VAT included in that invoice must be included in the March/April VAT return, which is due for submission and payment by 23 May, at the latest. This is the case even if the customer has not paid the invoice by 23 May. The business will therefore carry the cost of financing the VAT charge between the period when it is due for payment to Revenue, i.e. 23 May, and actual payment by the customer. If Neally Engineering Ltd's debtor balances are significant, then financing the VAT charges included in these debtor balances would be a very expensive exercise.

The alternative method of accounting for sales VAT is the 'cash receipts' basis, which requires that a business includes sales VAT in the VAT period in which its invoice is paid by the customer or when it receives a cash payment from the customer. Any business wishing to operate on the cash receipts basis, or to change from one basis to another, must have Revenue approval to do so.

As long as the annual turnover of a business is less than €2 million,[13] then the business owners will have a choice of operating either the cash receipts basis or the invoice basis. A business with a turnover exceeding €2 million must operate on an invoice basis. A change in turnover levels can necessitate a change in the accounting basis. ***Note:*** a move from the cash receipts basis to the invoice basis will likely require an adjustment to *increase* the sales VAT figure in the period of adjustment. The opposite is likely to be the case if turnover falls below €2 million and the business secures Revenue approval to revert to the cash receipts basis.

The other circumstance in which the cash receipts basis of VAT accounting may be used is when at least 90% of the business's supplies are made to unregistered customers, e.g. private individuals, or to VAT-registered customers that do not have an entitlement to full VAT recovery.[14]

[13] Section 80 VATCA 2010.
[14] *Ibid.*

### Case Study: Four Blue Ducks

As long as Four Blue Ducks supplies to the general public and no more than 10% of their turnover comes from, say, catering services provided to VATable business clients, then Four Blue Ducks would be entitled to operate on a cash receipts basis even if its turnover exceeded €2 million in a 12-month period.

***Note:*** the cash receipts basis of accounting may not be used for construction services supplied by a sub-contractor to a principal contractor. We have noted in **Appendix I** at the end of this chapter that supplies of these services are subject to the 'reverse VAT charge' mechanism. The cash receipts basis is also not available on invoices to parties that are connected to the business or to VAT on property transactions.

## *4.3.2 Timing of Claiming VAT Input*

Let us look now at the other side of this coin, i.e. the timing of claiming input VAT deductions for purchases. In general, once a business has received a valid VAT invoice, then it may claim input VAT in the VAT period in which the invoice is issued. For Revenue this means that there is potential for a serious timing mismatch if the purchasing business has an *immediate* entitlement to claim input VAT on purchases, yet the supplier business can delay paying the sales VAT to Revenue until their customer pays the sales VAT to them (because they are operating on a cash receipts basis).

For VAT periods from January 2014 onwards, there is a qualification to the general rule on the timing of claiming a VAT input deduction, which allows the deduction as normal but requires an adjustment if the business has not paid the supplier by the end of the third VAT period after the VAT period in which the VAT input deduction was claimed (generally six months later).[15]

### Case Study: Neally Engineering Ltd

Neally Engineering Ltd (which files VAT returns on a bi-monthly basis) receives a supplier invoice for €100,000 (plus VAT of 23%) dated 25 March 2014. It includes the €23,000 input VAT charge in its March/April 2014 VAT return. The company is in dispute with the supplier and initially refuses to pay the invoice. An agreement is finally reached and Neally Engineering pays 50% of the invoice in full and final settlement in January 2015. As the invoice is unpaid by the end of

[15] Section 62A VATCA 2010.

October 2014 (i.e. three VAT periods after the March/April 2014 VAT period), the company is obliged to adjust the input VAT figure in the September/October 2014 VAT return, reducing the figure by €23,000. As the company ultimately pays half of the original invoice value in January 2015, it may include an input VAT deduction of €11,500 (being 50% of €23,000) in its January/February 2015 VAT return.

The requirement for adjustments to VAT input figures are a feature of Revenue audits for post-2013 VAT periods, with auditors focusing on large and/or aged creditor listings. A business taxpayer may well argue that there is no loss to Revenue where the creditors are ultimately paid in full. In the case of creditors paid after the third VAT period after the VAT period of the supplier invoice, however, Revenue are likely to seek interest (and penalties) on the unadjusted VAT input for the period from that six-month deadline to the ultimate date of payment of the invoice.

Revenue acknowledge that there may be some exceptional circumstances where an adjustment to the VAT input figures is not required, despite the fact that the creditor remains unpaid after the six-month deadline. In this situation, the taxpayer business has the option to contact their local Revenue District to request confirmation that no adjustment is required.[16]

### *4.3.3 Proper Paperwork*

It is very important that invoices and credits notes accurately reflect the transactions for which the documents have been issued. The invoice or credit note reflects the sales (output) VAT charge that must be returned by the supplier, and the purchases (input) VAT deduction that may be taken by the purchaser. Failure to get these documents right could result in interest and penalties or, in more serious cases, in prosecution. Note also that the amount of the sales VAT charge included on the invoice becomes a VAT liability that the supplier must pay to Revenue. For a business operating on an invoice basis of VAT accounting, it is irrelevant whether or not the business's customer has paid the VAT charged to it, as the business is still liable to Revenue for that VAT charged. For full details, see the relevant section of Revenue's *Guide to VAT*.[17]

#### *4.3.3.1 Invoices*

**Appendix II** to this chapter lists all of the information that must be included on a valid VAT invoice. It is extremely important that VATable businesses meet these requirements and produce complete invoices, as it

[16] Revenue *eBrief* 55/2014, *VAT – Adjustment of VAT deductible where consideration is unpaid after six months (section 62A)* (July 2014). Available at www.revenue.ie/en/practitioner/ebrief/archive/2014/no-552014.html

[17] See www.revenue.ie/en/tax/vat/guide/credit-notes.html

is entirely possible for the tax authorities (in Ireland or elsewhere) to refuse to allow VAT input deductions to customers in possession of incomplete invoices. Simplified invoicing requiring less detail may only be applied if the value of the invoice is less than €100 or the commercial/administrative practices of the specific business sector make it difficult to comply with the usual requirements.

The latest date for issuing invoices is 15 days after the end of the month in which *the goods/services were supplied*, e.g. 15 March for supplies made during the month of February.[18] Note that it is not necessary to issue a VAT invoice on the date of the supply of goods/services; depending on the date of supply, there may be anything up to a six-week window until the associated invoice must be issued. This may provide some cash-flow benefit where, for example, an invoice is issued on a date (e.g. 15 March) later than the date of supply (e.g. 1 February), thereby pushing the invoice into a business's subsequent VAT period (March/April).

This 15-day deadline can be displaced where, for example, an advance amount (deposit) is paid before the supply is made; in this case, an invoice must issue within 15 days of the end of the month in which *the advance payment is made* and this invoice should be for the amount of the advance payment only (and not the full value of the supply).

CASE STUDY: NEALLY ENGINEERING LTD

Neally Engineering Ltd's terms and conditions require a total 80% payment before delivery to a new customer: 20% on placement of the order and 60% before delivery. The company delivers €75,000 worth of goods to a new customer on 20 June, in relation to which the customer has paid a deposit of €15,000 on 3 April and €45,000 on 18 May. Neally Engineering Ltd must issue invoices for the deposit of €15,000 by 15 May, for the deposit of €45,000 by 15 June and a balancing invoice for €15,000 by 15 July.

#### *4.3.3.2 Credit Notes*

Where an invoice has been issued and the values shown on the invoice are reduced by reason of an allowance/discount, generally the supplier must issue a credit note setting out the adjustment to both the value of the supply and the VAT amount.[19] **Appendix II** lists the information that must be included on a valid credit note.

For a supplier operating on the cash receipts basis of accounting (outlined at **Section 4.3.1** above), a credit note must always issue where the value of

[18] Regulation 23 of the Value-added Tax Regulations 2010 (S.I. No. 639 of 2010) (the '2010 VAT Regulations').

[19] Regulation 20 of the 2010 VAT Regulations.

an invoice is to be reduced. It is possible, however, for a supplier on the invoice basis of accounting and its VAT-registered customer to agree that the VAT charge on an invoice is not to be adjusted even though the value of the goods/services contained in that invoice is to be reduced. In this case, it will not be necessary for the supplier to issue a credit note. While the VAT rules do allow a supplier to avoid the necessity of issuing a credit note in these specific circumstances, in our view it is better practice to issue the credit note as this will make the VAT bookkeeping process easier.

#### *4.3.3.3 Incorrect Invoices and VAT Invoices Not Required*

If a supplier issues an invoice that includes a higher VAT rate than is actually required, the supplier must issue a credit note for the entire amount of the original invoice and then raise a fresh invoice that includes the correct VAT rate. If this paperwork is not corrected, the supplier will be liable to pay the higher VAT charge to Revenue, even though the customer may only pay the lower VAT charge.

***Note:*** if a business that is not VAT-registered issues an invoice that includes a VAT charge, then the business will be obliged to return and pay that VAT charge to Revenue. The business may then be subject to penalties for issuing the invoice when it was not VAT-registered.

#### *4.3.3.4 Electronic Invoicing (E-invoicing)*

Provided certain conditions are met, e-invoices and e-credit notes have equal standing with their paper equivalents. These conditions include a requirement that the supplier and customer agree to the use of e-invoicing. It is necessary to have an electronic storage system that is robust enough to ensure the integrity of the data transmitted, allows easy interrogation of the data and retrieval of detailed information, and has storage capacity that allows retention of records for the usual timeframes (e.g. six years in the case of VAT on business activities).

***Note:*** where a business that uses an e-invoicing system is the subject of a Revenue audit, the Revenue auditors will likely require access to that system in order to run diagnostic tests.

### *4.3.4 Change in VAT Rates*

A change in VAT rates sometimes causes confusion as to the appropriate VAT rate to be applied. This confusion can be especially acute where the supply and the issue of the invoice/credit note for that supply straddle the date on which the VAT rate has changed.

The following is a general summary of the rules pertaining to a change in VAT rates:

- For supplies to VAT-registered customers, the correct VAT rate is the rate of VAT in force on the invoice issue date or the date the invoice should have been issued, whichever is the earlier.

- For supplies to VAT-registered customers by businesses operating on a cash receipts basis, the correct VAT rate is the VAT rate in force on the date of supply.
- For supplies to unregistered customers, the correct VAT rate is the VAT rate in force on the date of supply.
- Where credit notes are issued to VAT-registered customers after a rate change and relate to invoices issued before the rate change, the VAT rate to be included is the one in force on the invoice issue date.
- Credit notes issued to unregistered customers should include the VAT rate in force on the date of supply.
- Where payments in advance are made by VAT-registered customers to suppliers on an invoice basis, the VAT rate to be included on the advance payment invoice should be the one in force when the advance payment invoice is/should be issued, whichever is the earlier.
- For payments in advance from VAT-registered customers to suppliers on a cash receipts basis, or payments in advance from unregistered customers, the correct VAT rate is the one in force on the date of the advance payment.

For more information, see the "Changes in rates of VAT" section of Revenue's *Guide to VAT*.[20]

## 4.4 Selling Online

The internet is increasingly important to more and more businesses, from multinational corporations to corner-shop sole traders. For VAT purposes, there is a distinction between the use of the internet to facilitate communications or to take orders, i.e. online purchasing and email, and the use of the internet to actually deliver a service, i.e. 'electronically supplied services'.

Where a business uses the internet merely to facilitate communications, then there are no specific VAT rules and the business must apply the usual VAT rules for the supply of its goods or services.

For an Irish business supplying 'electronically supplied services' to either VAT-registered or non-VAT-registered (private) customers in Ireland, the 'place of supply' of these services will be Ireland and Irish VAT, at the appropriate rate, will apply. In **Chapter 12** we will review the VAT rules for Irish businesses that supply electronically supplied services to VAT-registered and non-VAT-registered customers based both within the EU and outside of it.

[20] See www.revenue.ie/en/tax/vat/guide/changes-rates.html (accessed May 2016).

## 4.5 Filing Proper VAT Returns

The importance of filing all necessary VAT returns must be mentioned. A VAT-registered business will be obliged to file electronically (using the Revenue On-Line Service (ROS)) the following returns, at a minimum:

- **Regular VAT return (Form VAT3)** Depending on the size of the business, this may be required on a bi-monthly, quarterly, half-yearly or yearly basis. Revenue will make a determination as to the frequency of the returns. These returns typically generate a VAT liability or a VAT refund.
- **Annual Return of Trading Details (RTD)** This return is required for statistical purposes only and sets out a summary of supplies and purchases made during the year, as well as the value of intra-Community supplies and acquisitions. No VAT liability or refund attaches to this return.

In addition to these requirements, an Irish business may also be required to file EU-wide statistical returns (INTRASTAT and VIES) in relation to intra-Community supplies and acquisitions where certain thresholds are breached. As with the Irish RTD, these returns are required for statistical purposes only and will not generate a VAT liability or refund. We will review the obligations to file INTRASTAT and VIES returns in **Section 4.6.1.2** below and in **Chapter 12**.

***Note:*** an Irish business ignores the filing of these statistical returns at its peril. Failure to file them may result in penalties of €4,000 *per unfiled return*.[21] These fixed penalties also apply to a range of VAT offences, including failure to register for VAT when required to do so, failure to issue proper invoices and credit notes and failure to keep proper books and records.

Thus far in this chapter, in **Sections 4.1** to **4.5**, we have discussed VAT compliance for a business that purchases all inputs and makes all sales in Ireland. **Figure 4.1** below summarises the steps such businesses should take to be fully VAT compliant, starting with the consideration of when to register for VAT.

Figure 4.1: The Steps to VAT Compliance

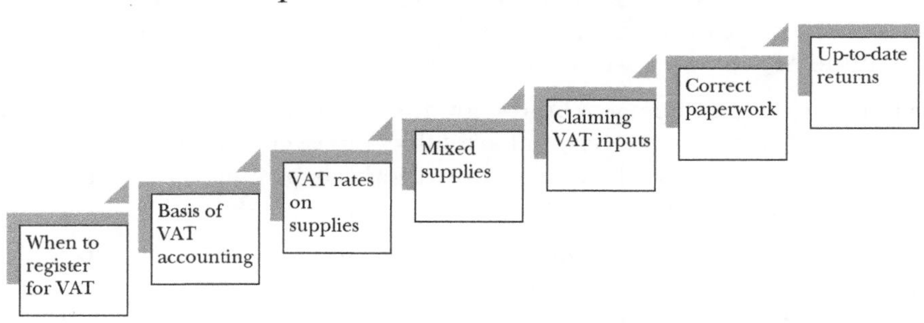


[21] Section 115 VATCA 2010.

## 4.6 Foreign VAT Aspects for Irish Businesses

Increasingly, more Irish businesses have an international dimension, whether on the sales side or the purchases side, or both. VAT is an EU-wide tax, which means that there are certain EU-wide VAT rules that apply where the foreign supplier/customer is based in a EU Member State. Irish VAT can also apply where the foreign supplier/customer is based outside of Ireland and outside of the EU.

In this section we will look at foreign purchases, i.e. where an Irish business purchases goods/services from a supplier based in another EU Member State or based outside of the EU for use in the Irish business. The VAT implications of an Irish business making foreign sales, to customers located both within and outside of the EU, are set out in **Chapter 12**.

### *4.6.1 VAT Implications of Intra-Community Acquisitions*

We mentioned above that VAT is an EU-wide tax, which means that each EU Member State operates within the same broad framework of VAT rules, both in relation to domestic purchases/supplies and purchases/supplies between businesses located in different Member States. Movements of goods and services between Member States are known as 'intra-Community acquisitions' (i.e. purchases) and 'intra-Community supplies'. Our focus in this section is on the VAT implications for an Irish business making intra-Community acquisitions of goods or services.

#### *4.6.1.1 Impact on Irish VAT Registration Thresholds*

**Goods** Where the value of these intra-Community acquisitions exceed, or is expected to exceed, €41,000 in a 12-month period, then the Irish business must register for VAT. We noted at **Section 4.2.1** that an Irish business supplying goods is not usually required to register for VAT unless its turnover exceeds, or is expected to exceed, €75,000 in a 12-month period. Where that business is purchasing goods from another EU Member State, however, this €75,000 goods *sales* threshold may be superseded by the lower €41,000 goods *purchases* threshold.

An Irish VAT-exempt business (which ordinarily may not need to register for VAT) must also register for VAT in respect of these EU purchases if the value of the purchases exceeds the €41,000 threshold.

Where the goods being acquired by the Irish business are either new means of transport or goods that are subject to excise (e.g. alcohol), then no registration threshold applies and the Irish business must automatically register for VAT in Ireland.

**Services** Where the Irish business is receiving services from within the EU that are VATable in the location where they are received (i.e. Ireland), then it must register for VAT in Ireland. In this situation, the Irish business's turnover level is irrelevant and the sales thresholds set out at **Section 4.2.1** are ignored.

#### *4.6.1.2 Requirement to File INTRASTAT Returns*

One of the implications of the Irish VAT system being part of an EU-wide VAT system is that the EU authorities want to ensure that all transactions between EU Member States are correctly treated for VAT purposes; and to record reliable statistics on trading between Member States.

Where an Irish business acquires goods (not services) from VAT-registered businesses in other EU Member States (i.e. intra-Community) and the ex-VAT value of these acquisitions exceeds €500,000 on a calendar-year basis, the Irish business is required to file a detailed monthly INTRASTAT return setting out full details of these intra-Community acquisitions. This is a filing exercise only and does not trigger VAT liabilities.[22] Details of such intra-Community acquisitions of goods must also be included in the Irish business's usual Irish VAT return.

#### *4.6.1.3 VAT Treatment on Purchases from another EU Member State*

**Goods** When an Irish business acquires goods from another EU Member State, generally the EU supplier charges VAT at 0% on the supply, as long as the following conditions are met:

1. the Irish business is registered for VAT in Ireland;
2. the VAT numbers of both the Irish business and the EU supplier are recorded on the VAT invoice; and
3. the goods are actually transported from another EU Member State to Ireland.[23]

The Irish business purchaser must then self-account for VAT on the purchases, at the appropriate Irish VAT rate. This self-accounting for VAT is also known as the 'reverse VAT charge' and was previously outlined in **Section 3.4.4** of **Chapter 3** where we reviewed the 'reverse VAT charge' that arose when Neally Engineering Ltd agreed to exercise a 'joint option to tax' the purchase of its business premises. This 'reverse VAT charge' should be included in the sales VAT figure (Box T1) of the business's regular VAT return. Where the Irish business's activities are fully VATable, it may take a VAT deduction of the same amount in the input VAT figure (Box T2) of its VAT return. Of course, if the Irish business does not have full VAT-recovery status, then a full VAT deduction cannot be taken, and a net VAT cost will arise.

The impact of these VAT rules on intra-Community acquisitions of goods is clear. The fact that the supply of certain goods may attract different

[22] For full details, see Revenue's *VIES and INTRASTAT Traders Manual* (Replacement 8, January 2016) available at www.revenue.ie/en/customs/businesses/vies-intrastat.html (accessed May 2016).

[23] Sections 3 and 24(1) VATCA 2010.

VAT rates in different EU countries will be irrelevant, as the purchasing business (in this case, based in Ireland) will be subject to Irish VAT rates on the purchases, irrespective of where in the EU the goods are coming from.

There are different VAT rules where the customer is a private, non-VAT-registered individual, but these are outside the scope of this book. Our focus here is on an Irish VAT-registered business acquiring goods from another EU Member State.

As well as the potential obligation to record these intra-Community acquisitions in an INTRASTAT return (if the €500,000 value threshold is exceeded), the Irish business must also record the value of these purchases in its Irish VAT return in the box marked 'E2 – Total goods received from other EU countries'.

### Case Study: Neally Engineering Ltd

Neally Engineering Ltd purchases a piece of equipment costing €100,000 from France. The company provides the French supplier with the relevant information and the French invoice is subject to the French equivalent of the 0% rate of VAT. As the equipment is subject to the standard rate of 23% in Ireland and as Neally Engineering Ltd's activities are fully VATable, it includes a 'reverse VAT charge' of €23,000 in Box T1 of the VAT return and a VAT input of €23,000 in Box T2. These two entries cancel each other out, so no net VAT liability arises.

The company also includes the ex-VAT value of the goods, €100,000, in Box E2 of the VAT return.

If Neally Engineering Ltd makes further EU purchases of goods with a value of at least €400,000 within the same calendar year, then it is obliged to file an INTRASTAT return setting out full details of its EU acquisitions.

We have seen that an Irish VAT-exempt business is obliged to register for VAT in relation to the purchase of EU goods only if the value of these goods exceeds €41,000 in a 12-month period. Where this turnover threshold is breached and the Irish VAT-exempt business has registered for VAT, then the business must 'reverse charge' the appropriate Irish VAT rate as set out above, but it will not be in a position to take a corresponding VAT input of the same amount.

**Services** In general, where an Irish business purchases services from a supplier established in another EU Member State, then in most cases the EU supplier will not charge VAT and the Irish business must 'reverse charge' VAT at the appropriate Irish VAT rate. The documentation requirements are similar to those required in the intra-Community acquisition of goods.

Again, as with an intra-Community acquisition of goods, an Irish business that makes VATable supplies may take a simultaneous VAT input deduction for the same value as the VAT 'reverse charge', leaving no net VAT liability on this transaction. An Irish VAT-exempt business may not claim this input deduction and will be liable to pay the amount of the 'reverse charge' VAT to Revenue. The Irish business must record the value of these services in its regular Irish VAT return in the box marked 'ES2 – Total services from other EU countries'.

The theory behind the 'reverse charge' VAT mechanism applying to the supply of services across EU borders is that, generally, the 'place of supply' of that service is deemed to be the country where the business purchaser is located.[24] For the narrow focus of this section of the chapter, i.e. that the location of the business purchaser is Ireland, it is the appropriate Irish VAT rate that applies to the transaction.

There are exceptions to this 'place of supply' rule, including the following:

- supply of services connected with immovable goods (i.e. property);
- admission to cultural, artistic, sporting, scientific, educational and entertainment services;
- restaurant and catering services; and
- hiring out of means of transport.

Taking a closer look at the first exception, i.e. the supply of services connected with immovable goods, examples would include construction works carried out on property, as well as property agent/valuation services and the services of architects and engineers. The 'place of supply' of these services is the place where the property is located. An example of how this exception to the general 'place of supply' rule operates to trigger a foreign VAT charge for an Irish business is set out in the case study extract below.

### Case Study: Neally Engineering Ltd

Neally Engineering Ltd quickly becomes very successful in Ireland and, after analysing the domestic market, Danielle and Martin realise that if they wish to expand their business, they must look at additional markets. Martin had previously spent time working in Madrid; he speaks fluent Spanish and keeps in contact with old business associates who encourage him to open a new factory near Madrid. Martin makes a number of trips to the region, spending some of his time assessing two possible factory premises. As part of this assessment, he employs a local architect to provide reports on the buildings' existing status and potential. As the Spanish architect's services are connected with the Madrid property, she is obliged to charge Spanish VAT on the invoices she issues to Neally Engineering Ltd.

[24] Sections 3 and 34 VATCA 2010.

#### *4.6.1.4 Refund of EU VAT Charged to an Irish Business*

We have seen that for a significant amount of EU cross-border business transactions the reverse VAT charge mechanism applies, meaning that no VAT charge is applied by the supplier and the business customer self-charges VAT at the appropriate local VAT rate, i.e. the Irish VAT rate in the case of the Irish business purchaser.

But what about the situation where an Irish business purchases goods or services from another EU Member State and the reverse VAT charge mechanism does not apply? (An example of this situation is the Spanish VAT charge that arises on the services provided by the Spanish architect to Neally Engineering Ltd set out above.) If the Irish business receives an EU invoice that includes foreign VAT, and the Irish business has full entitlement to reclaim input VAT, then how does the Irish business secure a VAT refund for this foreign VAT?

As VAT is an EU-wide tax, there is an EU-wide mechanism to enable businesses to recover the foreign VAT applied by a supplier located in another Member State.[25] An Irish business that suffers a VAT charge in another Member State may make an application for a refund of that VAT charge through the Revenue On-Line Service (ROS) system.[26] A number of conditions must be met in order for the refund to be processed, including:

- the refund claim must be lodged within nine months of the end of the calendar year in which the VAT was charged;
- an Irish business may only reclaim the foreign VAT charge to the extent that it relates to the VATable activities of the business; and
- the VAT charge must not relate to goods/services that are treated as 'non-deductible items' (see **Section 4.2.4**) under the VAT rules of the other Member State.

Case Study: Neally Engineering Ltd

We noted above that the invoice issued to Neally Engineering Ltd by the Spanish architect had to include Spanish VAT. As the Irish company makes VATable supplies and has incurred the Spanish architect's fees in the course of its VATable business, it can make a claim to the Irish Revenue for a refund of the Spanish VAT charge. The invoice is dated 13 April 2015, which means that the refund claim should be made by 30 September 2016.

[25] Section 101 VATCA 2010.

[26] See www.revenue.ie/en/online/ros/

### 4.6.2 VAT Treatment on the Receipt of Goods/Services from Outside the EU

**Section 4.6.1** focused on the VAT implications of an Irish business purchasing goods or services from another EU Member State (i.e. intra-Community acquisitions). We look now at the VAT implications arising when an Irish business purchases goods or services from suppliers based outside of Ireland and outside of the EU.

**Goods** The importation of goods from outside the EU to Ireland is generally subject to VAT, at the appropriate Irish VAT rates applicable to the goods, at the time of importation (this is known as 'VAT at the point of entry').[27] Unless the business importing the goods is authorised to use the deferred VAT payment facility, VAT and all other import charges must be paid before the goods will be released by the Customs authorities to the Irish business.

A deferred payment system is available to ease the cash-flow impact of having to pay VAT upfront on each importation in order for the goods to be released to the Irish business. Full details of this system are set out in the 2010 VAT Regulations. In overview, authorisation for payment deferral requires the Irish importing business to secure a Customs deferral number and to provide a direct debit voucher, drawn on the Irish business's bank and guaranteed by the bank, to the Collector of Customs and Excise. If the Irish business secures this deferral, it is not required to pay VAT at the time of importation, but it must do so by the 15th of the month following importation, i.e. 15 September for August imports.

There are some specific exemptions to the general rule that VAT must be paid on the importation of goods from outside the EU, as well as 'free zones' where goods are treated as remaining outside of the EU and therefore not subject to VAT. In Ireland, these 'free zones' are Shannon Customs-Free Airport and Ringaskiddy Free Port. Further information is set out in the "Imports" section of Revenue's *Guide to VAT*.[28]

**Services** Where an Irish business is receiving services from outside of the EU that are VATable in the location where they are received (i.e. Ireland), then it must register for VAT in Ireland. The Irish business must reverse charge VAT at the appropriate Irish VAT rate and the business's status, as regards full/partial/no VAT recovery, will determine whether or not it is entitled to a VAT input in respect of this reverse VAT charge.

[27] Sections 3, 53 and 54 VATCA 2010.

[28] See www.revenue.ie/en/tax/vat/guide/imports.html (accessed May 2016).

### 4.6.3 VAT Regime Applicable to the Purchase of Goods/Services by Certain Irish Businesses

An Irish business that makes intra-Community supplies of goods, or exports goods outside of the EU, will generally subject these supplies to VAT at 0% (i.e. 'zero-rated supplies'). If the business's suppliers charge VAT to that business under general VAT rules, then it may be in a permanent VAT refund position.

In order to avoid the administrative burden and cash-flow cost of constant VAT refund claims, the business can apply for a specific authorisation, known as a 'VAT 56A authorisation', which allows that business's suppliers to zero-rate their supplies to it.[29] We will expand on this further in **Chapter 12**.

This entire section has focused on the VAT implications of an Irish business *purchasing* goods and services from another EU Member State and from outside the EU. In **Chapter 12** we will look at the VAT implications of an Irish business *supplying* goods and services to customers based in other EU Member States and to customers based outside of the EU.

## Appendix I: Specific VAT Schemes for Certain Types of Business

- **Farmers' 'flat-rate addition'** Referred to above at **Section 4.2.1**, this scheme applies to unregistered farmers and provides compensation for the input VAT that the farmer does not reclaim. In addition, an unregistered farmer may secure a VAT refund in relation to the expenses of construction of farm buildings, underpasses, hedgerows, land drainage or land reclamation.[30] Freshwater fishermen are defined as carrying out 'farming activities' and are subject to the same VAT treatment as farmers.

- **Sea fishermen** In general, sea fishermen who supply unprocessed fish are not obliged to register for VAT although they may elect to do so. If not VAT-registered, fishermen are entitled to secure a VAT refund on the costs of: marine diesel (where they operate in a Bord Iascaigh Mhara-registered fishing vessel); the purchase or hire of a sea-fishing vessel; the purchase, hire or repair and maintenance of fishing equipment; and the repair and maintenance of sea-fishing nets.

[29] Section 56A VATCA 2010.

[30] Revenue *eBrief* 22/2011, *Value-Added Tax (Refund of Tax) (No. 25) Order, 1993* (April 2011).

- **Pharmacists** This scheme provides a method for assessing allowable input VAT for pharmacies with turnover of less than €1.5 million that do not have a full electronic point of sale (EPOS) system.[31]
- **Margin scheme – second-hand goods** This is an optional scheme open to dealers and auctioneers of second-hand movable goods (e.g. art, collectors' items and antiques), second-hand vehicles (excluding EU cross-border supplies) and agricultural machinery. The scheme allows a dealer to return sales VAT on the profit margin generated on individual sales. The dealer does not claim input VAT and instead treats the profit margin as inclusive of the relevant VAT rate.[32]
- **Margin scheme – travel agents** This operates in a manner similar to the margin scheme for second-hand goods above, in that the travel agent is subject to VAT on the profit margin only. An added feature of this scheme is that the travel agent can register for VAT and file VAT returns in one EU Member State only, which will cover all travel services supplied in all EU Member States.[33]
- **Retail export scheme – tax-free shopping for tourists** This scheme allows a person who is visiting Ireland and who is normally resident outside of the EU to make a purchase in Ireland without incurring the usual Irish VAT charge. The item purchased must be exported outside of Ireland and the EU within three months of purchase and the scheme may be operated either as a 'VAT-off' arrangement, where the retailer does not charge the usual VAT charge, or by way of a VAT refund secured after purchase.[34]
- **Principal contractors and sub-contractors involved in construction operations** Where the services provided by the sub-contractor to the principal contractor come within the operation of the relevant contracts tax (RCT) regime, the sub-contractor does not charge VAT on its invoices. Instead, the principal contractor 'self-charges' the relevant VAT charge; this is known as a 'reverse charge'.[35] (We highlight the VAT treatment applicable to a sub-contractor operating within the RCT

[31] More information can be found on the website of the Irish Pharmacy Union at www.ipu.ie/about-the-ipu/ipu-vat-scheme.html

[32] The section of the Revenue's *Guide to VAT* relevant to this margin scheme is available at www.revenue.ie/en/tax/vat/leaflets/margin-scheme-second-hand-goods.html

[33] The section of the Revenue's *Guide to VAT* applicable to travel agents is available at www.revenue.ie/en/tax/vat/leaflets/travel-agent-margin-scheme.html

[34] The relevant section ("Retail Export Scheme (Tax-Free Shopping for Tourists)") of the Revenue's *Guide to VAT* is available at www.revenue.ie/en/tax/vat/leaflets/tax-free-shopping-tourist.html

[35] The "Reverse Charge Construction" section of the Revenue's *Guide to VAT* is available at: http://www.revenue.ie/en/tax/vat/guide/reverse-charge.html

regime here for the sake of completeness only. The RCT regime is outside the scope of this book.)

- **Supply of gas or electricity by VAT-registered businesses** The reverse charge mechanism also applies to the supply of gas/electricity to a VATable dealer in Ireland, and to the supply of a gas/electricity certificate to a VATable customer in Ireland. These new rules came into effect from 1 January 2016.[36]
- **Tourist transport by coaches** VAT refunds may be reclaimed in relation to the cost of purchasing or hiring transport coaches, where those coaches are used to transport groups of tourists.
- **Other VAT refunds to unregistered persons** There are a variety of further entitlements to VAT refunds and these are set out in the "Repayments to Unregistered Persons" section of Revenue's *Guide to VAT.*

## Appendix II: Information Required on Valid VAT Invoices and Credit Notes[37]

***Information required on a Valid VAT Invoice***

1. Date of issue.
2. A sequential number, based on a series, which uniquely identifies the invoice.
3. Full name, address and VAT registration number of the supplier.
4. Full name and address of customer.
5. Where the 'reverse VAT charge' mechanism applies, the VAT registration number of the customer and a statement that the 'reverse VAT charge' mechanism applies.
6. Where the supply constitutes an intra-Community supply of goods to a VAT-registered business in another EU Member State, the VAT registration number of the customer and a statement that the supply is an intra-Community supply of goods.
7. The quantity and nature of the goods/services that make up the supply.
8. The date the goods/services were supplied, or, where an advance payment has been made, the date of that advance payment.
9. Where an invoice is issued in a currency other than euro, the corresponding euro amounts for the VAT charges.
10. In relation to the goods/services supplied: the unit price (ex-VAT), any allowances or discounts not included in the unit price, and the total consideration (ex-VAT).
11. In relation to the goods/services supplied: the VAT rate applicable to each supply of goods/services and the amount of consideration

[36] Section 52 of the Finance Act 2015.

[37] Excerpted from Revenue's *Guide to VAT.*

(ex-VAT) applicable to each VAT rate. This requirement does not apply where the 'reverse charge mechanism' applies to the supply.

12. The total VAT charge payable on the supply.
13. Where a tax representative is liable to pay the business's VAT liabilities in another EU Member State, the name, address and VAT registration number of that tax representative.

***Information Required on a Valid VAT Credit Note***

The information set out at points 1, 2, 3 and 4 above are required, along with the VAT registration number of the customer.

Also required is the reason why the credit note is being issued and a cross-reference to the original invoice. The note must then list the consideration (ex-VAT) to be credited, the rate of VAT applicable to each element of the supply to be credited and the relevant VAT amount for each portion of the consideration. These last requirements in relation to VAT rates and amounts do not apply where the 'reverse charge mechanism' applied to the original invoice.

Note that there are specific rules in relation to invoices/credit notes supplied by the following:

- the supply of construction services by a sub-contractor to a principal contractor;
- the supply of means of transport;
- supplies under the margin scheme;
- hire-purchase transactions;
- supplies by flat-rate farmers; and
- supplies of scrap metal.

More information on these specific requirements can be found in the relevant VAT leaflets on Revenue's website.

# CHAPTER 5

# PAYROLL ISSUES AFFECTING EMPLOYEES AND DIRECTORS OF CLOSE COMPANIES



Aside from the obvious employee 'benefit' of salary, you may ask what else may trigger a tax charge if it is paid for by the employer on behalf of the employee. The glib answer is "well, potentially, everything". We will see that although this may seem like a rather extreme position, it is a good starting point when considering employer payroll tax obligations, as the tax legislation in this area is very widely drawn.

'Payroll taxes' will be charged to "every person having or **exercising an office or employment** ... or to whom any annuity, pension or stipend ... is payable, in respect of all salaries, fees, wages, perquisites or profits ... and shall be computed on the amount of all such salaries, fees, wages, perquisites or profits".[1] The reference to a person having or exercising an 'office' means that directors of a company are also treated as employees for the purposes of payroll taxes.

When it comes to benefits provided to employees by the employer, benefits-in-kind (BIK) are also subject to payroll taxes. Again, employee benefits are widely defined as an expense incurred by a company:

> "in or in connection with the provision, for any of its directors or any person employed by it in an employment ... of:
> (i) living or other accommodation,
> (ii) entertainment,
> (iii) domestic or other services, or
> (iv) other benefits or facilities of whatever nature".[2]

The taxable BIK rules also extend to employers who are sole traders or partnerships. Other tax rules make it clear that where benefits are provided directly to an employee's *family*, the employee will be subject to payroll taxes on those benefits as if she had received them directly.

There are many specific rules relating to payroll taxes on certain benefits. The employer's PAYE page of the Revenue website includes detailed information in this regard.[3]

***Note:*** throughout this chapter we will refer to wages, fees, salaries, perquisites, profits and benefits received by employees by the all-encompassing term 'employment income'.

When we talk about 'payroll taxes', we are referring to Pay As You Earn (PAYE) income tax, Universal Social Charge (USC) and employer's Pay Related Social Insurance (PRSI). In addition, most employees must pay employee's PRSI on employment income. For almost all individuals employed by private business, these taxes and charges are currently set at the following rates, with effect from 1 January 2016:

| | |
|---|---|
| **Income tax** | 20% and, thereafter, 40% once the standard rate band has been surpassed.<br>The standard rate band is:<br>€33,800/€37,800 for an individual; and<br>€42,800/up to €67,600 for married couples/civil partners. |

[1] Section 112 of the Taxes Consolidation Act 1997 (TCA 1997) (emphasis added).
[2] Section 118 TCA 1997.
[3] See www.revenue.ie/en/business/employers-paye.html (accessed June 2016).

| | |
|---|---|
| **USC** | Rate of 0% (where total income is less than €13,000 per annum).<br>*Otherwise:*<br>1% – on first €12,012 of income;<br>3% – on next tranche of income from €12,013 to €18,668;<br>5.5% – on next tranche of income from €18,669 to €70,044;<br>8% – on next tranche of income from €70,045 to €100,000; and<br>11% – on excess over €100,000 for certain types of non-PAYE income.<br>*Reduced rates may apply on the basis of age or medical card status.* |
| **Employer's PRSI** | Class A employees: 8.5 % (where income is €376 per week or less) and 10.75%.<br>A rate of 0.5% may apply to some employees aged 66 years or over.<br>*Certain company directors (Class S) are not subject to employer's PRSI.* |
| **Employee's PRSI** | Class A employees: 0% (where income is €352 per week or less) and 4%.*<br>* With effect from 1 January 2016, a new PRSI credit, which will reduce the amount of employee's PRSI, will be available to many employees who earn between €352 and €424 per week.<br>*Employees aged 66 years or over are generally exempt from paying employee's PRSI.* |

## 5.1 The Employment Status of an Individual Hired by a Business

The employment status of an individual is a fundamental question and the starting point for any employer in working out their payroll tax obligations for an employee. For a large part of the working population, it is obvious whether someone is an employee of a particular business or not. If she comes to work for regular hours, works exclusively for one business, gets a regular salary and is entitled to sick leave, holiday pay, etc., surely that person is an employee? But what about another person who has control over their working environment and hours – should they be treated as a self-employed contractor to the business? Can that person really be regarded as "exercising an office or employment"? The crux of this question is whether the person is engaged in a 'contract *of* service' or a 'contract *for* services'.

### *5.1.1 Revenue's* Code of Practice

Revenue have produced a *Code of Practice for Determining Employment or Self-Employment Status of Individuals.*[4] This lists various factors that are relevant in determining whether an individual is "in business on their own account" (i.e. is engaged in a 'contract for services'), or whether he or she is under the control of an employer (i.e. a 'contract of service'). The *Code of Practice* emphasises that all aspects of the relationship between the business and the employee/self-employed person should be looked at, and any statements as to the employment status or otherwise of the person (in any contract between them) will be disregarded. What this means is that the circumstances of the relationship will determine employment status, and that any attempted manipulation of the contractual paperwork will be ignored.

Relevant questions in this regard include:

- Does the individual bear her own financial risk and does she have the opportunity to increase her profits from the work if she manages it well?
- Can the individual control her hours and how/where she performs the work?
- Can the individual arrange for the work to be done by another person?
- Does she have a number of clients or customers?
- Is she obliged to provide her own insurance cover for her work?
- How embedded is the individual in the contracting business; for example, does she have an email address with or direct-dial number at the business? Does she hold herself out as representing the business?
- If there is a contract between the business and the individual, what does it say?

FIGURE 5.1: EMPLOYED VS SELF-EMPLOYED?

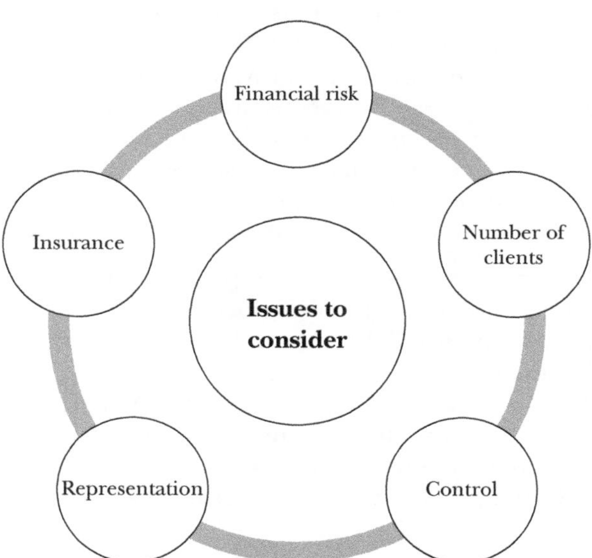


[4] See www.revenue.ie/en/practitioner/codes-practice.html (accessed May 2016).

The conclusion reached on an individual's employment/self-employment status will impact on both the tax treatment to be applied and whether the protections of employment law, and some social welfare law, will be available to her.

### *5.1.2 Tax Implications of Employment/Self-employment Status*

An employee will be subject to payroll taxes on all employment income due to her so that she receives net amounts, after these deductions, in her regular pay. The opposite is the case for a self-employed person; no deductions are applied and she receives her remuneration on a gross basis. The self-employed person is obliged to include this untaxed income in her income tax return, which must be filed by 31 October of the year following the tax year in which she received the remuneration.

In relation to a self-employed person, as there is no employer/employee relationship, no employer PRSI (at current rates of 8.5% and 10.75%) will be payable. The self-employed person will be obliged, however, to pay self-employed PRSI and this is currently set at a rate of 4% (the same as employee's PRSI). Self-employed PRSI is included in the income tax return calculations and is payable at the same time as the income tax and USC liabilities. Therefore, employer's PRSI represents an additional cost for employers that does not arise when an individual is treated as self-employed.

Where a self-employed person is treated as being "in business on their own account", then in calculating her taxable income (profit), she may take deductions in relation to all expenses paid "wholly and exclusively ... for the purposes of the trade or profession".[5] In contrast, an employee is subject to payroll taxes on all expenses paid to her by her employer unless those expenses come within strict parameters and are properly documented. Employee expenses will not be subject to payroll taxes only if those expenses are shown to have been "wholly, exclusively and necessarily"[6] incurred in the course of the employee's duties. This test for employee expenses is generally considered to be more restrictive and self-employed people are regarded as having more scope to claim business expenses and reduce their taxable income. (See below, however, for comments in relation to a recent Revenue investigation into so-called 'personal service companies'.)

Where the self-employed person is supplying VATable goods/services, she will be obliged to register for VAT once her turnover passes a certain threshold. At this time, the VAT threshold is generally €37,500 turnover per 12-month period in the case of services supplied by a business established in Ireland. The self-employed person must charge her client/customer VAT, at the appropriate VAT rate, on her invoices and include this sales VAT in her regular VAT returns. We have already looked at a summary of the VAT obligations arising for businesses in **Chapter 4**.

[5] Section 81 TCA 1997.
[6] Section 114 TCA 1997.

Where an individual operating in the construction, forestry or meat-processing industries is treated as self-employed, then she will be subject to the relevant contracts tax (RCT) regime. This regime is outside the scope of this book but, in broad terms, it requires the registration of contractors (known as sub-contractors) who have a 'relevant contract' with a 'principal contractor' and the registration of the contracts themselves. If proper RCT registration is not put in place, then the principal contractor is obliged to deduct RCT at 35% on all payments made to the sub-contractor and to pay this amount to Revenue. For more on the operation of the RCT regime, see Revenue's website.[7]

### 5.1.3 Some Employment Law/Social Welfare/Pension Implications

The determination of an individual's status as an employee or as a self-employed person will have far-reaching implications beyond tax. The more important implications are as follows:

- An employee will be entitled to unemployment, disability and invalidity benefits payable by the Department of Social Protection (DSP); a self-employed person will not.
- In general, an individual employee who has worked for an employer for at least two years will be eligible for tax-free statutory redundancy payments; a self-employed person has no such entitlement.
- The protections of employment legislation in relation to working time, holidays, protection from unfair dismissal, etc. are not available to self-employed people.
- A self-employed person operating their business through their own company will be in a position to shelter profits from income taxes and charges by making significant pension contributions into a company scheme. An employee will not generally have the same scope in this regard. (See the comments in **Chapter 1, Section 1.2.3** in relation to pension provision for company owners.)

### 5.1.4 Recent Revenue Reviews of Individual Employment Status

There is the potential for significant loss of tax revenue where individuals are incorrectly treated as self-employed. First, the loss of employer's PRSI at current rates of 8.5% and 10.75% will certainly add up. Secondly, there is also the potential for a self-employed person to receive their remuneration on a gross basis and then fail to return some or all of this income in an annual income tax return.

Over the years, Revenue has focused its attention in relation to the employment/self-employment status issue on a number of different sectors, including the construction and personal services sectors. Within the construction industry, Revenue have combined an increasingly robust (and streamlined) RCT regime (see above) with unannounced

[7] See www.revenue.ie/en/tax/rct/index.html (accessed June 2016).

on-site visits and review of third-party information, such as city and county council planning information, recruitment advertising, etc. In August 2015, Revenue announced another programme of focus on the construction industry and encouraged businesses operating in the sector to self-review their tax affairs before they become the subject of Revenue audit/intervention.[8] At the time of writing, this programme is ongoing and Revenue has issued an e-Brief highlighting some of the errors that it is frequently encountering.[9]

The personal services sector includes individuals who 'hire out' their services to a client/customer (for example, engineers, project managers, advisors and consultants of all types), and as such this sector is at the heart of the 'employed versus self-employed' debate. Recent Revenue audit programmes on the employed/self-employed issue have targeted 'locums' and 'personal service companies'.

##### *5.1.4.1 'Locums' Operating in the Medical, Health Care and Pharmacy Sectors*

A practice had developed over a number of years whereby 'locums', i.e. professionals operating in the medical, health care and pharmacy sectors and hired typically on a short-term basis, were treated as self-employed contractors and paid on a gross basis. These individuals worked on a 'locum' basis in a variety of ways, including:

- covering holiday periods;
- regular part-time, or sometimes almost full-time, hours with the hiring business, being paid on an hourly/piecemeal basis; and
- groups of medical locums coming together and putting more formal structures in place, whereby a medical practice could contact them looking for locum cover for a defined period of time and the group would decide which individual would provide the services.

Believing that these practices resulted in the loss of tax revenue, Revenue adopted a strong position in 2009, which initially involved the issue of a statement that, in their view, the majority of these locum arrangements should be reclassified as employer/employee relationships, with the resultant tax obligations. In early 2011, Revenue allowed employers of locums to correct their payroll tax obligations (where necessary) for 2009 and 2010, without the imposition of penalties. Revenue also stated that businesses that hired locums, and that had dealt with any outstanding payroll tax obligations for 2009 and 2010, should review previous years to determine if there were any outstanding payroll tax obligations for those years. Many of these hiring businesses were the subject of subsequent Revenue audits, while others made voluntary disclosures to deal with outstanding payroll tax liabilities.

[8] Revenue *eBrief* 77/2015, *Increased compliance interventions in the construction sector* (25 August 2015).

[9] Revenue *eBrief* 33/2016, *Increased compliance interventions in the construction sector – application of the Reverse Charge for VAT and other matters* (23 March 2016).

There are two key points to note from the locums project:

1. Statements included in any written contract between the hiring businesses and the locums to the effect that 'X is a self-employed contractor and not an employee of Y hiring business' were ignored; Revenue specifically stated that the circumstances of the individual's working situation would determine their employment status.
2. Despite the fact that Revenue only adopted this strong position in 2009, many hiring businesses were obliged to make tax settlements in relation to tax years prior to that.

#### *5.1.4.2 Professionals Providing their Services Through 'Personal Services Companies'*

While Revenue's focus with the 'locum project' was on the employed/self-employed status of individuals working in the medical, health care and pharmacy businesses, Revenue's next project on this issue focussed on individuals who provided their services through a company (known as a 'personal services company') to a small number, or potentially only one, business(es).

In a letter of January 2013, the Revenue South West Region responded to queries about a review it was carrying out of the corporation tax affairs of companies and the income tax affairs of their directors in circumstances where:

> "the main source of income is a contract or contracts 'for service' with a larger company or companies (directly or through intermediaries), the company in question does not appear to have a substantial business separate from these contracts, and in most cases the director(s) are the only employees of the company and pay tax through PAYE".[10]

While this letter stated that, at that time, Revenue was not expressing an opinion on whether directors should in fact be treated as direct employees of the (larger) company awarding the contract, it reserved the right to revisit the issue at a later date. This review was rolled out country-wide over the following months and, like the locums project discussed above, has had serious implications for a large number of 'personal services companies'.

While the initial review was focused on engineers, IT consultants and other consultants, its scope widened as it proceeded to include all types of professional service providers. Revenue's particular focus has been on the expenses deducted by these companies in calculating corporation tax liabilities – including on 'exaggerated' expenses, non-deductible personal expenses, expenses of the directors that are not incurred "wholly, exclusively and necessarily" for the purposes of their employment, family members as employees and travel expenses relating to trips between home and office.[11] **Chapter 8** includes a detailed account of how Revenue audits, reviews and enquiries are handled.

[10] From 22 January 2013 letter from Revenue South West Region to the Irish Tax Institute (available at the Tax Policy and Practice section of www.taxinstitute.ie).

[11] Revenue *Tax Briefing* 4/2013, *Revenue's Contractors Project* (November 2013).

## 5.2 Other Payroll Obligations for Employers

At the beginning of this chapter, we reviewed two excerpts from the tax legislation that clearly demonstrate how widely drawn are an employer's payroll obligations. In general terms, all employment income and benefits-in-kind paid by an employer to, or on behalf of, an employee are subject to payroll taxes. Certain exemptions and specific regimes for certain expenses apply and we will discuss these below.

Recent tax changes have introduced further payroll tax obligations on employers that do not relate to employment income or benefits-in-kind paid by the employer. Instead, these payroll tax obligations relate to:

- payments due from the employee directly to Revenue, e.g. local property tax (LPT);
- payments paid directly to the employee by the Department of Social Protection (DSP) that are subject to tax, e.g. maternity benefit and illness benefit.

In both these instances, the employer is obliged to act as the collection agent for Revenue, even though the taxes arising do not relate to any payments paid by the employer to, or on behalf of, an employee.

### *5.2.1 Local Property Tax*

While local property tax is generally outside the scope of this book, we refer to it here in the context of employer payroll tax obligations. LPT in respect of residential property was introduced in 2013, when a half-year charge was levied on all owners of residential property as at 1 May 2013. Property owners were obliged to file their LPT return by the end of May 2013 and pay by July 2013. One payment *option* was to have the LPT deducted at source from salary payments, in which case the LPT charge could be spread evenly over the period July to December 2013. From 2014 on, the LPT charge is deducted at source over the period January to December. Where an individual liable to LPT chooses the 'deduction at source' option, the employer receives a revised tax credit certificate (known as a P2C) from Revenue, which is coded to include the employee's LPT charge.

If a residential property owner has not filed their LPT return or has not paid their LPT liabilities (including any outstanding Household Charge that has been converted to LPT), then Revenue has a number of collection options at its disposal. One of these is *mandatory* deduction at source from salary payments, in which case Revenue will issue a revised P2C to the property owner's employer.

Where an employer has received a P2C requiring deduction of LPT from an employee's salary and the employer either fails to make the deduction, or fails to pay the deduction over to Revenue, then the employer may be subject to penalties.[12]

[12] Revenue *eBrief* 48/2016, *Non-Filing of Returns – Prosecution and Penalty Programmes* (6 May 2016).

### 5.2.2 Benefits Paid by the Department of Social Protection

Illness benefit and occupational benefit are payable directly by the DSP to the employee and, since January 2012, are subject to income tax but not to USC and PRSI. An employer is obliged to collect the income tax liabilities arising on these benefits through the payroll system. The DSP issue a notice to the employer setting out the amount of taxable benefit to be included in the employee's payroll calculations. If this notice does not issue, the employer should assume that the employee has received the benefit, commencing six days after the period of absence started, at the basic personal rate, which is, at the time of writing, €188 per week for a new applicant (assuming the employee receives average weekly earnings of €300 or more).[13]

Since July 2013, maternity, adoptive and health & safety benefits are also subject to income tax, but not to USC and PRSI. As with the other DSP benefits noted above, the income tax liabilities arising must be collected through the payroll system. At the time of writing, maternity and adoptive benefits for new applicants are €230 per week, for up to 26 and 24 weeks respectively.[14]

## 5.3 Specific Rules for Taxation of Employee Benefits/Expenses

### 5.3.1 General Concepts

The first point to note here is that a sole trader will not be subject to the specific regimes relating to employee expenses. Instead, the sole trader will take deductions in her business accounts for the business element of the expenses she incurs, e.g. fuel costs, motor tax, meals and accommodation. For the purposes of assessing the tax implications of payment/reimbursement of these types of expenses to a company director, however, the director is treated as an employee of the company.

Where an employer pays/reimburses employee expenses, there are specific rules for taxing (or not taxing) these expenses depending on the nature of the expenses and how the expenses are paid/reimbursed by the employer. The following sections set out a general overview of the tax treatment applicable to the payment of:[15]

- travel and subsistence expenses;
- round-sum expense payments and allowances;

[13] For more information, see www.welfare.ie/en/Pages/345_Illness-Benefit.aspx (accessed June 2016).

[14] For more information on maternity and adoptive benefit, see: www.welfare.ie/en/Pages/SW11.aspx (accessed June 2016).

[15] There is a significant amount of detail in this area, which is beyond the scope of this book, but can be found in the *Employers' Guide to PAYE* on the Revenue website.

- general expenses other than expenses of travel and subsistence;
- provision of a company car;
- provision of a company van;
- provision of home office equipment and supplies.

### *5.3.2 Travel and Subsistence Expenses*

Travel and subsistence (i.e. meals and accommodation) expenses may be reimbursed by an employer when an employee carries out the duties of her employment away from her 'normal place of work'. (This concept is important to this discussion and is set out in some detail below.) Revenue's *Income Tax Statement of Practice on the Tax Treatment of the Reimbursement of Expenses of Travel and Subsistence to Office Holders and Employees,*[16] sets out the conditions that must be met in order for these expenses to be paid/ reimbursed on a tax-free basis:

- the employee must be temporarily away from her 'normal place of work' in the performance of her duties; and
- the expenses of travel and subsistence must be necessarily incurred in the performance of these duties; and
- the employee must bear the costs of the travel and subsistence.

A significant issue to note is that expenses incurred in travelling between home and work are *not* treated as necessarily incurred by the employee in the performance of her duties.

Essentially, there are two methods of reimbursing travel and subsistence expenses on a tax-free basis, either:

- by way of flat-rate allowances; *or*
- by reference to actual vouched expenses.

An employer should choose one of these methods and stay with that method. Having a mix of the two methods will cause confusion and is likely to result in incorrect payroll tax calculations – outstanding tax liabilities caused by mixing (or doubling-up) the methods of paying these expenses are a feature of many Revenue audit settlements.

The flat-rate allowances that may be paid without seeking specific Revenue approval are the Civil Service rates for travel and subsistence, which can be found on the Revenue website in leaflets IT51 and IT54. In relation to subsistence expenses, note that:

- Where the employee is assigned to a location that is not her 'normal place of work' for more than 56 nights, employers should make an application to Revenue to agree the correct subsistence rate. In general, there is a cap of six months on the period of subsistence.
- Where the employee is assigned to a location outside of Ireland, there are Civil Service rates specific to each of Ireland's main trading partners.

[16] Income Tax Statement of Practice, SP – IT/2/2007, revised July 2015.

These can be obtained by contacting a Revenue regional office. (See **Chapter 12** for further information on subsistence expenses for foreign travel.)

In order to support the reimbursement of either flat-rate allowances or actual vouched expenses on a tax-free basis, it is imperative that the employer retain detailed records for six years after the end of the tax year to which the records relate. Again, a failure to retain detailed records for travel and subsistence expense claims is a feature of many Revenue audit settlements.

**'Normal Place of Work'** We have seen that travel and subsistence expenses may be reimbursed on a tax-free basis where an employee performs their employment duties away from their normal place of work.[17] This is assumed to be at one fixed location, which is usually noted in the employment contract. There are a number of issues to highlight here.

First, it is acknowledged by Revenue that for certain employees (known as 'site-based employees'), their normal place of work is not a fixed base but a series of different locations. Employees operating in the construction industry, who work on successive sites, are an obvious example here. Under the terms of various employment agreements negotiated by their trade unions, many of these employees receive tax-free flat-rate allowances (known as 'country money') on a weekly basis. Where other site-based employees (who are not covered by these registered employment agreements) are paid 'country money' at rates that do not exceed those accepted by Revenue, they also may receive these payments on a tax-free basis.[18]

In recent times, there has been a distinct focus on the normal place of work. This arose initially in the context of the 2013/14 Revenue project in relation to professionals who provide their services through a personal services company (as discussed in **Section 5.1.4.2** above). Many of these companies have only one employee and are based in the employee's home; and many are professionals operating in a highly mobile environment, which involves them travelling to various client locations as well as performing a significant amount of client work at their home office. Revenue are extremely slow to accept that the individual's normal place of work is their home. As the expenses of travel between work and home are not covered by this regime, the consequence is that Revenue auditors have disallowed significant amounts of claims for travel and subsistence expenses.

The Revenue position has been the subject of many submissions by the Irish Tax Institute, amongst others, which has highlighted that "[t]he working patterns of people have changed hugely in the modern

[17] Income Tax Statement of Practice, SP – IT/2/2007, revised July 2015, Section 2.1.

[18] *Ibid.*, Section 4.6.

world and technology has had a profound impact on the mobility of employees. As a result, our relevant tax law on travel and subsistence allowances has become completely out of date".[19] The Irish Tax Institute's August 2015 submission was in response to a consultation paper released by the Department of Finance. Following this consultation, the only specific change to date to the travel and subsistence expenses regime related to the expenses of a non-tax-resident non-executive director attending board meetings in Ireland.[20] At the time of writing, we understand that the Department of Finance is still considering the tax treatment of travel and subsistence expenses, so there may be further changes.

### 5.3.3 Round-sum Expense Payments and Allowances

Where an employee receives an agreed rounded lump sum (a 'round sum') for expenses on a regular basis, e.g. €500 per month, this lump sum payment will be subject to the usual payroll taxes. Likewise, an agreed regular amount payable in relation to a 'car allowance', e.g. annual car allowance of €8,000, will also be subject to the usual payroll taxes. These 'round sum' expenses/allowances are characterised by the fact that they do not relate to specific expenses or the Revenue-approved Civil Service rates, and their claim is not typically supported by documentation.

An alternative to the provision of a 'car allowance' may be the provision of a 'company car'. A summary of the tax implications arising in relation to the provision of a company car is set out at **Section 5.3.5** below.

### 5.3.4 General Reimbursement of Expenses other than Expenses of Travel and Subsistence

It is possible for an employer to reimburse an employee on a tax-free basis for other expenses; the only method of doing so is on the basis of actual vouched receipts. The reimbursement of these expenses may be tax-free if they meet the general rule on employee expenses, which is that they must be incurred "wholly, exclusively and necessarily"[21] in the performance of the employment duties (see comments in **Section 5.1.2**).

Revenue's *Employer's Guide to PAYE* specifically refers to business entertainment expenses as an example of other expenses that may be incurred by the employee and reimbursed by an employer. The Guide

[19] Irish Tax Institute's August 2015 submission (available at the Tax Policy and Practice section of www.taxinstitute.ie).

[20] Section 6 of the Finance Act 2015.

[21] Section 114 TCA 1997.

states that as these expenses do not pass the "wholly, exclusively and necessarily" test, they may not be reimbursed on a tax-free basis. However, in our experience, it is not Revenue practice to treat the reimbursement of business entertainment expenses as taxable BIK.

### 5.3.5 Provision of a Company Car

Where an employer provides a company car to an employee and the employee may use that car for private use also, a taxable BIK will arise. We have seen above that a journey between home and work is not treated as a business journey, so an employee who has use of a company car for that purpose will also have a taxable BIK. In practical terms, what happens is that an amount of notional pay (known as the 'cash equivalent') is included in the employee's gross pay and payroll taxes are then calculated in the normal way.[22]

For company cars provided since 1 January 2009, in order to calculate the amount of the 'cash equivalent', there are three relevant factors:

- the original market value (OMV) of the car;
- the employee's annual business mileage; and
- any contribution made by the employee to either the acquisition of the car or its annual running costs.

The first step is to take the OMV of the car and multiply this by the relevant percentage, which is determined by the level of annual business mileage, as follows:

| Business Mileage – Lower Limit (km) | Business Mileage – Upper Limit (km) | Cash Equivalent (% of OMV) |
|---|---|---|
| 0 | 24,000 | 30% |
| 24,000 | 32,000 | 24% |
| 32,001 | 40,000 | 18% |
| 40,001 | 48,000 | 12% |
| 48,001 | and upwards | 6% |

The OMV of the car is generally the list price of the car, including VAT and vehicle registration tax (VRT), at the time of its first registration. Some specific rules apply where the car was the subject of a discount on its purchase price. ***Note:*** this method of calculating the car's OMV must be applied irrespective of whether or not the car was actually bought as new. The next step is to take a deduction for any general contribution that the employee makes to the employer to cover the car's running costs. Any specific running costs paid directly by the employee will not impact on the BIK calculations.

[22] Section 121 TCA 1997.

## Case Study: Neally Engineering Ltd

Consider, for example, a product developer, Adam, working for Neally Engineering Ltd, who spends a significant amount of his time visiting client premises to discuss sales and new product development. In 2014, he is provided with a new company car with an OMV of €30,000, in respect of which he makes an annual general contribution of €1,000 and pays his own private fuel costs. In 2014, Adam drives 35,000 business kilometres and spends €600 on his private fuel costs. His 2014 'cash equivalent' for BIK purposes is as follows:

| | | € |
|---|---|---|
| OMV × relevant percentage | €30,000 × 18% | 5,400 |
| No deduction for private fuel costs | | – |
| Less: general contribution | | (1,000) |
| Taxable BIK | | 4,400 |

The employer is obliged to collect the relevant payroll taxes arising on the taxable BIK throughout the year. This means that there must be a best estimate of expected business mileage set at the beginning of the year so that an appropriate percentage can be applied to the car's OMV to generate the 'cash equivalent', which is then spread evenly across the year's payroll periods. This best estimate should be reviewed just before year-end to see if any adjustment to the 'cash equivalent' is required.

Revenue's *Employer's Guide to PAYE* includes weekly and monthly ready reckoners, which will calculate the 'cash equivalent' amount that must be added to an employee's employment income across the year's payroll periods to capture this taxable BIK.

Maintenance of detailed records, by way of logbook or regular odometer readings, is imperative if the employer is to apply a reduced percentage to the car's OMV because the employee is claiming business mileage exceeding 24,000 km in any given tax year. Where such records are incomplete, the employer should look at the total kilometres travelled by the employee in a given tax year and reduce this by a minimum of 8,000 km for assumed private use. ***Note:*** a Revenue auditor reviewing 'cash equivalent' calculations for payroll tax purposes will take a dim view of incomplete business mileage records and is likely to challenge reduced 'cash equivalent' calculations based on those records.

An alternative basis of calculating the 'cash equivalent' may be used where an employee drives between 8,000 and 24,000 business km per annum. This alternative basis, which reduces the cash equivalent to 24% of the car's OMV, may apply if the employee works at least 20 hours a week and spends at least 70% of their time away from their employer's place of business in a given tax year.

The provision of a hired car would also give rise to taxable BIK for an employee if there is private use. A car provided by an employer as part of a 'car pool' arrangement will not trigger payroll taxes if certain conditions are met.[23]

### *5.3.6 Provision of a Company Van*

Similar rules arise in relation to the provision of a 'company van' for private use. In that situation, the 'cash equivalent' is a straightforward 5% of the van's OMV, and the amount of business kilometres travelled by the employee is irrelevant.[24] As with a company car, no payroll taxes are triggered if the van is provided by an employer as part of a 'van pool' arrangement.

Where an employee spends at least 80% of their time away from their employer's place of business in a given tax year, no taxable BIK may arise in relation to private use of a company van. This exemption requires the following conditions to be met:

- the van is necessary for the performance of the employment duties;
- the employee is required to bring the van home after work; and
- the only private use is travel between home and work; other private use is prohibited.[25]

### *5.3.7 Provision of Home Office Equipment and Supplies*

Where an employer provides certain office equipment and supplies to an employee who is regarded as being an 'e-worker', no taxable BIK may arise as long as any *private use is incidental.*[26] Office equipment supplies can include: computers, scanners, printers, fax machines, software, telephone line, broadband connection and office furniture. An employee will not be regarded as an 'e-worker' if they merely bring some work home from their employer's premises in the evenings or at weekends. Typical traits of an 'e-worker' include:

- working away from the employer's premises for significant time, either at home or on the move;
- logging on to the employer's computer, and sending/receiving emails, data or files, remotely; and
- developing ideas, products or services remotely.

[23] For more information on the taxation of company cars, see *Private Use of Company Cars,* available at www.revenue.ie/en/tax/it/leaflets/benefit-in-kind/private-use-cars.html (accessed June 2016).

[24] Section 121A TCA 1997.

[25] For more information on the taxation of company vans, see *Private Use of Company Vans.* Available at www.revenue.ie/en/tax/it/leaflets/benefit-in-kind/private-use-vans.html (accessed June 2016).

[26] Section 118(5B) to (5D) TCA 1997.

Employers may pay a daily flat-rate allowance of €3.20 on a tax-free basis to cover the additional utilities costs arising because the employee is working at home. Where higher costs are incurred, these may be reimbursed on a tax-free basis where the employee provides actual vouched receipts.[27]

## 5.4 Some Opportunities to Reduce Payroll Taxes

We know that PAYE income tax, employee's PRSI and USC are all deductions from an employee's gross pay; in effect, these taxes and charges do not cost the employer anything and the employer's role is merely to act as collection agent. Employer's PRSI, however, is an additional charge that is suffered by the employer. So, for example, if an employer agrees a salary of €50,000 with an employee, the cost to the employer will be €50,000 plus the employer's PRSI charge of 10.75%, giving a total cost of €55,375. This means that where there are opportunities to pay employee benefits on a tax-free basis, these may result in tax savings for both employers and employees.[28]

### *5.4.1 Travel Passes*

Monthly or annual bus, train, LUAS and ferry passes provided by an employer will not be subject to payroll taxes in certain circumstances. The cost of the travel pass must be incurred directly by the employer. Often, the employer and employee will agree to reduce the employee's salary by the value of the travel pass – this is known as a 'salary sacrifice'. In general, a 'salary sacrifice' is subject to payroll taxes.[29] For example, if an employee agrees to reduce her annual salary by €1,000 in exchange for the employer paying her gym subscription of €1,000, then this €1,000 benefit will be included in the employee's gross pay for payroll tax purposes. Where certain conditions are met in sacrificing salary in favour of a travel pass, however, the benefit of the travel pass will not be taxable.

### *5.4.2 Bicycle Scheme (Cycle to Work Scheme)*

Another specific tax saving through a temporary 'salary sacrifice' arrangement can be achieved where an employer buys a new bicycle for an employee, who uses it mainly to travel between home and work, or between working locations. A cap of €1,000 applies and the employee may avail of

[27] For more information on e-working and tax, see Revenue's leaflet IT69, *e-Working and Tax*. Available at www.revenue.ie/en/tax/it/leaflets/it69.html (accessed June 2016).

[28] Further information is available in Revenue's *Employers Guide to Benefit-in-kind.* Available at http://www.revenue.ie/en/tax/it/leaflets/benefit-in-kind/index.html (accessed June 2016).

[29] Section 118B TCA 1997.

this scheme once every five years.[30] The employee repays the 'salary sacrifice' over an agreed number of payroll periods (which cannot exceed 12 months) and, as the repayments are deducted from gross pay, effectively no payroll taxes arise on this benefit.

### 5.4.3 Small Benefit

Where an employer provides a one-off, non-cash benefit (e.g. a voucher) with a value not greater than €500, no taxable BIK will arise. If the value of the non-cash benefit breaches the €500 threshold, then all of the benefit will be taxable and not just the excess over €500. This type of benefit can be provided on an annual basis.[31] This applies to 'qualifying incentives' provided from 22 October 2015; prior to this date, the maximum value of the benefit was €250.

### 5.4.4 Life Assurance and Permanent Health Insurance

Where certain conditions are met, it is possible for an employer to provide life assurance and permanent health insurance to an employee without triggering payroll taxes.

### 5.4.5 Employer Pension Contributions

Pension contributions made by an employer in respect of an employee into Revenue-approved pension schemes and personal retirement savings accounts (PRSAs),[32] will not be treated as taxable BIK as long as certain limits are not breached.

### 5.4.6 Employing Spouse or Civil Partner

Where a spouse/civil partner of the business owner is working in the business, careful consideration should be given to the spouse/civil partner's income. As the Irish income tax system is based on the concept of 'individualisation' (i.e. it deals with people primarily as individuals and not as members of households), a higher standard rate band is available for two-income couples than for one-income couples. On the rates effective from 1 January 2016, a one-income couple will start paying income tax at 40% when the taxable income of the income earner exceeds €42,800. A two-income couple will not be subject to the 40% rate until the combined taxable income is €67,600 – this assumes that each spouse/civil partner earns at least €24,800 in their own right.

[30] Section 118(5G) TCA 1997.
[31] Section 112B TCA 1997, introduced by section 11 FA 2015.
[32] PRSAs are only exempt from USC since a change in section 2 FA 2015.

### Case Study: Four Blue Ducks

An example is the case of Jim and Cathy, both of whom are working for Four Blue Ducks, which is owned by Jim. If there is a pot of €60,000 of net profits available to 'pay out' of the business, then instead of all of this amount being taken by Jim as taxable profits, there is a tax advantage to dividing it between Jim and Cathy. In this case, Cathy would be registered as an employee of Jim, the sole trader.

If the full €60,000 is allocated to Jim, then excluding any other income/tax credits, Jim will pay estimated income tax of €15,440 – being €8,560 (€42,800 × 20%) plus €6,880 (€17,200 × 40%). Where the profits are allocated as €35,200 to Jim and €24,800 salary to Cathy, then the two-income couple 20% band of €67,200 will be available to the couple. The estimated income tax liabilities would be €7,040 for Jim (€35,200 × 20%) and €4,960 for Cathy (€24,800 × 20%) – a total of €12,000, generating an estimated tax saving of €3,440.

***Note:*** the business owner should be 'allocating' salary to her spouse/civil partner only if they are genuinely working in the business. As part of the 2013 Revenue sectoral project into personal services companies (see **Section 5.1.4.2**), in some cases Revenue auditors did not accept that the shareholder/director's spouse/civil partner was actually working for the company, or they concluded that the spouse/civil partner was overpaid given the work that they were doing. Revenue require that the employment of a spouse/civil partner must "have been put in place on an arm's length basis. This means that the [spouse/civil partner] must be performing services or duties in the business and rates of pay must be similar to the rates paid to other employees doing the same type of work".[33]

During this sectoral project, where Revenue auditors were not satisfied that a spouse/civil partner's employment/salary level was bona fide, then the auditors re-allocated the salary of the spouse/civil partner to the shareholder/director themselves, resulting in higher tax liabilities.

## 5.5 Close Company Tax Implications

In **Chapter 1** we briefly referred to the concept of the 'close company' and noted that a company treated as a close company will be the subject of additional tax obligations. In this section, we will look at the tax implications arising on transactions between the owners/directors of the company and the company itself.

[33] Revenue *Tax Briefing* 4/2013, *Revenue's Contractors Project* (November 2013).

A 'close company' is a company that is under the control of either:

- five or fewer 'participators' (a '**participator**' is a person who owns any type of share or voting right in the company, or is a loan creditor of the company); *or*
- 'participators' who are also directors of the company.[34]

In summary, where a company has up to five shareholders and is controlled by those shareholders, or where a company is controlled by its directors/shareholders, then it will be treated as a 'close company'. As you would expect, this close company status attaches to the vast majority of Irish SME companies.

The 'close company rules' set out below are measures designed to reinforce the fact that a company's financial affairs are completely separate to those of its individual shareholders and directors. By triggering additional tax obligations on transactions between them and the company, the rules discourage those shareholders and directors from dipping into company assets for their personal benefit.

In relation to transactions between a close company and its directors/shareholders, there are three specific rules, as set out in the following sections.

### *5.5.1 Expenses Paid on Behalf of Participators and their Associates*

Where a close company pays the cost of any benefit for a 'participator' (e.g. a shareholder) or a participator's 'associate', (being a relative or business partner of a 'participator') then the company will be treated as having paid a dividend to that shareholder.[35] For the shareholder, the tax implications are that she must include the grossed-up value of this 'deemed dividend' in her personal tax return and pay income taxes and charges on this income. The company cannot take a tax deduction for this 'deemed dividend', so it will effectively incur a corporation tax charge on the amount, as well as having incurred the cost of the benefit. It will also be obliged to pay over dividend withholding tax (DWT), at the current rate of 20%, to Revenue on the grossed-up value of the benefit.

These rules apply only to benefits paid to the participator (or 'participator's associate') of a close company who is not a director or employee. If the participator (or 'participator's associate') is also a director or employee, then the usual payroll taxes would be applied to the benefit under general BIK rules on taxable benefits. The case study extract below sets out the tax implications for both the participator and the close company, where that company pays a personal expense of the participator.

[34] Section 430 TCA 1997.

[35] Sections 436 and 436A TCA 1997.

### Case Study: Tigim Language Learning Ltd

We look here at the potential tax implications for Tigim Language Learning Ltd (a company controlled by its three shareholders) if the company paid €6,000 in January 2016 for a Croke Park tenure ticket for the personal use of one of its shareholders, Aoife.

If Aoife was not a director/employee at the time that the benefit was paid by the company, the deemed dividend rules would apply as follows.

The company would not be entitled to take a tax deduction for this €6,000 deemed dividend, so it would suffer the ticket cost of €6,000 plus an additional corporation tax charge of €750 (€6,000 × 12.5% trading corporation tax rate). The company would also be obliged to pay over DWT of €1,500 (20% of the grossed-up value of the benefit, i.e. €6,000/0.80 = €7,500) to Revenue.

Aoife would be treated as having received a dividend of €7,500 in 2016. If we assume that Aoife pays income taxes and charges at a marginal rate of 49.5% for 2016, then including a dividend amount of €7,500 in her personal tax return for the year would generate additional personal tax liabilities of €3,713 for her. Aoife could take a credit for the DWT of €1,500 paid by the company, so her net tax liabilities would be €2,213.

Total tax costs arising (not including the cost of the ticket) because Aoife instructed the company to pay for the ticket are an estimated €4,463.

### *5.5.2 Interest Paid on Loans from Directors and their Associates to a Close Company*

These deemed dividend rules will also apply where loan interest is payable by a close company to a director of the company (or her associate) who controls at least 5% of the company's shares and the loan interest exceeds a certain limit.[36] The limit is a sum equal to 13% of the lower of the following amounts:

- the total value of the loans from company directors on which interest was paid in the period; and
- the nominal value of the issued share capital account and share premium account at the beginning of the accounting period.

[36] Section 437 TCA 1997.

CASE STUDY: NEALLY ENGINEERING LTD

Let's look again at the €50,000 loan that Danielle provided to Neally Engineering Ltd during the company's start-up phase. She has been charging a 2% annual interest rate to the company, which has issued share capital of €2,000 (1,000 ordinary shares of €2 each). As Neally Engineering Ltd is controlled by the company's director/shareholders, Danielle and her brother Martin, the deemed dividend rules will apply to any interest amount paid to Danielle that exceeds 13% of the *lower* of the following amounts:

- the total value of directors' loans (as Danielle's is the only director's loan, this cap is €6,500); and
- the total value of the ordinary shares (€2,000 × 13% = €260).

Danielle receives interest of €1,000 per annum from the company. As only €260 of this may be treated as 'normal' interest, the balance of €740 will be treated as a deemed dividend, with the following implications for interest paid in 2016:

- no corporation tax deduction will be available to the company, which means that an additional corporation tax charge of €92.50 (€740 × 12.5%) will arise;
- the company must pay DWT of €185 (20% on the grossed-up value of the benefit, i.e. €740/0.80 = €925) to Revenue;
- Danielle will be deemed to have received a dividend of €925, on which she will pay income taxes and charges – say, €458 at a marginal rate of 49.5%. She will include this deemed dividend in her personal tax return for the year and can claim a credit for the DWT of €185 already paid by the company.

### *5.5.3 Loans to Participators and their Associates*

Where a close company makes a loan to its participator (or her associate) and where that loan-making does not form part of the company's ordinary business, then the company will be obliged to make an income tax payment to Revenue, calculated at 20% of the grossed-up amount of the loan value.[37] You could think of this payment to Revenue as a 'loan' in itself, as it is repayable if and when the participator repays the loan to the company. If, however, the participator's loan is forgiven by the company, then the company's payment to Revenue will not be refunded. Instead, the grossed-up value of the loan will be subject to tax in the participator's hands and must be included in the participator's income tax return for the year of the loan forgiveness. Credit will be given to the borrower for the tax already paid by the company to Revenue.

[37] Sections 438, 438A and 439 TCA 1997.

In addition, where the participator is also a director of the company and the loan is interest-free, she must pay BIK on the annual benefit to her of the 'free use of money', i.e. the benefit to her of not having to pay for the loan. This annual BIK is calculated by applying a deemed interest rate to the value of the loan provided. The current deemed rates are 4%, where the loan is used to purchase, repair or improve the participator/director's private home; and 13.5% where the loan is used for any other purpose.

### Case Study: Tigim Language Learning Ltd

Suppose that, instead of instructing her company Tigim Language Learning Ltd to purchase her Croke Park tenure ticket, Aoife borrows €6,000 on an interest-free loan from the company and buys the ticket herself. Aoife is a director of the company and holds 40% of its shares. The loan is taken out in January 2016 and is forgiven by the company in June 2017.

The company is obliged to make a payment to Revenue, calculated as 20% of the grossed-up amount of the loan value, being €6,000 × 20/80 = €1,500. As the loan is not used for the purchase, repair or improvement of Aoife's residence, the BIK charge arising on the loan will be applied at 13.5% per annum. This generates a taxable BIK amount of €810, on which income taxes and charges will arise for 2016 and for half of 2017. Assuming that Aoife has a marginal tax rate of 49.5%, she will have estimated tax liabilities of €401 for 2016 and €200 for 2017.

When the loan is forgiven in 2017, Aoife will be subject to income taxes and charges on the value of the grossed-up loan, being €6,000/80 = €7,500. Again, assuming a 49.5% marginal tax rate, this will trigger an estimated €3,713 of tax liabilities. Aoife may claim a credit of €1,500, being the tax already paid by Tigim Language Learning Ltd to Revenue. As the loan is forgiven, Tigim Language Learning Ltd will not be entitled to a refund of the payment it made to Revenue in this regard.

In this situation, the total estimated tax costs arising (not including the cost of the forgiven loan) because the company initially loaned the money for, and then ultimately bore the cost of, the ticket are €4,314.

***Note:*** these rules relating to loans to participators (or their associates) do not apply in the following circumstances:

- where the amount of the loan to a director or employee does not exceed €19,050; *and*
- where the borrower works full-time for the close company or its associated companies; *and*
- where the borrower does not hold more than 5% of the ordinary share capital of the close company or its associated companies.

## 5.6 Other Income and Payroll Tax Issues for Directors of Close Companies

In general, an employee whose income is subject to payroll taxes will be entitled to a PAYE tax credit at the current rate of €1,650. Despite the fact that a director's salary is also subject to payroll taxes, this tax credit is not available to a 'proprietary director', who is defined as a director who either owns all of the company shares or who can directly/indirectly control at least 15% of the company shares. This credit is also not generally available to the spouse, civil partner or child of the proprietary director where those individuals receive employment income from the company, though there are certain circumstances where the child of such a director may be entitled to this credit.[38]

There has been recognition that the fact that a proprietary director was not entitled to a PAYE credit was discriminatory and so a new 'earned income' credit of €550 was introduced for proprietary directors and self-employed persons in Finance Act 2015.[39] The Department of Finance's *Summer Economic Statement,* issued in June 2016, includes a commitment to increase the 'earned income' credit to €1,650 by 2018.[40]

We know that an employee in receipt of employment income will be subject to payroll taxes and receive only the net after-tax amounts from their employer. Where this employment income is the individual's only income, the individual will not generally have an obligation to file an income tax return and the fact that she receives her salary after deduction of payroll taxes will generally be taken as evidence that she is tax compliant.

This is not the case, however, for proprietary directors (as defined above). The deduction of payroll taxes from the employment income of proprietary directors will not be taken as evidence of tax compliance unless there is documentation that shows these payroll taxes actually having been paid to Revenue. Where a company pays employment income to directors and employees (non-directors), and the company has outstanding payroll tax liabilities, then payroll taxes already paid to Revenue will be deemed to have been paid in respect of the non-directors first.[41] Without this tax rule, the director could arrange for the company to delay payment to Revenue of the payroll taxes withheld on their salary, and yet secure credit for the withheld payroll taxes in their personal tax return.

[38] Section 472 TCA 1997.

[39] Section 472AB TCA 1997, as introduced by section 3 FA 2015.

[40] See www.budget.gov.ie/Budgets/2017/Documents/SES/Summer-Economic-Statement-2016.pdf (accessed June 2016).

[41] Section 997A TCA 1997.

## 5.7 PRSI Classification for Directors of Close Companies

We noted previously that company directors are treated as employees for payroll tax purposes. As detailed above, the current employer's PRSI rates under Class A classification are 8.5% and 10.75%. The Class A PRSI classification generally applies to employees within the private sector.

The PRSI classification of Class S applies to self-employed people (e.g. sole traders) and to certain working directors who are also treated as 'self-employed' for the purposes of the Social Welfare Acts. The current Class S PRSI rate is 4%. A company director who is subject to Class S PRSI classification will not have access to certain social welfare benefits, such as unemployment benefit, as set out in **Section 5.1.3** above.

Section 16 of the Social Welfare and Pensions (Miscellaneous Provisions) Act 2013 states that Class S classification applies to individuals who:
- are employed by a company under a written or oral contract; *and*
- are the beneficial owner of the company (i.e. own 100% of the company); *or*
- are able to control 50% or more of the company's share capital, either directly or indirectly.

The Social Welfare Act 2013 did not include any specific provisions in relation to the correct PRSI classification where a director owns or controls less than 50% of the company's shares. In this case, employers are directed to the general principles set out in the Revenue *Code of Practice for Determining Employment or Self-Employment Status of Individuals.* If there is uncertainty as to the appropriate PRSI classification that should apply to an individual director/shareholder, then the employer company may make a submission to the SCOPE section of the Department of Social Protection, setting out the director's circumstances and requesting a determination.

The rules outlined above relate to executive, or what we might call 'working', directors. These are the people who manage the company on a day-to-day basis. There is another type of director, called a **non-executive director**, who is not involved in the daily business; instead, this person may provide specific expertise at meetings of the board of directors. In the absence of an employment contract, directors' fees paid to a non-executive director will be subject to Class S PRSI.

In recent years there have been increasing calls for the full benefits of the employee PRSI scheme to be made available to self-employed persons and directors who are treated as self-employed for PRSI purposes. The Department of Finance's June 2016 *Summer Economic Statement* (as referenced above) included a commitment to introduce a PRSI scheme for self-employed people.[42]

[42] Further information in relation to PRSI and DSP benefits can be found on the DSP website, www.welfare.ie.

CHAPTER 6

# KEEPING TAXES ON PROFITS DOWN



This chapter will focus on taxes arising on the profits of a trading business or profession: income tax for sole traders and partnerships; and corporation tax for companies. Note that, in tax terms, a 'profession' is generally treated in the same way as a 'trade' and the same tax rules in relation to calculating the taxable profits of a trade will apply to calculating the taxable profits of a profession.

One of the main ways to keep taxes on profits as low as possible is to focus on maximising all available tax deductions; it is this issue that will occupy us for much of this chapter. In addition, we will look at the surcharges aspect of the 'close company' rules, which we referred to in **Chapters 1** and **5**. We will also look in more detail at the corporation tax exemption for start-up companies, briefly referred to in **Chapter 1**.

## 6.1 Calculating 'Taxable Profit'

While the concept of profit, i.e. income less expenses, is generally understood, we must distinguish in this context between 'accounting profit' and 'taxable profit'. In Ireland, 'accounting profit' is the profit figure produced by applying the rules of accounting, either Irish and UK GAAP (Generally Accepted Accounting Practice) or IFRS (International Financial Reporting Standards), to a business's accounts. Taking the 'accounting profit' as the starting point, various adjustments required by the tax rules must be made to arrive at the 'taxable profit' for the accounting period.[1] An obvious example of a tax adjustment is the tax rule requiring the addback of accounting depreciation and the deduction of capital allowances (so-called 'tax depreciation'). We will review many of the rules relating to capital allowances below.

The next general concept to understand is that many of the basic rules relating to calculating taxable profit for corporation tax purposes follow the rules for calculating taxable profit for income tax purposes. For example, the basic rules relating to capital allowance deductions will be the same, whether the business is a sole trader or a company. Once the taxable profit is calculated, the appropriate rate of income tax (20/40%) or corporation tax (12.5/25%) is then applied, depending on the form of the business, i.e. sole trader, partnership or company.

***Remember***: the basis for claiming a tax deduction when calculating taxable profit is that the expense must be "wholly and exclusively laid out or expended for the purposes of the trade".[2]

Combining these concepts, we can generally say that as long as an expense of the business is incurred "wholly and exclusively" for the purposes of the trade then, unless it is the subject of a specific tax adjustment rule, the expense will be a valid tax deduction in calculating the taxable profit for the accounting period.

## 6.2 Pre-trading Expenses

The process involved in creating and starting a new business can take quite some time and the business owners may well be paying for various expenses before the business 'opens its doors'. What is the tax treatment of these 'pre-trading expenses'? The tax rules state that a deduction can be claimed for pre-trading expenses as long as the following conditions are met:

- the expenses were incurred for the purposes of the trade;
- the expenses were incurred within three years of commencement of the trade; *and*

[1] Section 76A(1) of the Taxes Consolidation Act 1997 (TCA 1997).
[2] Section 81(2)(a) TCA 1997.

- there is no other method of deducting the expenses in calculating taxable profits of the business.[3]

The tax deduction for pre-trading expenses can only be used to reduce taxable income of the trade for which the expenses were incurred. It cannot be used to reduce other taxable income, e.g. rental income. Set out in the case study extract below is an example of how a company's pre-trading expenses may arise and how they may be dealt with from both tax and accounting perspectives.

Case Study: Tigim Language Learning Ltd

Tigim Language Learning Ltd starts as a classroom-based language learning business and later morphs into a fully online language learning service. The classroom-based sessions require individual computers for each student as well as the presentation of information by the class lecturer. During the three-month preparation period for starting the business, rent must be paid on the newly leased premises and money spent on fitting out some of the open-plan space, leasing new computers, creating a website and printing promotional material. All told, approximately €12,500 is spent before the company starts trading on 1 November 2009, when the first language courses commence.

When the company is incorporated in 2009, the three shareholders take nominal share capital, i.e. 100 shares at €1 each, which means that the company does not have any cash invested by way of share capital. In order to bridge the gap until the company starts trading, Aoife pays all of the pre-trading expenses, carefully ensuring that all of the invoices for these expenses are made out to Tigim Language Learning Ltd and retaining all the invoices. When the company is up and running, the total amount of pre-trading expenses paid by Aoife is reflected in the company accounts as a loan from Aoife. This means that the expenses are treated as company expenses and included as deductions when the taxable profit for the first accounting period is being calculated, and Aoife is treated as having made a loan of €12,500 to Tigim Language Learning Ltd.

## 6.3 Capital Allowances

We noted above that capital allowances, sometimes called 'tax depreciation', are a type of tax deduction available to a business when calculating its taxable profit.

[3] Section 82 TCA 1997.

Before looking at capital allowances in more detail, we will look at the difference between 'revenue' and 'capital' expenses. In general, a 'revenue' expense is an expense that provides a short-term benefit, usually covering a period of a year or less. Examples include insurance, utility bills, advertising costs and rental payments. As these expenses provide only a short-term benefit, the full value of the expense is usually included as an accounting deduction in the profit and loss account of the business for the accounting period in which the expense was incurred. Unless there is a specific tax rule requiring an adjustment to this accounting deduction, the deduction will stand when calculating the taxable profit.

On the other hand, a 'capital' expense is one which provides a longer-term benefit to the business. The expense of these longer-term benefits is spread across a number of accounting periods through deductions known as 'depreciation charges'. In preparing a business's accounts, the business owners/directors will agree suitable depreciation policies with the accountant/auditor for the capital expenses it has incurred.

Take, for example, a company that purchases computer equipment and decides to depreciate these assets over a four-year term. **This means that a depreciation charge of 25% of the cost of the asset will be included in the company's profit and loss account for four accounting periods** (assuming the accounting periods are 12 months long).

And what about the tax treatment of this depreciation charge? This is an area where a specific tax adjustment is required to the accounting profit; the taxpayer is required to add back the depreciation charge (increasing the taxable profit) and take a deduction for capital allowances on the same asset (reducing the taxable profit).

### Example 6.1: Depreciation Charges vs Capital Allowances

We referred above to a company that chose a four-year accounting depreciation policy for its computer equipment and noted that no tax deduction is available for accounting depreciation; instead capital allowances may be claimed in respect of this equipment. Under tax rules, computer equipment is eligible for capital allowances on the basis of an eight-year timeframe, i.e. an allowance of 12.5% of the cost of the asset over eight accounting periods (assuming the accounting periods are 12 months long). If we compare a four-year accounting depreciation policy and the eight-year capital allowance entitlement, we can see that, for the first four years, the depreciation charge is double the capital allowance for the computer equipment.

Take an item of computer equipment worth €100,000, which is subject to an accounting depreciation policy of four years, i.e. a depreciation charge of 25% (€25,000) per annum. As capital allowances are available at the rate of 12.5% per annum (€12,500), this means that in the first four years the addback of the depreciation charge and the claim for the capital allowance will result in increased taxable profits for the business.

The depreciation charges and capital allowances available on the computer equipment valued at €100,000 would have the following effect on taxable profit:

| | Depreciation Addback | Capital Allowance | Net Effect on Taxable Profit |
|---|---|---|---|
| | € | | € |
| Year 1 | 25,000 | (12,500) | 12,500 |
| Year 2 | 25,000 | (12,500) | 12,500 |
| Year 3 | 25,000 | (12,500) | 12,500 |
| Year 4 | 25,000 | (12,500) | 12,500 |
| Year 5 | – | (12,500) | (12,500) |
| Year 6 | – | (12,500) | (12,500) |
| Year 7 | – | (12,500) | (12,500) |
| Year 8 | – | (12,500) | (12,500) |
| Total | 100,000 | (100,000) | NIL |

We can see that the total depreciation charges and the total capital allowances are €100,000. This means that, over the course of the eight-year period, the full cost of the computer equipment is fully depreciated in the accounts and is also the subject of full tax deductions (capital allowances). Note also that the cumulative effect on taxable profit over the eight-year period is NIL, which highlights that in this case the tax rules affect only the *timing* of tax deductions for the computer equipment.

### *6.3.1 Different Types of Capital Allowance*

For most trading businesses, the two most relevant categories of capital allowance are:

- plant and machinery (including motor vehicles) wear and tear allowances; and
- industrial buildings allowance.

#### *6.3.1.1 Plant and Machinery Wear and Tear Allowances*

To be eligible for a wear and tear (W&T) allowance for expenditure on plant and machinery, the following conditions must be met:

- the expense must have been incurred for the purpose of the trade;
- the plant and machinery must be used wholly and exclusively for the purposes of the trade; *and*

- the plant and machinery must be in use at the end of the accounting period.[4]

The current rates of W&T allowances are:

- Plant and machinery: 12.5% of cost per 'chargeable period'. (Broadly, 'chargeable period' refers to a 12-month accounting period in the case of a company taxpayer, or a tax year in the case of an individual taxpayer.)
- Motor vehicles (excluding taxis/car-hire vehicles): 12.5% of cost per chargeable period.

  For motor vehicles purchased after 1 July 2008, the allowable cost for W&T allowances is capped by reference to the car's $CO_2$ emission levels. For cars in the low emission categories of A–C, the maximum allowable cost will be €24,000. This maximum amount is halved for cars in the D–E categories, i.e. maximum allowable cost will be €12,000, and no wear and tear allowances are available for cars in the F–G categories.
- Taxi/car-hire vehicles: 40% per chargeable period on a 'reducing-balance basis', which means that instead of taking a percentage of the cost every period, the W&T allowance is calculated by taking a percentage of what *remains of the cost* after reduction by prior period allowances. This remainder amount is known as the 'tax written-down value'.

### Example 6.2: Capital Allowances Calculated on a 'Reducing-balance' Basis

A taxi costs €50,000. The W&T allowance available on it in Year 1 is €50,000 × 40% = €20,000. The calculation of subsequent years' W&T allowance is:

Year 2: (Cost minus Year 1 allowance) × 40%
(€50,000 – €20,000) × 40% = €12,000
Year 3 allowance: ((Cost minus Year 1 allowance)
minus Year 2 allowance) × 40%
((€50,000 – €20,000) – €12,000) × 40% = €7,200

We can see that when this reducing-balance basis is used, W&T allowances are not spread evenly across the chargeable periods. The restriction on the maximum allowable cost of the motor vehicle (see above) for W&T allowances does not apply to taxis or car-hire vehicles.

***Note:*** W&T allowances are only available on the actual net cost to the taxpayer. This means that if the asset cost is reduced by, say, state grants, then the W&T allowances will be available on the cost less the amount of the grant.

[4] Section 284(1) TCA 1997.

### *6.3.1.2 Industrial Buildings Allowance*

An annual allowance (known as a writing-down allowance) at the rate of 4% of the 'qualifying cost' per chargeable period is available to a taxpayer who holds the 'relevant interest' in an industrial building at the end of the chargeable period, where the building is being used by the taxpayer for the purposes of a trade being carried on by him.[5]

There are a number of points to note in relation to 'qualifying cost':

- As with plant and machinery W&T allowances (see above), any state grants provided to assist the purchase/construction of the industrial building must be deducted from the cost.
- If the building has been constructed by the taxpayer, then the qualifying cost *includes* construction costs, site preparation costs and professional fees, but *excludes* site acquisition costs. Where the industrial building includes an element of offices, showrooms, retail shops or dwellings, then these elements are excluded from the qualifying cost if their cost exceeds 10% of the total costs.
- If the building has been bought by the taxpayer from a builder, then the 'qualifying cost' will be:

$$\text{Purchase price} \times \frac{\text{Construction costs}}{\text{Construction} + \text{site costs}}$$

- If the building has been bought by the taxpayer from a non-builder, then the qualifying cost will be the lower of the amount produced by the above formula and the construction costs.[6]

The list of buildings that may be treated as 'industrial buildings' is set out in **Appendix I** to this chapter; note that offices, retail units and showrooms are not regarded as industrial buildings. It is extremely important that a taxpayer identify if there is an entitlement to the industrial building allowance (IBA) in relation to any newly purchased or newly constructed premises to be used for the purposes of the trade.

Note also that certain types of 'industrial building' were/are entitled to accelerated IBA, i.e. higher rates of annual allowances available over a shorter period of time. For this purpose, certain types of building were deemed to be 'industrial buildings', including, for example, multi-storey car parks and holiday camps/tourism infrastructure in the 'Shannon Corridor'.

Many of these accelerated allowance schemes have now expired and/or are the subject of a 1 January 2015 'guillotine', after which any unused allowances carried forward are no longer available for deduction. As this is an extremely convoluted area, it is outside the scope of this book; however, a taxpayer considering the purchase of a building that appears to meet the definition of 'industrial building' (as described in **Appendix I**) should take professional advice as to the availability of IBA.

[5] Section 272 TCA 1997.

[6] Section 279 TCA 1997.

### *6.3.1.3 Balancing Allowances/Charges*

It bears repeating that in order to be eligible for capital allowances, the relevant asset must be in use by the business at the end of the chargeable period. But what happens when the asset is sold or written off? It is no longer in use at the end of the chargeable period and, in fact, will never be used by the business again.

In this situation, the tax rules require the calculation of either a 'balancing allowance' (which will reduce the taxable profit) or a 'balancing charge' (which will increase the taxable profit). We noted earlier, in **Section 6.3.1.1** when we reviewed the capital allowance rules applicable to taxis/car-hire vehicles, the concept of 'tax written-down value' (TWDV), which is the amount of asset cost that has not yet been the subject of a capital allowance. When an asset is disposed of or written off, then in order to determine whether a balancing allowance or balancing charge is required, the asset's TWDV must be compared with the sale price of the asset. The examples set out below compare the results when the asset's TWDV is higher or lower than the sale price.

CASE STUDY: TIGIM LANGUAGE LEARNING LTD

Consider, for example, a computer server bought for €8,000 on 1 October 2012 by Tigim Language Learning Ltd. It was immediately brought into use and subject to 12.5% annual wear and tear allowances (€1,000 per annum). The company's year-end is 30 September. By 2 October 2014, two years' wear and tear allowances will have been claimed so that the equipment's TWDV on 2 October 2014 will be €6,000.

The rules on capital allowances are aimed at ensuring that the taxpayer only receives a tax deduction (in the form of a capital allowance) for the actual net cost to them of the asset. On the disposal of the asset, the taxpayer is required to compare the TWDV with the sales proceeds. Where the sales proceeds are less than TWDV, the taxpayer will be entitled to a balancing allowance for the shortfall.

If the computer server was sold for €2,000 on 2 October 2014, then the taxpayer would be entitled to a balancing allowance of €4,000 in the chargeable period ended 30 September 2015. We can see that the net cost of the asset to the taxpayer would be €6,000 (€8,000 less €2,000) and the total capital allowance entitlement would match this cost as follows:

| | |
|---|---|
| 2013 W&T allowance | €1,000 |
| 2014 W&T allowance | €1,000 |
| 2015 balancing allowance | €4,000 |
| | €6,000 |

Conversely, a balancing charge would be triggered if the sales proceeds exceeded the TWDV and this would be calculated as the 'excess' of the sales proceeds over the TWDV, limited to the amount of allowances already granted.

If the computer server was sold for €6,500 on 2 October 2014, then the taxpayer would suffer a balancing allowance of €500. The net asset cost was €1,500 (€8,000 less €6,500) and the total capital allowances matched this cost as follows:

| | |
|---|---|
| 2013 W&T allowance | €1,000 |
| 2014 W&T allowance | €1,000 |
| 2015 balancing charge | (€500) |
| | €1,500 |

*Note:* there is a measure of relief in respect of balancing charges in relation to small disposals, i.e. no balancing charge will arise where the amount of the sales proceeds is less than €2,000.[7]

### 6.3.2 Maximising Capital Allowance Claims

Having set out the basic tax rules in relation to W&T allowances, IBA and balancing allowances/charges, we look now at how to maximise these allowance claims.

The more efficient type of capital allowances are W&T allowances, in that the tax deductions available for plant and machinery are spread over an eight-year period, as opposed to the 25-year period for the normal IBA. Therefore, it is in a business's interest to classify as much expenditure as possible as being incurred on plant and machinery. Moveable plant and machinery is fairly easy to identify (e.g. computer laptops or office furniture); it is the immoveable plant that is embedded in buildings that is much more difficult to classify, though this is often where the really valuable tax deductions (i.e. capital allowances) will be found. Modern factory premises, laboratories and office buildings sometimes seem like living, breathing organisms as their fabric contains so much plant and machinery; anything up to 30–40% of the expenditure on new commercial premises may constitute 'plant'.

There is no comprehensive list of 'plant' that is eligible for W&T allowances; instead, the meaning of the term has evolved through the decisions made in various court cases. In general, to be treated as 'plant', an asset must be:

- integral to the building (meaning that the owner would not seek to remove it from the property on sale of the property);
- used in carrying on a business;
- kept for permanent use in the business (and not as trading stock); and
- *functional* in the context of the business and not part of the *setting* in which the business is carried on.

This last test, the test of 'functionality', has been interpreted in different ways in various court decisions. Examples of assets that have been treated

[7] Sections 288 and 289 TCA 1997.

as plant include petrol station canopies and hotel light fittings and murals. On the other hand, suspended ceilings in a department store and tennis courts have not been treated as plant.

Further listings of assets that may or may not meet the definition of plant are set out at **Appendix II** to this chapter.

***Note:*** there are advisory firms that specialise in analysing detailed building specifications and associated expenditure in order to attribute as much expenditure as possible to plant so that maximum W&T allowances may be claimed. This type of analysis will be even more worthwhile if the building is not classified as an 'industrial building'.

### *6.3.3 Interaction of Industrial Buildings Allowance with Wear and Tear Allowances*

In certain circumstances, the taxpayer business may have a choice as to the type of allowance claims to be made. This could arise in a situation where a building that is classified as an 'industrial building' (for IBA purposes) contains plant that would qualify for W&T allowances. In this case, the taxpayer can choose to claim IBA (at the rate of 4% per annum for 25 years) or claim W&T allowances (at the rate of 12.5% per annum for eight years). Choosing the W&T allowances will, of course, accelerate the tax deductions for this asset, giving a cash-flow advantage to the taxpayer business.

### *6.3.4 Leasing Assets and the Claim for Wear and Tear Allowances*

We noted at **Section 6.3.1.1** that the general rules in relation to wear and tear allowances require that in order to be entitled to this claim the taxpayer must have incurred the cost of providing the plant or machinery and be using the asset for the purposes of their trade. But what about the situation where an asset is leased by the owner (lessor) to a business that uses the asset for the purposes of its (the lessee's) business?

In this situation, the key question is who has the so-called 'burden of wear and tear'. In other words, who will be affected by the asset losing its value over the course of its life, and who would be required to replace the asset once it is of no further use? There is a differentiation here between 'general/fair' wear and tear, i.e. the day-to-day deterioration of an asset by reasonable use, which can be made good by repairs, and the more extreme breaking-down, damage or destruction of an asset, which cannot. Where the 'burden of wear and tear (fair wear and tear excepted)' remains with the lessor, then it is the lessor that has the entitlement to wear and tear allowances.[8] In this case, the lessor is deemed to be carrying on the trade of leasing. (A leasing trade is subject to specific rules as to

[8] Section 298 TCA 1997.

the calculation of capital allowances, the detail of which is outside the scope of this book.)

In other circumstances, it is the lessee that will have the entitlement to claim wear and tear allowances on the leased asset. This entitlement will arise if the lessee is carrying on a trade, bears the burden of wear and tear on the asset and is obliged to maintain the asset and hand it over in good condition at the end of the lease.[9] In this case, the lessee is deemed to have incurred the cost of acquiring the asset and is deemed to own the asset, thus entitling it to the claim for wear and tear allowances.

***Note:*** lessees that do not have an entitlement to claim wear and tear allowances on leased assets may be in a position to claim a tax deduction for leasing payments as long as they are incurred 'wholly and exclusively' for the purposes of the trade. See **Chapter 2, Section 2.1.4** for further information on this aspect.

### *6.3.5 Timing Issues and Maximising Wear and Tear Allowances Claims*

We noted above that the difference between claiming deductions by way of depreciation charges and capital allowances may be one of timing only, i.e. that where an asset that is the subject of accounting depreciation is eligible for capital allowances, then the total deductions available will be the same amount but the timing of the depreciation charges and capital allowances may differ. Where capital allowance claims can be accelerated this will not change the total tax deductions available, but it will give a cash-flow boost to the business. We highlight some possibilities for accelerating capital allowance claims below.

#### *6.3.5.1 Purchasing Assets just before Accounting Period End*

While it is a condition of an allowance claim that the asset must be in use by the taxpayer at the end of the chargeable period, there is no requirement for the asset to have been in use for the entire chargeable period in order to claim a full year's allowances. Purchasing an asset and putting it into use just before the chargeable period-end, as opposed to early in the following chargeable period, would increase the taxpayer's allowances claim in the chargeable period.

#### *6.3.5.2 Reviewing Lists of Older Plant and Machinery*

Certain assets depreciate more quickly than the wear and tear allowance rules acknowledge, so there may be situations where an asset is obsolete and/or has been destroyed and yet the full wear and tear allowances have not been claimed. An example of this is a computer laptop, which may only have a useful life of four to five years and yet the wear and tear

[9] Section 299 TCA 1997.

allowances are spread over an eight-year period. (A computer laptop is treated as 'machinery' for the purposes of wear and tear allowances.) If the laptop is thrown out after four years, then a balancing allowance equalling the laptop's TWDV should be claimed in the accounting period in which it is thrown out. For businesses with large plant and machinery listings, it is worth reviewing the older assets to determine if any of them are no longer in use and could be the subject of balancing allowances.

### *6.3.6 Accelerated Capital Allowances*

In addition to the 25-year (for the IBA) and eight-year (for W&T allowances) timeframes for claiming capital allowances, certain assets may be the subject of accelerated allowance claims. Taxpayers should be aware of the types of asset involved so that they can amend their purchasing behaviour if possible.

#### *6.3.6.1 Energy-efficient Equipment*

The first point to note here is that the accelerated allowances available for 'energy-efficient equipment' may only be claimed by corporate taxpayers; sole traders and partnerships cannot secure these accelerated allowances. This is an extremely useful tax deduction, as it comprises a 100% capital allowance that is available in the first year the expenditure is incurred – in effect, a full deduction is available in the year of purchase.

To qualify, the asset must:
- be a new asset;
- be used by the company for the purposes of its trade;
- be owned by the company – it cannot be leased or hired;
- meet certain energy-efficiency criteria and fall within one of 10 classes of equipment; *and*
- be from a list of approved products.[10]

The approved list of products is set out in the relevant section of the website of Sustainable Energy Authority of Ireland (SEAI).[11]

The categories of 'energy-efficient equipment' are:
- motors and drives;
- lighting;
- building energy management systems;
- information and communications technology;
- heating and electricity provision;
- process and heating, ventilation and air-conditioning control systems;
- electric and alternative-fuel vehicles;

[10] Section 285A and Schedule 4A TCA 1997.

[11] See www.seai.ie/Your_Business/Accelerated_Capital_Allowance (accessed June 2016). Further information can also be found in Revenue's *Tax & Duty Manual*, Part 09-02-04, available on the Revenue website.

- refrigeration and cooling systems;
- electro-mechanical systems; and
- catering and hospitality equipment.

***Note:*** the allowance is available in respect of energy-efficient equipment purchased no later than 31 December 2017.

### *6.3.6.2 Development or Acquisition of Intangible Assets*

This type of wear and tear allowance is also restricted to corporate taxpayers only.

Unlike, say, plant and machinery W&T allowances or allowances for energy-efficient equipment, the accelerated W&T allowances for 'intangible assets' may follow the accounting depreciation policy of the taxpayer business, e.g. if the business depreciates a qualifying asset over a five-year period (at the rate of 20% per annum), then the allowance will match this depreciation charge and be available at the rate of 20% per annum. Alternatively, the taxpayer business may elect to claim these allowances at the rate of 7% per annum for 14 years and 2% in the final year.[12]

The definition of 'intangible asset' is quite broad and includes: patents, designs, inventions, brands, trademarks, domain names, customer lists (as long as these are not provided in connection with the transfer of a business as a 'going concern'), copyrights, research and authorisation allowing the commercial exploitation of a medicine or product deriving from a design or invention, know-how, etc., and associated rights and goodwill attributable to any one of these qualifying items. Items that are excluded from the definition include some marketing intangibles, e.g. internally generated brands and goodwill, that are not linked to one of the qualifying items listed above.

In order to claim these accelerated W&T allowances, the intangible asset must be in use by the company for the purposes of its trade and the company must prepare its accounts under IFRS or Irish GAAP. Pre-trading expenditure on intangible assets that will be used by the company for the purposes of its trade will also be eligible for these allowances. Where the asset ceases to be used by the trade within five years of acquisition, a balancing charge will arise. After this five-year anniversary, no balancing charge will arise.

While the summary above refers to a trading company that acquires an intangible asset for use in its trade, these accelerated W&T allowances may also be claimed by a company whose business is the management, development or exploitation of intangible assets. This type of company is more likely to be one of a number of companies within a corporate group that licenses intangible assets, e.g. patents, to other group companies.

[12] Section 291A TCA 1997.

***Note:*** it is not possible to claim capital allowances on the development of intangible assets where the company already has an entitlement to claim the research and development (R&D) tax credit for the development of these assets. (We will review the R&D tax credit in detail in **Chapter 11**.)

#### *6.3.6.3 Certain Commercial Buildings*

Many of the tax-incentivised commercial property developments of the 1990s and 2000s were accelerated capital allowance schemes. The types of buildings subject to these allowances included: multi-storey car parks, hotels, holiday camps, holiday cottages, guest houses, holiday hostels, nursing homes, housing units for the aged and infirm, private convalescent facilities, childcare facilities, student accommodation, buildings used for third-level education, private hospitals, mental health centres, palliative care units, sports injury clinics and park-and-ride facilities.

Many of these capital allowance schemes are 'closed' to new developments although the allowances arising from existing developments may yet be available. Since 2007, the so-called 'high earner's restriction' has impacted on non-trading investors in accelerated allowances schemes by restricting the amount of allowances the investor can use in a given tax year; the purpose being to ensure that each investor pays a minimum effective tax rate of 30%.[13] Many of the unused allowances arising under these schemes were the subject of a 1 January 2015 guillotine, after which date unused allowances carried forward can no longer be used to reduce taxable income.

Bucking the general trend towards the wind-down of these property schemes, Finance Act 2015 introduced a new scheme of accelerated allowances for expenditure incurred on aviation services facilities at Irish airports during the period from 13 October 2015 to 12 October 2020.[14] These allowances are also subject to the 'high earner's restriction.'

## 6.4 Illustration: Tax Deductions for Computer-related Expenditure

In the introductory paragraph on capital allowances, we looked at the difference between 'revenue' and 'capital' expenditure and also noted the impact of the accounting treatment of an item of expenditure on its tax treatment.

To illustrate how these different concepts interact across one type of expenditure, we will look briefly at computer-related expenditure to see how tax deductions may be claimed in respect of websites, computer hardware and software.

[13] Sections 485C–G TCA 1997.

[14] Section 268 TCA 1997, as amended by section 27 of the Finance Act 2015 (FA 2015).

### 6.4.1 Website Development

The costs associated with website development and maintenance fall squarely into the revenue versus capital debate for the business's accountants (and/or auditors) when preparing the financial statements. Should these costs be expensed to the profit and loss account, on the basis that they are a type of advertising cost, so that a full deduction is taken in the accounting year in which they are paid? Or should these costs be capitalised on the balance sheet and the capitalised amounts made subject to an annual depreciation charge, on the basis that the benefit arising from the expense endures for more than one accounting period?

The relevant accounting standard will determine whether these costs will be expensed or capitalised and, in general, the tax treatment of the costs will follow the accounting treatment. This means that where the website costs are expensed to the profit and loss account, a full tax deduction should be available in the year that the expenses were incurred.

### 6.4.2 Computer Hardware

Computer hardware is usually treated as a type of plant and machinery, so a tax deduction for expenditure incurred on it is claimed by way of a W&T allowance at the rate of 12.5% per annum over a period of eight years.[15]

Some computer hardware has a much shorter useful life and is scrapped long before this eight-year timeframe has expired. In this case, the taxpayer business will have secured full allowances by the end of the hardware's useful life, being W&T allowances for the accounting periods of use and a balancing allowance in the accounting period in which the hardware is scrapped. In effect, the 'useful life' of the hardware has determined the length of time it takes to secure full tax deductions for the asset. (See **Section 6.3.1.3** for a reminder of how the balancing allowance is calculated.) At **Section 6.3.5.2** we noted that it is good practice to review lists of older plant and machinery that may have become obsolete or have been scrapped before the end of their eight-year allowance period in order to claim the applicable balancing allowances as soon as possible. This is particularly relevant to computer hardware.

### 6.4.3 Computer Software (Internal and External Use)

Where a business spends money on acquiring or developing computer software for use in its trade, or the business acquires the right to use computer software (i.e. a software licence), this expenditure will be treated as a type of plant and machinery.[16] W&T allowances at the rate of 12.5% per annum, over an eight-year period, should be available.

[15] Section 284 TCA 1997.
[16] Section 291 TCA 1997.

Where the software is no longer used, or the software licence period ends, within this eight-year period, then balancing allowances will be triggered as outlined above.

Where the computer software acquired or developed is for commercial exploitation, i.e. where the trade will involve the licensing of the software to third-party customers, then the rules set out at **Section 6.3.6.2** in relation to intangible assets will apply. This means that the allowance may follow the accounting amortisation policy of the company: if the company depreciates the asset over five years, then the capital allowances would be available over a five-year period at the rate of 20% per annum. Alternatively, the company could choose to claim the capital allowances over a 15-year period, at the rate of 7% in Years 1 to 14 and 2% in Year 15. ***Remember***: this type of allowance is only available to a corporate taxpayer.

## 6.5 Corporation Tax Exemption for Start-up Companies

We briefly referred to this tax relief in **Chapter 1**, **Section 1.2.2.2**, noting that, as the tax relief applies to corporates only, an entrepreneur expecting to make profits right from the beginning of trading may decide to run the new business through a company so that the corporation tax (CT) exemption could be utilised. We look now in more detail at this tax relief, which is available to qualifying companies that commence trading before 31 December 2018.[17]

The tax relief operates to fully exempt taxable profits of a new trade that do not exceed €320,000 for a trading year, i.e. without the relief the company would have a CT liability of up to €40,000 for that year. The tax relief is subject to a condition requiring the company to have paid employer's PRSI totalling at least €40,000 for the year. Partial relief (known as 'marginal relief') is available where the company's taxable profits for the year are between €320,000 and €480,000 (a CT liability of between €40,000 and €60,000). The exemption from CT is available in respect of the first three years of trading.

The CT relief is not available to 'service companies' or to companies involved in dealing in or developing land, or exploration and extraction of natural resources (see **Chapter 1**, **Section 1.2.2.2** for further information on this aspect). It is also not available to a company that takes over a trade/profession previously operated by another person; it is due to this restriction that the CT relief may not be claimed where a sole trader later incorporates their business. (The tax implications of certain business restructuring are dealt with in detail in **Chapter 9**.)

[17] Section 486C TCA 1997, as amended by section 30 FA 2015.

In order to encourage start-up companies to employ staff, the full CT exemption is only available where the company pays €40,000 employer's PRSI for each year of the exemption. A further condition states that in determining whether the €40,000 threshold is reached, the maximum employer's PRSI per employee is €5,000. This means that if the employer's PRSI payable in respect of a specific employee is, for example, €8,000, only €5,000 of that PRSI is taken into account when assessing whether the €40,000 threshold is reached. Employers with a total PRSI liability of less than €40,000 in a qualifying year will secure a lower exemption from CT, relative to the amount of employer's PRSI paid.

The current rates of employer's PRSI are 10.75% and 8.5% (the latter on earnings of €376 per week/€19,552 per annum or less). Based on current rates, in order to meet the €40,000 threshold of employer's PRSI in any one year, the employer is required to employ at least eight employees on salaries of at least €46,600 each per annum (or more employees, if any salary levels are lower than €46,600). This is a 'big ask' for many start-up companies and may significantly reduce the usefulness of this CT exemption.

Of course, an exemption from CT liabilities for start-up companies is only relevant if the company is making taxable profits (and generating CT liabilities) in its early years and this is often not the case for start-up businesses. To acknowledge this reality, a further amendment to the tax relief was introduced for accounting periods beginning on or after 1 January 2013, which allows the company to carry forward any tax relief, unused in the first three years of trading due to insufficient taxable profits, to subsequent years.[18] This would mean, for example, that if the company was loss-making in Years 1 to 3 but began making taxable profits in Year 4, then the unused tax relief could be used in Year 4 and subsequent years to reduce net taxable profits. This carry-forward of unused tax relief is also subject to the condition that the maximum tax relief available for any one year is the amount of employer's PRSI paid for that year.

### Case Study: Neally Engineering Ltd

Neally Engineering Ltd has the following results and employer's PRSI contributions for the first four years of trading. The company meets all of the conditions attaching to the corporation tax exemption.

[18] Revenue *Tax Briefing* 02/2013, *Finance Act 2013 Changes to the 3-Year Tax Relief for Start-up Companies.* Available at www.revenue.ie/en/practitioner/tax-briefing/archive/2013/no-022013.html (accessed June 2016).

| | **Accounting Period Ended 30 June ...** | | | |
|---|---|---|---|---|
| | **2014** | **2015** | **2016** | **2017** |
| | **€** | **€** | **€** | **€** |
| Taxable profits | NIL | 30,000 | 75,000 | 300,000 |
| CT liability @ 12.5% | – | 3,750 | 9,375 | 37,500 |
| Total employer's PRSI | 17,500 | 30,000 | 35,000 | 35,000 |
| CT relief applied | – | (3,750) | (9,375) | (35,000)* |
| Revised CT liability after CT relief is applied | – | – | – | 2,500 |
| Carried forward unused CT relief in each of Years 1 to 3 | 17,500 | 26,250 | 25,625 | – |
| Aggregate amount carried forward to Years 5 *et seq.* | | | | 34,375 |

* Relief is capped at the amount of the employer's PRSI liability in Year 4.

In this case, Neally Engineering Ltd has a tax relief worth €34,375 to be used in Years 5 *et seq.* to reduce or eliminate the company's CT liabilities. The maximum amount of the relief that may be used in each of the Years 5 *et seq.* is limited to the amount of employer's PRSI paid in each year of use.

## 6.6 Surcharges for Close Companies

We have previously referred to the payroll tax issues for 'close companies' (see **Chapter 5, Section 5.5**). We will now consider the other significant impact of a company having close company status, i.e. 'close company surcharges'. In effect, a company may attract surcharges simply by virtue of its close company status and not as a result of filing tax returns late. The impact of the surcharge rules may reduce the tax efficiency of accumulating after-tax profits in a close company, which is of course the aim of these tax rules.

Before proceeding, it is worth reminding ourselves that a 'close company' is a company that is under the control of either:

- five or fewer 'participators' (a 'participator' is a person who owns any type of share or voting right in the company, or is a loan creditor of the company); *or*
- participators who are also directors of the company.[19]

We can quickly see that the majority of SMEs in Ireland will be treated as 'close companies' under these definitions.

[19] Section 430 TCA 1997.

### 6.6.1 Surcharge on Undistributed Passive Income

'Passive income' refers to unearned income, i.e. income that is not earned from a trade or profession. Examples include rental and interest income. As the profits arising from this type of income source are not trading profits, the applicable corporation tax rate is 25%. ***Note:*** this rate applies to passive income profits, irrespective of whether or not the company is treated as a close company.

A close company that generates taxable profits on passive income must distribute the after-tax amount of these profits within 18 months of the end of the accounting period in which they are generated, or suffer a 'close company surcharge'. The usual way to satisfy this requirement for a distribution is to make a dividend payment to the shareholders of the appropriate amount, though there are other types of 'distributions'. The rate of the close company surcharge is 20% of the after-tax amount of the undistributed passive income[20] and there is a 7.5% reduction in the surcharge level for trading companies, i.e. companies who generate the majority of their income from trading activities.

There is an exemption from the surcharge where the undistributed passive income is €2,000 or less. Marginal relief will apply above the level of €2,000, which means that a reduced surcharge will arise where the undistributed passive income level is between €2,000 and €2,667.

Returning to the Tigim case study, we will look at the practicalities of calculating the surcharge and the concept of the after-tax 'passive income' profits.

CASE STUDY: TIGIM LANGUAGE LEARNING LTD

Tigim Language Learning Ltd is treated as a close company on the basis that it is controlled by its three directors/shareholders. The company generates €135,000 of trading profits and €9,000 of rental profits (on the sub-let of classroom space) in the accounting period to 30 September 2014. By the deadline of 31 March 2016, it has not declared any dividends to its shareholders.

The corporation tax charge and close company surcharge on the rental profits will be as follows:

| | € |
|---|---|
| Corporation tax at 25% on rental profits of €9,000 | 2,250 |

[20] Section 440 TCA 1997.

Close company surcharge on undistributed after-tax passive income of €6,750 (being €9,000 less CT of €2,250):

| | € |
|---|---|
| Distributable passive income | 6,750 |
| Less: 7.5% deduction for trading company | (506) |
| Less: dividends/distributions | 0 |
| Amount subject to surcharge | 6,244 |
| Surcharge at 20% | 1,249 |
| Total CT liabilities (including surcharge) on rental profits | 3,499 |

We can see that if the company makes a dividend (or other type of distribution) to its shareholders during the 18-month window, then the amount of this dividend will reduce the after-tax income subject to surcharge. Where the dividend is greater than the amount subject to surcharge, then no surcharge will arise.

Note also that the surcharge is calculated by looking at whether there is any after-tax passive income that is undistributed by the end of the 18-month window. If there is, a surcharge will arise. Even if the company distributes that income after the 18-month deadline, it may not claim a refund of the surcharge.

Excluding the small 7.5% deduction for trading companies, we can see that, including the surcharge, the effective rate of corporation tax on undistributed passive income is approximately 40%, being 25% + 15% (i.e. after-tax profits (100% – 25%) × 20%). This is the rate that would apply, for example, to a property investment close company that did not distribute its after-tax rental profits. While the exemption from surcharge for passive income of €2,000 or less is limited, it would cover, for example, the interest income earned by a trading company with up to €100,000 on deposit, earning an annual interest rate of say 2%. The surcharge rules therefore allow a trading company with retained profits to generate a certain amount of passive income on these retained profits before triggering a close company surcharge.

### *6.6.2 Surcharge on Undistributed Trading Profits of Service Companies*

The surcharge rules set out above relate to undistributed passive income of *any* type of close company, trading or otherwise. In addition to this type of surcharge, a 'services close company' will also suffer a surcharge on its undistributed after-tax *trading* profits.[21] This surcharge is

[21] Section 441 TCA 1997.

calculated by dividing the undistributed after-tax trading profits in half and multiplying this by 15%, giving a net surcharge rate of 7.5%. Therefore, the effective rate of corporation tax on this type of undistributed income is approximately 19%, being 12.5% + 6.5625% (i.e. after-tax profits (100% – 12.5%) × 7.5%).

This type of surcharge is levied on a 'service company', which is defined as a close company that:

- carries on a profession or provides professional services; *or*
- exercises an office or employment, e.g. the company itself provides directorship services; *or*
- provides services or facilities to professional service providers or businesses who exercise an office or employment.

Examples include companies that provide services in the areas of: accountancy, actuarial services, architecture, auctioneer/estate agent services, auditing, engineering, financial services, management consultancy, private education, veterinary, etc. (***Note:*** this is a sample list and is not exhaustive.)

The exemption from surcharge when the undistributed after-tax trading profits of the service company is lower than €2,000, as well as the 'marginal relief' between the level of €2,000 and €2,667, may also apply when calculating a company's exposure to this type of surcharge.

### Case Study: Tigim Language Learning Ltd

When Tigim Language Learning Ltd first begins to trade, Aoife takes professional advice as to its corporation tax status. The advice concludes that the company is a service company for the purposes of the close company rules.

Assuming no 'distributions', the total CT liabilities arising on the €135,000 of trading profits in 2014 will be:

| | € |
|---|---|
| CT at 12.5% on €135,000 | 16,875 |
| Close company surcharge on undistributed after-tax trading profits of €118,125 (being €135,000 less CT of €16,875): | |
| Undistributed after-tax income | 118,125 |
| Divide by 2 | 59,062 |
| Less: dividends/distributions | 0 |
| Amount subject to surcharge | 59,062 |
| Surcharge at 15% | 8,859 |
| Total CT liabilities (including surcharge) on trading profits | 25,734 |

***Note:*** where a service company is subject to the two types of close company surcharge, i.e. in relation to passive income and 'service-company trading profits,' and the company makes a distribution within the 18-month window, then the distribution will reduce the passive income first. This is to the company's advantage, as the surcharge rate on passive income (20%) is higher than the surcharge rate applicable to 'service-company trading profits' (7.5%).

### *6.6.3 Reducing Exposure to Close Company Surcharges*

While the focus of our review of surcharges has been on the imposition of a surcharge on the undistributed after-tax passive income of a close company and undistributed after-tax trading profits of a service company, there is a broader consideration that may impact on whether surcharges are due at all.

In order for a surcharge to apply to undistributed after-tax income/profits, the company must have sufficient 'distributable reserves' to do so. This is a company law concept and is broadly defined as a company's 'accumulated realised profits' less its 'accumulated realised losses'.[22] While the actual amount of a company's distributable reserves are calculated by either Irish GAAP or IFRS, it is worth keeping in mind that a company with, for example, trading losses generated in current or previous accounting periods may not have sufficient distributable reserves to make a distribution, thereby avoiding a close company surcharge for not having done so.

For a group of companies that includes a company potentially subject to close company surcharges, it may be possible to manage the location of distributable reserves across the group in order to minimise the exposure to surcharges.

A service company may reduce its distributable reserves by making pension contributions to a company scheme established for the benefit of the working shareholder(s)/director(s). This approach can be particularly suitable for a 'one-person company' that is set up by a professional who is an employee of the company and who hires the company out to various clients.

An obvious way of managing exposure to surcharges is to ensure that sufficient levels of dividends are made within the 18-month window after accounting period-end. Note, however, that these dividends will trigger tax implications of their own. For Irish tax-resident shareholders, the dividend will be subject to their marginal rate of income tax and charges (potentially 55% at the top rate), thus swapping a tax liability for the company, at an effective rate of 15% or 6.562% (the effective rates for each type of surcharge), for a personal tax liability of, potentially, 55%.

[22] Section 117 of the Companies Act 2014.

In some instances, company management, looking to avoid triggering a close company surcharge, may consider swapping a part of a shareholder's/director's regular salary for a dividend, thereby reducing the amount of undistributed passive income or undistributed service company trading profits. For example, if a dividend of €10,000 must be paid to a company's two shareholders/directors in order to avoid a surcharge, then the company could reduce each person's salary by €5,000 in exchange for the issue of a €5,000 dividend. While this will generally not impact on the personal tax position of the two shareholders/directors – they pay the same level of income tax and charges on either salary or a dividend – it will impact on the tax position of the company. As far as the company's tax liabilities are concerned, there are two differences between the payment of a salary and a dividend:

- Unlike for a salary payment, no CT deduction may be taken for a dividend payment. For a trading company, payment of €5,000 salary will generate a CT saving of €625 (€5,000 × 12.5%) – the saving could be doubled if the company is taxed at the 25% CT rate, i.e. €1,250. No such tax deduction/saving arises from the payment of a €5,000 dividend.
- A salary payment will be subject to employer's PRSI (potentially at the rate of 10.75%), generating potential, additional payroll charges of approximately €538 on a salary payment of €5,000. No PRSI charge arises on the payment of a dividend.

## Appendix I: Summary List of Industrial Buildings or Structures Eligible for Industrial Buildings Allowance

A building or structure in use by the taxpayer business for the purposes of:

1. A trade that is carried on in a mill, factory or other similar premises.
2. A dock undertaking, which would include, for example, a harbour, pier or jetty, as long as these were not used primarily for recreational purposes.
3. A trade that consists of the operation or management of an airport.
4. A trade of growing fruit or vegetables or any other produce which would be defined as 'market gardening'.
5. A trade involved in the intensive production of cattle, sheep, pigs, poultry or eggs (other than the trade of farming).
6. A trade of hotel-keeping, including a holiday cottage, holiday camp, holiday hostel and guest-houses, registered under the Tourist Traffic Acts.
7. A trade of running a private, registered nursing home.
8. The use of laboratories for the analysis of minerals for future exploration.
9. Providing for the recreation or welfare of a trader's employees.
10. A trade of running certain private convalescent homes.
11. A trade of running a qualifying hospital.
12. A trade of running a qualifying mental health centre.

13. A trade of running specialist palliative care units.
14. A building or structure comprised in, and in use as, part of premises that are registered in the Register of Caravan Parks and Camping Parks.
15. A trade of running a qualifying sports injuries clinic.
16. Childcare facilities.
17. Buildings used for third-level educational purposes.

## Appendix II: Availability of Wear and Tear Allowances for Certain Items of Plant

Examples of assets that *may* be treated as 'plant' for the purposes of wear and tear allowances include:

- moveable partitions in an office;
- swimming pools in a caravan park;
- a dry dock for ships;
- an automated hen house;
- petrol station canopies;
- light fittings and murals in a hotel;
- grain silos;
- racecourse stands;
- books of tax cases;
- lifts;
- heating and ventilation systems;
- air-conditioning systems;
- electricity/gas distribution services;
- water and waste services;
- alarm and security systems;
- firefighting/prevention systems;
- any wiring ancillary to the above group of items;
- fish cages;
- commercial marina equipment, including pontoons, anchors, gangways and access bridges.

Examples of assets that *may not* be treated as 'plant' for the purposes of wear and tear allowances include:

- suspended ceiling in a department store;
- electrical installations for a department store;
- ship used as a floating restaurant;
- taxi plates;
- refuse trucks;
- tennis courts;
- car-wash sites;
- glasshouses.

# CHAPTER 7

# MANAGING TAX PAYMENTS AND RETURNS



Much of this book focuses on tax efficiency, i.e. keeping tax liabilities as low as possible by having a clear understanding of tax deductions and reliefs, and using them to their utmost. The focus in this chapter, however, is on **timing** or, more specifically, timing issues that can be used to a business's advantage to delay the trigger/payment date of tax liabilities and give the business some leeway in managing its working capital. Though clichéd, there is a lot of truth in the saying that "cash is king"; it is the unwise business owner who focuses on profit figures but does not properly manage cash flow.

Matching our tax head focus throughout the rest of the book, in this chapter we will examine timing issues around taxes on profits (income tax and corporation tax), as well as payroll taxes and VAT. We will also look at what happens when a business is struggling to keep its tax payments up to date and Revenue's approach in this situation.

Figure 7.1 below shows the range of negative consequences of a business not managing its tax payments and returns correctly.

FIGURE 7.1: WHEN TAX PAYMENTS AND RETURNS ARE NOT MANAGED

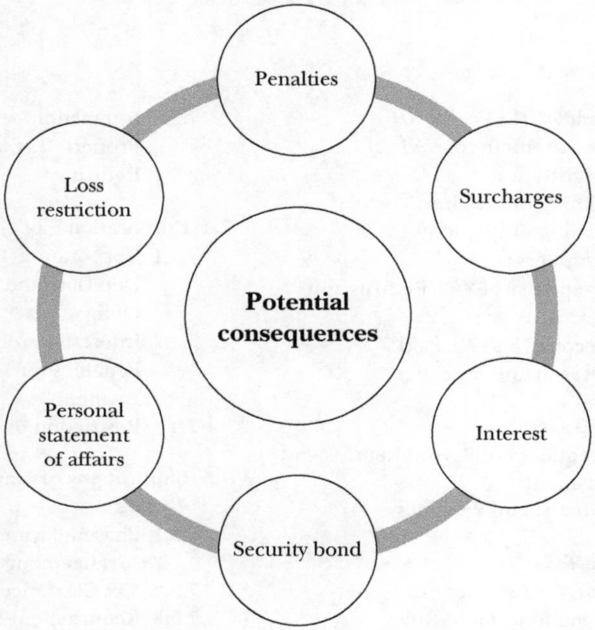

Penalties

Surcharges

Interest

Security bond

Personal statement of affairs

Loss restriction

**Potential consequences**

# 7.1 Value-added Tax

## *7.1.1 Requirement for VAT Registration*

In **Chapter 4**, we reviewed the various turnover thresholds that apply to the supply of different goods/services and noted that, where a business's 12-month turnover is lower than the relevant threshold, no VAT registration is required. There are a couple of points to note on this:

- A business owner must make a decision as to whether the business should be registered for VAT purposes from the commencement of trading. It may be decided that as the expected turnover will be less than the relevant turnover threshold (generally, €37,500 for services and €75,000 for goods) for the first 12 months of trading, it is not necessary to register for VAT purposes. The business may decide to register for VAT purposes anyway, to allow a reclaim of VAT charged on purchases.
- For a VAT-registered small business whose turnover drops below the relevant threshold, it is possible to change the VAT registration status and deregister for VAT. While this appears to give a tax and cash-flow

advantage, in that all payments made by customers will now be retained by the business, do not forget the other side of the coin: the business will also lose entitlement to reclaim VAT on its purchases and this could be significant for a low-margin business if, for example, it charged mostly reduced VAT rates on its supplies (e.g. 9% or 13.5%) and yet reclaimed VAT at the standard rate of 23% on some or all of its purchases.

- A business wishing to deregister for VAT purposes must apply for cancellation to the local Revenue district. Businesses that elect to register for VAT and later wish to deregister must pay the 'excess VAT refund' for the 'relevant period', which is the lower calculation for either:
  - the VAT periods during which the VAT registration was in effect; *or*
  - the three-year period prior to the date of applying to cancel the VAT registration.
- The amount of the 'excess VAT refund' is calculated, for the 'relevant period', by adding the VAT claimed on purchases to the VAT claimed on intra-Community acquisitions and subtracting the net VAT paid by the business.
- A business that has previously deregistered for VAT purposes will be obliged to re-register once the relevant turnover threshold has been breached in a 12-month period.[1]

### *7.1.2 Timing of VAT Invoices*

One of the questions that must be answered on the VAT registration form is whether the business will be registered on a cash-receipts basis (also referred to as the 'monies received basis of accounting') or on an 'invoice basis'. If an election is not made at the time of registration, the business will automatically operate on an invoice basis. As we have seen in **Chapter 4**, the difference between the two bases of accounting for VAT is very significant and the owner/managers should be careful to choose the most suitable basis for the business. In general, businesses with an annual turnover of less than €2 million, or businesses where at least 90% of the turnover comes from supplying unregistered customers or customers who cannot reclaim VAT in full, may elect to use the cash-receipts basis of accounting.

There are certain rules as to the timing of VAT invoices, the most basic of which is that the invoice must issue 15 days after the end of the month in which the goods/services are supplied or payment is received, whichever is the earlier ('the 15-day rule'). While the date on which goods are supplied is readily determined, this may not be so straightforward for the supply of services. Below is an example involving a supply of professional services through various channels over a number of weeks.

[1] For more information, see the "VAT Registration" section of Revenue's *Guide to VAT* at www.revenue.ie/en/tax/vat/guide/registration.html (accessed June 2016).

### Example 7.1: Date of Supply of Services

A tax advisor provides inheritance tax advice to a client by writing reports and having meetings and telephone calls with the client. Assuming the tax advisor issues only one invoice to the client, what is the date of supply? Is it the date the report(s) issued or the date of the first (or last) meeting or telephone call to review or explain the report(s)?

This type of business may have some flexibility as to when invoices are issued. A business operating on an invoice basis will prefer to issue invoices at the beginning of a VAT period, so as to give as much time as possible to be paid by the client/customer before the business must pay the VAT charge over to Revenue. Longer VAT periods will assist here also.

Similarly, a business operating on an invoice basis that provides a continuous supply of services and/or receives periodic payments over the course of a long project may be in a position to influence when it must pay a sales VAT charge to Revenue. Where the supply has not been completed, the business may issue a 'request for payment' (RFP), which typically contains the statement:

> "This is not a VAT invoice. A VAT invoice will be issued when payment has been received."

The issue of a RFP will not, of itself, trigger a VAT charge immediately.[2] Instead, it should prompt the client or customer to make a payment and it is the payment that will then trigger the VAT charge (which is effectively the same treatment for a business operating on the cash-receipts basis of accounting for VAT).

### Example 7.2: The Impact of a RFP on the Timing of the VAT Charge

Referring again to the tax advisor who provides inheritance tax advice, say, over a period of two years: if the billing arrangements agreed with the client are based on work-in-progress requests every three months, then the tax advisor may issue a RFP every three months but only include the sales VAT charge applicable to each RFP in the VAT return of the VAT period in which the invoice is raised, to reflect a payment made.

***Note:*** if the services supplied can be separated into distinct services, then the '15-day rule' must be applied to each completed service.

[2] Regulation 23 of the Value-Added Tax Regulations 2010 (S.I. No. 639 of 2010) (the VAT Regulations 2010).

### *7.1.3 Timing of Payments to Suppliers*

Where a business is operating on a cash-receipts basis of accounting for VAT, then the VAT sales charge on an invoice is only triggered in the VAT period in which payment is received. Generally, the VAT input charge included in the business's supplier invoices may be included in the VAT period in which the invoice is received, even if it has not yet been paid. This may give rise to a cash-flow advantage for the business, but it must be careful not to delay the payment to the supplier for too long! Changes to VAT rules in 2014 require that an adjustment must be made to a business's VAT returns in relation to VAT input charges on supplier invoices that remain unpaid approximately six months after their issue.[3] Effectively, this means that the business must add back the VAT input charge already taken in relation to the unpaid invoice, but can include that input charge in a later VAT return if the invoice is ultimately paid. (See **Chapter 4** for more on this.)

### *7.1.4 Frequency of VAT Returns and Payments*

Having reviewed some ways in which the 'trigger' date for a VAT sales charge can be postponed by pushing the charge into a future VAT period, let us look now at the length of the VAT period, as this can also assist in pushing out VAT liabilities and giving the business more time to collect payment before it must pay over the sales VAT to Revenue.

The standard VAT period is two months, with payment for each VAT period due by the 23rd day of the month following the end of the VAT period. The general rule is that businesses have bi-monthly VAT periods, which are:

- January/February (due for filing and payment by 23 March);
- March/April (due for filing and payment by 23 May);
- May/June (due for filing and payment by 23 July);
- July/August (due for filing and payment by 23 September);
- September/October (due for filing and payment by 23 November); and
- November/December (due for filing and payment by 23 January of the following year).

Where a business's *net* VAT liabilities (i.e. sales VAT less input VAT) are below certain annual levels, it is possible to file returns on a less frequent basis. This can reduce the amount of administration involved in preparing VAT returns, as well as potentially giving a longer timeframe to pay over net VAT liabilities to Revenue. These less frequent bases are as follows:

- businesses with annual VAT payments (i.e. net VAT liabilities) of €3,000 or less – six-month VAT periods (i.e. two VAT returns and payments per annum); and
- businesses with annual VAT payments of €3,001 to €14,400 – four-month VAT periods.

[3] Section 62A of the Value-Added Tax Consolidation Act 2010 (VATCA 2010).

A new VAT-registered business commencing to trade will automatically have bi-monthly VAT returns for at least the first 12 months of trading. After this time, Revenue will review the level of regular VAT liabilities and will inform the business that it can file VAT returns on a less frequent basis, as appropriate. If the business meets the conditions for filing less frequent VAT returns but Revenue have not contacted it, then assuming that it would suit the business to file less frequently, an application can be made to the business's Revenue district.

An example of a situation where less frequent returns would *not* suit the business is a business that tends to be in a regular VAT refund position, perhaps because a significant part of its turnover is subject to VAT at 0%. This type of business would want more frequent filing so as to secure VAT refunds more quickly.

It is possible for a business to file one 12-month VAT return where its net VAT liabilities do not exceed €300,000 per annual VAT period and the business is making *monthly* direct debit VAT payments. While this would significantly reduce the amount of VAT administration, businesses should take great care when setting the amount of the monthly direct debit payment, which is at their own discretion. The total of the 12 payments should be sufficient to cover at least 80% of the actual net VAT liabilities for the 12-month period; otherwise interest will be charged on the shortfall from the mid-point of the year.

### Case Study: Four Blue Ducks

Four Blue Ducks' turnover tends to be quite seasonal with sharp spikes over the Christmas period and during the summer months. In order to smooth out the VAT payments throughout the year, Jim and Cathy have been advised to pay VAT on a monthly direct debit basis. In the first year of monthly payments, Cathy estimates the total net VAT liabilities for the VAT period March 2015 to February 2016 will be €18,000, so she decides to pay €1,500 per month for the 12-month period. It turns out that the total VAT liabilities for the 12-month VAT period amount to €24,000, so interest is charged on the underpayment of €6,000 from 23 September 2015 to the date the underpayment is actually paid.

The way to avoid interest charges is, of course, to monitor net VAT liabilities throughout the year and to adjust the monthly direct debit payment where necessary. In order to move onto this basis of annual filing and monthly direct debit payments, the business should apply to the Direct Debit Unit of the Collector-General, Revenue's tax collection division.

### 7.1.5 Recovery of VAT Paid

There are certain situations in which a business will have paid a sales VAT charge, to either the Irish Revenue or the tax collection authorities in another EU Member State, and later have an entitlement to reclaim this VAT. Set out below are three situations in which this can arise.

#### 7.1.5.1 Adjustment for Bad Debts

In the case of a business that has paid VAT on sales to Revenue on the basis of the invoices it has issued, what happens when a customer never pays the invoice? In this situation, while relief for the VAT charge paid to Revenue on these specific bad debts is available, certain conditions must be met, including:

- the supplier business must have taken all "reasonable steps" to recover the bad debt;
- the bad debt is allowed as a deduction in calculating the taxable profits of the business;
- the bad debt has been written off in the accounts of the supplier business – these can be either the year-end financial accounts or the (interim) management accounts of the business; *and*
- the supplier and the customer are not 'connected persons'.

Bad debt relief may be claimed in the VAT period in which the bad debt meets the conditions listed above; it is not necessary to wait until the business's accounting year-end. This relief is claimed by including the unpaid VAT charge in the 'VAT on purchases' (Box T2) section of the VAT return. If the customer later pays some or all of a debt for which VAT bad debt relief has already been claimed, then the business must make an adjustment to the VAT return to pay back the VAT relief already granted. This adjustment is made by reducing the 'VAT on purchases' figure (Box T2) by the amount of the VAT charge paid over by the customer. This latter adjustment must be made in the VAT period in which the payment is received.

Where bad debt relief is claimed, the business should not issue a credit note to its customer.[4]

***Note:*** the question of whether a supplier has taken all 'reasonable steps' to recover a bad debt before claiming VAT relief will likely be an area of focus during a review of the treatment of bad debts as part of a Revenue audit. The Revenue auditor will require written evidence of the efforts made, including correspondence with the customer and if appropriate, referral to a solicitor or debt collection agency. If the auditor is not

[4] For more information, see Revenue's VAT leaflet *Bad Debts (excluding hire purchase)*. Available at www.revenue.ie/en/tax/vat/leaflets/bad-debts-relief.html (accessed June 2016).

satisfied that bad debt relief is correctly claimed, then the relief may be denied, requiring repayment of the adjustment to Box T2, along with interest and penalties. **Chapter 8** includes a detailed review of Revenue audits.

### *7.1.5.2 Retention of Non-refundable Deposit where Sale is not Completed*

Where a business requires the payment of a non-refundable deposit in order to secure a customer order, then the payment of the deposit is regarded as an advance payment of the VATable supply of the goods/services ordered. This means that sales VAT must be charged on the deposit and included in the business's VAT return for that VAT period. If the customer then cancels the order, the deposit will be retained by the business though no VATable supply will have taken place. In this situation, the business may make an adjustment in the return for the VAT period in which the order is cancelled, reducing the sales VAT figure by the amount of VAT charged on the deposit. Effectively, the business gets to keep the deposit but does not have to pay VAT on it. In order to be entitled to this adjustment, the following conditions must be met:

- no supply of goods or services takes place due to the customer's cancellation;
- the cancellation of the order is noted in the business's accounts;
- the deposit is not refunded to the customer; *and*
- the business does not provide any other benefit or supply to the customer in lieu of refunding the deposit.[5]

The following case study extract illustrates how the cancellation of an order, on which refundable and non-refundable deposits have been paid, impacts on the VAT treatment of the cancelled order.

#### Case Study: Neally Engineering Ltd

Neally Engineering Ltd's standard trading terms to a new customer include the following payment deadlines:

- non-refundable 20% deposit on placement of the order;
- 60% payment in advance of order delivery; and
- 20% payment within 30 days of order delivery.

On 15 February 2016, the company takes an order from a new customer. The order is valued at €75,000 ex-VAT at 23%; the customer pays the €15,000 + VAT deposit on 28 February and is given an estimated delivery date of 15 July. The second 60% payment (€45,000 + VAT) is made on 5 May, but the customer abruptly cancels the order on 3 July, triggering a refund to the customer of €55,350 (the second payment) only.

[5] Section 74(4) VATCA 2010.

Neally Engineering Ltd files VAT returns on a bi-monthly basis, so the VAT charges and adjustments required in relation to this order are as follows:

- January/February 2016 – Sales VAT figure increased by €3,450
- May/June 2016 – Sales VAT figure increased by €10,350
- July/August 2016 – Sales VAT figure reduced by €13,800.

#### 7.1.5.3 *Recovery of Foreign VAT*

In **Chapter 4**, we looked at how an Irish business can secure a repayment of foreign VAT incurred in another EU Member State. The key point to note here is that the claim for repayment must be made **within nine months of the calendar year-end of the VAT charge**, e.g. by 30 September 2017 for a VAT charge arising in 2016. It is worth highlighting this deadline again, as the opportunity to claim a foreign VAT refund will be lost forever if the deadline is not met. ***Note:*** incorrectly including a foreign VAT charge as an input VAT charge in the business's regular Irish VAT return would be met with interest charges and harsh penalties in the case of a Revenue audit/inquiry.

### *7.1.6 Interest and Penalties*

An interest rate of 0.0274% per day (10% on a per-annum basis) is due on late payment of any VAT liability or on the amount of any VAT refund that was claimed and received by a taxpayer but was not due to it. The daily rate applies as follows:

- In the case of late payment of a VAT liability, the period from when the payment was due (the 23rd of the month following the end of the VAT period) to the actual date of payment.
- In the case of payment of an incorrectly claimed VAT refund, the period from the date of refund until the date the amount is paid back to Revenue.
- The same interest rate applies to the monthly direct debit scheme where, on a 12-month basis, the total monthly direct debits amount to less than 80% of the actual liability. In this case, interest is applied to the shortfall and will run from the 23rd of the month after the mid-point of the 12-month period (e.g. 23 July 2016 for an annual VAT period of January to December 2016) until the shortfall is actually paid.

In **Chapter 8** we will review the tax-based penalties that may arise in the context of VAT defaults – these range from 3% to 100% of the tax liabilities. Separate to these penalties are so-called 'fixed penalties' (generally charged at a flat rate of €4,000), which apply to a variety of issues including: failure to register for VAT when required to do so by the legislation; failure to comply with the rules for proper invoicing; failure to keep full and true records; and failure to charge proper VAT charges and pay them over to Revenue.[6]

[6] Section 115 VATCA 2010.

## 7.2 Payroll Taxes

In the preceding section, we reviewed timing issues for filing VAT returns and paying VAT liabilities. We now consider these timing issues for employer payroll taxes.

### *7.2.1 Frequency of Payroll Returns and Payments*

In relation to returns for payroll taxes, the general rule is that these are filed and paid on a monthly basis. The deadline for paying and filing is the 14th of the following month and where both the return and the payment are made online through ROS, this deadline is extended to the 23rd of the following month. These returns and payments will include all PAYE income tax, employee PRSI and USC (as well as any local property tax) deducted from all employment income for the previous month, as well as employer's PRSI contributions.

For those employers with payroll tax payments totalling less than €28,800 per annum, quarterly returns and payments may be made. An employer who wishes to move onto a quarterly basis must apply to the Collector-General to do so.

It is also possible for an employer with monthly payroll tax liabilities of up to €25,000 (annual liabilities of up to €300,000) to pay by monthly direct debit and to file just the annual Form P35 return. This may suit businesses with seasonal spikes in turnover that require additional staff, e.g. additional retail staff employed at Christmas time. As with VAT payments made on a monthly direct debit arrangement, attention should be paid to the amount of the direct debit to ensure that any shortfall at year-end will be small; otherwise interest may arise. A specific application to the Collector-General must be made by an employer who wishes to move onto a monthly direct debit arrangement. For more information on this method of payment, see Revenue's "Terms and Conditions of using the SEPA Direct Debit Scheme".[7]

### *7.2.2 Interest and Penalties*

Interest is charged on the late payment of payroll tax liabilities at a rate of 0.0274% per day (10% on a per-annum basis).

'Fixed penalties' of €4,000 also arise for a number of issues in this area, including: failure to produce records to a Revenue officer; failure to maintain a complete register of employees; and failure to notify Revenue of practicalities relating to a new employee.[8]

[7] Available as a pdf document on www.revenue.ie.

[8] Section 987 of the Taxes Consolidation Act 1997 (TCA 1997).

## 7.3 Income Tax

In the following two sections, we will review how and when taxes arising on business profits are assessed and paid. Where a business is unincorporated, i.e. a sole trade or partnership, then the business owners are personally liable for income taxes and charges on profits of the unincorporated business. These business owner(s) must self-assess their liabilities for income taxes and charges by calculating and paying these liabilities through their personal tax return. **Chapter 1, Section 1.1.3** referred to the partners of a partnership business being taxed on a personal basis for their share of the partnership's profits. Where a business is incorporated, the profits of that business will be subject to corporation tax, as set out in **Section 7.4** below.

### *7.3.1 Basis of Assessment*

We look now at the income tax rules that determine which profits of an unincorporated business (i.e. sole trade or partnership) are included in which personal tax return. This will give us an understanding of the timing link between earning business profits and the sole trader or partner's deadline for paying the income taxes and charges arising on these profits. All business owners should have a clear understanding of these rules so they can determine their tax payment obligations and plan their personal cash flow accordingly.

Unincorporated businesses generally prepare 12-month sets of accounts. Any profits arising in these 12-month accounts are then included in the business owner's personal tax return. Generally, the business owner has a choice as to the timing of the 12-month period – she could choose a 31 December year end (and many do) in order to tie in with the period covered by an income tax return and/or because her own sense of the 'year end' is the end of December. It is entirely possible, however, to choose a year-end date of 31 March, 30 June, 15 August, etc., and there may well be business/commercial reasons for doing so.

The tax rules state that where business profits are calculated by reference to annual accounts, tax is charged for a year of assessment on the profits of an *accounting period ending in the year of assessment.* 'A year of assessment' refers to a calendar year, i.e. the 2016 year of assessment covers the period 1 January to 31 December 2016. This means that, for the 2016 year of assessment, sole traders and partners of a trading business will be taxed on the profits arising in the accounts ending *at any time* during the period 1 January to 31 December 2016. A business with a 30 June year end, for example, will include the results of the accounting period 1 July 2015 to 30 June 2016 in the tax return for the 2016 year of assessment.

### *7.3.2 Commencement Rules*

The rules set out above in relation to which accounts are included in which year of assessment are set aside in the early years of a new unincorporated business. For the first three years of a new business, the specific rules[9] that determine the basis of assessment to tax are:

- **First year** The profits earned in the period from start date to the following 31 December.
- **Second year** There are three possibilities here:
  - o where there is a 12-month set of accounts made up to a date in that tax year, then the profits included in that set of accounts;
  - o where there are accounts for longer than a 12-month period ending in that tax year, or where there are two or more sets of accounts made up to a date in that tax year, then the profits of the 12-month period ending at the later set of accounts; *or*
  - o in any other situation (e.g. there are no accounts made up to a date ending in that tax year), the 12-month profits for the calendar year.
- **Third year** The profits earned in the 12-month set of accounts made up to a date in that tax year.

We will now look at how these commencement rules determine how the early years' trading profits of Four Blue Ducks café are assessed in the owner Jim's personal tax return.

### CASE STUDY: FOUR BLUE DUCKS

Four Blue Ducks starts trading on 2 March 2014 with Jim deciding on a 28 February year end. The first set of accounts is prepared for the period 2 March 2014 to 28 February 2015.

The taxable profits for the relevant accounting periods are as follows:

| | € |
|---|---|
| 12-month period to 28 February 2015 | 65,000 |
| 12-month period to 28 February 2016 | 55,000 |

The profits of the business will be taxed as follows in the first three years of assessment, being 2014, 2015 and 2016:

- First year (2014): Profits earned from 2 March 2014 to 31 December 2014: €65,000 × 10/12 = €54,167
- Second year (2015): Profits earned in the accounting period to 28 February 2015: €65,000
- Third year (2016): Profits earned in the accounting period to 28 February 2016: €55,000

In conjunction with the rules relating to the first three years of assessment, there is a specific tax relief that may be claimed if the amount of profits

[9] Section 66 TCA 1997.

*assessed* for tax for the second year exceeds the *actual* profits for that year. This relief is known as the 'second-year excess' and must be claimed by writing to the Inspector of Taxes by 31 October following the third year of assessment.

CASE STUDY: FOUR BLUE DUCKS

Reviewing Four Blue Ducks' position, we see that a 'second-year excess' claim of €8,334 is available:

Second year of assessment per general commencement rules: €65,000

Actual profits in the 12-month period to 31 December 2015:

[€65,000 × 2/12 (Jan/Feb 2015)] + [€55,000 × 10/12 (March to December 2015)] = €56,666

This tax relief can be used to reduce the assessable profit in the third year, i.e. reduce the €55,000 assessable profits for 2016, or, if there are not sufficient profits to absorb this claim in the third year, the claim can be carried forward to reduce future profits of the business. Jim must claim the 'second-year excess' relief by 31 October 2017, the deadline for filing the 2016 income tax return.

### *7.3.3 Income Tax Return Filing Due Date and Payment Obligations*

The general rules in relation to filing income tax returns and paying income tax liabilities are:

- Income tax return must be filed by 31 October in respect of the previous year of assessment, i.e. the tax return for the 2015 year of assessment must be filed by 31 October 2016.
- Where the tax return is filed online, and any associated tax liabilities are paid online through ROS, an extended deadline to mid-November is allowed, the exact date of which changes every year. In 2016, the extended ROS deadline will be 10 November. (To avoid confusion, we will continue to refer to the 31 October deadline only below.)
- In relation to income tax, a taxpayer has two payment obligations for the 31 October deadline:
  - payment of the balance of income tax, PRSI and USC (collectively 'income taxes and charges') due in respect of the previous year of assessment; and
  - payment of preliminary income taxes and charges (collectively 'preliminary tax') due in respect of the current year of assessment. For example, for the 31 October 2016 deadline, taxpayers will pay the balance of income taxes and charges due for 2015 (the previous year of assessment) and preliminary income taxes and charges for 2016 (the current year of assessment).

- Preliminary tax payments may be calculated by choosing the *lowest* of the following methods:
  - 90% of current-year liability: for the 31 October 2016 deadline, this would mean 90% of the estimated 2016 liability;
  - 100% of prior-year liability: for the 31 October 2016 deadline, this would mean 100% of the 2015 liability;
  - 105% of prior-prior-year liability: for the 31 October 2016 deadline, this would mean 105% of the 2014 liability. (The 105% preliminary tax option is only available where the taxpayer pays their preliminary tax through a regular direct debit arrangement, and there was a tax liability for the prior-prior year.)
- Where the preliminary tax payment paid in relation to a year of assessment is lower than the final liability for that year, the balance must be paid by the following 31 October. Where it exceeds the final liability, a refund will arise.
- For the owners of new sole trades/partnerships, the preliminary tax rules typically operate to alleviate them from paying any preliminary tax in the first year of trading. This is because these taxpayers can rely on the '100% of prior year' rule, even though this gives a nil result as the business was not trading in the prior year. The owners of new unincorporated businesses are given some breathing space before they must start paying tax on business profits; however, the result is that a 'double' payment of tax will be due the following year. This cash-flow issue should be closely monitored by new business owners.

### Case Study: Four Blue Ducks

For Jim, who opened the doors of Four Blue Ducks on 2 March 2014, this results in the following timing for payments of income taxes and charges based on the trading results set out above:

| | |
|---|---|
| 31 October 2014 | No preliminary tax payment required |
| 31 October 2015 | A. Income tax and charges on 2014 €54,167 profits – (est.) €19,000<br><br>B. Preliminary tax for 2015 – lower of:<br>• 90% of 2015 liability on €65,000 profits – €21,600 (€24,000 est. × 90%)<br>• 100% of 2014 liability – (est.) €19,000<br><br>Total (A + B) – €38,000 approx. |
| 31 October 2016 | A. Balance income tax and charges on 2015 €65,000 profits – €5,000 (being actual liabilities for 2015 of €24,000 less €19,000 preliminary tax already paid)<br><br>B. Preliminary tax for 2016 – lower of:<br>• 90% of 2016 liability on €55,000 profits – €15,750 (€17,500 est. × 90%) |

- 100% of 2015 liability on €65,000 profits – €24,000
- 105% of 2014 liability option not available as there was no income tax liability for this business in 2014

Total (A + B) – €20,750.

(*Note:* the calculations above assume no other sources of income and include Jim's separate tax band, personal tax credit and earned income credit, as appropriate.)

We can see that, for Jim, the big pressure on his cash flow comes on 31 October 2015. Once he has dealt with this 'double' payment of tax (being the full tax payment for 2014 and preliminary tax for 2015) and is in the system of paying preliminary tax, his tax liabilities should spread out on a more even basis.

If he has a significant jump in profits in a given year, however, then the preliminary tax payment already made for that year will be too low and the balancing payment for that year may be very significant. The choice of 28 February as year-end would potentially be helpful for Jim in dealing with a significant jump in profits. Assuming his business accounts are prepared within a few months of year-end, then by the time it comes to 31 October, Jim should have his current-year results to hand and can then make an accurate calculation of the '90% of current year' option for preliminary tax purposes.

You may recall from our review in **Chapter 1**, **Section 1.2** of whether or not to incorporate, that Jim and Cathy made a decision to start their business as a sole trade, owned by Jim. One of the reasons for this decision was that Jim was eligible for Start Your Own Business (SYOB) relief, which operates to exempt up to €40,000 of business profits per annum for the first 24 months of trading. For simplicity, we have not included this tax relief in the above calculations.

Again, in order to avoid confusion, we have excluded from the above calculations the 'second-year excess' relief (noted at **Section 7.3.2** above) to which Jim is also entitled.

### 7.3.4 *Interest, Surcharges and Penalties for Late Filing and Late Payment*

Interest, at the rate of 0.0219% per day (approximately 8% on a per-annum basis) arises on the late payment of income tax and charges in two instances:

- Balance of tax due for the prior year of assessment, in which case the interest period will run from the due date to the date of payment. For example, if Jim does not pay the balance of taxes payable on his 2015 profits (due on 31 October 2016) until 1 December 2016, he will pay interest on this balance for the one-month period at a rate of approximately 0.657% (0.0219% × 30 days).

- If the level of preliminary tax payment fails the 90%/100%/105% tests (set out above) or the monthly direct debit arrangement (which allows the use of the 105% test) is not fulfilled, then interest will arise on the shortfall from the due date of that preliminary tax payment until the date of payment.

### Case Study: Four Blue Ducks

On the basis of the figures set out at **Section 7.3.3** above, Jim's preliminary tax payment for 2015 is approximately €19,000. He does not have sufficient cash available on 31 October 2015 and pays only €1,000 towards this 2015 preliminary tax liability, leaving a shortfall of €18,000. If he were to make up that shortfall only when he was making his tax payments on 31 October 2016, then he would have an interest charge of approximately 8% on €18,000 for the period from 31 October 2015 to 31 October 2016.

- If no preliminary tax payment is made, then interest will arise on the minimum payment that should have been made in order to meet the 90%/100% tests from the preliminary tax due date until the date of payment. No 105% option is available in this situation as there has been no preliminary tax payment by direct debit.

Additional liabilities (known as 'surcharges') will arise when an income tax return has been filed late. These surcharges are calculated as a percentage of the tax liabilities set out in the return, so they can be very significant if the taxpayer is paying high levels of tax. The surcharges are calculated as follows:

- when the return is filed within two months of the return filing deadline of 31 October, the surcharge is 5% of the tax liabilities, up to a maximum of €12,695; and
- a return filed after this two-month period will be subject to a surcharge of 10% of the tax liabilities, up to a maximum of €63,485.[10]

In addition, fixed penalties of up to €4,000 may arise when an income taxpayer with an obligation to file an income tax return fails to do so or fraudulently/negligently makes incorrect returns. There are also other penalties for behaviour that prevents the correct assessment of a taxpayer.[11]

[10] Section 1084 TCA 1997.

[11] Sections 1052–1058 TCA 1997.

### *7.3.5 Interaction between Local Property Tax and the Income Tax Return*

There is now a link between an individual's local property tax (LPT) obligations and their income tax return. Though the detailed operation of this tax is outside the scope of this book, we briefly reviewed LPT as it affects employer payroll tax obligations in **Chapter 5, Section 5.2.1**.[12]

LPT also interacts with income tax by the trigger of a specific 'LPT surcharge' on the income tax return if an LPT taxpayer has not filed their LPT return or not paid their LPT by the time they file their income tax return.[13] For example, if a self-employed taxpayer owns her own home and either has not submitted her 2015 LPT return or has not paid her 2015 LPT liability by the 31 October 2015, an LPT surcharge will arise on her 2014 income tax return.

***Note:*** the LPT surcharge will trigger when the income tax return is filed. If the self-employed taxpayer decided to file her 2014 tax return early, on say 7 June 2015, and she has not met her LPT obligations by that date, then the LPT surcharge would trigger on 7 June 2015.

The surcharge is calculated as 10% of the income tax liability for the prior year of assessment (for example, 10% of the income tax liability for the 2014 year, which must be returned by the 31 October 2015 deadline), up to a maximum of €63,485. Where the LPT obligations are subsequently fulfilled, the amount of the surcharge will be capped at the amount of the LPT liability.

***Remember***: the surcharge for late filing/payment of the LPT return is a *second* potential surcharge; this may arise *in addition* to the surcharge for late filing of the income tax return itself.

## 7.4 Corporation Tax

In the preceding section, we reviewed the income tax rules that apply to trading profits earned by unincorporated businesses, i.e. sole trade or partnership. Where a business is incorporated, meaning that it is operated through a company, then the company will pay corporation tax on business profits arising. We set out the relevant corporation tax assessment, payment and return filing rules below.

[12] Full details of the operation of this tax are set out in *Surviving Local Property Tax* by Brian Keegan, Mary Roche and Norah Collender (Chartered Accountants Ireland, 2014).

[13] Section 38 of the Finance (Local Property Tax) Act 2012.

### 7.4.1 Corporation Tax Return Filing Due Date and Payment Obligations

As with a sole trade or partnership business, 12-month accounts are the usual basis for recording a company's trading results on a regular basis. However, unlike the income tax rules for filing and paying returns, there is no specified date by which corporation tax returns must be filed and paid; instead there are a number of deadlines that are driven by the date of the company's accounting period-end.

The general rules for filing corporation tax returns and paying corporation tax liabilities are as follows:

- A corporation tax return must be filed by a date that is eight months and 23 days after the company's accounting period-end, i.e. the 2015 corporation tax return for a company with a 30 June 2015 period-end must be filed by 23 March 2016.
- As with income tax rules, a company must make preliminary tax payments as well as final balancing payments by certain deadlines.
- The rules in relation to calculating preliminary tax payments differ, depending on whether a company is treated as a 'small' or 'large' company. For these purposes, a 'small' company is one which, in the previous accounting period, had a tax liability of less than €200,000. Note that the focus here is on tax liability and *not* on taxable profits or turnover. A regular trading company, which is subject to tax at 12.5% on its trading profits, would have to generate taxable trading profits of €1.6 million before it would be treated as a 'large' company for preliminary tax purposes.
- A 'small' company has a choice when calculating preliminary tax payments; these can be based on 100% of the liability for the previous accounting period or 90% of the estimated liability for the current accounting period. Using a 30 June 2015 period-end to illustrate, the deadlines for filing and paying corporation tax returns and payments are as follows:
    - o Preliminary tax payment – calculated on the basis of the 100%/90% thresholds outlined above – must be paid by the 23rd day of the month before the end of the accounting period (i.e. for a 30 June 2015 period-end, the deadline is 23 May 2015).
    - o Final balancing payment – to bring the total payment to 100% of the liability for the current accounting period – must be paid by the corporation tax return filing deadline, i.e. a date which is no later than eight months and 23 days after the accounting period end (i.e. 23 March 2016 for a 30 June 2015 period-end).
- A 'large' company must pay two instalments of preliminary tax (three payments in total) – again, we will use a 30 June 2015 period-end to illustrate:
    - o First preliminary tax payment – calculated on the basis of 50% of the liability for the previous accounting period or 45% of the estimated liability for the current accounting period – must be paid by a date that is five months and 23 days after the accounting period starts

(i.e. for a 30 June 2015 period-end, the deadline is 23 December 2014).

- Second preliminary tax payment – an amount which, added to the first preliminary tax payment, brings the total payment amount to 90% of the estimated liability for the current accounting period – must be paid by the 23rd day of the month before the end of the accounting period (i.e. for a 30 June 2015 period-end, the deadline is 23 May 2015).
- Final balancing payment – to bring the total payment to 100% of the liability for the current accounting period – must be paid by the corporation tax return filing deadline, i.e. a date that is no later than eight months and 23 days after the accounting period end (i.e. 23 March 2016 for a 30 June 2015 period-end).

- There is a specific rule for the calculation of preliminary tax by a new company. Where that company does not expect to have a tax liability exceeding €200,000 in the first year of trading, then no preliminary tax will be required in the first year.[14] This means that the tax liability for the first accounting period will be due for payment on the same date as the filing deadline for the corporation tax return covering that first accounting period.

### Case Study: Tigim Language Learning Ltd

Tigim Language Learning Ltd started trading on 1 November 2009 and the company directors nominated 30 September 2010 as the first accounting period-end. As the expected corporation tax liability for the first accounting period was approximately €5,000, the company did not have a preliminary tax payment obligation in that first year. The company was obliged to pay the €5,000 corporation tax liability by the same deadline date for filing the first corporation tax return, i.e. 23 June 2011 for the 30 September 2010 year end.

It is very important to note that the classification of a company for preliminary tax purposes as a 'large' or 'small' company is not a static test and the company's status must be reassessed on a continuous basis. The focus of the test is, after all, the level of corporation tax liability for the company's previous accounting period. It is perfectly possible to move back and forth between the two classifications from accounting period to accounting period.

- Note that a specific relief from corporation tax may arise for certain start-up companies whose corporation tax liabilities do not exceed €40,000 in the first three years of trading. This is discussed in more detail in **Chapter 6**, **Section 6.5**.

[14] Section 959AN TCA 1997.

### 7.4.2 Interest, Surcharges and Penalties for Late Filing and Late Payment

As with income tax, the late payment of corporation tax payments (including preliminary tax payments) and the payment of preliminary tax payments that do not meet the various 45%/50%/90%/100% tests set out above, will incur interest charges. The same interest rate applies as for late payment of income tax: 0.0219% per day (8% on a per-annum basis).

Where any of a company's preliminary tax payment(s) do not meet the relevant minimum thresholds, then the due date for the entire corporation tax liability will be moved back to the due date of the first preliminary tax payment. For a 'large' company, this would bring the due date to the date that is five months and 23 days after the accounting period commences, e.g. 23 December 2014 for a 30 June 2015 period-end.

Surcharges will also arise where the corporation tax return is filed late:

- When the return is filed within two months of the return filing deadline, the surcharge is 5% of the tax liabilities, up to a maximum of €12,695.
- A return filed after this two-month period will be subject to a surcharge of 10% of the tax liabilities, up to a maximum of €63,485.[15]

As with income tax obligations, failure by a company to file a corporation tax return or the fraudulent/negligent filing of incorrect returns will trigger 'fixed' penalties of up to €4,000. There are also other penalties for behaviour that prevents the correct assessment of a corporate taxpayer. Note that the registered secretary of a company may be personally subject to penalties of up to €3,000 if the company is liable to penalties for various Revenue offences.[16]

### 7.4.3 Restriction on Use of Losses

There is a further implication of late filing of corporation tax returns and it relates to the use of trading losses for offset against other income. Where a company has other sources of income, e.g. rental income, and the company generates both rental profits and trading losses in the same accounting period, the company will wish to deduct the losses from the profits when calculating the corporation tax liability. This means that a restriction to the amount of losses that may be deducted will actually cost the company in additional corporation tax charges.

A detailed discussion of the use of corporation tax losses is outside the scope of this book, but we do wish to highlight the restrictions on the use of current-year trading losses when the corporation tax return is filed late, as follows:

- Where the return is filed within two months of the filing deadline, a 25% restriction on loss relief arises, subject to a maximum restriction of €31,740.

[15] Section 1084 TCA 1997.

[16] Sections 1052 to 1058 TCA 1997.

- A 50% restriction arises where the return is more than two months late, subject to a maximum restriction of €158,717.[17]

Similar restrictions apply to the surrender of losses between group companies where either the surrendering company or the claimant company are late filing their corporation tax return.

## 7.5 Implications of Having Significant Tax Arrears

We have set out above the interest, penalties, surcharges and loss use restrictions that arise where VAT, payroll, income tax and corporation tax payments and returns are filed and paid after the due dates. There are more significant implications, however, for a business that is continually late with tax payments and/or tax returns, and businesses that have a significant amount of tax arrears. After a while, a business in this position may find it extremely difficult to conduct its day-to-day activities and ultimately may be forced into liquidation.

### *7.5.1 Phased Payment/Instalment Arrangements*

We look first at how Revenue may deal with a business that has a significant amount of tax debts. Given the economic difficulties that arose in the wake of the financial crisis, Revenue recognised that it needed to engage with viable businesses that were experiencing a (hopefully) temporary inability to pay their tax debts as they fell due. Where certain conditions are met and the outstanding tax debt is at least €5,000, a caseworker from the Collector-General's office may engage with a business that has significant tax arrears with a view to agreeing an instalment arrangement to deal with these arrears. Revenue highlight that as this approach is a concessionary one, it "must be fully justified by reference to the circumstances of each individual taxpayer or business".[18]

In order for Revenue to agree to an instalment arrangement, the caseworker will expect the taxpayer business to engage with them as early as possible and to provide detailed information on the business during the negotiation for such an arrangement. A taxpayer's previous approach to filing and paying tax returns, timeliness, etc., will also have an impact on whether Revenue will consider an instalment arrangement and, if so, the terms of the arrangement. All instalment arrangements will include interest charges (at the usual rates for outstanding tax liabilities) so they can be a very expensive way of financing the business.

[17] Section 1085 TCA 1997.

[18] "Collection of Tax Debts: The Collector-General outlines Revenue's approach", p. 4. Available at www.revenue.ie/en/business/running/tax-payment-difficulties.html (accessed June 2016).

In determining whether or not to agree a proposed instalment arrangement, Revenue's stated aim is to:

> "strike the necessary balance between ensuring payment of the debt due in the shortest possible timescale having regard to the circumstances of the taxpayer or business while at the same time ensuring that the arrangement is a viable way for the business to meet not just its obligation to pay the overdue debt but to have the capacity to meet future tax debts as they arise".[19]

To start the negotiation to secure an instalment arrangement, the taxpayer business must complete a Form PPA1 (Phased Payment Application)[20] and provide various detailed information. Where the tax debts amount to more than €100,000, a greater level of detail is required but, at the very least, the taxpayer will be expected to provide the following:

- Details of tax debts, why they have arisen and why they cannot be paid in one lump sum.
- Proposed instalment arrangement schedule, including down payment, monthly payments, duration, interest charges over the course of the proposed arrangement and any penalties.[21]
- Details of all bank accounts, existing bank loans and invoice discounting/factoring arrangements.
- List of current debtors, including value, age, payment schedule and bad debt provision.
- Explanation as to why the business is a viable one and why the business will be in a position to honour any instalment arrangements agreed and meet future tax debts as they fall due.
- Up-to-date bank statements for three to six months.
- List of business assets and any loans, etc. secured on them.
- Detail of what cost-cutting measures have been implemented in the business.

In our experience, Revenue may insist on a down payment of up to 40% of the outstanding liabilities. In general terms, a two-year timeframe is typically the longest period that Revenue will contemplate for a phased payment arrangement.

In order to avoid having to revisit the terms of an instalment arrangement soon after it is put in place, Revenue will require that all outstanding tax returns are filed up to date and that all tax debts are included in the instalment arrangement.

Revenue's document "Dealing with Tax Payment Difficulties and Engaging with Revenue"[22] notes that, once an instalment arrangement

[19] *Ibid.* p. 5.

[20] See www.revenue.ie/en/business/running/ppa1.pdf (accessed June 2016).

[21] An instalment calculator is available on Revenue's website at www.revenue.ie/en/business/running/phased-payment-arrangements.html (accessed June 2016).

[22] See www.revenue.ie/en/business/running/tax-payment-diffs-engaging-with-revenue.pdf (accessed June 2016).

is agreed, the expectation is that only minor changes can be made. If an instalment arrangement is not honoured, it may be adjusted only in very exceptional circumstances; otherwise the taxpayer's file will be sent for collection/enforcement to the Sheriff and/or the Revenue Solicitor's office immediately. The options available to these offices include forced liquidation of a company and forced cessation of a sole trade/partnership business.

### *7.5.2 Tax Clearance Certificates*

A tax clearance certificate is a statement from Revenue confirming that a taxpayer's tax affairs are in order.[23] Since 1 January 2016, a new electronic tax clearance (eTC) system has been in place. With the exception of a small number of taxpayers (for whom paper tax clearance may still apply), the entire system of applying for and receiving confirmation of tax clearance will now be processed through the ROS system or the 'myEnquiries' online system. The majority of Irish tax resident businesses will apply for tax clearance through the ROS system.

Prior to 1 January 2016, all tax clearance certificates were subject to relatively short time limits, but under the new eTC system, the tax clearance will be valid for four years, unless/until it is specifically rescinded by Revenue for non-compliance. The exception to this is where an eTC is required in order to secure a state grant, in which case clearance will issue for one year only. The online application process provides an immediate result: either the issue of an eTC on screen, or a notification that the application has been refused or is under review. If the application is refused, the reasons why, for example, outstanding tax payments or tax returns, will be set out, and these must be dealt with before the taxpayer can re-apply for clearance.

For many businesses, retention of an eTC is absolutely essential, so it can become a very significant issue for a business that falls behind with tax payments and/or tax returns. The production of a valid tax clearance certificate will be required in many situations, including:

- payment of state subsidies of a value of €10,000 or more, e.g. JobsPlus payments (see **Chapter 2, Section 2.3.1**);
- issue of public sector contracts for supplies of a value of €10,000 or more;
- securing trading licences in certain industries, e.g. liquor licence, taxi licence.

In general, Revenue will also issue an eTC to any taxpayer who requests one, as long as the taxpayer's tax affairs are compliant.

The tax affairs of parties that are treated as 'connected' to an applicant taxpayer will also be reviewed and no eTC will issue to the applicant

[23] Sections 1094 and 1095 TCA 1997.

taxpayer unless the tax affairs of all 'connected' parties are also in order. 'Connected' parties include spouses/civil partners, business partners and fellow directors/shareholders. Where the applicant for an eTC is a company and at least one of the company's shareholders owns, or is in a position to control, more than 50% of the company's shares, then the tax affairs of that owner must also be up to date in order for the company to secure an eTC.

It is now possible for a third party to secure online confirmation that a taxpayer has a valid eTC. This requires the third party to have the taxpayer's tax number and tax clearance access number, as well as the taxpayer's permission for this verification process.[24]

While the issue of an eTC requires that a taxpayer's returns and payments are up to date, a taxpayer operating within a payment instalment arrangement should be able to secure an eTC, as long as the arrangement is being honoured.

### *7.5.3 Requirement to Produce a Personal Statement of Affairs*

Where an individual taxpayer owes tax debts that remain unpaid and they do not engage with the Collector-General to deal with these tax debts, the Collector-General has the power to compel the taxpayer to produce a detailed personal statement of affairs (SOA) by issuing a notice to that effect.[25] The purpose of doing so is to allow the Collector-General to assess whether the outstanding tax debts are recoverable.

In general, the SOA must include details of all assets held by the taxpayer, the assets' current location, date and cost of acquisition, current market value, mortgages, etc. secured against them, and insurance policies on each asset. In addition, the SOA must include details of the taxpayer's income and outgoings for the period specified by the Collector-General.

The obligation to produce a SOA may extend to the spouse/civil partner of the taxpayer where the taxpayer and their spouse/civil partner are jointly assessed for income tax. There are two different types of SOA that may be required:

- a short statement of affairs; and
- a statutory statement of affairs.

Only a senior Revenue officer may request a statutory SOA and non-submission of a statutory SOA can result in prosecution of the taxpayer. The statutory SOA also requires details of assets owned by a minor child

[24] For further details in relation to the eTC system, see www.revenue.ie/en/online/tax-clearance.html and www.revenue.ie/en/about/foi/s16/collection/tax-clearance/electronic-tax-clearance.pdf, both on Revenue's website. Note also Revenue *e-Briefs* 11/2015, 97/2015, 115/2015 and 34/2016.

[25] Section 960R TCA 1997.

(i.e. an unmarried child who is under 18 years old) of the taxpayer or their spouse/civil partner, and trustees of the taxpayer or their spouse/civil partner.

The taxpayer will have 30 days from the date of the notice to produce the SOA.

### *7.5.4 Requirement to Produce a Security Bond*

In recent years, there has been a pattern of 'phoenix businesses' collapsing, leaving behind unpaid tax debts and a new business comprising the same/similar trade starting again. There is also the serious issue of businesses that have an ongoing history of falling behind with tax payments and/or of not engaging with the Collector-General. Amendments in the 2014 Finance Act allow Revenue wide flexibility where it appears "requisite to them to do so for the protection of revenue" to issue a notice requiring any taxpayer wishing to carry on a business to produce a security bond to cover payment of certain tax liabilities, being:

- PAYE income tax, PRSI and USC;
- LPT collected through the payroll system;
- relevant contracts tax (RCT) (outside the scope of this book);
- VAT.[26]

Note that under the Finance Act 2014 changes, there is no requirement that the business owner has any history of tax default or that a new business has been in default for non-payment of taxes.

In addition, Revenue guidelines state that taxpayers will be considered for a security bond requirement if:

- there is a previous unpaid Revenue debt of €50,000 or more; *and*
- one or more payroll, RCT or VAT returns and/or payments have been outstanding for 30 days or more.

The taxpayer has 30 days to comply with this requirement; if they do not, they are obliged to cease trading. If the taxpayer continues to trade without having produced the security bond to the Collector-General, they will be guilty of a Revenue offence, punishable by fines of up to €126,970 and/or imprisonment for up to five years. The security bond should comprise either a guarantee from a financial institution that a certain level of tax debt owing by the taxpayer will be paid by the financial institution or, alternatively, a bank draft for the same amount.

It is possible to appeal the requirement to produce a security bond to the Tax Appeals Commission (the independent authority to which a taxpayer can appeal a Revenue decision) and to continue trading while awaiting the outcome of this appeal. The fact that there is such an appeal pending

[26] Section 960S TCA 1997.

will not prevent the Collector-General demanding and enforcing payment of any unpaid tax liabilities of the business.[27]

### Case Study: Four Blue Ducks

In **Chapter 9** we will see that Jim decides to incorporate his sole trade business to facilitate business expansion and to provide opportunities to reinvest profits on a pre-tax basis – both valid commercial drivers for this decision. If the reason for incorporation of the business was, instead, to start operating the café through a new company so Jim could leave unpaid sole-trade tax debts behind, the Collector-General could invoke this requirement for a security bond from the new company. This would effectively prevent the new company from trading until either the bond was produced or the request for the security bond was withdrawn following an appeal to the Tax Appeals Commission.

[27] For further information, see "Requirement for Security Bonds Section 960S TCA 1997". Available at www.revenue.ie/en/about/foi/s16/collection/security-bonds (accessed June 2016).

## CHAPTER 8

# DEALING WITH A REVENUE AUDIT AND OTHER REVENUE APPROACHES



In the early part of this chapter we will review how a Revenue audit should be handled by a taxpayer and their agent, as well as looking at what the Revenue auditors will require. In addition to being provided with access to the relevant books and records, the Revenue auditors will expect *full* co-operation from the taxpayer if they wish to avoid the full rigours of the penalty regime, possible publication of the audit settlement and potential prosecution. In this regard, our case study extract below is a lesson in what not to do.

## Case Study: Four Blue Ducks

Jim McLachlan walked into the room, threw a brown envelope on the desk and slumped into a chair. "Why are they picking on me?" he asked. "I'm up to date; the returns are filed, the taxes are paid. What more do they want from me?"

Maeve, his accountant and tax agent, picked up the envelope, saw the official harp and said, "Don't feel persecuted, Jim. Revenue audits are a part of being in business. You might have been randomly selected; they do that sometimes." Maeve hesitated before continuing. "Though they do rely heavily on their risk-profiling system. It's called the REAP system, would you believe? So they might suspect some loss of tax, Jim. But let's talk about it – we can help you with this."

Over the next half an hour, Maeve talked Jim through the Revenue audit process and how he could prepare for it. However, Jim was not interested. "Listen", he said, "as far as I am concerned, the returns are right and they're up to date. Let them look at the files and try to find something wrong." Maeve tried to persuade Jim that it would be better to review the files before the audit and see for himself if there was anything that Revenue would have a problem with. She explained that Revenue now generally expect the taxpayer's tax agent to attend the audit. She explained the benefits of making a disclosure in advance to Revenue, but Jim wasn't listening. "I know you are trying to help, Maeve, but I don't see why I should spend my time and money doing their job for them. No, I'll just leave them at it. I'll look after it myself, thanks anyway."

The morning of the audit, two Revenue auditors arrived at Jim's café at the appointed time. They introduced themselves and then asked if he was making a disclosure before they started; Jim replied that he did not see any need to as he was sure his tax returns were correct. When they asked what information he had for review, he said that he had copies of returns, his purchases listings and his sales listings. "What about bank statements? Do you have the bank reconciliations? What about credit cards?" asked one of the auditors, to which Jim replied that he did not think they were necessary.

Then the questions started. They wanted to know all about the business: who were its customers and suppliers; what bank accounts did it use; how did it deal with petty cash; how were sales recorded? The questions continued and Jim was getting annoyed. "Listen", he said. "What's with all these questions? I'm not a criminal, but you're making me feel like one." One of the auditors responded "We're just doing our job, Mr McLachlan, there's no need to get annoyed". But this was like a red rag to a bull. "Don't tell me when I can get annoyed" Jim exploded. "I've had enough of your questions. Just stick to the files." The other auditor tried to pacify Jim, saying that it was in his interest to work with them; it would make the audit quicker and, if he had tax to pay, the penalty would be lower.

But Jim, again failing to listen, stormed out of the room saying, "I'll leave you at it. Call my accountant with your questions."

After a long conversation with one of the Revenue auditors, Maeve put down the phone and shook her head. "How am I going to talk Jim through all this?" She stared at the list of issues on her notepad, particularly the auditor's comment that they had found Jim very un-cooperative. They assumed that he had something to hide and were talking about at least 40% penalties on any underpaid tax. They had expanded the audit and were now reviewing Jim's personal tax returns, as well as the business's returns. They had also extended the number of tax years they were looking at, to two years, from commencement in March 2014 to February 2016. "This is going to be a tough one", thought Maeve.

Clearly, Jim is a hot-headed person and lost his temper with the wrong people. Many business people feel the same way about Revenue audits, however, initially obsessing over why they were selected and then adopting a fairly un-cooperative attitude towards the process. This is really not the best approach and this chapter will illustrate why.

We will review the audit process, from the audit notification letter to final settlement, and how best to approach a Revenue audit, including why advance disclosures can save money and prevent publication or prosecution. We will also focus on the types of issues that typically arise for start-ups and SMEs. Later in the chapter, our focus will shift to other types of Revenue intervention and other ways for businesses to correct errors in their tax returns.

All types of Revenue 'interventions', including audits, non-audit interventions and investigations, are conducted under the *Code of Practice for Revenue Audit and other Compliance Interventions*, issued in November 2015. Previous versions of this Code were issued in 2010 (updated August 2011) and 2014.[1] The *Code of Practice* is Revenue's interpretation of current tax law and best practice as they relate to Revenue interventions, and although not necessarily definitive, a taxpayer would have an uphill battle if they expected to conduct some aspect of a Revenue intervention outside of the *Code of Practice*'s guidelines.

Note that our focus in this chapter is to provide an overview of a Revenue intervention as typically experienced by a start-up or SME business. This information is provided in summary and full details are set out in the *Code of Practice.* It is not our intention to review the entire *Code of Practice* in these chapters and certain aspects of it are specifically excluded here, for example, the rules that relate to 'tax avoidance transactions' and the Mandatory Reporting Regime.

[1] All three versions of the *Code of Practice* are available on the Revenue website. See www.revenue.ie/en/practitioner/codes-practice.html (accessed June 2016).

## 8.1 The Scope of Revenue Audits

To start at the beginning and the receipt of the Revenue letter (Jim's 'brown envelope'), the first thing that should be confirmed is whether the Revenue intervention is an audit. If this is the case, then the letter should contain the phrase 'Notification of a Revenue Audit'.

The audit letter sets out the taxpayer(s) who will be subject to the audit and the scope of the audit, i.e. the type of tax it will cover and the time period, for example, corporation tax for the calendar year 2012 or VAT returns for the period March/April 2011 to January/February 2013.

Often the audit's scope is quite limited and refers to one or two taxes and to, say, a 12- or 24-month time period. In other cases, the audit can cover all tax types for a four-year period; and if fraud or negligence is suspected, it can cover an even longer period. The term 'tax head' will be used throughout this chapter and refers to a type of tax, e.g. corporation tax and VAT are two separate 'tax heads'. A tax agent advising a client who has received a notice of an all-tax-head audit (i.e. an audit of all taxes that the business is subject to) for a four-year period would assume that Revenue have specific suspicions of unpaid tax.

Under the terms of the 2015 *Code of Practice*, the question of how many tax periods/years are to be included in the audit is now determined by an assessment of the taxpayer's compliance history and whether their behaviour indicates a high or low risk of lost tax revenue. In general, most Revenue audits cover, say, a tax year or a year's worth of tax periods, unless a specific risk has been identified, in which case the audit may cover more than one year (or year's worth of tax periods).

A key issue here is the identity of the taxpayer that is to be subject to audit. Revenue cannot audit the tax returns of a taxpayer without issuing a specific audit notification letter to that taxpayer. While many company owners incorrectly tend to think of their personal and company financial affairs as 'one', they are separate and represent two separate taxpayers. Revenue often issue audit letters to the individual owners/directors of a company at the same time as they issue audit letters to the company itself, but they do not always do so. If no notification letter has issued to the company owners/directors, this means that queries arising during the audit of the company should not drift into gathering personal information on those owners/directors. However, Revenue do have the right to formally extend the audit of a company into an audit of its owners/directors if there is a reasonable suspicion of unpaid taxes in their tax returns.

The other significant issue to note is whether the audit notification letter includes a reference to e-auditing of the taxpayer's computer systems and electronic information (see **Section 8.3.2.1** below).

It is extremely important to be clear from the outset as to the scope of the Revenue audit:

- the tax heads to be covered;

- the time period to be audited;
- the identity of the taxpayer(s) who are subject to audit; and
- the access to computer systems required (where an e-audit is to take place).

Having clear audit scope should clarify what information should be included in any disclosure letter to Revenue and may enable a taxpayer to submit a second disclosure letter if the initial audit scope is later expanded.

## 8.2 Preparing for a Revenue Audit

### *8.2.1 When and Where?*

Once notified, the taxpayer should prepare for a Revenue audit of their tax returns, and the very first issue to be settled is the date and location of the audit. Typically, Revenue will set a date 21 working days from the date of the audit letter and will expect to conduct the audit at the taxpayer's address – at the taxpayer's home if the audit concerns a sole trade or partnership with no separate business premises, or otherwise at the business's main trading premises.

Many people would be uncomfortable having an audit in their own home, considering it an invasion of their personal space. Equally, many business people would prefer that a Revenue audit not be conducted on the business premises so as to minimise disruption. Historically, Revenue would generally agree to a request for a different location, as long as full books and records, and the taxpayer(s) and tax agent, were available at that address at the commencement of the audit. It was also quite typical to have the audit in the offices of the taxpayer's agent, i.e. accountant or tax advisor. Where the tax agent's office was used as a location for the Revenue audit, the Revenue auditor often visited the taxpayer's business premises in any event. The 2015 *Code of Practice* now states, however, that audits are "not normally carried out at an agent's office" and that if the taxpayer's business premises or home are not suitable, then the audit will be carried out at the local Revenue office. (As this does not reflect our experience to date, it remains to be seen if this results in a change in Revenue's practice.)

In relation to the date of the audit, it is usually possible to move this by a few days, subject to the Revenue auditor's work schedule. A phone call to the Revenue office listed on the audit letter is the best approach here. There is also a formal method for delaying the audit for up to 60 days, in the context of making a 'qualifying disclosure', which we will discuss below. If a qualifying disclosure is to be made, then the taxpayer may write to Revenue giving notice of an intention to make this disclosure. As long as the taxpayer's letter is submitted within 14 days of Revenue's audit letter, then the additional 60-day preparation time will apply. Securing the additional 60-day preparation time will likely create an expectation that there are (possibly significant) unpaid tax liabilities, though there may be other reasons why extra time is required to prepare the disclosure letter, e.g. the audit period stretches back a number of years and time is required to secure archived files.

### 8.2.2 *Taxpayer Review of the Books and Records*

When the date and location of the audit have been agreed, the taxpayer and their tax agent then review the books and records from three specific angles:

1. The first is to ensure that they are up to date and presented in an order that an external reviewer (i.e. Revenue auditor) can follow. Keeping good books and records is not just a matter of good business practice; a taxpayer is obliged by law to keep 'proper records',[2] which must be sufficient to "give a full and accurate account of the business so that correct tax liabilities can be calculated".[3] We will look at what constitutes 'proper records' later in the chapter.
2. The second reason the books and records should be reviewed by the taxpayer and their tax agent is to determine if there are any unpaid taxes and, if so, to quantify them.

   With regard to the scope of the taxpayer's review of the books and records, we have noted that it is more typical for Revenue audits to be limited in scope, i.e. to one or two tax heads, and usually for, say, a 12-month period. While the scope set out in the Revenue audit letter will certainly be the starting point for the taxpayer's review, it is good practice to widen that review to all tax heads and for the four previous years as well as the current year. This is especially the case if issues that arise in the tax year/tax periods under review also recur in other years. Depending on how the audit progresses, the Revenue auditor may widen the scope of the audit to this extent. However, in order to widen the audit beyond the previous four years, the Revenue auditor must believe that there are serious tax defaults in prior years (based on a pattern of tax defaults in the years under audit) or that fraud/negligence has taken place. Examples of how the scope of an audit can be extended because of the nature of the tax issues arising are set out in our case study extract below.

CASE STUDY: FOUR BLUE DUCKS

If Jim's audit covered the income tax head only and there is an issue of undeclared sales, this could impact on the level of income tax liabilities and also the VAT liabilities, thereby bringing the VAT tax head into the scope of the audit. Another example would be if Jim

[2] Section 886 of the Taxes Consolidation Act 1997 (TCA 1997).
[3] 2015 *Code of Practice*, section 3.21.

had a part-time cleaner that he paid gross, without deduction of PAYE, even though the cleaner should have been on the business's payroll. If the cleaner has been working for Jim for 2015 and 2016, yet the scope of the Revenue audit letter was payroll taxes for the 2016 tax year, then the fact that the payroll tax issue also arises in 2015 would mean that the scope of the audit on payroll taxes would be extended to the two-year period of 2015 and 2016.

3. The third reason for the taxpayer and their agent to carry out this review is to determine if there are any outstanding tax returns, or unpaid tax liabilities on outstanding or previously filed returns. The ideal situation is to ensure that all tax returns are filed and paid up to date before the Revenue audit commences. At the very least, all tax returns should be filed. Where there are outstanding tax liabilities, taxpayers should expect that the Revenue auditor will question them on when these liabilities will be paid. It would be wise to have prepared a payment schedule for these outstanding liabilities for discussion.

### *8.2.3 Dealing with Unpaid Taxes*

If there are unpaid taxes, then in order to complete the audit process, the unpaid taxes (known as 'tax defaults') must be paid, along with interest and penalties. Consideration should be given to making a disclosure of these defaults to the Revenue auditor.

While there is no legal obligation on a taxpayer to make disclosures on tax defaults to a Revenue auditor, there are very good incentives to do so. These are known as the '**three Ps**':

- penalties,
- publication, and
- prosecution.

Where a taxpayer makes a disclosure that is regarded as 'qualifying', they should be in a position to secure reduced *penalties* on tax defaults and to avoid both *publication* of the terms of the Revenue audit settlement and *prosecution* for tax defaults and/or filing of incorrect tax returns. ***Note:*** the disclosure must be made before the audit commences. In practical terms, this can be at any time from the issue of the audit letter to the beginning of the audit meeting.

We can see the importance of having a disclosure letter treated as a 'qualifying' disclosure letter by the Revenue auditor. Small errors or discrepancies in a disclosure letter will not, of themselves, undermine a disclosure letter's 'qualifying' status, though if the Revenue auditor decides that these were intentional, the letter may lose that status.

#### *8.2.3.1 Qualifying Disclosure Letter*

What should a qualifying disclosure letter contain?

- First, the letter should be addressed to the taxpayer's Revenue district and refer to the specific Revenue audit letter(s), including the audit scope set out in that letter(s). It should set out the tax defaults, giving a full explanation of the issues and calculations of the unpaid taxes arising. Interest arising on the tax defaults should also be calculated and included – the interest charges should cover the period from the tax due date to the date of the audit.
- The letter should include a declaration by the taxpayer that "to the best of [their] knowledge, information and belief [the disclosure is] correct and complete"[4] and should be signed by the taxpayer (or a company director/secretary where the taxpayer is a company).
- Finally, the letter should be accompanied by payment of the total sum of the unpaid taxes and interest liabilities. Penalties and/or surcharges will also arise on the unpaid tax amounts (but not on the interest amounts) and these are a matter for discussion with the Revenue auditor, though they need *not* be included in the disclosure letter for it to be regarded as 'qualifying'. However, the penalties arising must be paid within 30 days of the final agreement.

#### *8.2.3.2 Interest*

Taxpayers are often taken aback by the idea that interest must be calculated by them and included in the qualifying disclosure letter. Some ask whether a deal can be struck with Revenue over the interest charges. The 2015 *Code of Practice* is very definite on this, however, and baldly states that "interest due is not mitigated".[5]

Tax agents sometimes have differing experiences with this issue, depending on the individual Revenue auditor they are dealing with. In our experience, it is very difficult to get any reduction in interest charges, as the usual response from the Revenue auditor is that the interest charges are 'statutory', meaning that they are mandated by law and cannot be reduced. In practical terms, once tax defaults and calculations are set out in the disclosure letter, the Revenue auditor will not agree to reduce these figures. There is then the question of what to set out in the disclosure letter in respect of interest if the full interest charges are not to be included and a statement, to the effect that the taxpayer wishes to discuss interest, is made instead. It is possible that the Revenue auditor could treat the disclosure letter as incomplete and then refuse to accept it as 'qualifying'.

[4] 2015 *Code of Practice,* section 3.7.

[5] *Ibid.,* section 5.3.

In broad terms, there are two levels of interest rates for late payment of taxes:

- The rate applicable to late payment of so-called 'fiduciary' taxes (VAT, PAYE and RCT) is approximately 10% per annum (or 0.0274% per day).
- Late payment of income tax and corporation tax attract a lower annual interest rate of approximately 8% (or 0.0219% per day).

A simple example from our case study should illustrate this calculation.

CASE STUDY: FOUR BLUE DUCKS

If Four Blue Ducks had an undeclared VAT liability of €3,000 that should have been paid by 23 July 2014 and the date of the audit is 4 March 2016, then the interest charge arising must cover the period 23 July 2014 to 4 March 2016 and is calculated as follows:

591 days × 0.0274% = 16.19% × €3,000 = €485.80

### 8.2.3.3 *Tax-geared Penalties*

'Tax-geared penalties' will arise in addition to unpaid taxes and interest, and are calculated as a percentage of the unpaid taxes.[6] Updated in the 2015 Finance Act, the definition of unpaid tax (for penalty purposes) now also covers the *spread* between an incorrectly claimed refund and the tax liability that was actually due. For example, if a taxpayer claims a VAT refund of €2,000 when in fact there was a VAT liability of €2,000, then the penalty would be calculated as a percentage of the €4,000 spread.

**Table 8.1** below sets out the 'tax-geared penalties', the level of which is influenced by the following factors:

- whether a qualifying disclosure has been made;
- whether the taxpayer has been fully co-operative during the Revenue audit process; and
- the level of the taxpayer's intent in underpaying tax – was it deliberate or careless?

There are also separate penalty tables to cover situations where the taxpayer has made two or more qualifying disclosures **or** where the taxpayer makes a qualifying disclosure outside of a Revenue audit. (We will look at the latter situation in **Section 8.9** below.)

[6] Section 1077E TCA 1997, as amended by section 78 of the Finance Act 2015 (FA 2015).

Table 8.1: Tax-geared Penalties in a Revenue Audit[7]

| Category of Default | Prompted Qualifying Disclosure and Full Co-operation | No Disclosure but Full Co-operation | No Disclosure and Incomplete/ No Co-operation |
|---|---|---|---|
| Deliberate behaviour | 50% | 75% | 100% |
| Careless behaviour with significant consequences | 20% | 30% | 40% |
| Careless behaviour without significant consequences | 10% | 15% | 20% |

The 2014 *Code of Practice* introduced a new exemption from tax-geared penalties in the following specific circumstances:

- the total amount of the taxpayer's tax default is less than €6,000; *and*
- the tax default is treated as arising from *careless* behaviour and not *deliberate* behaviour.

### *8.2.3.4 Tax-geared Penalties and the Level of Intention*

In assessing penalties, Revenue distinguish between two types of behaviour: deliberate and careless. The key element that distinguishes the two types of behaviour is intent: effectively, the Revenue auditor assesses whether the taxpayer *intended* to default, or if the taxpayer behaved in such a way that, at the very least, tax defaults were likely to arise and the taxpayer's behaviour could not be characterised as careless.

Some obvious examples of 'deliberate behaviour' would include:

- failing to keep proper books and records;
- repeated omissions of transactions from the books and records;
- providing false or misleading information; and
- concealment of bank accounts or other assets.

'Deliberate behaviour' is a type of behaviour generally regarded as tax fraud, i.e. behaviour carried out in the full knowledge that it is wrong.

'Careless behaviour', on the other hand, is characterised as "the failure to take reasonable care" to ensure that any action or omission of the taxpayer would not give rise to a tax default. ***Note:*** a taxpayer cannot delegate

[7] This table refers to tax defaults that occurred on or after 24 December 2008.

the responsibility to submit correct tax returns to a tax agent; even if the returns prepared by a tax agent are incorrect, the responsibility remains with the taxpayer.

Referring to **Table 8.1** again, the difference between careless behaviour 'with' and careless behaviour 'without' significant consequences involves a straightforward mathematical equation. If the level of unpaid tax is less than 15% of the tax liability as correctly calculated, then the careless behaviour will not be regarded as having significant consequences. An example from our case study should illustrate this point.

CASE STUDY: FOUR BLUE DUCKS

Suppose Jim applied the wrong sales VAT rate on a small portion of his sales for the VAT period January/February 2015. He says that this was a simple calculation error that arose because he was extremely busy (and tired) when he was preparing that VAT return. If he declared sales VAT of, say, €1,500 and the amount of sales VAT correctly calculated for that VAT period should have been €1,750, then the default should be in the category of 'careless behaviour without significant consequences'. This is because the percentage of the unpaid amount relative to the correct amount is 14.3%. Securing agreement that the default should attract the lowest category of penalty requires that this default is regarded as a 'one-off'. A pattern of charging lower than the required rate of sales VAT could, however, indicate deliberate behaviour on Jim's part, even if each incident accounts for only a small amount of unpaid tax.

(***Note:*** an appropriate level of penalty can be applied to each separate tax default; it should not be assumed that one penalty rate automatically applies to all tax defaults.)

As behaviour can often be interpreted in different ways, we can see that establishing a working relationship with the Revenue auditor from the outset and providing full co-operation will assist when it comes to arguing the appropriate level of penalty.

### *8.2.3.5 Impact of Intention on the Scope of Disclosures*

While the cost of penalties payable in relation to unpaid tax is a very significant issue in and of itself, there is another important element to the question of penalties, specifically the type of taxpayer *behaviour* (deliberate or careless) that is assessed as having generated the different levels of penalties. The type of tax behaviour will, in fact, determine the *scope* of the tax defaults that must be set out in a disclosure letter in order for it to be regarded as 'qualifying'.

We noted, at **Section 8.2.2** above, that when the taxpayer is reviewing the files in advance of the Revenue audit, best practice suggests they should not limit this review to the scope set out in the audit notification letter, i.e. they should review files for all tax heads for the previous four tax years and the current tax year. This is because the following tax defaults must be included in a qualifying disclosure letter:

- Disclosures in the *deliberate behaviour* category must state the unpaid taxes and interest in respect of **all tax heads and all tax periods** in which these defaults arose, meaning that where *deliberate* defaults have arisen for any tax head and in any tax year, the fact that the scope of a Revenue letter is limited to, say, one tax head for one tax year is irrelevant, as all of these defaults must be included.
- Disclosures in the *careless behaviour (with or without significant consequences)* category must state the unpaid taxes and interest in respect of the tax heads and tax periods within the scope of the audit notification letter.

In practical terms, what this entails is that a taxpayer (and their tax agent) must self-assess the likely category of penalty for all tax defaults so that they can be clear on the extent of the disclosures to be included in the disclosure letter. In particular, the taxpayer must determine if there are any tax defaults in the *deliberate behaviour* category.

#### *8.2.3.6 Fixed Penalties*

In some circumstances, a taxpayer may be liable for fixed penalties, although not where tax-geared penalties arise. These fixed penalties are typically set at €4,000 per breach of an obligation under tax legislation and will arise in situations including:

- failure to complete full and true VAT records;
- failure to register with Revenue as an employer when required to do so;
- failure to maintain a register of employees; and
- failure by an employer to deduct local property tax (LPT) at source when instructed by Revenue to do so.

#### *8.2.3.7 Late Filing Surcharges*

In **Chapter 7** we detailed the surcharges that arise when an income tax return, a local property tax return and a corporation tax return are filed late. A Revenue audit settlement will always include 'late filing surcharges' if the taxpayer's income/corporation/LPT tax return(s) were actually filed late.

In relation to an incorrect return that is treated as having been filed 'deliberately' or 'carelessly', there is also the potential for application of a 'late filing surcharge', even if that incorrect return was, in fact, filed on time. This is because the return is *deemed* to have been filed late. Note that a 'late filing surcharge' for *deemed* late filing will not arise if tax-geared penalties are applied to the settlement and the incorrect return was, in fact, filed on time.

#### *8.2.3.8 Payment with the Disclosure Letter*

The *Code of Practice* states that in order to be accepted as 'qualifying', disclosure letters must be accompanied by payment of the total sum of the unpaid taxes and interest charges. While this is certainly the ideal position, it is not always possible. Revenue understands the realities of this and may accept the implementation of a phased payment schedule once the terms of the final settlement are agreed. The final settlement should include agreed tax defaults and interest charges and, where relevant, tax-geared penalties, fixed penalties and/or late filing surcharges. This schedule should be realistic, considering the taxpayer's circumstances. In reviewing a request for such a method of payment, Revenue will require certain current and projected financial information on the taxpayer's business. Details of these requirements are set out in **Chapter 7, Section 7.5.1**.

***Remember***: the Revenue auditor is entitled to charge interest until the *date of payment* of the Revenue audit settlement. This means that, where a phased payment schedule is agreed, the overall cost of the settlement will be increased.

We commented above on the desirability of ensuring that all tax returns are up to date and that all outstanding tax liabilities are paid up to date before the commencement of the audit. If there are outstanding liabilities at the time of the audit, you can expect the Revenue auditor to request immediate payment or to include these liabilities in a payment schedule also.

Once a payment schedule has been agreed (and the deposit paid), this will fulfil the requirement that the disclosure letter be accompanied by payment in order to be treated as qualifying. However, if the payment schedule is not subsequently honoured, then Revenue will not accept that the disclosure letter was a qualifying one, thus leaving the taxpayer potentially exposed to the 'three Ps': (higher) penalties, publication and prosecution.

## 8.3 The Revenue Audit

Once the taxpayer has prepared for the Revenue audit, readied the books and records for review, and perhaps prepared and signed a disclosure letter, they are ready for the initial meeting. As required by the *Code of Practice*, the taxpayer's agent should attend the initial meeting and, if the audit is an e-audit, the business's IT support staff should also be ready to attend.

The initial meeting usually runs along the following lines. First, the Revenue auditor(s) introduce themselves and produce their personal ID cards. At this point they typically ask whether a disclosure letter is being presented by the taxpayer – if so, this is the right time to hand this over. If the Revenue auditor does not inquire about a disclosure letter at the outset, the taxpayer should produce it at the beginning of the meeting in any event. This is because the time for disclosure is up until the point that the audit commences and it is now commencing. Typically, the Revenue auditor will briefly review any disclosure letter presented, to ensure that they understand the tax defaults being disclosed.

### *8.3.1 Profiling the Taxpayer's Business*

The first phase of the audit will involve the auditor profiling the taxpayer; this means asking a lot of questions about how the business is run, who its customers and suppliers are, the maintenance of books and records, how the business is staffed, the identity of the business owners (and directors, if it is a company) and how the business is funded. The auditor will also want to get an understanding of where the business operates and what assets it holds. There will be some detailed questions about the business's bank accounts and credit cards, how customers pay their bills and how cash is handled (if this is relevant).

The auditor may have copies of tax returns or other information to hand with details of the business they wish the taxpayer to explain. This information will have come from Revenue's databases, but may also come from many other sources (e.g. other state bodies, media and general internet searches, etc.). The auditor will want to understand the business's activities and results for analysis, and for comparison with other businesses operating in the same industry. For example, a Revenue auditor who is auditing a café and who has particular expertise on small food businesses will have certain expectations on profit margins, staff numbers, VAT inputs, etc. for such a business.

The profiling part of the audit may take a number of hours/days, depending on the size and complexity of the business.

A word on the extent of the auditor's profiling questions. As we have seen, a taxpayer will only be subject to an audit if a formal audit notification letter has been received. In the case of a small owner/director company, for example, it is entirely possible that the company is the subject of an audit but that the owner/director is not. In this situation, care should be taken if it appears that the Revenue auditor's questions are drifting into the personal financial affairs of the company's owner/director. While questions about the owner/director's income or expenses from the company are entirely appropriate in the context of the company's audit, questions about other sources of income (e.g. from unrelated rental properties) are not. It is perfectly reasonable to ask why such questions are being raised and to emphasise that the audit is of the company only. A balance needs to be struck here, however, as the taxpayer is expected to give full co-operation to the auditor, especially if they will be arguing for reduced tax-geared penalties later in the audit.

Another issue is the people that attend the initial audit meeting. While the 2015 *Code of Practice* requires that the taxpayer's tax agent attends the audit, it is not acceptable for the tax agent to attend on their own. The

Revenue auditor will want to meet at least one senior person from the business so that profiling questions may be put to them. If a senior person does not attend, the Revenue auditor may treat this as a lack of full co-operation by the taxpayer.

### *8.3.2 Review of Books and Records*

The other phase of the initial audit meeting is used to explain the books and records available for inspection by the Revenue auditor, to highlight where all the relevant information is and to clarify who can provide further information or answer queries for the auditor as the audit progresses.

#### *8.3.2.1 Revenue's E-auditing Programme*

Over the past few years, Revenue have embraced new technology as a means of providing more effective ways to carry out its role. One such application is in the use of 'e-auditing' techniques as part of a Revenue audit. E-auditing refers to the use of Revenue computer programs to interrogate the taxpayer's computer systems and electronic records. Where e-auditing techniques are to be used as an extensive part of a Revenue audit, this will be noted in the audit letter. E-auditing techniques usually include the examination of the taxpayer's electronic systems and the copying/downloading of electronic data for analysis by the auditor. The *Code of Practice* assures taxpayers that such confidential business information is stored on encrypted storage devices "in accordance with safeguards outlined in Revenue's data security policy and ICT guidelines".[8]

Where the Revenue audit letter advises the taxpayer that e-auditing techniques will be used, it will usually note that the Revenue auditor wishes to have a preliminary pre-audit meeting to identify and understand:

- the accounting and electronic point of sale (EPOS) systems that the taxpayer uses;
- the format and extent of electronic records that are available; and
- the electronic records that will be required to be made available at the Revenue audit meeting(s).

This pre-audit meeting will normally be held at the business premises where the computer systems can be accessed. Both the taxpayer's tax agent and IT support staff may also be required to attend. It is important to note that this pre-audit meeting is *not* the Revenue audit meeting and the taxpayer is still entitled to present a qualifying disclosure letter at the initial audit meeting itself.

In **Section 8.1** above we emphasised the importance of having clarity on the scope of the audit and this is even more important when an e-audit is to be carried out. It is critical that the scope of the e-audit, i.e. the tax

[8] 2015 *Code of Practice*, section 1.9.

periods to be covered and the type of information that the auditor expects to access at the e-audit meeting, is agreed in advance. The best way to confirm this is for the taxpayer to prepare a note of what was agreed at the pre-audit meeting and for the Revenue auditor to confirm their agreement to this note. Doing so is the best insurance against later disagreement/ confusion, which could ultimately lead to the auditor concluding that there was a lack of full co-operation during the audit.

### 8.3.2.2 *Types of Information Required*

The taxpayer is required to produce sufficient records to "give a full and accurate account of the business so that correct tax liabilities can be calculated".[9] Linking papers, i.e. documents that are drawn up when preparing the taxpayer's accounts showing details of the calculations that link the records, the accounts and the tax returns, are regarded as part of the books and records.

Set out below is a (non-exhaustive) sample list of the types of records that may be required. In our view, even if the Revenue auditor looks for further information later, handing over the following information at the initial audit meeting should provide a fully **co-operative** start. The information should cover the tax heads and tax periods set out in the audit notification letter, unless a qualifying disclosure letter from the taxpayer has widened this scope. In that case, the information should cover the expanded scope.

Where taxes on profits – income tax or corporation tax – are included in the scope of the Revenue audit, the following information should be provided by the taxpayer at the initial meeting:

- copies of tax returns and notices of assessment, as well as all computation and preparation papers associated with these returns;
- copies of the business's year-end accounts;
- proof of payment for each of the tax returns (a printout from ROS will usually suffice here);
- bank statements for all business accounts;
- credit card statements for all business credit cards (and personal credit cards of the business owner/director where business expenses are paid using these cards);
- where the business has disposed of any capital item (e.g. a piece of machinery, equipment or property) full details of the purchase and sale of the capital item, including capital gains tax computations and assessments (where relevant); if any tax relief has been claimed in relation to this disposal, information that supports this claim;
- details of how assets or liabilities in the business balance sheet are valued, including back-up documentation, if relevant; and
- detailed information supporting tax reliefs claimed by the business, e.g. a claim for research & development tax credit.

[9] 2015 *Code of Practice*, section 3.21.

Where VAT is included in the scope of the Revenue audit, the following should be provided, at the initial meeting:

- copies of VAT returns;
- purchase listings that reconcile to VAT returns, purchase invoices and statements;
- sales listings that reconcile to VAT returns, sales invoices and statements;
- where the business enters into contracts with their customers, copies of these contracts;
- where the business uses a cash register or EPOS system, reports from these systems that link to VAT returns;[10] and
- bank reconciliations that reconcile to VAT returns.

Where payroll taxes – PAYE income tax, PRSI and USC – are included in the scope, the following should be provided:

- copies of payroll returns;
- a register of employees, setting out personal details, dates of employment commencement and cessation for all employees;
- tax credit certificates and any other formal payroll documentation (e.g. Form P45 from previous employment, maternity leave information, etc.) for all employees;
- copies of all payslips that reconcile to payroll returns, as well as the payroll calculations; and
- calculations of all benefits in kind paid to all employees that reconcile to payslips and payroll returns.

A taxpayer may be subject to other taxes that are outside the scope of this book. Examples include relevant contracts tax, capital gains tax, customs duties, professional services withholding tax and LPT. Each of these taxes may also be included within the scope of a Revenue audit. For a full list of all taxes covered, see Section 1.2 of the 2015 *Code of Practice*.

### *8.3.2.3 Importance of Good Books and Records*

As we have seen, keeping good books and records is an obligation under law and incomplete documentation can create serious difficulties for taxpayers subject to a Revenue audit. In general, all taxpayers must retain tax records for six years. This six-year period is extended where an inquiry, investigation, appeal, judicial process or claim is ongoing, until such time as this process is completed.[11]

A new business should use appropriate accounting computer software from the start and ensure that transactions are input on a very regular basis.

[10] A specific information leaflet in relation to record-keeping for cash registers/ EPOS systems is available on the Revenue website at www.revenue.ie/en/tax/vat/leaflets/cash-registers.html (accessed May 2016).

[11] Section 886 TCA 1997.

While it is entirely possible for a new small business to take care of its own bookkeeping and accounting matters, it is advisable that:

- an accountant advises on the most suitable accounting software for the business; and
- the person with responsibility for bookkeeping and accounting matters (often the owner/director in the early days) gets sufficient training in using the accounting software.

In addition to the legal obligation to maintain good books and records, a savvy business person will want accurate, up-to-date records in order to be able to see how the business is doing and to make effective management and operating decisions.[12]

### *8.3.3 Expansion of the Audit Scope*

We highlighted earlier the importance of clarity around the scope of the audit. As we have seen, the scope of the audit will impact on the books and records required for the audit, the amount of pre-audit review that must be undertaken and the types of tax default (if these are present) that must be included in a disclosure letter so that it will be treated as a qualifying disclosure.

There are instances where an audit is expanded after it has commenced, typically because of information discovered by the Revenue auditor during their review. Examples include the situation where an audit starts out in relation to, say, a subsidiary company, and is then formally extended by the Revenue auditor to the entire group of companies, or where an audit of a small director-owned company is expanded to include the personal financial affairs of the owner/director. Where an audit is expanded to include another taxpayer, that taxpayer can make a qualifying disclosure at the time of extension of the audit. In such circumstances, the Revenue auditor will generally allow a 21-working-day period to prepare a qualifying disclosure.

Another potential situation is where the Revenue auditor draws the taxpayer's attention to tax defaults not within the initial scope of the audit, but does not formally extend the scope of the audit. Where these tax defaults are *unrelated* and there is no *deliberate behaviour* on the part of the taxpayer, the taxpayer should have the opportunity to make an 'unprompted qualifying disclosure' in relation to these unrelated tax defaults. We will look at what constitutes an 'unprompted qualifying disclosure' in **Section 8.9** below.

### *8.3.4 Full Co-operation during the Audit Process*

The 2015 *Code of Practice* has placed more emphasis on the importance of providing *full* co-operation during the Revenue audit. The *Code of Practice*

[12] For detailed and practical advice on keeping good books and records, see June Menton's *Crack the Books: Accounting for Non-Accountants* (Chartered Accountants Ireland, 2009).

lists specific requirements that must be met in order for the taxpayer to be regarded as 'fully co-operative':

- "having all books, records and linking papers ... available for Revenue at the commencement of the audit
- having appropriate personnel available at the time of the audit
- responding promptly to all requests for information and explanations
- responding promptly to all correspondence
- prompt payment of the audit settlement liability".[13]

If, during the course of the audit, the Revenue auditor forms an opinion that the taxpayer is not providing full co-operation, then they will formally write to the taxpayer (and the tax agent) noting the lack of full co-operation and highlighting the fact that if this lack is not rectified then increased penalties will apply, giving 21 days to rectify the situation.[14]

## 8.4 Bringing the Audit to a Conclusion

For smaller businesses, the auditor's review of the books and records usually takes two or three days and the taxpayer can expect to field queries and requests for further information during this time. The Revenue auditor will expect full co-operation in dealing with queries and, in fact, one of the examples of non-co-operation highlighted in the 2015 *Code of Practice* is a failure "to provide Revenue ... with information known to the taxpayer which would be used in determining whether a tax underpayment arises".[15] Often, the auditor will finish their review of files at the taxpayer's (or their tax agent's) office and deal with outstanding queries in the following days by correspondence.

When the Revenue auditor is satisfied that all queries are answered – and they will allow reasonable time to do so – the auditor will set out their findings to the taxpayer. This may occur by way of a phone call, correspondence or at a further meeting. The auditor will highlight any tax defaults that they have uncovered, provide calculations for these tax defaults and (if they believe it necessary) provide revised calculations for tax defaults set out in any disclosure letter. The auditor will also comment on whether they regard any disclosure letter to be a 'qualifying' one and whether they think that they have received full co-operation during the audit.

Acknowledging the fact that most taxpayers will want to have a Revenue audit concluded in as short a timeframe as possible, a 'three-month rule' applies. Revenue commit to updating the taxpayer/tax agent with the status of the audit and the likely timeframe for completion where the

[13] 2015 *Code of Practice*, Section 3.16.

[14] See Revenue's *Tax & Duty Manual*, Compliance – Audit And Other Compliance Interventions – Failure to Cooperate Fully with a Revenue Compliance Intervention (March 2015). Available on the Revenue website.

[15] 2015 *Code of Practice*, Section 3.16.

taxpayer has dealt with all outstanding queries and the audit remains open three months later. Where a taxpayer's entitlement to credits or refunds has been held up pending audit completion, then, unless there is a clear cause for delay in completing the audit, these credits or refunds cannot be delayed any further.

Once the calculations regarding all tax defaults and interest charges are agreed between the taxpayer and the Revenue auditor, the conversation about penalties will commence. The question of the taxpayer's intention – whether deliberate or careless – in relation to the tax defaults, and their level of co-operation, may become a subject of hot debate. In the majority of audits, however, the taxpayer will come to an agreement with the Revenue auditor on penalties. The following extract from our case study illustrates just how expensive tax defaults can be.

CASE STUDY: FOUR BLUE DUCKS

Following on from the example at **Section 8.2.3.2** above in relation to Four Blue Ducks' €3,000 underpayment of VAT for the VAT period May/June 2014, as this is a default in the category of 'careless behaviour without significant consequences', Jim has not submitted a qualifying disclosure letter and is not treated as having co-operated with the auditor, and a penalty of 20% would apply. Including the interest calculations above, Jim's €3,000 underpayment of VAT could result in him being charged €4,086 in total, being €3,000 unpaid VAT + €486 interest + €600 penalty.

(***Note***: with regard to the level of autonomy enjoyed by individual Revenue auditors, while they are the people attending the audit meetings, making decisions on which avenues of inquiry to pursue and gathering any information they feel is necessary, it is not the auditors who make the final decision as to whether an audit settlement is sufficient. All Revenue auditors are obliged to report their findings to Revenue senior management, who make that decision. There are instances, therefore, where the Revenue auditor's recommendation in relation to penalties is not accepted and they are instructed to revert to the taxpayer with a higher bill.)

The final step in the audit process is the payment of the audit settlement bill (whether at the time of the audit or by way of phased payment arrangement) and the issue of a letter of audit settlement by the Revenue auditor.

## 8.5 Disagreement over the Tax Defaults or Penalty Levels

It is entirely possible that the taxpayer will not agree with either the Revenue auditor's assessment of tax defaults (the calculations themselves or that they arise at all) or the penalty levels being proposed by the auditor.

The auditor will detail the tax defaults in written correspondence to the taxpayer. Where these are not accepted, the auditor will raise the necessary notices of assessment for the relevant tax heads. The taxpayer will then be required to appeal these assessments to the Tax Appeals Commission. This will allow an oral hearing before the Tax Appeals Commission, which may take many months to secure. In order to make a valid appeal to the Commission, the taxpayer must pay what *they* regard as the correct tax liabilities arising (if any).

Where the tax defaults are agreed but the penalty levels are not, the auditor will issue a Notice of Opinion to the taxpayer setting out the penalty levels. The taxpayer may decide to accept the penalty levels at that point, and to pay them; they can then secure a letter of audit settlement. If the taxpayer does not accept the penalty levels then, after 30 days the auditor may apply to the relevant court (District, Circuit or High Court, depending on the amounts involved) to secure a determination that these penalties are due. Securing a court ruling gives Revenue the right to pursue collection of these penalties in the usual way. (The office of the Collector-General (Revenue's tax collection division) has a variety of methods to pursue collection of unpaid tax/interest/penalty liabilities, including: seizure of assets; registration of judgement mortgages against taxpayer property; forced sale and notice of attachment against taxpayer bank accounts.)

## 8.6 Publication

Where a Revenue audit settlement includes the payment of penalties, then Revenue are obliged to publish the taxpayer's name, address and occupation, and details of the audit settlement, in a List of Tax Defaulters. Where penalties are court-determined, Revenue are also obliged to publish details of the Revenue audit settlement, whether or not the penalties have been paid.

There are exclusions from publication in the specific circumstances where:

- the taxpayer has presented a disclosure letter as part of the audit process and this has been accepted as a qualifying disclosure; *or*
- the total value of the settlement (unpaid taxes, interest and penalties) does not exceed €33,000; *or*
- the penalty level is 15% or less of the total amount of tax ultimately due.

Details of the audit settlement will be published in *Iris Oifigiúil* (the State gazette), which is available online and posted on the Revenue website. It is also quite typical to see reports of the names of tax defaulters in the general media. For many businesses, potential reputational damage is sufficient incentive for them to ensure that any relevant tax defaults are set out in a qualifying disclosure letter.

## 8.7 Prosecution

### 8.7.1 Taxpayers

Prosecution is usually reserved for revenue offences committed by the most serious and unyielding tax offenders – in addition to being required to pay all unpaid taxes, interest and penalties, those convicted are liable to a fine or imprisonment, or both. Again, a disclosure letter accepted as 'qualifying' will ensure that prosecution will not arise. Included in the 2015 *Code of Practice* is a specific list of offences for which Revenue "pursues a vigorous prosecution policy".

In recent years, Revenue have been active in pursuing prosecution cases. Examples include:

- Two directors of a company providing professional door staff were each sentenced to two years in prison on sample counts of failure to submit a corporation tax return, submission of incorrect VAT returns and knowingly producing incorrect invoices.
- A sole trade block-layer was sentenced to three years in prison, with two of those years suspended, for a total of 32 counts of failure to submit VAT returns and the annual payroll return (Form P35), as well as knowingly submitting incorrect VAT returns.
- A security firm and one of its directors were found guilty on the same six counts of submitting incorrect VAT returns and P35 forms, submitting incorrect information and failure to keep proper books and records. The company was fined €30,000 and the director was sentenced to three years in prison, with one of those years suspended.

### 8.7.2 Tax Agents

A tax agent may be charged with the revenue offence of:

> "Knowingly aiding, abetting, assisting, inciting or inducing another person to make or deliver knowingly or wilfully any incorrect return, statement or accounts in connection with any tax."[16]

Successful prosecution for this offence will also lead to the imposition of a fine and/or imprisonment. While this offence has been part of tax legislation for some time, it has not been generally pursued. According to the 2015 *Code of Practice,* charging tax agents with this offence (where appropriate) will now form part of Revenue's prosecution policy.

## 8.8 Some Typical Tax Defaults in Small and Medium-sized Businesses

There are certain issues that arise regularly during audits of small and medium-sized businesses. In addition to their general search for errors in

[16] Section 1078(2)(b) TCA 1997.

the calculation of tax liabilities, Revenue auditors are *likely* to be looking out for some or all of the tax defaults listed below.

(a) Payment of wages without payroll deduction to casual staff who should be on the business's payroll. To rectify this default, payroll taxes will be collectable, though these may be somewhat offset by reduced taxes on profits, as these payroll taxes will become a taxable deduction in calculating corporation tax/income tax (see **Example 8.1**).

EXAMPLE 8.1: PAYROLL TAXES NOT APPLIED TO CASUAL STAFF

For a part-time cleaner who is paid cash of €10 an hour and works 10 hours per week, the €100 weekly payment will be regarded as having been paid 'net' or after tax, meaning that the amount must be grossed-up using the employee's personal tax rate and then subjected to payroll taxes. Additionally, employer's PRSI must be paid on the taxable amount.

If we assume the cleaner is subject to a 20% income tax rate, 3% USC charge and 0% employee PRSI rate, then the cleaner has an effective tax rate of 23%. The payroll taxes arising on that €100 payment will be as follows:

€100 divided by 77% (100 – 23) = €129.87, which is the amount subject to payroll taxes

€129.87 × 23% (cleaner's effective tax rate) = €29.87

€129.87 × 8.5% (lower employer PRSI rate) = €11.04

Total payroll taxes payable = €40.91

(***Note***: tax credits were ignored for the purposes of these calculations.)

If the business paid corporation tax for the year when this payroll tax arose, it should get an offset of overpaid corporation tax against this liability. This offset arises because the company is entitled to a deduction in its profit and loss account for the additional payroll taxes payable. The amount offset will be €40.91 × the trading corporation tax rate of 12.5% = €5.11, so that the net amount due to Revenue on the €100 weekly payment will be €40.91 – €5.11 = €35.80.

If the business is a sole trade, meaning that the taxable profits are subject to income taxes and charges, then the amount offset will be higher, i.e. €40.91 × owner's marginal tax rate.

(b) Payments without payroll deduction to individuals who style themselves as 'consultants' or 'contractors' to the taxpayer business but who, in fact, should be regarded as employees of the business.

Similar calculations will be required as in (a) above and the relevant tax rates will be determined by the individual's personal tax status.

(c) Payment of the owner/director's personal expenses from the business's bank account or using the business's credit card. Only expenses that are wholly and exclusively incurred for the purposes of the business may be paid by the business. Additional payroll taxes will arise (similar to the calculations at (a) above) and increased corporation tax may also arise as the business should not take a deduction for these expenses in assessing taxable profits. For a sole trade business, the additional taxes will be limited to income taxes and charges only.

(d) Payments of travelling expenses, to the owner/director or any employee, that are not supported by invoices or do not fall within the civil service mileage and subsistence rates. Alternatively, payment to employees of any personal expenses that have not been subjected to the rules for payroll tax on benefits in kind. Similar calculations will be required as in (a) above.

(e) Suppression of turnover, e.g. by treating some sales as 'cash sales' and excluding them from the business's declared sales figures. This default will generate additional VAT liabilities and also additional taxable profits/reduced losses.

### Example 8.2: Multiple Tax Implications of Suppressed Sales

A business has undeclared sales of €10,000 where the standard VAT rate of 23% applies. On the basis that it is too late to charge VAT on the sales, the sales figure of €10,000 will be treated as inclusive of VAT at 23%. The VAT liabilities are calculated as €1,869.92, being €10,000 divided by 1.23 and multiplied by 0.23. The VAT-exclusive sales amount of €8,130.08 (€10,000 – €1,869.92) will also potentially generate either corporation tax liabilities of €1,016.26 (applying the 12.5% trading corporation tax rate) or income tax liabilities of up to €4,471.55 (applying the maximum income tax, USC and PRSI rates totalling 55%).

(f) Applying the incorrect VAT rate where the business supplies a combination of goods/services that attract different VAT rates. An example of this, which often causes a problem within the food industry, is the supply of a 'meal deal' that includes a soft drink. While the food element of the 'meal deal' may be subject to a VAT rate at 0% or 9%, the soft drink will be subject to VAT at 23%. Often the business will have treated the entire 'meal deal' as subject to the 0% or 9% rate. In this case, the value of the soft drink must be isolated from the value of the entire 'meal deal' and the difference between the VAT rate applied and the 23% VAT rate actually applicable paid over.

EXAMPLE 8.3: INCORRECT VAT TREATMENT ON A MULTIPLE SUPPLY

A pizza delivery business sells a 'meal deal' for €8.45 that includes pizza and a can of a soft drink, and the business incorrectly treats the entire supply as inclusive of a 9% VAT charge.

If the value of the soft drink including VAT is €0.75, then the VAT charge on the soft drink should be €0.14 (€0.75 divided by 1.23 and multiplied by 0.23) and the charge on the pizza should be €0.64. As the taxpayer has only returned a sales VAT amount of €0.70 on the entire 'meal deal', an additional VAT charge of €0.08 will arise.

(g) Where a business uses a cash register or EPOS system that is coded incorrectly so that incorrect VAT rates are applied to sales of goods/services. Similar calculations to those set out at (f) above will be required.

(h) Including non-deductible VAT charges in the purchases VAT claims, e.g. VAT charges arising on employee entertainment, purchase or hire of cars, or expenses incurred in relation to a VAT-exempt element of the business. The total value of the incorrectly claimed purchases VAT must be repaid to Revenue.

(For other types of common VAT errors and more detailed information regarding employee benefits, see **Chapters 4** and **5**.)

While the focus of this chapter has thus far been on Revenue audits, there are other types of Revenue intervention that have different consequences. The implications of these other types of intervention are set out below in **Section 8.9**, as is some information on Revenue investigations. Revenue investigations arise where Revenue are of the opinion that serious tax offences have taken place that may lead to prosecution. The conduct of non-audit interventions and investigations is also covered by the *Code of Practice for Revenue Audit and other Compliance Interventions*, updated in November 2015.[17]

## 8.9 Opportunity to Make Unprompted Qualifying Disclosure

The most important aspect to note in relation to Revenue interventions that are neither Revenue audits nor Revenue investigations is that a taxpayer should be entitled to make an '*unprompted* qualifying disclosure' to Revenue *after* the inquiry has commenced. By contrast, where a Revenue audit letter

[17] Both this *Code of Practice* and its previous versions are available on Revenue's website.

has been issued, any qualifying disclosure subsequently made will be treated as a '*prompted* qualifying disclosure'. The significance of the distinction between prompted and unprompted disclosures is in the huge variation in penalty levels. Set out in **Table 8.2** below are the penalties that will arise where an 'unprompted qualifying disclosure' is made and full co-operation is given. (Again, these relate to tax defaults that occurred on or after 24 December 2008.) For the purposes of comparison, the penalties applicable to 'prompted qualifying disclosure' with full co-operation are also set out:

### Table 8.2: Penalties for a Qualifying Disclosure with Full Co-Operation

| Category of Default | Unprompted Qualifying Disclosure and Full Co-operation | Prompted Qualifying Disclosure and Full Co-operation |
|---|---|---|
| Deliberate behaviour | 10% | 50% |
| Careless behaviour with significant consequences | 5% | 20% |
| Careless behaviour without significant consequences | 3% | 10% |

There are various types of Revenue intervention that are not treated as Revenue audits. The first piece of Revenue correspondence or phone call in a non-audit Revenue intervention typically includes an explicit statement that the opportunity to make an 'unprompted qualifying disclosure' is still available.

Just as with a prompted qualifying disclosure letter, a taxpayer wishing to submit an unprompted qualifying disclosure letter may secure a 60-day period in which to prepare this letter. To do so, a written notice of intention must be given to Revenue. As one might expect, if either an audit letter has issued or the taxpayer has been notified of a Revenue investigation into their tax affairs, the opportunity to make an unprompted qualifying disclosure letter is no longer available.

Information discovered by Revenue during these non-audit interventions may trigger a subsequent audit or investigation. In a situation where tax defaults have been highlighted and it is clear that Revenue's next step will be to issue an audit letter, taxpayers would be well advised to submit a qualifying disclosure letter immediately, before the issue of the audit letter, so that the disclosure letter will be treated as unprompted.

Discussed below are various types of non-audit interventions that do not constitute Revenue audits or investigations.

### 8.9.1 Aspect Queries and Assurance Checks

These are sometimes known as 'desk audits' and comprise detailed inquiries on a specific aspect of a tax return or requests for back-up information on a specific tax issue. These interventions occur because Revenue consider that there is a risk of tax loss arising as a result of a specific transaction or claim in a specific period(s). The inquiries are generally carried out by phone or correspondence, and may or may not involve meeting with a Revenue official.

An aspect query may involve a request to a taxpayer to prove entitlement to a specific tax relief, e.g. a claim for accelerated capital allowances on the purchase of energy-efficient equipment.

A typical example of an assurance check would include queries where discrepancies arise between various tax returns submitted by a taxpayer, e.g. where there is no match between the annual payroll liabilities noted in the Form P35 payroll return and the sum of that year's monthly Form P30s. Another example would be where a taxpayer has claimed a VAT refund that is outside the normal trading pattern; in this case the Revenue official may require copies of the relevant purchase invoices before they will authorise payment of the refund.

The taxpayer will usually be given at least 30 days to provide the required information.

### 8.9.2 Unannounced Visits

Revenue officials will not normally arrive at a taxpayer's business premises unannounced. However, they do periodically carry out 'spot checks' where, for example, on a given day they will visit all the business premises on a particular city street or in a town or village. Typically, the issues that they are looking at include: the accuracy of cash registers or EPOS systems, the standard of record-keeping in the business, or the identity and employment status of all staff present in the business on the day. Alternatively, an unannounced visit may signal the start of a Revenue investigation, in which case a letter notifying the taxpayer of a Revenue investigation will be handed over at the beginning of the visit. It is critical for the taxpayer (or tax agent) to clarify the type of intervention at that time.

The Revenue official will want to speak to the owner or manager of the business, and will explain the purpose of the visit. It would not be wise to have a junior member of staff answering Revenue inquiries, so if the owner/manager is not available, the taxpayer (or tax agent) could consider requesting a postponement of the visit. The Revenue official will have various questions and may take copies of tax records. A clear note of the discussions and a note of the information copied should be taken by the taxpayer/staff member.

As long as the visit is not part of a Revenue investigation, the taxpayer continues to have the opportunity to make an unprompted qualifying disclosure.

### 8.9.3 *Profiling Interviews*

We referred previously to Revenue's use of the REAP system to select taxpayers for interventions. There are times when REAP will highlight a particular taxpayer as showing increased risk of tax default, but instead of immediately proceeding to audit, a Revenue official will decide to interview the taxpayer/company directors. The official will write to the taxpayer setting out the risk areas that they wish to discuss and the interview will usually take place 21 working days after the issue of the letter. The taxpayer may make an unprompted qualifying disclosure before or at the time of the interview.

The taxpayer should receive a letter from Revenue within 14 working days of the interview noting the outcome of the interview.

### 8.9.4 *Sectoral or Industry Reviews*

Periodically, Revenue announce a review of a specific sector/industry in which a pattern of unpaid taxes has emerged. Recent sectoral reviews include: the 'contractors project' (referred to in **Chapter 5**), which is aimed at individual consultants operating through personal service companies with often only one customer/client, and the construction industry. Prior to this, Revenue focused on the employed/self-employed status of medical locums who were treated as self-employed contractors and paid gross without payroll deduction (also discussed in **Chapter 5**).

Where a sectoral/industry review is announced in the general media, a taxpayer operating in that area will continue to have the opportunity to make an unprompted qualifying disclosure, assuming that they have not yet received an audit letter. In the situation where the sectoral/industry review is ongoing, the importance of the taxpayer securing a 60-day period to prepare an unprompted qualifying disclosure (as long as they notify Revenue in writing) cannot be overstated.

## 8.10 Revenue Investigations

Revenue investigations are a more serious matter as they arise in situations where Revenue suspect serious tax offences have taken place. A letter notifying a taxpayer of an impending Revenue investigation will clearly state that the intervention is an investigation. It is possible for a Revenue audit or non-audit intervention to become an investigation where information discovered during the earlier intervention merits it. The notification letter will outline the specific tax period(s) under scrutiny and the matter being investigated. An investigation may be finalised by way of financial settlement, but there is also the possibility that it will lead to criminal prosecution. Prosecution for tax evasion now comes with a recommendation of a three-year custodial sentence.

While a taxpayer under investigation may make a disclosure of tax defaults, this will not be treated as a qualifying disclosure and none of the benefits of making a qualifying disclosure will apply. This means the penalty level will be 100% of the tax default, and both publication and prosecution may also arise. During the course of the investigation, the taxpayer may be formally cautioned by the Revenue official, who will say the following:

> "You are not obliged to say anything unless you wish to do so, but whatever you say will be taken down in writing and may be given in evidence."

A taxpayer who is faced with this situation would be well advised to speak to their lawyer.

## 8.11 Other Methods of Dealing with Errors in Tax Returns

Revenue have stated that they wish to encourage self-review of tax returns as part of good compliance practice by taxpayers. To this end, there are a number of ways of correcting errors in tax returns that may attract low penalties or no penalties at all. ***Note:*** in these situations statutory interest continues to apply.

### *8.11.1 Innocent Error*

No penalties will arise where a taxpayer can satisfy Revenue that they have made an innocent error in the preparation of their tax returns. Factors that Revenue will consider in this regard include:

- the materiality of the error relative to the overall value of tax payments made by the taxpayer;
- whether they are satisfied that the taxpayer keeps good books and records;
- whether the taxpayer takes reasonable care in preparing their tax returns;
- the taxpayer's compliance record; and
- the frequency of the error.

The unpaid tax and statutory interest must be paid in full.

Where the error is not regarded by Revenue as 'innocent', the disclosure will be treated as an unprompted qualifying disclosure and be subject to the lower level of penalties noted at **Section 8.9** above.

### *8.11.2 Self-correction*

In general, a taxpayer may make a 'self-correction' adjustment to an income/corporation tax return for a period of up to 12 months after the due date for filing the return. This means, for example, that a corporation tax return for the accounting year ended 31 December 2014 may be the subject of self-correction up to no later than 23 September 2016. Different deadlines apply for self-correction of VAT and payroll tax returns.

Note that, in some limited circumstances, the general deadline of 12 months after the return filing deadline may be extended to four years from the end of the chargeable period.[18]

In order for an adjustment to a return to qualify as self-correction, the taxpayer must set out in writing to Revenue details of the unpaid tax and the statutory interest charges. The total liabilities must then be paid in full, though a phased payment schedule may be put in place at Revenue's discretion. No penalties should arise. As with a claim of 'innocent error', self-correction will not apply where Revenue assess the taxpayer as having behaved deliberately in triggering the tax default.

For cases of self-correction in relation to VAT, where the taxpayer prepares VAT returns on a bi-monthly/quarterly/half-yearly basis and there is a net underpayment of VAT of no more than €6,000 for a VAT period, this underpayment may be included in the next VAT period return without notifying Revenue and without the need to pay interest.

Once the time limit for making a self-correction has elapsed, it is still possible for a taxpayer to make an unprompted qualifying disclosure, assuming no notice of audit or investigation has issued, though this will attract some level of penalties.

### *8.11.3 Unprompted Qualifying Disclosure*

Taxpayers can avail of the benefits of an unprompted qualifying disclosure at any time as long as no audit or investigation of their tax affairs is underway. No prior contact from any Revenue official is required to make such a disclosure.

### *8.11.4 Technical Adjustment*

There is recognition of the fact that Revenue and a taxpayer may have differing interpretations of the tax legislation and/or how it is applied. While there is scope for correcting, without penalties, a difference in interpretation that leads to a lower tax liability having been paid by the taxpayer, Revenue expect that the taxpayer will have taken 'due care' in adopting that position and that the misinterpretation was not based on *deliberate behaviour*. The more significant the amounts of tax that are in play, the more 'due care' will be expected.

[18] Section 959V TCA 1997.

Where legal precedent exists (including Revenue guidance, case law and published decisions of the Tax Appeals Commission) that clearly sets out the correct interpretation of the issue, Revenue will not treat the unpaid tax as a 'technical adjustment' and will demand payment of penalties.

Statutory interest will be applied to the unpaid tax liabilities, in any event.

## 8.12 No Loss of Revenue

There are instances where, despite the fact that a taxpayer did not pay a tax liability, Revenue do not suffer a loss. An example of this would be the failure of a VATable business to charge VAT to a VAT-registered business. In the normal course, the supplier would include the sales VAT charge in their VAT return (resulting in a tax payment to Revenue) and the customer would include the purchases VAT charge in their VAT return (resulting in a tax refund/reduction of the same amount from Revenue). The net position would be nil.

As long as certain conditions are met, Revenue may not insist on the payment of the unpaid tax liability, but will charge reduced penalties. Their rationale for doing so is that the integrity of the tax system must be maintained. Some of the conditions are:

- the unpaid tax must be either VAT or relevant contracts tax (RCT) – in exceptional circumstances, a claim for 'no loss of revenue' may be considered for other tax heads; *and*
- the taxpayer must satisfy Revenue that it has suffered no loss; *and*
- the claim for 'no loss of revenue' must be made in writing, in the form of a qualifying disclosure, and accompanied by relevant supporting documentation; *and*
- the taxpayer must have a good compliance history and there must have been no *deliberate behaviour.*

The *Code of Practice* states that where there is a mismatch in timing between the tax payment due date from one taxpayer and the tax refund due to another taxpayer, interest will arise for the period of the temporary loss of revenue.

It is possible that no penalties at all will arise if a 'no loss of revenue' claim can be justified as part of a claim for 'innocent error' or 'technical adjustment'.

Otherwise, there is a separate schedule setting out the penalty rates that apply where a 'no loss of revenue claim' is accepted. The penalties range from 3% to 9% and fixed amount caps can operate to limit these penalties. For example, the penalty rate applicable to a no loss of revenue claim where there has been an unprompted qualifying disclosure and full co-operation is 3% of the unpaid tax, but it is capped at a maximum of €5,000.

Further details on these penalty rates and the issues set out above may be found in the 2015 *Code of Practice for Revenue Audit and other Compliance Interventions.*

## Chapter 9

# BUSINESS STRUCTURES FOR EXPANSION AND THEIR TAX IMPLICATIONS



In **Chapter 1**, we looked at how to determine the best structure for a new business in its early days. For some businesses, a more formal or complex structure is required from the start. An ambitious entrepreneur may decide to incorporate a company and operate through it from day one. Alternatively, she may consider operating two or more different businesses, and, for commercial reasons, have these operate via separate companies. These separate companies could each be directly owned by her or she could establish a group structure. Generally, the more complicated the structure, the higher the administration and compliance costs, so many entrepreneurs will adopt a simpler structure at the outset and introduce more complexity as the need arises.

In this chapter, we will look at three different scenarios in which businesses have been operational for some time and the business owners realise that a more complex structure is required. The scenarios are: the incorporation of a sole trade/partnership; the creation of a group structure; and the introduction of key employees as shareholders.

## 9.1 Incorporation of a Sole Trade or Partnership

It is entirely possible to incorporate a company and use this as the business structure from the beginning, and in **Chapter 1** we reviewed the different tax implications that arise from doing just that. But what if, after a few years of trading as a sole trade or partnership, the business owner(s) decide that a company structure is required? **Figure 9.1** below shows the ownership of the business before and after its incorporation. Note that, after incorporation, the business owners become shareholders of the new company that now owns the business.

FIGURE 9.1: BUSINESS OWNERS BECOME SHAREHOLDERS OF THE NEW BUSINESS OWNER (THE COMPANY)

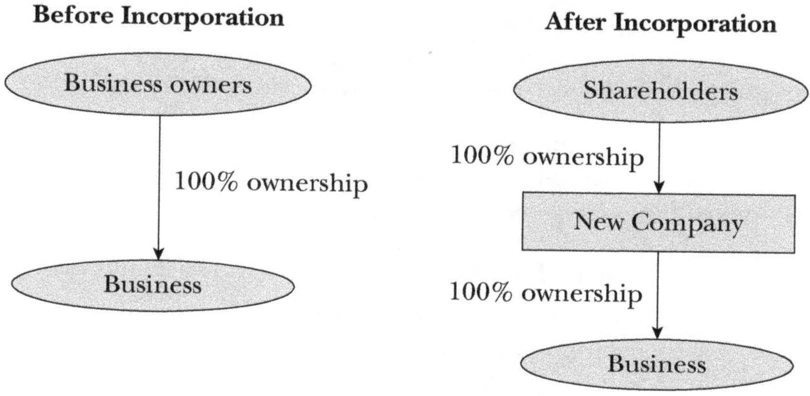


The owners can take either of **two approaches**, depending on the circumstances:

1. they can sell the business to the company for cash; *or*
2. they can transfer the business to the company in exchange for shares in the company.

### *9.1.1 Some Comments on Valuing a Business*

Before we present an overview of the different tax implications of these two approaches, we will look briefly at an important practical issue that arises in both cases: the valuation of the business. A key point to note is that as the business is being transferred between 'connected parties', i.e. the business owners and the company that they control, then, under tax rules, the sale must take place at market value. In these circumstances, 'market value' is often difficult to establish – in relation to capital gains tax (CGT), the tax legislation defines market value as the "price which those assets might reasonably be expected to fetch on a sale in the open market".[1] But of course, the issue here is that this transaction is not going to take place on the open market, so unless a professional advisor is consulted, there will be no external assessment of the business.

[1] Section 548 of the Taxes Consolidation Act 1997 (TCA 1997).

**(*Note:* the following paragraphs set out a basic framework for valuing a business, but this is not something that business owners can do for themselves. In all cases requiring a business valuation, an external valuation should be secured.)**[2]

As the assessment of market value is difficult in these circumstances, and there is no one set method of establishing this valuation, we will look at one possible approach.

The first step is to look at the current value of all assets and liabilities of the business. While some of these assets may be worth their face value only, e.g. cash (a deposit balance of €20,000 is generally worth €20,000), other assets may have increased/decreased in value since their acquisition (e.g. property or equipment) and formal valuation reports may be required for them. A business's liabilities and potential liabilities (e.g. a threat of litigation) must also be assessed. Once the current values of all of the business's assets and liabilities have been assessed, this will produce a minimum valuation for the business, as we can usually say that the value of the business is worth at least the value of its net assets (its assets less its liabilities).

The next step is to look at an 'earnings/profit' method of valuing the business, i.e. reviewing the annual profits for the previous years of trading, averaging these figures, and then taking a multiple of them to produce a valuation. The question, of course, is how do we average and what multiple of earnings should be applied? This is where a professional expert's experience will come into play, and why, if you ask three different advisors for a business valuation, you may get three different valuations (or more, if one of the valuations is prepared on the basis of a valuation range!).

In relation to averaging, the two methods most often used are:

- Simple average, e.g. the annual profit of the five previous years divided by five.
- Weighted average, e.g. the average annual profit is weighted towards the more recent years, to reflect the fact that the business is more profitable latterly. A five-year weighted average for the years 2009 to 2013 could be calculated as follows:

$$\frac{(2013 \text{ profit} \times 5) + (2012 \text{ profit} \times 4) + (2011 \text{ profit} \times 3) + (2010 \text{ profit} \times 2) + (2009 \text{ profit} \times 1)}{15}$$

(***Note:*** there are other methods of calculating weighted averages.)

As for the multiple to be applied to this average annual profit, this will depend on the strength, profitability and market share of the business and the market in which it operates. Within the Irish private business sphere, we most typically see profit multiples in the range of three to eight. Note that certain profit multiples may be regarded as the 'norm' within particular industries; however, each business should be valued by reference to its

[2] For more information on business valuations see *The Valuation of Businesses and Shares* by Des Peelo (2nd Edition, Chartered Accountants Ireland, 2016).

own circumstances. This requirement to focus on the particularities of the business itself in assessing the appropriate profit multiple also arises in relation to the annual profit figures that are averaged and subject to these profit multiples. It is quite typical, for example, to drill down into annual profit figures and make adjustments for any unusual items of income or expenditure in any of the relevant trading years.

Assuming that the business is trading reasonably well, the 'earnings/profit' method of valuation will often produce a higher figure than the current value of the business's net assets, and the difference here is treated as the business's '**goodwill**'. In other words, if the current valuation of a business's net assets is €700,000 and the 'earnings/profit' method of valuation produces a figure of €1,000,000, then the €300,000 difference is the goodwill figure. This is not usually recorded in the business's accounts as an asset, but it does exist and is generated by the fact that the business and its relationships with customers and suppliers are already established.

We have noted that, where a business is being transferred to a company owned by the business owners, the business is not put on the open market and the business owners should secure an external valuation of the business from their advisors. We will see below that a tax advantage can arise to the business owners on this transaction and so there may be a temptation to over-value the business. Note, however, that while Revenue will not give advance clearance or pre-approval to a business valuation, they can certainly query and test the valuation *after* the transfer has taken place. If they take the view that the business has been over-valued, then significant tax liabilities, penalties and interest may arise. Revenue may query any such transaction as part of their usual audit/inquiry programme, but they may also focus on these transactions as part of a targeted sectoral project. An example of this was the Dublin Region 2013 programme that focused on the transfer of all or part of the business of medical practitioners into companies. In that instance, Revenue specifically stated that they believed that many of these businesses were valued at a "highly inflated and unrealistic price".[3]

We look now at the differing CGT implications of the two methods of transferring a sole trade/partnership business into a company. While in general CGT is outside the scope of this book, we consider it here purely in the context of these specific transactions. We will also briefly refer to other tax implications that may arise.

### *9.1.2 Tax Implications of Selling a Business to a Company*

The first step for business owners selling their business to a company is for the business owners to incorporate a new company, with the business owners as shareholders. As the company will soon own the business,

[3] Letter from Revenue Dublin Region to Irish Tax Institute, 7 May 2013, "Tax Affairs of Medical Consultants". Available at the Tax Policy and Practice section of www.taxinstitute.ie.

the business owners – soon to be shareholders – must make a decision as to whether they will continue to own the business in the same ownership ratio as previously, i.e. if two people own the business on a 50/50 basis, does this mean that each of them will own 50% of the shares in the new company? It is possible to change this ownership ratio when making a straightforward sale of the business to a company.

### *9.1.2.1 Capital Gains Tax*

The sale of the business will be treated as a disposal for CGT purposes, which means that a CGT computation must be prepared along the following lines for any assets subject to CGT:

| | € |
|---|---|
| Sales proceeds | Market value of assets chargeable to CGT |
| Less: | Purchase price of business (if any) |
| Less: | Associated costs of acquiring business |
| Less: | Associated sale costs |
| Chargeable gain/loss | Profit subject to CGT/capital loss |

Where a chargeable gain arises, CGT at the current rate of 33% will be payable by the business owners.

We commented above on a business's market value, which will represent the 'sales proceeds' for this sale. The purchase price for the business refers to a situation where a sole trader/partnership bought the business from a previous owner. Where the business was started by the sole trader/partnership themselves, then no deduction will arise. The associated costs of acquiring the business (if relevant) would typically refer to stamp duty and the fees of professional advisors – lawyers, accountants, business agents, etc. Likewise, the associated costs of sale would refer to the fees of professionals providing advice on the sale of the business to the company.

The purchase of the business by the company must be funded by the company, which will owe the business owners an amount equal to the 'sales proceeds' or market value of the business. If one of the business's assets is a large amount of cash, then this cash may be transferred to the company along with all the other business assets and may be used by the company to pay the business owners. However, it is more typical for the owners to transfer sufficient cash to keep the business fully functioning (its working capital) and to retain any 'excess' cash. In this situation, the company may take out a bank loan to fund the purchase price and/or create a loan account balance in the company's accounts in favour of the business owners, now shareholders. The loan account balance can then be paid off by the company as and when the company's finances allow. In general, *no tax implications* arise on the repayment of these shareholder loans, as the tax implications of the sale of the business have been dealt with at the time of the sale, when the business owners' CGT liabilities/capital losses are calculated. **Example 9.2** below involves part-payment for a business by way of a shareholder's loan account balance.

### Example 9.1: Company Pays for a New Business

A business owner, Patrick, sells his business to his new company, MountPatrick Ltd, for the market value of €1,000,000 and after taking various deductions into account, this triggers a CGT liability of €220,000. This means that Patrick owes Revenue €220,000 and his company owes him €1,000,000. MountPatrick Ltd has available cash of €150,000 and borrows another €150,000, so, at the time that the sale closes, the company pays Patrick €300,000, the majority of which he uses to pay Revenue. The company still owes Patrick €700,000 but does not have the cash to pay this in the short term, so it creates a loan account balance of €700,000 in Patrick's favour. Over the following years, the company pays off this loan in various instalments as and when cash flow allows.

Of course, the key practical point here is that there must be sufficient cash available (either from company resources or bank borrowings) to pay Patrick at least the amount of his CGT liability, as this must be paid within months of the transaction. The fact that Patrick will not receive some of the sales proceeds for a number of years does not generally impact on the due date for the CGT payment.

The straightforward sale of the business to the company will trigger a CGT liability (at the current rate of 33%); however, such a sale has the benefit of generating a cash payment to, or creating a loan account balance in favour of, the business owners/shareholders. This loan account balance may entitle the shareholders to certain future profits of the company, by way of loan repayments, up to the value of the outstanding loan. If we compare the CGT rate with the potential income tax, USC and PRSI rates (of up to 55%) chargeable on the taxable profits of sole traders/partners, we can see that this once-off transaction can crystallise some significant tax benefits for the business owners.

### *9.1.3 Transfer of Business to Company in Exchange for Shares in the Company*

In the introductory comments to this section, we noted that there are two methods of incorporating a business. We reviewed the first method, i.e. the sale of the business to the company, in **Section 9.1.2** above. In this section, we will look at the alternative method of incorporating a business, which involves the swap of the business for shares in the new company that will own the business.

### *9.1.3.1 Capital Gains Tax*

When incorporating a sole trade or partnership, an alternative approach involves the *deferral* (not the elimination) of some or all of the CGT liabilities that would arise on the straightforward sale of the business to the company. This deferral of CGT liabilities is subject to a number of conditions, including:

- all of the assets of the business must be transferred to the company (though some cash may be excluded);
- the business must be transferred as a 'going concern'; *and*
- at least some of the consideration for the transfer must be company shares, which are issued to the person(s) transferring the business.[4]

The implications of deferring some or all of the potential CGT liabilities is that, in the future, these deferred liabilities could be triggered if the company were sold *and* the sale price was at least the value placed on the shares when the business was originally transferred into the company.

The first point to note is that, if the business owner wishes to rely on this CGT deferral, then the ownership of the business before transfer, when it is directly owned, and after transfer, when it is indirectly owned, must match. This means that if the business was owned, say, by a partnership on a 50/50 basis, then each of the partners must hold 50% of the company shares after the business is transferred into the company. This ownership match is not required in a straightforward sale of the business to the company, as set out in **Section 9.1.2** above.

Secondly, it is entirely possible for the business owners to retain significant business cash balances, but if they do so this will reduce the effectiveness of the CGT deferral. An important question here is the treatment of business creditors; if the company takes these over when it is taking over all the assets of the business, then this is a cash benefit for the business owners who no longer have the obligation to pay these creditors. A strict reading of the conditions for the CGT deferral would conclude that where a company takes over business creditors, this would also reduce the effectiveness of the CGT deferral. However, a Revenue concession allows bona fide trade creditor balances to be transferred with the business while not requiring that the value of these creditors reduce the amount of the CGT deferral. These trade creditor balances must relate to previous supplies of goods or services to the business being transferred and cannot include bank loans or tax liabilities taken over by the company.[5]

Our case study example below sets out the significantly different tax implications of incorporating a business by the two methods noted, i.e. the sale of the business to a new company versus the 'swap' of the business for shares in a new company.

[4] Section 600 TCA 1997.
[5] Revenue *eBrief* 111/2014.

## CASE STUDY: FOUR BLUE DUCKS/BLUE LACHA LTD (JIM AND CATHY DECIDE TO INCORPORATE)

Husband-and-wife team Jim and Cathy decided to start their business Four Blue Ducks as a sole trade owned by Jim, with Cathy employed by the business. Some of the reasons for this included: Jim's ability to reduce his income tax liability by relying on Start Your Own Business relief; Jim and Cathy's understanding that they would need to use all business profits to fund their own lifestyle in the early years; and the lower compliance costs associated with operating as a sole trade.

After the difficult early years of developing the business, they were pleased to see that the café had started to generate 'excess' profits, i.e. profits that they did not need to support their lifestyle. They were also interested in expanding their food production to create new income streams, supplying other food businesses/small supermarkets, etc. Jim and Cathy had spent some time on these ideas and were convinced that, with third-party investment, they could create a modern food production facility in a new premises near their home in Kildare. When their accountant outlined the potential of the Employment Investment and Incentive Scheme (EIIS) to facilitate that third-party investment, and noted that operation of this scheme required investment in a company, they decided that it was time to incorporate the business.

Jim and Cathy sat down with their tax advisor, Maeve, to look at the assets and liabilities of the business, and to discuss the tricky concepts of market value and goodwill. Maeve produced the following figures:

| | **Current Value €** | **Original Cost €** |
|---|---|---|
| Goodwill | 220,000 | – |
| Tenant's fixtures | 40,000 | 50,000 |
| Stock | 8,500 | |
| Cash in current account | 12,000 | |
| Cash on deposit | 25,000 | |
| Trade creditors | (7,500) | |
| Current value of all business assets | 298,000 | |

The next question was what was the best approach to take: a straight sale of the business to a company or the transfer of the business to a company in exchange for shares? Maeve advised that the following tax implications could flow from the two approaches.

**(a) Sale of the Business to the Company**

Jim and Cathy were happy that the business's ongoing cash requirement would be covered by the €12,000 balance in the current account, so the deposit balance of €25,000 could be retained by Jim and used to part-pay his CGT liability. They also wished to have the company take on the trade creditors of €7,500. This would mean that Jim would be selling his business for €273,000 (current value of all assets of €298,000 less €25,000 cash on deposit).

Jim's net chargeable gains are €210,000 – on the goodwill and tenant's fixtures – on which he has an estimated CGT liability of approximately €69,000 (at the current rate of 33%). This would mean that the company would have to pay Jim at least €44,000 in the short term, so that he could pay his CGT bill of approximately €69,000. Once this €44,000 amount was paid by the company to Jim, he would have a loan account balance of €229,000 in his favour that could be repaid over the following years as the company's finances allowed.

**(b) Transfer of the Business to the Company in Exchange for Shares in the Company**

The alternative approach was to transfer the business in exchange for shares and cash, and to rely on the CGT deferral as set out above at **Section 9.1.3.1**. Again, Jim and Cathy wished to retain the €25,000 cash on deposit owned by the business.

Maeve set out two scenarios in relation to cash balances for Jim from this transaction:

(i) in exchange for €70,000 cash plus company shares; and
(ii) in exchange for €150,000 cash plus company shares.

*(i) In exchange for €70,000 cash plus company shares*

In this first scenario, the business would be transferred for €70,000 cash and shares in the new company. As we saw above, the net chargeable gains were calculated at €210,000. On the basis that all conditions for CGT deferral are met, the deferral would be calculated as:

$$\frac{\text{Consideration taken in the form of shares}}{\text{Total value of consideration}} \times \text{Chargeable gain}$$

$$\frac{€203{,}000}{€280{,}500} \times €210{,}000 = €151{,}978$$

On the basis that the €25,000 cash on deposit is retained and all other business assets and liabilities are transferred in exchange for

€70,000 in cash and shares in the new company, approximately €152,000 of the chargeable gain arising may be deferred, leaving approximately €58,000 of a gain on which CGT would be payable within months. In this scenario, Jim would have a CGT liability of approximately €19,000, which would be covered by the €25,000 cash on deposit he has retained. Jim would also have a €70,000 loan account balance in his favour, which could be repaid as the company's finances allow.

Some or all of the CGT on the deferred gain of approximately €152,000 could become payable in the future if Jim sold the company. The amount that could become payable would depend on the value of that future sale.

*(ii) In exchange for €150,000 cash plus company shares*

To illustrate the impact of including a higher cash payment as part of the exchange, Maeve also set out the tax implications if Jim were to transfer the business for €150,000 cash and shares in the new company. The CGT deferral would now be calculated as:

$$\frac{€123{,}000}{€280{,}500} \times €210{,}000 = €92{,}086$$

In this situation, €92,000 approximately of the gain would be deferred, leaving €118,000 subject to CGT of approximately €39,000. Jim would have a €150,000 loan account balance in his favour, at least €14,000 of which would have to be repaid in the short term to cover the balance of his CGT liability.

Some or all of the CGT on the deferred gain of approximately €92,000 could become payable in the future if Jim sold the company. The amount that could become payable would depend on the value of that future sale.

In considering how they wished to proceed, Maeve encouraged Jim and Cathy to focus on two fundamentals. The first of these was tax, i.e. the tax costs they were prepared to absorb in order to incorporate the business, and the tax benefit of creating a loan account balance in Jim's favour for the future. Jim could see that as he and Cathy were now paying income taxes and charges at the rate of 52%, a strong loan account balance in his favour could reduce the amount of income taxes and charges they would pay for some years to come. He was also of the view that the deferred tax liability might never arise as it could only trigger if he sold the company.

The second fundamental that Maeve discussed with Jim and Cathy were the realities of looking for EIIS investment into a company with a large shareholder loan balance and the fact that this could dissuade potential EIIS investors. (We will see Jim and Cathy's approach to EIIS investment in **Chapter 10**.)

Ultimately, Jim and Cathy decided to transfer the business into a new company called Blue Lacha Ltd in exchange for a shareholder loan balance of €70,000 and shares. Note that as this transaction constituted the transfer of a business in exchange for shares, the shares of the new company, Blue Lacha Ltd, were all issued to Jim. This ensured that ownership pre- and post-transfer matched, i.e. Jim previously owned 100% of the sole trade and now owns 100% of the company shares.

### *9.1.4 Other Tax Implications of the Transfer*

#### *9.1.4.1 Stamp Duty*

As a general rule, the sale or transfer of the business will be subject to stamp duty at the rates applicable to commercial property, currently 2%. However, it may be possible to avoid stamp duty on the transfer of some assets, i.e. those that are not listed in a written document recording the transfer and which are said to pass 'by delivery'. Specific stamp duty advice should be secured in this regard.

#### *9.1.4.2 VAT on Transfer of Business*

There is a specific exemption from a charge to VAT on the transfer of a business, as long as the assets transferred constitute an 'undertaking' or part of an 'undertaking' that is capable of being operated on an independent basis.[6]

#### *9.1.4.3 Impact on Assessment of Sole Trade/Partnership to Income Taxes and Charges*

When the business is transferred to the new company, the sole trade or partnership will cease trading in its own right and this will trigger the application of the *cessation* rules for income tax purposes. These rules require the taxpayer to review the level of profits subject to income tax in the year before the business ceased (penultimate year) and, potentially, to revise that year's taxable profits upwards.[7] Note that an upward revision of

[6] Section 20(2)(c) of the Value-Added Tax Consolidation Act 2010 (VATCA 2010).
[7] Section 67 TCA 1997.

taxable profits in the penultimate year would typically arise if taxable profits were increasing during the final two or so years of trading.

There is also an income tax relief that may be available to a so-called 'short-lived business', which is a business that starts and ceases within three tax years.[8] This could potentially apply to the business of Four Blue Ducks, as the business started in March 2014 and ceased on transfer to Blue Lacha Ltd in June 2016.

#### *9.1.4.4 Terminal Loss Relief Claim*

Where the profits of the business had been falling and losses were generated in the last year of trading before cessation, then it may be possible to use these losses to generate refunds of income tax paid for any of the three tax years before the year of cessation.[9] Application of this relief obviously requires that there were taxable profits in at least one of those three tax years.

If we look at the potential application of the income tax cessation rules and a potential claim for terminal loss relief, we can see that careful consideration should be given to the timing of the incorporation of a sole trade or partnership.

#### *9.1.4.5 Capital Allowances: Balancing Allowances and Charges*

In **Chapter 6**, we looked at the concept of capital allowances, which are a type of tax deduction for the cost of certain property, e.g. equipment, plant and machinery. We noted that where an asset is eligible for capital allowances, the tax cost of the asset is reduced by the amount of the capital allowance available for deduction in each tax year. The cost of the asset, net of capital allowances already claimed, is known as the 'tax written-down value' (TWDV) of the asset.

CASE STUDY: FOUR BLUE DUCKS/BLUE LACHA LTD

Jim owns a commercial fridge–freezer that he uses for the purposes of his café business. He bought the equipment in 2014 and was entitled to claim an annual capital allowance of 12.5% on the equipment. This means that, as the equipment cost €8,000, the annual capital allowance available was €1,000 and, at the beginning of March 2016, the TWDV of the equipment was €6,000. This is calculated as €8,000 less the 2014 and 2015 allowances of €1,000 each.

8 Section 68 TCA 1997.
9 Sections 385–390 TCA 1997.

To recap on our discussion of balancing allowances/charges in **Chapter 6**, we know that when an asset is transferred while it is still within its tax life for capital allowances purposes, then a balancing allowance or balancing charge will arise, depending on the value at which the asset is transferred.

CASE STUDY: FOUR BLUE DUCKS/BLUE LACHA LTD

We look again at the example of Jim's fridge–freezer with a purchase cost of €8,000. If this piece of equipment were transferred at a lower value than the TWDV of the equipment at the time of transfer, i.e. lower than €6,000, Jim would be entitled to a balancing allowance (effectively, an additional tax deduction) that would ensure that he gets full capital allowances for the net cost of the equipment. Conversely, if the equipment was transferred at a higher value than its TWDV of €6,000, a balancing charge (equivalent to an increase in taxable profit) would arise.

We can see that where a business is incorporated, the transfer values noted on assets eligible for capital allowances matter as they will have an effect on tax liabilities.

The first point to note is that when a business is being incorporated the business owners and the company can elect to transfer all assets eligible for capital allowances at TWDV.[10] This would mean that the sole trade/partnership would not have to make any adjustment to taxable profits because of balancing allowances and charges, and the company would be entitled to claim capital allowances only on the remaining TWDV of the assets.

The two parties can elect to make the transfer at TWDV values, but they are not obliged to do so. If not transferred at TWDV values, then the assets should be transferred at 'open market value'. The 'open market value' and TWDV of assets should be carefully considered before a decision is made on transfer values, as the extent to which the business was subject to income taxes and charges before incorporation could provide an opportunity for tax savings.

There are many other non-tax implications of incorporating a business that are outside the scope of this book, including: company law requirements; legal agreements; tax registrations and dealing with suppliers; customers; employees; licensing authorities; and banks. The advice of both an accountant/tax advisor and a lawyer are critical to ensuring a smooth and effective transfer of the business.

[10] Section 312(5) TCA 1997.

## 9.2 Creation of a Group Structure

It is worth re-iterating that a new business can create a group structure before trading starts. Doing so at the outset would be straightforward from a tax perspective, in that the structure would be put in place before any value had been created in the business, meaning that no tax implications should arise from its creation. However, to do so before the business is operational would be expensive and perhaps not suited to entrepreneurs who may change their business strategy depending on how the business progresses.

We look now at the second of our restructuring scenarios, where a business is initially operated through a single company and the owners subsequently wish to put a group structure in place. This involves them 'swapping' their *direct* ownership of the **trading** company for *indirect* ownership of the company through direct ownership of a **holding** company, which owns the trading company. This is represented in **Figure 9.2** below:

FIGURE 9.2: SHAREHOLDERS IN A TRADING COMPANY BECOME SHAREHOLDERS IN A HOLDING COMPANY

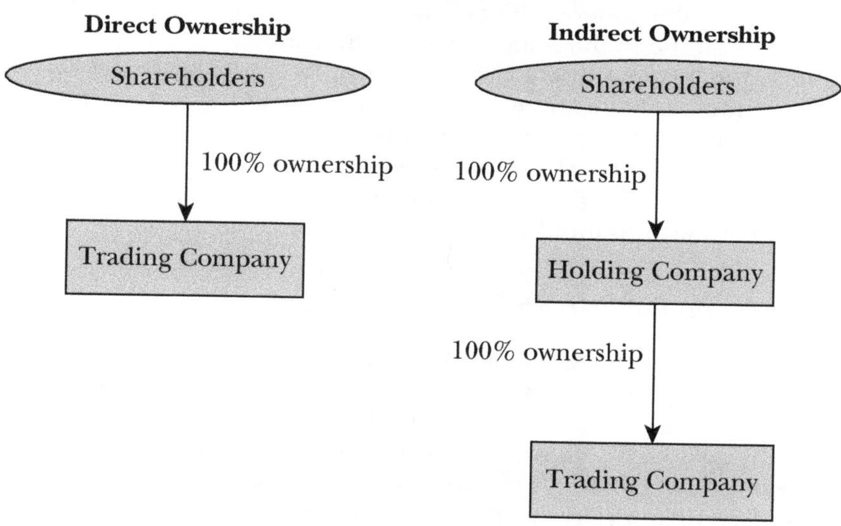


Though we have not shown it here, it is quite normal for the holding company to own numerous subsidiary companies. A 'subsidiary' company is a company owned directly by a holding company; so in **Figure 9.2** the trading company is a 'subsidiary' of the holding company.

So, why would a business need a group structure? Set out below are some of the reasons why more than one company may be established, as well as the possible rationale for these companies to be owned indirectly by the shareholders through a holding company (i.e. in a group structure), as opposed to being directly owned by the shareholders.

### *9.2.1 Reasons for Establishing more than One Company*

Business owners may decide to operate their business(es) through more than one company for a variety of commercial, legal or tax reasons. Some of these reasons include:

- The business operates different trading activities, which for commercial reasons (e.g. protection of brand name/goodwill), should be separated and operated through different companies. An example of this is Jim and Cathy's business, which expands to include both food retail (the café) and food production for both the café and for third-party customers.
- The business operates from a number of locations and the owners wish to be able to assess each location separately, e.g. a group of pizza production and delivery businesses that trade from six separate premises around Cork and operate through six trading companies.
- The business operates both within and outside of Ireland, in which case the foreign business may be operated through a company incorporated in that foreign location under local laws.
- There are valuable assets in the business that the owners wish to protect from liabilities of the trading business, e.g. business premises that have significant value independent of the trading business and could be sold separately if the trading business ran into trouble.
- Where the business operates a number of trading activities or operates from a number of locations, the owners may wish to have separate management for each business unit so that key employees of an individual unit could be given a share in that business unit.
- Allied to this is the possibility that the owners may wish to develop a particular business unit for future sale.

### *9.2.2 Reasons for a Group Structure*

Where business owners decide to operate their business(es) through a number of companies, these companies can each be owned directly by the business owners, which would mean that the companies have no relationship with each other. Alternatively, a group structure may be put in place. Some benefits of creating a group structure include:

- Where companies are in a group structure, i.e. owned by a holding company, this allows for much more flexibility in transactions between subsidiary companies, and between subsidiary companies and the holding company. One obvious and important example of this is in relation to loans between the companies. There are strict company law rules in relation to loans between companies that are not in a group, which do not apply within a group structure.
- Where a group company makes losses, these can be surrendered to other group companies that are profit-making and so reduce overall corporation tax liabilities.
- Group companies may transfer assets to each other without triggering capital gains taxes.

- Trading subsidiary companies may be sold by the holding company without triggering tax charges and the full sales proceeds reinvested in further business activities within the group. This is a specific CGT relief, which is subject to a number of conditions and is outside the scope of this book.
- Some groups use the holding company as more than just a 'holder' of shares. Central management and control of all group activities may be operated through the group holding company, which may also carry out the group finance function. This can be more cost-effective, with specialist knowledge developed in one location, and can result in a more co-ordinated business strategy for the group as a whole.

### *9.2.3 Creation of a Group Structure by Share-for-share Exchange*

A tax-efficient mechanism of achieving the group structure set out in **Figure 9.2** above is for the shareholders of the trading (subsidiary) company and the holding company to make a swap/exchange. This involves the shareholders of the trading company giving the holding company their shares in the trading company and, in exchange, the holding company issuing shares in itself to the shareholders of the trading company. This is known as a 'share-for-share exchange'. **Figure 9.3** below shows the movement of shares envisaged by this share-for-share exchange.

Figure 9.3: Exchange of Trading Company Shares for Holding Company Shares

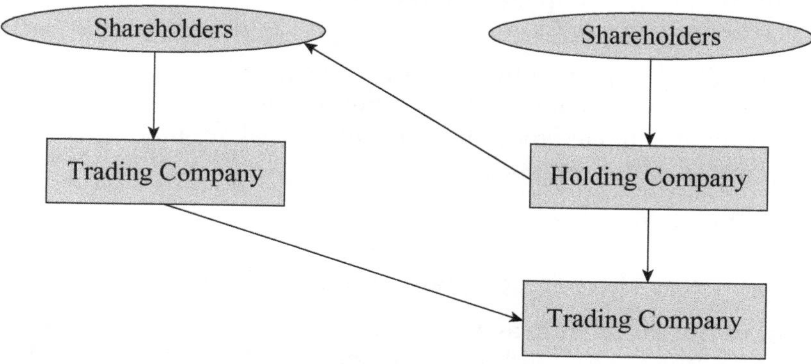


As this transaction involves the **disposal** of the shares of the trading company in exchange for the **acquisition** of the shares of the holding company, various tax implications will arise. Some tax rules have been specifically written to facilitate this type of corporate restructuring and so the restructuring may not trigger any immediate tax liabilities as long as the conditions of two specific tax reliefs are met, as discussed below.

#### *9.2.3.1 Capital Gains Tax*

The first tax relief that may apply is a relief from CGT for the shareholders of the trading company, without which the *disposal* of shares in the trading company to the holding company could trigger CGT liabilities calculated by reference to the market value of the trading company's shares. The conditions that must be met in order for the relief to apply include:

- an offer to acquire the shares of the trading company must be made to *all* the shareholders of the trading company; and
- the holding company must acquire control of the trading company.[11]

#### *9.2.3.2 Stamp Duty*

The other tax that typically applies to the **acquisition** of shares is stamp duty, which is payable by the party that acquires the shares (in this case, the holding company). A specific relief from stamp duty may arise where various conditions are met, including:

- the holding company must acquire at least 90% of the shares of the trading company;
- the maximum cash consideration that the holding company may pay the shareholders of the trading company for their shares is 10% of the value of the trading company;
- the holding company issues shares in itself to the (former) shareholders of the trading company in the same proportion as their shareholding in the trading company. For example, if there had been four shareholders in the trading company, each of whom owned 25% of the company's shares, then each of those shareholders should be issued with 25% of the shares in the holding company; and
- there are specific company secretarial requirements that must be met if this relief is to apply.[12]

Other conditions apply to the operation of this relief, including a condition that applies to many CGT and stamp duty tax reliefs, i.e. that the transactions are effected for bona fide commercial reasons and not for the main purpose of avoiding tax.

#### *9.2.3.3 Other Taxes*

There is no VAT charge on the transfer or issue of shares.

We saw in **Chapter 5** that, as a general statement, payroll taxes will arise where an employee (including a director) receives any benefit, whether cash or benefit-in-kind (BIK), from their employer. Payroll taxes do not typically apply to the shareholder/director of the trading company on the shares they receive as part of this restructuring, however, as the shareholder/director of the trading company does not receive the shares in the holding company "in connection with their employment".

[11] Section 586 TCA 1997.
[12] Section 80 SDCA 1999.

## CASE STUDY: NEALLY ENGINEERING LTD BECOMES THE NEALLY GROUP

The business of Neally Engineering Ltd is initially run through one company, owned on a 50/50 basis by brother and sister, Martin and Danielle. The company originally produces metal tools for the aviation industry. Once the shareholder/directors have made the decision to develop a new business line, being the production of silicone tools for the life science industry, they take some advice as to the effectiveness of their business structure.

As part of their plans to develop this new business line, Martin and Danielle recognise the importance of keeping Dirk, the chemical engineer who is leading the 'silicone project', in the business and highly motivated. They discuss giving Dirk a part of the proposed silicone business, though they do not wish to give him a part of the original metal tools business. The directors also consider it important from the perspectives of business development and sales/marketing that the two businesses be kept separate. After discussing their business strategy with their accountant/tax advisor, Martin and Danielle decide the following:

- a group structure should be put in place by way of a share-for-share exchange. As a result of this, Martin and Danielle will own 50% each of Neally Holdings Ltd, which will own 100% of Neally Engineering Ltd;
- a new subsidiary company of Neally Holdings Ltd will be incorporated, Neally Silicone Ltd, through which the silicone business will be run; and
- Danielle and Martin will discuss with Dirk the possibility of issuing him shares in Neally Silicone Ltd at the time of incorporation of that company.

The new Neally Group structure may look like this:

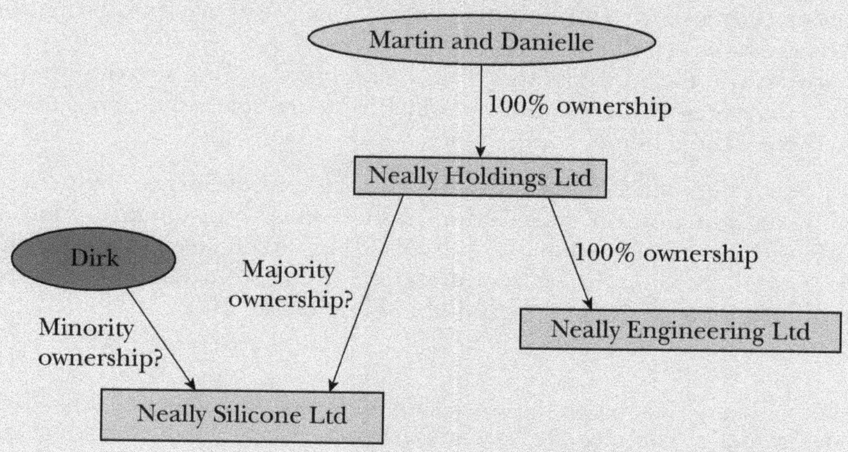

## 9.3 Introduction of Key Employees as Shareholders

Every successful entrepreneur knows that they cannot do everything themselves and must rely on the experience and talents of a good team in order to move the business forward. In building that team, the entrepreneur may consider giving certain employees a share in the business in order to ensure that they stay and are motivated in developing the business for the medium to long term.

In this section we consider how to go about giving an employee shares in a tax-efficient manner since, as a general rule, all benefits provided to employees are subject to payroll taxes. The first option is to give the employee shares in the company when the company first commences. This may have the benefit of triggering low/no payroll taxes and charges (on the assumption that the business is worth nothing at the outset); but is it realistic? Is it likely that the employee will have worked for the business, demonstrating ability and commitment, from the start? Would the entrepreneur want to commit to a long-term relationship with an employee as a fellow shareholder so soon in the life-cycle of the business?

More realistically, on the assumption that the business is already operational and already has value, we will look at some of the more typical methods of incentivising key employees of an Irish SME by way of a part share of the business.

The first thing to note is that for many Irish start-ups and SMEs, the more well-known types of employee incentive schemes will not be suitable, either because of the level of administration and costs involved or because the terms of the scheme require that it is made available to all employees, so that it is not possible to reward a small number of key employees only. These schemes include:

- Employee share ownership trusts (ESOT) – more typically used by semi-state bodies. Well-known examples include the legacy ESOTs operated by Aer Lingus and eir (formerly Eircom).
- Approved profit-sharing schemes (APSS) – these typically require that *all* employees with a minimum number of years' service must be allowed to access the scheme.
- Save As You Earn (SAYE) share option schemes – these also require that *all* employees with a minimum number of years' service must be allowed to access the scheme.

It is worth highlighting here that the Department of Finance launched a public consultation on the taxation of share-based remuneration in May 2016, with submissions due by 1 July 2016. Should changes to the existing tax regime for share-based remuneration result from this consultation, then these changes may be included in Finance Act 2016.[13]

[13] For more information on this consultation, see www.finance.gov.ie/what-we-do/tax-policy/consultations/taxation-share-based-remuneration-consultation (accessed June 2016).

Before reviewing some of the more typical methods used by Irish SMEs to introduce a select number of employees as shareholders, we must highlight yet again the importance of taking professional advice before doing so. At a minimum, an external valuation of the company must be secured before shares are issued to the key employees and the tax implications of the share issue properly assessed. ***Remember***: if the tax implications are not properly dealt with, both the employee in receipt of the shares and the employer may be liable for unpaid taxes (and interest and penalties).

In addition, company secretarial requirements must be met and in some instances, legal agreements will be required. When introducing employees as shareholders, another issue to consider is the creation of a shareholders' agreement. This would set out how the shareholders can deal in the company shares: can they sell them to third parties?; what happens in the event of the death of a shareholder, etc.? A shareholders' agreement can also set out what happens to the shares of the key employee if they leave the company: do they receive cash for their shares or is there an automatic buyout?

### 9.3.1 Share Option Schemes

A share option scheme allows an employer company to incentivise key employees by giving them a future option to acquire shares in the company at a price that is fixed at the grant of the share option (the 'option price'). The timing of when the share option may be exercised, the number of shares that may be purchased and the option price are all controlled by the employer company, which may link these to performance. Typically, a share option scheme will require that the share options are exercised within seven years of the option becoming exercisable. In this case (known as a 'short option'), no tax is triggered on the *grant* of the option[14] and the employee has full control over whether they will ever exercise that option. (***Note:*** a different tax treatment applies to the grant and exercise of options in a share option scheme that allows options to be exercised more than seven years after their grant.)

If, by the time the short option is exercisable, the market value of the shares is lower than the option price, then the employee is unlikely to exercise the short option. If the market value of the shares rises, then the employee may decide to exercise the option, though they are not obliged to do so. If they do, they will personally have to finance both the cost of buying the shares (at the option price) as well as paying the tax liabilities triggered by the purchase. These tax liabilities comprise income tax, USC and employee PRSI, and are charged on the difference between the option price and the market value price on the date the option is exercised. The tax liabilities

[14] Section 128 TCA 1997.

must be paid directly by the employee to Revenue within 30 days of the exercise of the option. Unlike other employee benefits-in-kind, no employer PRSI (at the current rates of 8.5%/10.75%) will arise. We set out below a brief example of how the taxable benefit arising on the exercise of a short option is calculated.

### Example 9.2: Tax Implications of Exercising a 'Short' Share Option

Nora was granted 5,000 share options, at a price of €1.25 per share, on 2 February 2014. These options were exercisable at any time up to 1 February 2019. Nora exercised all of her options on 31 March 2016 when the share price was €1.35 per share.

| | | € |
|---|---|---|
| Value of shares when exercised | (€1.35 × 5,000) | 6,750 |
| Value of shares at option price | (€1.25 × 5,000) | 6,250 |
| Taxable benefit subject to income tax, USC and employee's PRSI | | 500 |

Share option schemes may be made available to a small number of employees and, on the face of it, achieve the aim of allowing key staff to have a stake in the company. The difficulty here is that the employee must not only personally finance the acquisition of the shares but must also finance the income taxes and charges arising on the option exercise, which could be as high as 52% at current rates. In order to cover costs, employees may need to take out a loan to finance the share purchase or, alternatively, sell some of the shares acquired (assuming they can secure a buyer). This can defeat the aim of introducing employees as shareholders and merely turns the whole transaction into a more tax-efficient (for the employer) way of giving employees some benefits.

The practical issue highlighted above, whereby employees may be obliged to take out a loan or sell some of their shares to fund the tax costs arising, may be alleviated where a 'Save As You Earn' (SAYE) scheme is introduced along with a share option scheme. This scheme includes an employee savings element to cover the costs of acquiring shares under a share option scheme. The potential downsides are that an SAYE scheme will be more complex and costly, requires Revenue approval and must be made available to all employees with a minimum number of years' service.

Other practical issues with the use of share option schemes, particularly those faced by smaller companies, include the difficulty of determining the appropriate market value for the shares at the date on which share options are exercised, as well as the need to provide a ready market for employees to be able to sell their shares if they wish or need to do so.

### 9.3.2 Share Award Schemes

The alternative, and more straightforward, method of introducing employees as shareholders is to have the company issue new shares directly to them. As discussed above, these share awards will almost certainly be linked to performance and, as in the case of a share option scheme, require a valuation of the company at the time the shares are acquired.

The award of the shares will be treated as a taxable employee BIK, meaning that PAYE income tax, employee PRSI and USC will arise on the award. No employer PRSI will arise on this benefit. These liabilities will also be payable by the employee (by withholding through the payroll system), who may have the same practical difficulties around financing these tax costs as an employee exercising an option under a share option scheme. Given that the employer chooses to award the shares to the employee, the obvious solution may appear to be that the employer also covers the payroll taxes arising. The difficulty with this approach is that if the employer does so, then the employer is providing a further benefit to the employee (i.e. the value of the payroll taxes), which will trigger a further BIK, also subject to payroll taxes.

We focus our attention now on the valuation of the employee shares, as there are some methodologies available to reduce their value and therefore, the associated tax liabilities. ***Note:*** the company issuing the shares must first be valued on a market-value basis to provide a starting point in assessing the taxable BIK arising.

#### *9.3.2.1 Minority Shareholdings*

In **Section 9.1.1**, we looked at some typical methods of valuing businesses, i.e. net asset value and the 'earnings/profit' basis. These methods are also relevant when valuing private companies, as is an additional method of valuation based on the level of dividends being paid on the shares, if dividends are in fact being paid (the 'dividends' basis). There are other important considerations when valuing private company shares, particularly small or minority percentage holdings of those shares.

Revenue acknowledge that, in the case of shares in a private company, there is often a limited (or perhaps non-existent) market to sell these shares. There is also acknowledgement of the fact that a minority shareholder is not in a position to control the company or prevent decisions being made that may reduce the value of their shares. Because of these issues, a specified discount factor may be applied to the share valuation, depending on the size of the individual's percentage shareholding, along the following lines.

## Revenue Capital Acquisitions Tax Manual – Valuation of Unquoted Shares[15]

**21.13 Majority Shareholding/Influential Minority Shareholding**

**21.13.1 Holdings of 50% and above**

Value by reference to the value of the whole company less a suitable discount, e.g.

| [Percentage shareholding] | [Appropriate discount factor] |
|---|---|
| 75% + | Nil discount or perhaps 5% at most |
| 50% + 1 | 10 – 15% |
| 50% | 20 – 30% |
| 25% + 1 | 35 – 40% |

**21.13.2 Minority Shareholding**

Up to 25% – value by reference to dividends if a realistic level of dividend is being paid. If no dividend, look at discounted earnings with a discount range of 50–70%, as these are influential minority holdings.

The above is for guidance only and the circumstances of the market in which the company operates, the company itself, its shareholders and their relationship to each other, must be taken into account when choosing an appropriate discount factor (if any). An example of how a discount factor may be applied to a minority share valuation is set out in the case study extract below.

## Case Study: Neally Silicone Ltd

Following from the developments discussed at **Section 9.2.3** above, if, instead of issuing shares in Neally Silicone Ltd to Dirk at the time the company is incorporated, shares are issued to him after a year of trading which results in him owning 26% of the company at a time when the market value of the company is assessed at, say, €250,000, then Dirk's shareholding would be initially valued at €65,000. If the maximum discount factor of 40% set out in Revenue's guidance above were to be applied, this would reduce his taxable BIK value to €39,000, meaning that Dirk would pay payroll taxes on this reduced amount.

[15] Revenue Commissioners, *Capital Acquisitions Tax Manual*, Paragraph 21.13, Part 21 – Valuation of Unquoted Shares. Available at www.revenue.ie/en/about/foi/s16/capital-acquisitions-tax/ (accessed June 2016).

### 9.3.2.2 Share Clog Schemes

In general, an asset is valuable to its owner if the owner has full unrestricted rights to deal with it as they wish, e.g. to derive income from it, sell it, use it as loan security, etc. Where these ownership rights are restricted in some way, then the asset is generally worth less. In relation to the issue of shares that are subject to restriction, specific tax rules set out a range of discount factors that will apply when valuing these restricted shares for BIK purposes. This type of scheme is called a 'share clog' scheme and typically includes a set timeframe during which the employee cannot deal with the shares and cannot use the shares as security – this is known as the 'period of retention'. The discount factors are as follows:[16]

| Period of Retention | Appropriate Discount Factor |
|---|---|
| 1 Year | 10% |
| 2 Years | 20% |
| 3 Years | 30% |
| 4 Years | 40% |
| 5 Years | 50% |
| 5+ Years | 60% |

CASE STUDY: NEALLY SILICONE LTD

Assume that Dirk's shares are subject to a 'share clog' scheme, which in his case means that he would not be in a position to sell his shares for four years. The €39,000 valuation arrived at by applying a discount factor for a minority shareholding would be further reduced by a discount factor of 40% to reflect this four-year period of retention. The taxable BIK value would now be reduced to €23,400. Assuming the current 40% rate of PAYE income tax, 8% USC charge and 4% employee PRSI charge, the tax costs for Dirk would be approximately €12,000, a figure he may be quite happy to pay to secure 26% of Neally Silicone Ltd.

Such schemes require certain formalities, including the holding of the shares in trust for the benefit of the employee and the requirement that the employee sign a contract to say that they will not try to deal with the shares during the retention period. However, these formalities are not hugely onerous. The big advantage of these schemes is that, in addition to

[16] Section 128D TCA 1997.

being used to reduce payroll taxes arising on the issue of the shares, the schemes can be used in a targeted way to retain key employees.

### *9.3.2.3 Differing Classes of Shares*

Most company shares are 'ordinary shares', which attract all the rights usually attaching to the ownership of shares, being:

1. voting rights;
2. right to participate in dividends;
3. right to receive a share of the net assets on a winding-up of the company; and
4. right to information on the company.

It is entirely possible, however, for a company to have a more complicated share structure, with different types of shares attracting different share rights. For example, it is possible to have shares that have voting rights, but no other rights. It is also possible to have shares that have a right to participate in dividends from a certain date forward, or to have shares that have no rights at the time of issue but which may convert into 'ordinary shares' at some point in the future if certain events happen.

The valuation of differing types of shares is a complex issue, but there is scope for tax planning here that may result in low BIK valuations on share issues, meaning lower tax liabilities for the employee. This is an area for specialist tax advice, as advisors must take care to avoid triggering the anti-avoidance legislation introduced in Finance Act 2008, which mandates higher share valuations in certain circumstances.

CHAPTER 10

# EXTERNAL INVESTMENT THROUGH THE EMPLOYMENT AND INVESTMENT INCENTIVE SCHEME (EIIS)



The Employment and Investment Incentive Scheme (EIIS) is another example of a tax policy that is used to encourage certain behaviour. The scheme is designed to encourage individuals to invest in a company with a view to assisting its business development and the expansion of employee numbers, or to assist in the company's research and development (R&D) activities. The individual investors subscribe for shares in the company, which they retain for a minimum four-year holding period and in return receive an income tax deduction representing the amount of their investment. The expectation is that these shares are then bought back after the holding period has expired, at a price at least equal to their initial purchase price. As with any share investment, the investor is exposed to the commercial risk of the company declining and, in the worst-case scenario, failing. In fact, exposure to this risk is a key requirement for the availability of the income tax relief.

In **Chapter 2**, we reviewed the Startup Refunds for Entrepreneurs (SURE) scheme, which is a variation of the EIIS. An important difference is that, while the EIIS is aimed mainly at incentivising the external private investor, the SURE scheme is aimed solely at the internal investor, i.e. the company shareholder who can secure income tax relief for their investment. We will see below, however, that in some limited circumstances *existing* shareholders of a qualifying EIIS company may themselves invest in the company. Another significant difference is that the EIIS income tax deduction is available either in the tax year in which the shares are issued or a future tax year, whereas the tax deduction available under the SURE scheme is a retrospective deduction available against the six tax years prior to the year in which the shares are issued, resulting in a refund of income tax already paid.

As you would expect, there are many conditions set out in the tax legislation[1] that must be met in order for the EIIS relief to apply. These conditions have two foci:

- the individual investor must be a 'specified (i.e. qualifying) individual'; and
- the company receiving the investment (which we will call the 'investee company') must be a 'qualifying company' that carries on 'relevant trading activities' and issues 'eligible shares'.

This tax relief is subject to Revenue approval. The usual approach is to secure *outline* Revenue approval of a proposed EIIS in advance of the investment being made, with *final* approval being secured post-investment. It would be unusual for outline approval to be granted and then rescinded after the EIIS investment has been made.

As the intention behind this scheme is to encourage private investors to invest in the development of Irish companies, the tax relief specifies the use to which the investment monies must be put, being:

- the relevant trading activities of the investee company; *or*
- where the investee company has not commenced its trade, the monies must be used on "research and development activities" (the definition of these activities is the same as that provided in the tax rules underlying the R&D tax credit, details of which are set out in **Chapter 11**).

In addition to these requirements, the use of the monies must also "contribute directly to the creation or maintenance of employment in the company".[2]

An EIIS investment is really a type of private loan, with the potential return coming in two forms: income tax relief and a buyback price that is, hopefully, higher than the initial subscription price.

[1] Sections 488–507 of the Taxes Consolidation Act 1997 (TCA 1997), as amended by section 18 of the Finance Act 2015 (FA 2015).

[2] Section 489(1) TCA 1997.

Use of the EIIS compares positively with other types of financing. As this is a form of equity financing, there are no debt financing costs (i.e. interest) to be paid by the investee company (though this saving will be somewhat offset by the fees to be paid to the company's advisors to put the scheme in place).

As the EIIS shares will be a different class of shares to those owned by the original shareholders, the latter will retain control of the company during the holding period. By facilitating the company in commencing or expanding its business, the EIIS investment monies should increase the value of the company's balance sheet, which may make it more attractive for banks and other finance providers, e.g. Enterprise Ireland, to finance the company after the EIIS investment has been made.

From the perspective of the investee company (and its shareholders) EIIS investment can be seen as attracting lower risk than a straightforward bank loan because the buyback price for EIIS shares will be driven by the value of the investee company at the time of buyback. If the company has not done well during the holding period, then the buyback price will be low (or potentially nil). This is the risk that the EIIS investor takes when investing in EIIS shares. The other significant potential benefit for the original shareholders of the investee company is that, in the current economic cycle, securing a *company* bank loan often requires the provision of *personal* guarantees by the shareholders to the bank. These are not required with an EIIS investment.

On the downside for the investee company, the four-year timeframe for investment may be so short as to prevent potential EIIS companies from going down this route. This is because such companies may need a longer timeframe for return on investment and may not produce sufficient funds to allow repayment of the investment after four years. In addition, the original shareholders will generally be prevented from selling the company during the EIIS holding period.

The EIIS is usually used by established companies that are looking to bring the business to another level, e.g. by moving into a new market, by adding a new income stream or production line, etc. We will see that many conditions must be met in order to secure the income tax relief and that a fairly significant amount of paperwork must be created/ processed in order to put the scheme into effect. For these reasons, there should be a solid commercial rationale for the company seeking external financing; the tax relief potentially available should be regarded as a bonus.

***Note:*** the EIIS is the successor to the old Business Expansion Scheme (BES) and its related tax relief, which was similarly structured. The EIIS is generally regarded as a more expansive scheme, potentially available to more companies, allowing higher investment levels and adopting a more simplified approach to establishing the investment.

## 10.1 Overview of the Employment and Investment Incentive Scheme

The conditions attaching to the EIIS have been quite significantly amended in Finance Acts 2014 and 2015. The information set out below is relevant to a new EIIS, established after 12 October 2015, by a company that has never created such a scheme previously and has been operating for less than seven years:

- The EIIS is available to 31 December 2020.
- Where a 'qualifying individual' makes an EIIS investment in a 'qualifying company', they will be entitled to tax relief (by way of tax deduction) up to a maximum of 40%, spread over two tranches:
  - 30% tax relief is available in the year in which the EIIS investment is made; and
  - a further 10% tax relief *may* be available in the year after the end of the investment-holding period, provided that either the investee company has increased its employee numbers and total wages since the investment was made or the investee company has increased its R&D expenditure.

  ***Note:*** if neither of these conditions is met then the second tranche of tax relief will not be available, but this will not impact on the 30% tax relief already claimed.
- The private investor makes their EIIS investment by purchasing (subscribing for) a class of ordinary shares which is separate to the share class owned by the company's existing shareholders.
- The private investor must retain their shares for a four-year holding period, which runs from the date of the shares being issued or, if the company was not at that date carrying on 'relevant trading activities', from the date when those activities commenced. After the holding period has expired, the investor and/or the company/promoter will exercise a 'put and call option' agreement to sell the shares. (A 'put and call option' agreement gives the investor the right to oblige the company/promoter to purchase (to 'put') the EIIS shares, and also gives the company/promoter the right to oblige the investor to sell (to 'call') the EIIS shares to them.) If the investor does not hold the shares for the full extent of the holding period, then some (or all) of the tax relief already secured may be clawed back.
- Tax relief is available against the private investor's income tax only; it will not reduce USC or PRSI liabilities.
- The maximum investment amount on which income tax relief may be claimed by an individual investor for any tax year is €150,000. Where the investment exceeds this value or the investor does not have sufficient income to absorb the tax deduction in the year of investment,

the investor may carry forward this relief to following tax years, up to and including 2020.

- The maximum EIIS investment in any company and/or associated companies is €15 million, subject to a limit of €5 million of investment in any 12-month period. Where previous EIIS funds have been raised, then the maximum amount of the new investment will be €15 million less the value of the previous EIIS funds. Funds raised under the SURE scheme (as set out in **Chapter 2**) will be included in assessing this €15 million threshold.
- An investor may invest in a single qualifying company or in an EIIS designated investment fund that will invest in a pool of qualifying EIIS companies.
- In general, the tax relief available to an EIIS investor under the scheme is regarded as a 'specified relief' under the rules limiting the availability of tax reliefs to so-called high earner taxpayers. As a temporary measure to encourage the use of the EIIS, the tax relief attaching to shares issued during the period to 31 December 2016 will not be treated as a 'specified relief'.
- No claim(s) for EIIS relief will be allowed unless, at the time of the claim(s), the investee company qualifies for a tax clearance certificate.

Figure 10.1 below shows the building blocks required for a successful EIIS investment.

FIGURE 10.1: THE BUILDING BLOCKS OF EIIS

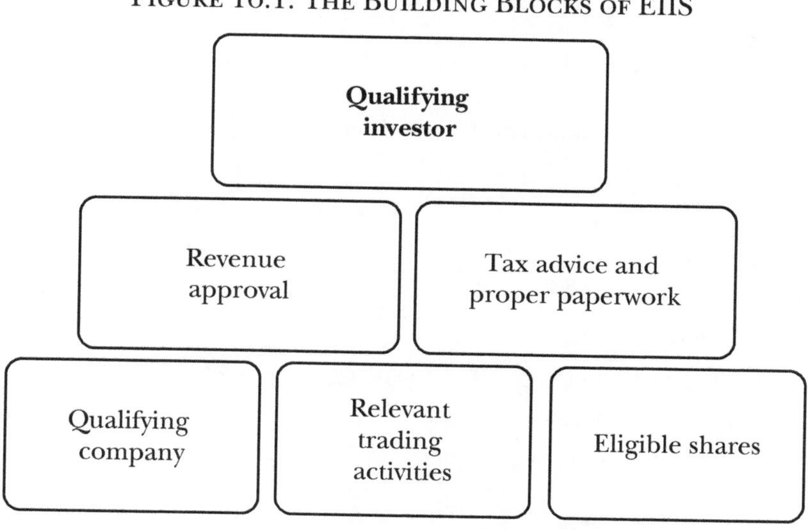


We will now look at the potential income tax savings that may be achieved by two EIIS investors in Jim's newly-incorporated Blue Lacha Ltd, the new owner of the Four Blue Ducks café. The incorporation of this sole trade business was detailed in **Chapter 9, Section 9.1**.

## Case Study: Blue Lacha Ltd

Two investors in the EIIS funding scheme for Blue Lacha Ltd, Mr Elevate and Mr Propel, subscribe €35,000 each for EIIS shares, which are issued to them in late 2016 at which time the company is carrying on 'relevant trading activities'. We look now at how the income tax relief operates for Mr Elevate, who earns €150,000 annually, and Mr Propel, who earns €50,000.

We noted that a 30% tax deduction is given in the year of investment (2016), which is calculated at 30/40ths of the value of the investment. A further 10% tax deduction, or 10/40ths of the investment value, is given after the four-year holding period has ended (in 2020), on the basis that an increase in employee numbers and total wages has been achieved during the period.

**Claim for Tax Deduction in 2016**

| | Mr Elevate | Mr Propel |
|---|---|---|
| | € | € |
| Total income | 150,000 | 50,000 |
| Income tax liability* | 49,940 | 9,940 |
| Less: EIIS tax relief: | | |
| (Investment of €35,000 × 30/40 × 40%) | (10,500) | |
| (Investment of €35,000 × 30/40 × mix 40% & 20%) | | (8,490) |
| Net income tax liability | 39,440 | 1,450 |

**Claim for Tax Deduction in 2020**

| | Mr Elevate | Mr Propel |
|---|---|---|
| | € | € |
| Total income | 150,000 | 50,000 |
| Income tax liability* | 49,940 | 9,940 |
| Less: EIIS tax relief: | | |
| (Investment of €35,000 × 10/40 × 40%) | (3,500) | |
| (Investment of €35,000 × 10/40 × 40%) | | (3,500) |
| Net income tax liability | 46,440 | 6,440 |

* Assuming single person 20% band and the availability of personal and PAYE tax credits at rates/bands/credits applicable to tax year 2016 (current at the time of writing). USC and PRSI are excluded from these calculations as EIIS will not reduce these liabilities.

*Note*: the 2016 income tax relief secured by Mr Elevate, who has annual income of €150,000, is greater than the 2016 relief secured by Mr Propel, with annual income of €50,000 (being €10,500 compared to €8,490). The reason that the tax deduction is lower for Mr Propel is that he does not have sufficient income taxable at the 40% rate of income tax to ensure that only '40% taxed income' is sheltered by this tax relief. This difference in tax relief does not arise in relation to the 2020 tax deduction, as the value of this deduction is €8,750 (€35,000 × 10/40) and Mr Propel has at least this amount of '40% taxed income' in 2020. This illustrates the point that, in order to take full advantage of the income tax relief available under the EIIS, a potential EIIS investor should ensure that they will have sufficient income taxed at the higher 40% rate of income tax in the year of EIIS investment *and* the year after the end of the four-year holding period.

## 10.2 Conditions to be Met by the Company

In order to secure EIIS relief, there must be an issue of 'eligible shares' in a 'qualifying company' that is carrying on 'relevant trading activities'. Some of the main requirements supporting these definitions are set out in the list below (which is not exhaustive). In general, these requirements must be met throughout the four-year holding period.

### *10.2.1 'Qualifying Company' Carrying on 'Relevant Trading Activities'*

Setting out the conditions that must be met by a putative EIIS investee company, sections 488 and 494 TCA 1997 provide that:

(a) The company must be carrying on, or intend to carry on, '**relevant trading activities**' from a fixed place of business in Ireland. Alternatively, the company may hold shares in, or make loans to, qualifying subsidiary companies *or* it may carry out a mix of these holding-company activities and 'relevant trading activities'. The general definition of 'relevant trading activities' is a regular trade, the profits or losses of which are subject to the trading corporation tax rate. Finance Act 2014 brings 'internationally traded financial services' into the definition of 'relevant trading activities', though a company involved in these activities will require a specific certificate from Enterprise Ireland in order to be treated as a 'qualifying company'.

    Some company activities will not qualify for the EIIS and these are set out at **Appendix I** to this chapter.

(b) The company must come within the definition of 'micro', 'small' or 'medium-sized' enterprises, as set out in European Commission Regulations.[3] A 'medium-sized' enterprise is one with fewer than 250 employees **and** *either* an annual turnover not exceeding €50 million *or* an annual balance sheet not exceeding €43 million. A 'small' enterprise is defined as one with fewer than 50 employees **and** an annual turnover *and/or* balance sheet of less than €10 million. The parameters for a 'micro' enterprise are set at staff numbers of less than 10 **and** annual turnover *and/or* balance sheet that does not exceed €2 million.

(c) The company must be an unlisted SME, and *either*:
   (i) it has not been operating in any market (i.e. it is a start-up company); *or*
   (ii) it has been operating in a market for less than seven years following its first commercial sale; *or*
   (iii) the company requires initial risk finance which, based on a business plan prepared with a view to entering a new product or geographical market, is greater than 50% of the average annual turnover in the previous five years.

(d) The company must be incorporated in Ireland or in any European Economic Area (EEA) state, which comprises the EU Member States plus Iceland, Liechtenstein and Norway. Irish branches of companies incorporated in another EEA state may also qualify.

(e) During the relevant period, the company must be tax resident in Ireland or another EEA state, and carry on business through an Irish branch or agency.

(f) As noted at (a) above, it is possible for a group holding company to qualify for the EIIS; however, in this case, the company's subsidiaries must also meet all of the conditions for it to be regarded as a qualifying company.

(g) Where a company has not commenced to trade and is seeking EIIS investment to carry out R&D activities, that company will lose their EIIS status unless, either:
   - all of the monies invested in EIIS shares are used within one month of the end of the four-year holding period and the company has created, and then disposed of, an 'intangible asset' (as defined by section 291A TCA 1997) that arises directly from the R&D activities; or
   - the company commences 'relevant trading activities' within two years of the EIIS investment and uses all of these EIIS monies for either these activities or R&D activities by the end of the four-year holding period.

### 10.2.2 *Anti-avoidance Rules Preventing a Company being Regarded as 'Qualifying'*

There are some specific anti-avoidance rules in place to prevent the exploitation of an EIIS company by an individual or company with a

[3] See Annex 1 to Commission Regulation (EU) No. 651/2014 of 17 June 2014.

controlling interest in the EIIS company. These rules prevent other EIIS investors in the company from having the value of their shares reduced by the actions of those controlling the company.

The main anti-avoidance rule relates to a period defined as beginning three years before, and ending two years after, the date of the issue of the EIIS shares or, if later, the date when the EIIS company began to trade. During this defined period, if an individual has a '*controlling interest*' in the EIIS company and a controlling interest in another trade, and the two trades are broadly similar in products, services or markets, then the company will not be treated as a qualifying company. In addition, an investee company will also lose its otherwise qualifying EIIS status if *transactions which are not at market value* occur between the company and either: a company that was the former employer of one of the EIIS investors; or a company that controls or is controlled by the former employer company.

### 10.2.3 Eligible Shares[4]

The shares issued to the EIIS investor must be newly issued ordinary shares that hold the right to a dividend, but do not hold a preferred right to dividends, a preferred right to the company's assets on a winding-up *or* a preferred right to be redeemed. These conditions must be met during the four-year investment-holding period.

Note that, although the EIIS shares have the right to an (ordinary) dividend, no dividend is typically expected or declared. This is because accumulating profits are usually retained by the EIIS company in order to support the buyback price for the EIIS shares after the end of the holding period. This is a more tax-efficient approach as the EIIS investor would be subject to income tax, USC and PRSI on receipt of a dividend, whereas a gain on the buyback of shares should be subject to capital gains tax, at lower rates. If a dividend is declared on the EIIS shares during the holding period, then often the buyback price will be reduced by the value of the dividend.

EIIS shares generally do not have voting rights.

As noted, the EIIS investor's exit comprises a 'put and call option' agreement with the EIIS company/promoter, whereby the shares are bought back after the holding period (which must be a minimum of four years) has expired. The purchase price set out in the put and call option agreement must be 'market value' (as defined by section 548 TCA 1997). As a minimum holding period of four years must pass before the EIIS shares may be bought back, it is not possible to set a buyback price at the outset. Instead, the put and call option agreement will typically note that the market value of the EIIS shares should be agreed between the parties, set by the company auditors, or, in case of disputes, be the subject of arbitration. It is quite typical for the buyback price to be defined as the market value of the EIIS share, subject to a specific cap.

[4] Sections 488 and 489 TCA 1997.

EXAMPLE 10.1: DEFINITION OF BUYBACK PRICE INCLUDED IN A PUT AND CALL OPTION AGREEMENT

The buyback price for a €1 EIIS share could be defined as market value, subject to a cap of €1.10 per EIIS share. This would mean that the buyback price will not exceed €1.10 per share, though it may, ultimately, be lower.

The investee company must be in a position to demonstrate to Revenue that the proceeds of the issue of EIIS shares are used for one of the purposes set out at the start of this chapter, i.e. the relevant trading activities of the company or the company's R&D activities.

We referred previously to the fact that the EIIS investor must carry the usual commercial risk associated with the ownership of shares, i.e. the possibility that no dividends will be paid on the shares and/or that the company will collapse and some or all monies invested will be lost. A specific anti-avoidance rule broadly states that where there is an agreement that could "reasonably be considered to eliminate the risk" of the investor losing some or all of the value associated with the EIIS shares, then no tax relief will arise for the investor.[5]

## 10.3 Conditions to be Met by the Individual Investor

In **Section 10.2** above, we reviewed a summary of the conditions that must be met by a putative EIIS company in order that EIIS relief may be claimed. In this section we will review the conditions that must be met by the putative EIIS investor. The key point to note here is that, as with a company that seeks to be a qualifying EIIS company, many of the conditions attached to becoming a 'qualifying individual' for the purposes of claiming EIIS relief persist throughout the four-year holding period.

### *10.3.1 'Qualifying Individual'*

In order to be treated as a 'qualifying individual' eligible for EIIS relief, the individual investor must be tax resident in Ireland for the tax year in which they make the claim for income tax relief. The investor must subscribe for 'eligible shares' in a 'qualifying company' and, during the four-year holding period, they must not be 'connected' to the EIIS company.[6]

The tax legislation relating to EIIS relief sets out specific rules to define the concept of 'connected' for the purposes of this relief. An individual

[5] Section 489(9) TCA 1997.
[6] Section 492 TCA 1997.

will be 'connected' to an EIIS company if they are, or their 'associate' (i.e. relative or business partner) is:

- a partner of the company; or
- a director or employee of the EIIS company, or of a company that is a partner of the EIIS company. It is, however, possible for a director or employee to be a 'qualifying individual' as long as: any payments received by the director or employee from the EIIS company do not exceed the normal levels of business expense reimbursement; any dividend received from the EIIS company does not exceed a normal rate of return; and any salaries/payments received are reasonable and necessary remuneration for services rendered to the EIIS company.

In addition, an individual will be regarded as 'connected' to an EIIS company if:

- they are a direct or indirect holder of (or entitled to acquire) 30% or more of the EIIS company's ordinary share capital, loan capital or voting rights, or, in the event of the company winding up, they hold or are entitled to acquire 30% or more of the company's assets; or
- they are entitled to ensure that the affairs of the EIIS company are conducted in accordance with their wishes.

These latter two methods of 'connection' to the EIIS company will not arise where the entire EIIS investment received by the company does not exceed €500,000.

Another anti-avoidance rule states that an individual will be regarded as 'connected' to an EIIS company if they are an investor in another (unrelated) company under an 'arrangement' whereby a person connected with that other company invests in the EIIS company.

### *10.3.2 Investment by Directors, Employees or Shareholders of SMEs*

To summarise the potential availability of EIIS relief to directors, employees and existing shareholders of an EIIS company, we can see that:

- a director or employee of an EIIS company may invest in that company, as long as the director or employee does not receive, for example, business expenses, dividends or salary/remuneration that exceed normal levels;
- an existing shareholder of the EIIS company may invest if, at the time of the investment, their direct/indirect ownership (or entitlement to ownership) is less than 30% of the company's ordinary shares, loan capital, voting rights or assets on a winding up;
- where this 30% threshold is exceeded at the time of investment, it may still be possible for an existing shareholder of the EIIS company to invest as long as the total investment received by the company does not exceed €500,000; and
- an attempt to get around these conditions by making an arrangement with another investor which involves a parallel investment in another unrelated company will be defeated by the anti-avoidance rules.

### 10.3.3 Anti-avoidance Rules that may Negate the Tax Relief

There are some expansive anti-avoidance rules in place that may disallow a claim for income tax relief or trigger a clawback of income tax relief already secured by an EIIS investor, in the situation where the investor 'receives value' from the EIIS company.[7] Clearly, these rules are aimed at preventing a scenario where the EIIS investor has secured tax relief and also secures some sort of refund of some or all of the monies invested in the EIIS shares. There is a broad list of different ways of receiving value; in general, the amount of income tax relief to be disallowed/clawed back will be determined by the following formula:

$$\text{Income tax relief} \times \frac{\text{Amount of value received by EIIS investor}}{\text{Total EIIS investment made by investor}}$$

The definition of 'receipt of value' includes:

- the redemption, repayment or repurchase of any of its share capital or securities owned by the EIIS investor;
- the repayment by the company of a debt to the EIIS investor, other than an ordinary trade debt;
- the company making a payment to the EIIS investor to give up their right to the repayment of any debt, other than an ordinary trade debt;
- the company releasing the EIIS investor from any debt owed to the company or discharging any debt owed by the EIIS investor to a third party;
- the company making a loan to the EIIS investor;
- the company transferring an asset to the EIIS investor for a price that is less than market value or acquiring an asset from the investor at a price in excess of market value; and
- the company making any payment to the EIIS investor, other than repayment of an ordinary trade debt or the payment of usual expenses and remuneration to a company employee or director.

In general, these rules will apply if the EIIS investor is in receipt of value at any time during a period beginning two years before the issue of the EIIS shares (or since incorporation of the EIIS company, if this is sooner) and ending three years after the issue of the shares.

## 10.4 Practicalities of Setting up an EIIS

### 10.4.1 Creating and Marketing the EIIS to Investors

Though not comprehensive, this chapter has thus far given an overview of the way in which an EIIS scheme works and some of the many conditions that must be met so that the income tax relief may be secured. It is obvious that proper advice must be taken in order to put this scheme together,

[7] Section 497 TCA 1997.

usually from a solicitor and accountant/tax advisor, both of whom are experienced in this area.

Given the costs of professional advice required to establish a scheme, it is also worth considering the levels of investment that the existing shareholders of the potential EIIS company are hoping to secure. In general, we would say that the minimum investment level should be in the region of €100,000 in order to make the scheme worth the company's while. The next question that should be considered is: who are the target investors? It is clear that there is no point in going through the process and expense of putting a scheme together and then being unable to secure sufficient EIIS investors.

The Revenue website contains a list of all companies that have issued BES/EIIS/SURE shares since 1 January 2007, as well as the value of the BES/EIIS/SURE share investment. It is interesting to note that in relation to EIIS shares the amounts range from less than €20,000 up to €1 million. So, what about the companies that raised less than €20,000? It is possible that they paid experienced solicitors/tax advisors, at their usual rates, to produce the scheme, in which case the whole exercise was probably a waste of time. Alternatively, they may have tried to put the scheme in place 'on a shoestring', with relatively little or inexperienced professional advice, and then tried to sell the EIIS shares themselves to friends and family. In such a case, they may have significant headaches unwinding the scheme after the holding period.

When creating an EIIS scheme, the best approach is to secure the advice of an experienced tax advisor who can consider whether the company's proposals (regarding business plans, rate of return for EIIS investors, etc.) are marketable, suggest changes to improve their marketability and analyse the target investor market. This advisor may also act as an intermediary and source investors for the EIIS shares. In the current economic climate, a potential EIIS investor will focus on issues such as the quality of the EIIS company's management, whether the EIIS company will have good asset backing and the level of its actual/expected borrowings from other sources. The experienced tax advisor advising on the creation of an EIIS scheme will give guidance on these and other issues.

The key point here is that before the process of creating the EIIS scheme begins and significant professional fees are incurred, the focus should be on the proposed scheme's marketability.

### *10.4.2 Overview of the Documentation Required*

We have seen that the EIIS investor makes their investment by subscribing for (purchasing) a new class of ordinary shares (what we have called 'EIIS shares'). This means that the company's constitutional document(s) must be amended to provide for the new class of EIIS shares and to set out the rights attaching to the new shares and the original shares in the company. In addition, documentation must be put in place setting out what the EIIS investor may do with the shares during the holding period and providing an exit for the EIIS investor once the minimum four-year holding period has expired. Finally, the promoter of the EIIS investment will need to create a 'placing memorandum' that can be presented to potential investors. As there can be no guarantee of the availability of the second tranche (10%) of income tax relief, a potential EIIS investor will need to be convinced that the company's management has the ability to ensure an increase in employment numbers or R&D expenditure during the holding period, in order to secure this second tranche of income tax relief.

In our experience, the documentation required will include the following:

- Placing memorandum, which may include information on the company's history and promoters/shareholders, details of the company's management team and their experience, a business plan covering the use to which the proceeds of the EIIS share issue will be put, projected profit and loss accounts, balance sheets and cash-flow projections.

### Example 10.2: EIIS Shares – Return on Investment Calculation

The placing memorandum will usually include a 'return on investment calculation', an example of which is set out below. For the purposes of this example, assume that the maximum buyback price for the EIIS shares is €1.10 per €1 share.

Indicative cash position in relation to an investment of 10,000 €1 EIIS shares:

| | € |
|---|---|
| Current outlay | (10,000) |
| Income tax relief in year of investment: 30/40 × 40% | 3,000 |
| (assuming marginal income tax rate of 40%) | |
| Income tax relief after four-year holding period: 10/40 × 40% | 1,000 |
| (assuming marginal income tax rate of 40% *and* conditions for award of second tranche of tax relief are met) | |
| Buyback of shares at maximum €1.10 price | 11,000 |
| Net positive cash position | 5,000 |

- Tax advice in relation to the proposed EIIS investment, including confirmation that it meets all the requirements of the legislation to secure the income tax relief for the investors.
- All company secretarial paperwork required to amend the investee company's constitutional documents and to issue the new EIIS shares.

- Put and call option agreement between the EIIS investor and the investee company and/or its promoters.
- Shareholding agreement (optional) setting out how the EIIS investors may deal with their shares during the holding period, e.g. whether they may gift or sell the EIIS shares, what happens in the event of their death, etc.

There are two types of activity/business where 'advance clearance' is required from another state agency (in addition to Revenue):

1. 'Tourist traffic undertakings' – these must secure clearance from Fáilte Ireland.
2. 'Internationally traded financial services' – where clearance must be secured from Enterprise Ireland.

All other companies that wish to secure EIIS funding (and that do not carry on any of the excluded activities set out in **Appendix I**) will usually proceed to the first stage of securing Revenue approval, i.e. the application for outline approval, which typically takes approximately six to eight weeks to secure, assuming all the paperwork is in order. ***Note:*** when considering an application for outline approval, it is quite normal for Revenue to request a copy of some draft documentation, e.g. placing memorandum, amended company constitutional document(s), and put and call option agreement. This means that it would be unwise to submit an application for outline approval on a speculative basis without having the scheme documentation in draft form.

The order of events as regards Revenue, the investee company and the investors is as follows:

- Company applies for outline approval, which is generally required in order to market the EIIS investment.
- Investors subscribe for the new class of shares that are expected to be confirmed as EIIS shares.
- Company submits claim for EIIS relief.
- Revenue issues authorisation to company to issue certificates of relief to EIIS investors.
- Company issues certificates of relief to EIIS investors.[8]

### *10.4.3 Timing of Claims*

#### *10.4.3.1 Timing for Companies*

EIIS status may be claimed immediately by companies that are already trading or, for newly established companies, after they have been trading

[8] For more information on the operation of the EIIS scheme, see Revenue leaflet IT55 *The Employment and Investment Incentive (EII) – Relief for Investment in Corporate Trades*. Available at www.revenue.ie/en/tax/it/leaflets/it55.html (accessed June 2016).

for four months.[9] Where the company is not trading at the time of issuing the EIIS shares (because it is using the funds to carry out R&D activities), EIIS status may not be claimed until either it:

- commences trading, and it must commence trading within two years of the share issue; *or*
- spends at least 30% of the monies invested on R&D activities connected with carrying on 'relevant trading activities'.

#### *10.4.3.2 Timing for Individual Investors*

Once the investor has secured a certificate of relief, they can make a claim for income tax relief for the tax year in which they subscribed for the EIIS shares.

Where the investor invests in an EIIS designated investment fund (DIF), which holds a pool of funds and invests them in a number of EIIS companies, the investor may be issued with shares in the tax year following the year in which they invest in the EIIS DIF. If this happens, then the investor can choose to claim the income tax relief in the tax year of investment as opposed to the tax year in which the shares are issued to them.[10]

## 10.5 Case Studies: Different Attitudes to Seeking EIIS Funding

Each of our three case-study businesses considered EIIS funding and whether it should form part of the mix of funding for their business.

CASE STUDY: FOUR BLUE DUCKS/BLUE LACHA LTD

We saw in the previous chapter that, after the early years, Jim and Cathy looked again at the structure of Jim's café business (a sole trade) and considered their business expansion plans. The business had reached a stage where some of the trading profits could be retained and reinvested in developing the business, so the business's tax advisor, Maeve, advised that it would be more tax efficient to do this through a company. She also outlined the possible use of the EIIS as a source of funding and the fact that it can only be utilised where the EIIS investment is made in a 'qualifying company'. Jim and Cathy were keen to pursue the EIIS funding route, and incorporate Jim's business into a new company called Blue Lacha Ltd in June 2016.

[9] Section 489(4) TCA 1997.
[10] Section 489(3) TCA 1997.

The EIIS funding would be used to lease new factory premises, employ qualified catering staff and construct food production lines that would create 'home cooking' ready meals, including meat, fish and vegetarian options, which could be cooked by customers in their own homes. Jim and Cathy had been very encouraged by the constant requests from their café customers to provide a takeaway service of the meals served in the café, and felt that they had a ready market. They also felt that some of the customers would be interested in supporting their business by making an EIIS investment in Blue Lacha Ltd. Jim and Cathy's ultimate plan is to have four different food production lines and they had estimated the total cost of buying the production equipment for each line at €45,000. While Cathy was keen to construct all four new production lines immediately, Jim was very concerned about the four-year investment timeframe, after which Blue Lacha Ltd would have to buy the EIIS shares back from the investors. He was conscious that some of the EIIS investors would be friends or family.

After working with Maeve on a business plan for this new phase of the business, Jim and Cathy concluded that Blue Lacha Ltd should plan to lease new premises, construct two food production lines and employ two staff in the short term. The company would then rely on trading profits to construct the third and fourth production lines. Jim and Cathy intended to keep their Four Blue Ducks café business open as an element of their business in its own right and also as a marketing and distribution tool for the new food production business. They were, therefore, confident that the staff numbers employed by Blue Lacha Ltd would be increased during the four-year timeframe of the EIIS and strongly emphasised this aspect, and the resale value of the food production equipment, to potential EIIS investors. Jim and Cathy were hoping to secure EIIS funding of €150,000, but were ultimately happy to receive €125,000 investment in their business in late 2016/early 2017.

## Case Study: Tigim Language Learning Ltd

We saw in **Chapter 2** that Aoife subscribed for shares in Tigim Language Learning Ltd on the basis that she would secure income tax relief under the Startup Refunds for Entrepreneurs (SURE) scheme. She did not take any professional advice on whether the company was eligible for the scheme and was very disappointed when her claim for income tax relief was rejected. This was on the basis that Revenue regarded Tigim Language Learning Ltd's activities as excluded from the definition of 'relevant trading activities'. We noted previously that many of the definitions relevant to a claim for EIIS also apply to the SURE scheme. The list of excluded activities (for both SURE and EIIS purposes) are set out in **Appendix I** to this chapter and Tigim Language Learning Ltd was treated as falling within exclusion (d), being "the provision of services, which would result in a close company ... being treated as a service company and subject to the close company services surcharge".

Once Aoife's claim for SURE scheme tax relief had been rejected, she knew that the company could not create a valid EIIS scheme.

### Case Study: The Neally Group

Danielle and Martin have big plans for developing a new business stream of manufacturing silicone tools for the life sciences industry. We will see in **Chapter 11** (about the R&D tax credit) that the company's chemical engineer, Dirk, and his staff had spent some time establishing a method of stabilising a type of silicone, with the intention of being able to use it to produce the tools. After a couple of months of initial testing, funded out of the company's own trading profits, Danielle and Martin thought that they could see a promising future for this research and that they would need a plan for funding it.

They considered the EIIS and noted that the type of work being carried out by Dirk and his team would fall squarely within the type of R&D activities covered by the scheme. The intention was that these R&D activities would ultimately generate a new income stream for the company. Funding would be required in order to fit out a mezzanine floor to be built into the company's existing factory premises, as well as paying for all relevant equipment and covering salaries for Dirk and his staff. But there was also the question of how long it would take Dirk to finish his research and then apply it for commercial use. Dirk was hard to pin down on timeframes and talked vaguely about 12 to 18 months.

Danielle and Martin initially rejected the option of EIIS funding as they thought that the four-year timeframe would be too short to allow for completion of the research, the development of commercial applications and the generation of trading profits from products resulting from the research.

Instead, the company applied to Enterprise Ireland (EI) for a grant from their R&D Standard Projects fund. EI saw potential in the silicone research being carried out by Dirk, but were keen to see if there would be interest from the life sciences industry for this type of product. As a result, EI committed to providing a €150,000 grant from the R&D Standard Projects fund if the Neally Group first created an EIIS scheme and secured €250,000 of EIIS investment. Danielle and Martin took professional advice and considered whether some of their proposed future silicone tools customers would be interested in investing in this type of research. With Dirk's input, they also put together what they considered a reasonable timeframe to get from research to saleable product. They went ahead with the EIIS scheme on the basis of a longer holding period of five years, which was compensated for by a higher maximum buyback price for the EIIS shares than usual. On this basis, the EIIS scheme raised €250,000 in EIIS funding, which allowed the release of the EI grant.

## Appendix I: Activities Not Regarded as 'Relevant Trading Activities' for EIIS Purposes[11]

(a) Adventures or concerns in the nature of trade;
(b) dealing in commodities or futures or in shares, securities or other financial assets;
(c) financing activities;
(d) the provision of services that would result in a close company ... being treated as a service company and subject to the close company services surcharge (see **Chapter 6** for explanation of the 'close company' and 'services company' concepts);
(e) dealing in or developing land;
(f) the occupation and use of woodlands in this State;
(g) operating or managing hotels, guesthouses, self-catering accommodation or comparable establishments or managing these types of properties used for these purposes. Since 1 January 2013, this exclusion does not apply to these properties if they are classed as a 'tourist traffic undertaking'; essentially this refers to tourist accommodation registered by Fáilte Ireland;
(h) operations carried out in the coal industry or steel or shipbuilding sectors; and
(i) the production of a film.[12]

[11] Section 488 TCA 1997, as amended by section 18 FA 2015.
[12] Note that these activities are also excluded from eligibility for the SURE scheme, set out in **Chapter 2**.

## CHAPTER 11

# THE R&D TAX CREDIT AND THE 'KNOWLEDGE DEVELOPMENT BOX'



While the research and development tax credit (colloquially known as 'the R&D credit') has been on the statute books for more than 10 years, it is only in the past few years that claims for this tax credit have really accelerated. Most people are aware of the 'R&D credit' but assume, wrongly, that it is only available to a limited number of specialised companies and that it is only the companies themselves that can benefit from it.

More recently, the 2015 Finance Act introduced the 'Knowledge Development Box', a tax incentive whereby a lower corporation tax rate will apply to profits arising from the exploitation of certain intellectual property assets, which are the result of qualifying R&D activity carried out in Ireland.

We will see that the 'R&D credit' and the Knowledge Development Box (KDB) are part of a broad range of supports, both tax-based and financial, offered by state authorities to encourage Irish companies to pursue research and development activities that:

- seek to achieve scientific or technological advancement; and
- involve the resolution of scientific or technological uncertainty.[1]

In this chapter, we will overview the current R&D tax regime, including:

- the corporation tax credit available to a company for both R&D activities and the business premises housing those R&D activities;
- surrender of this tax credit by a company to a 'key employee';
- the Knowledge Development Box (KDB), introduced in relation to accounting periods commencing on or after 1 January 2016; and
- tax deductions for expenditure on 'scientific research'.

A fundamental question that must be determined from the outset is whether or not an individual company (or group of companies) is actually engaged in R&D activities. While this chapter sets out, in broad strokes, the types of activity that may be defined as R&D activities, any claim should be supported by technical analysis prepared by relevant experts. This is necessary because R&D tax credit claims require two types of expertise: tax and scientific/technical.

The aim of this chapter is to explain how the R&D tax credit works, outline some of the most important conditions that must be met and outline the processes that must be followed and documentation that must be generated (and retained) in order to justify the claim in a Revenue audit. We will see that the KDB regime piggybacks on the R&D tax credit regime, borrowing its definition of 'eligible expenditure'; the section of this chapter that relates to the KDB regime aims to provide an overview only of how that regime will operate.

## 11.1 Overview of the R&D Tax Credit Available to a Company

Set out below is a summary of the key features of a claim for an R&D tax credit.

- The R&D tax credit is available to an Irish tax-resident company (or group of companies) that incurs expenditure on 'qualifying R&D activities' in Ireland or in a country located in the European Economic Area (EEA), being the EU Member States plus Iceland, Liechtenstein and Norway.
- Where a company receives direct or indirect grant assistance that covers qualifying expenditure, then the company will not be regarded as having incurred that expenditure, so no tax credit may be claimed.

[1] Section 766 of the Taxes Consolidation Act 1997 (TCA 1997).

The better-known state and EU authorities providing such grants include Enterprise Ireland, IDA Ireland, Science Foundation Ireland and the EU Horizon 2020 programme.

- The R&D tax credit may be claimed on 'eligible expenditure', which includes revenue and capital expenditure incurred wholly and exclusively for R&D purposes.
- The cost of a limited amount of outsourced R&D activities may also be eligible for the tax credit.
- The rate of the tax credit is 25%, which is in addition to the usual corporation tax deduction or capital allowance applicable to the expenditure (currently 12.5% for trading companies). This means that the total tax credit available for qualifying expenditure will be at a rate of 37.5%. Another way of looking at this is that the company gets three times the usual deduction or allowance for this expenditure.
- The R&D tax credit may be claimed on expenditure incurred on buildings used to house the R&D activities, as long the R&D activities constitute at least 35% of all activities in these buildings over a four-year period.
- From 1 January 2009 forward, the tax credit must be claimed within 12 months of the end of the accounting period in which the expenditure was incurred.

We have already noted that the R&D tax credit is available to a company or a group of companies. Where a group situation arises, there are detailed rules in relation to allocation of the R&D expenditure and the associated tax credit, as well as how to deal with group accounting issues. In order to get to grips with the fundamental rules for claiming an R&D tax credit, we will not refer to group situations here but will focus only on an R&D tax credit claim by an individual company.

### *11.1.1 Calculating the 25% Tax Credit*

In later sections of this chapter we will review the conditions that must be met in order for a company to claim an R&D tax credit on qualifying R&D expenditure. But first, we will confirm the extent of the credit, assuming that all of these conditions are met. Changes in the 2014 Finance Act have drastically simplified the calculation of qualifying R&D expenditure as this now refers to *all* expenditure in a 'relevant period' that meets all of the conditions set out in Section 11.1.5 below. This new definition of qualifying R&D expenditure applies to 'relevant periods' commencing on or after 1 January 2015.[2] In most cases, the relevant period will match the company's current accounting period, but it will not always do so.

***Note:*** a rather complicated method of calculating the R&D tax credit applied to expenditure incurred in 'relevant periods' commencing before 1 January 2015.

[2] Section 766 TCA 1997.

### 11.1.2 Use of the Tax Credit: Reduce Corporation Tax Liabilities or Secure a Cash Refund

When the R&D tax credit has been calculated, the company must then determine how that tax credit will be used. There are a number of possible outcomes, which must take the following order:[3]

1. Reduction of the company's corporation tax (CT) liability for the accounting period in which the expenditure was incurred.
2. Reduction of the prior accounting period's CT liability.
3. Where the CT liabilities of the current and prior accounting periods are not sufficient to absorb the tax credit, then the company has two options, either to:
   (a) carry the tax credit forward against future CT liabilities of the company; or
   (b) elect to have the tax credit *paid* to the company in the form of a cash refund from Revenue.

If the cash refund option is chosen, then the cash refund may be paid out in three tranches over a period of 33 months from the end of the accounting period in which the qualifying R&D expenditure was incurred, subject to very specific rules. For the purposes of illustrating these dates below, the expenditure is taken to have been incurred in the accounting period ended 31 October 2013.

- The first tranche of 33% of the excess tax credit will be paid out after the CT return filing deadline for the accounting period in which the expenditure was incurred, e.g. after 23 July 2014 for a 31 October 2013 accounting period.
- Any excess tax credit will be used to reduce the CT liability of the next accounting period, i.e. period ending 31 October 2014.
- If there is any excess tax credit, then 50% of this excess (second tranche) will be paid out 12 months after payment of the first tranche, i.e. after 23 July 2015.
- The remaining excess tax credit will then be used to reduce the CT liability of the next accounting period, i.e. period ending 31 October 2015.
- Any excess tax credit still remaining (third tranche) will be paid out 24 months after payment of the first tranche, i.e. after 23 July 2016.

This opportunity to turn the tax credit into a cash payment is an extremely attractive aspect of the R&D tax credit regime as it may be used by loss-making companies to improve their cash-flow position.

#### *11.1.2.1 The Cash Refund*

There are two important issues to note about this refund. First, in addition to all of the usual conditions that must be met in order for the tax credit

[3] Sections 766(4), 766(4A) and 766(4B) TCA 1997.

to arise (i.e. the requirements for qualifying R&D activities, eligible expenditure, etc.), if the tax credit is used by way of a cash-refund claim, then there is a further condition/rule to be met. This rule states that the value of the cash refund is capped at a figure which is the *greater* of:

- the company's CT liabilities for the 10 accounting periods before the accounting period before the period in which the expenditure was incurred; *or*
- the payroll tax liabilities of the company in relation to employees employed during the accounting period in which the expenditure was incurred and the prior accounting period.

***Note:*** both of these thresholds may be subject to complicated adjustment, further details of which are set out in Revenue's *Research & Development Tax Credit Guidelines* (the '2015 Revenue Guidelines').[4]

The impact of this cap could be very significant for more recently established companies that do not have a 10-year history of paying corporation tax, or for companies that operate with a small, highly skilled staff. Either or both of these traits would typically characterise a start-up business. ***Note:*** potentially, this cap applies to the cash refund only; where it operates to restrict a company from claiming a cash refund, the company still retains the tax credit claim and can use it to reduce future CT liabilities.

The second issue to note is that, in accounting terms, the cash refund can be recognised 'above the line'. What this means is that the cash refund is treated as being similar to a grant and can be shown in the company's profit and loss account as a type of income, thereby boosting the company's operating figures. This accounting treatment is often used by companies competing internationally for R&D projects, as they can present the cost of basing the project in Ireland on a 75%-of-total-cost basis (i.e. 100% cost less 25% R&D cash refund). This accounting treatment does not apply to a tax credit that cannot be translated into a cash refund.

In **Section 11.1.1** and **Section 11.1.2** above, we reviewed the extent of the R&D tax credit and how the tax credit may be used by a company. We now delve more deeply into the conditions that must be met in order for an R&D tax credit claim to arise.

> To make a valid claim for the R&D tax credit, the following broad conditions must be met:
>
> - the activities carried out by the company must be 'qualifying R&D activities'; *and*
> - the company must be a 'qualifying company'; *and*
> - the expenditure incurred on these activities must be 'eligible expenditure'.

[4] Updated April 2015. See www.revenue.ie/en/tax/ct/research-development.html (accessed June 2016).

### 11.1.3 'Qualifying R&D Activities'

The tax rules define 'qualifying R&D activities' as:

"... systematic, investigative or experimental activities in a field of science or technology, being one or more of the following—

(i) **basic research**, namely, experimental or theoretical work undertaken primarily to acquire new scientific or technical knowledge without a specific practical application in view,

(ii) **applied research**, namely, work undertaken in order to gain scientific or technical knowledge and directed towards a specific practical application, or

(iii) **experimental development**, namely work undertaken which draws on scientific or technical knowledge or practical experience for the purpose of achieving technological advancement and which is directed at producing new, or improving existing, materials, products, devices, processes, systems or services including incremental improvements thereto:

but activities will not be research and development activities unless they—

(I) seek to achieve **scientific or technological advancement**, and

(II) involve the resolution of **scientific or technological uncertainty**".[5]

The 2015 Revenue Guidelines make clear that the scientific/technological advancement sought must be an overall advancement and not an advancement in the company's own state of knowledge or capability alone. If a competent professional working in the field could reasonably be expected to have that knowledge or capability, then the fact that the company's R&D activities advance the company's own knowledge or capability will not, of itself, result in those activities being treated as qualifying R&D activities.

The scientific/technological uncertainty to be resolved could relate to:

"a. Uncertainty as to whether a particular goal can be achieved, or
b. Uncertainty (from a scientific or technological perspective) in relation to alternative methods that will meet desired specifications such as cost, reliability or reproducibility."[6]

We can see that the first category of potential R&D activity, 'basic research', is research for its own sake as there may be no attempt to secure a practical application for scientific or technological advance. The second category, 'applied research', covers work that involves both the pursuit of a scientific/technological advance and a practical application of that knowledge. The final category covers work that looks to produce new or improved results from existing knowledge or experience.

As few commercial companies will pursue knowledge for its own sake and without looking for a practical application, the majority of R&D tax credit claims will fall into categories (ii) and (iii) outlined above.

[5] Section 766 TCA 1997 (emphasis added).

[6] 2015 Revenue Guidelines, Section 3.5.

***Note:*** the tax rules require only that one of these three categories of activities is *pursued* by the company – they do not require the pursuit to be successful or fully realised.

A list of science and technology fields in which qualifying R&D activities may be carried out are included in the 2015 Revenue Guidelines and are set out in **Appendix I** to this chapter. The broad categories are natural sciences, engineering and technology, medical sciences and agricultural science. Also set out, both in the 2015 Revenue Guidelines and in **Appendix II**, is a non-exhaustive list of activities that are *not* treated as research and development activities.

As a general rule, there is no correspondence with Revenue in advance of a claim for the R&D tax credit, which means that a company's management team (and their tax advisors) must self-assess whether or not the company is entitled to claim the tax credit. The procedure for claiming the tax credit is as simple as including the relevant figures in the relevant box of the company's corporation tax return.

Many R&D tax credit claims are the subject of a Revenue audit and the Revenue auditor may withdraw some or all of the credit previously claimed if they view some or all of the claim as being ineligible. The withdrawal of an R&D claim is likely to result in the payment of additional corporation tax liabilities (or repayments of R&D tax credits paid out as cash refunds) as well as penalties and interest. We will review the elements of a Revenue audit that are specific to the review of an R&D tax credit claim below in **Section 11.3**.

So, what can management do to ensure that company activities that they believe to be qualifying R&D activities stand up to Revenue scrutiny? There are three possible approaches that can be taken to minimise risk on the R&D tax credit claim:

1. Reliance on the opinion of the company's own technical staff who are involved in the R&D activities. If there is doubt, the company could secure a second opinion from an external technical expert.
2. Request an advance opinion from Revenue as to whether or not the intended activities would be regarded as R&D activities. This option is available only in limited circumstances and Revenue may decline to provide an advance opinion. Company management (and the company's tax advisor) must assess the likelihood of securing an advance opinion and whether the request for an opinion may increase the possibility of a later Revenue audit. It is understood that very few requests for advance opinions are made in this regard.
3. There is a general facility available to taxpayers who are not regarded as acting with a view to evading or avoiding tax and which would, at least, protect the taxpayer from interest on late payment of tax and penalties. Any underpayment of tax (as a result of an R&D tax credit being withdrawn) would still be payable. This facility is called an '**expression of doubt**' and may be relied upon where the taxpayer is genuinely in doubt as to the correct tax treatment of a particular item. In this case, the taxpayer must provide a 'letter of expression of doubt'

setting out the full details. Company management (and the tax advisor) must consider whether it is appropriate to rely on this facility if no doubt exists in their minds as to the eligibility of the activities. There is also the question of whether the inclusion of an 'expression of doubt' in the company's corporation tax return will increase the possibility of a later Revenue audit.

Below we explain how the directors of two of our case study businesses, the Neally Group and Tigim Language Learning Ltd, became aware of the R&D tax credit and how they assessed whether their company could have an entitlement to make an R&D tax credit claim.

### Case Study: The Neally Group

In the initial phase of Neally Engineering Ltd's life, the company focused on producing metal products for the aviation industry. As an experienced chemical engineer, Danielle thought that the company had more opportunity to expand if they developed products for the life sciences industry. Danielle and Martin honed in on a particular type of silicone, which until then had been regarded by the industry as too unstable for commercial use. Danielle knew a brilliant chemical scientist, Dirk, who had carried out an academic research project on the developmental potential of this silicone and was willing to come and work on it. Neally Engineering Ltd constructed a specialised laboratory facility on the company's new mezzanine level and, after a number of months of work, Dirk and his staff had developed a commercial method of stabilising the silicone product. Buoyed by the huge interest expressed by potential life science customers, a newly incorporated group company, Neally Silicone Ltd, developed a system that could stabilise the silicone product and mould it into new silicone tools.

As Danielle had been involved in claims for R&D tax credits in previous jobs, she did not hesitate in employing tax advisors to liaise with Dirk, whose professional opinion would be the basis for claiming that the company was carrying out qualifying R&D activities. The tax advisors also provided advice on project documentation and prepared the tax credit claims.

In the case of the Neally Group, Danielle's previous experience of R&D tax credit claims ensured that she was immediately aware of the potential tax benefits of Dirk's research.

### Case Study: Tigim Language Learning

For Tigim Language Learning Ltd the opposite was the case and, in fact, company management only thought to consider the R&D tax credit after a chance meeting that Aoife had with Cillian, a friend of a friend. Aoife told him about Tigim Language Learning Ltd and the company's cash-flow pressure, so Cillian suggested that Aoife look at the R&D tax credit. He told her, "You would be amazed how many companies do not claim this tax credit, even though they are perfectly entitled to it. Everyone thinks that it only applies in businesses with people in white coats, working in a sterile laboratory, but it is much more widely available than that. It sounds to me like there might be some R&D activity in those online apps for language teaching you were telling me about. Why don't you check it out?"

When Aoife raised the question with the company's tax advisor, however, she was not encouraged. He outlined that it can be quite difficult to secure the R&D tax credit for the development of computer software. Aoife decided that she would be better off spending her time on other aspects of the business.

### *11.1.4 'Qualifying Company'*

In order to be regarded as a 'qualifying company' eligible to claim the tax credit, the company must meet various criteria, including:
- during the relevant period, the company must carry on a trade;
- the company must carry out qualifying R&D activities in the relevant period; and
- the company must maintain a record of the expenditure incurred by it in carrying out these activities.

The requirement to maintain a record of the expenditure should not be underestimated – extensive and detailed records must be kept. It is not unusual for a Revenue auditor to disallow R&D tax credit claims on the basis of a lack of documentation, even where they are in agreement that, on the face of it, the activities clearly fall squarely within the definition of qualifying R&D activities. Poor record-keeping, especially a lack of contemporaneous records, are regularly cited by Revenue auditors as the reason that R&D tax credit claims are disallowed.

We referred above to the fact that, in order to qualify for the tax credit, the company's activities must be regarded as qualifying R&D activities (known as 'the science test') and the expenditure must be regarded as 'eligible expenditure' (known as 'the accounting test').

The 2015 Revenue Guidelines set out a series of requirements for documentation in order for a company to pass both the science test and accounting test.[7] The Guidelines emphasise that records must be kept on a continuous and contemporaneous basis; the entries into the records should be made on a timely and consistent basis; and 'linking papers', which link the R&D documentation to the R&D tax credit claimed, must

[7] 2015 Revenue Guidelines, Section 8.

be retained. The company must be able to demonstrate the aims of the R&D project, the progress towards those aims and the outcomes of the activities, and whether or not it achieved these aims.

### *11.1.5 'Eligible Expenditure' on R&D Activities*

Once it has been determined that the company is a qualifying company and that the specific activities can be regarded as qualifying R&D activities, the next question is what expenditure on these activities will be eligible for the R&D tax credit.

The tax rules define 'eligible expenditure' as expenditure "incurred by the company wholly and exclusively in the *carrying on by it* of research and development activities in a relevant Member State"[8] and lists various eligible items. The expenditure that is most typically the subject of an R&D tax credit claim by a qualifying company includes: expenses deductible for trading purposes; plant, machinery and buildings eligible for capital allowances; and royalties.

The 2015 Revenue Guidelines note that the use of the phrase "carrying on by it" is regarded as narrowing the scope of eligible expenditure and that expenditure incurred to *enable* a company to carry on R&D activities will not be eligible for a tax credit claim. ***Note:*** 'eligible expenditure' is not limited to profit and loss account items only; expenditure capitalised in the company's balance sheet may also be eligible.

The types of expense that will be regarded as 'eligible' or 'ineligible' for the purposes of the tax credit are set out in detail below:

- **Eligible *direct* costs** Include:
  - full cost of salaries of staff directly involved in the R&D activity, plus a 'just and reasonable' portion of the salary costs of staff who spend part of their time on the R&D activity. The 2015 Revenue Guidelines distinguish between elements of a staff member's reward package, which are eligible for the tax credit, e.g. health insurance, pension contributions or bonus arrangements, and overheads associated with the employment, e.g. HR costs, which are not eligible;
  - fuel and utilities used in the R&D activity;
  - materials and laboratory equipment used in the R&D activity.
- **Eligible *indirect* costs** that are incurred in-house, include, under certain conditions, the costs of hiring part-time or short-term-basis consultants operating as sub-contractors to the company, which can be treated as direct employee costs. One of the conditions is that the period of engagement cannot exceed six months; otherwise the consultants will be treated as agency staff and be subject to the limitations on outsourcing set out below.
- **Costs that are specifically ineligible for the tax credit** Include:
  - costs not wholly and exclusively incurred in the carrying on of the R&D activity, including indirect overheads such as recruitment fees,

[8] Section 766 TCA 1997 (italics added).

  insurance, travel, equipment repairs or maintenance, shipping, business entertainment, legal fees, telephone and bank charges;
  - outsourced R&D activities, though see exception below.
- **Outsourced R&D activities** The general position is that expenditure incurred in outsourcing R&D activities to a third party will not be treated as eligible expenditure. This rule is subject to two exceptions:
  - for amounts paid to universities or institutes of higher education, the claim is limited to the *greater* of €100,000 *or* 5% of the expenditure incurred by the company itself on R&D activities, subject to the company incurring at least the same level of R&D expenditure itself; and
  - for amounts paid to any other *unconnected* third parties, the claim is limited to the *greater* of €100,000 *or* 15% of the expenditure incurred by the company itself on R&D activities, subject to the company incurring at least the same level of R&D expenditure itself.[9]

  ***Note:*** in order for the outsourced expenditure noted above to be eligible for R&D tax credit, the outsourced activity must constitute qualifying R&D activity in its own right.
- **Plant and Machinery** A 100% 'upfront' deduction may be claimed in relation to plant and machinery that is eligible for the usual capital allowances available to a company that uses the equipment for the purposes of its trade.[10] (For a summary of the conditions attaching to a typical claim for capital allowances, see **Chapter 6**.) The 100% deduction is available only if the company uses the equipment solely for its R&D activities. If the equipment has dual use, e.g. R&D activities and production, then a 'just and reasonable' apportionment must be made to determine the percentage use of the equipment for R&D activities.
- **Pre-trading Expenditure** A claim in relation to eligible pre-trading expenditure may be made once the company's trading activity has commenced. The claim must be made within 12 months of the end of the accounting period in which the trade commenced.

For more information on whether expenditure is 'eligible' for the purposes of the tax credit claim, see the 2015 Revenue Guidelines.

### *11.1.6 'Relevant Expenditure' on Buildings Used for R&D Purposes*

Many of the rules set out above that determine when expenditure on R&D activities may be eligible for the tax credit also apply in determining eligible expenditure on buildings that are used for R&D purposes.

Just as in the case of the 100% 'upfront' deduction in relation to plant and machinery used for R&D purposes, so the cost of buildings used for R&D purposes will only be eligible for the tax credit if the buildings are already eligible for capital allowances, in this case, industrial buildings allowance.

[9] Sections 766(1)(b)(vii) and (viii) TCA 1997.

[10] Part 9 TCA 1997.

(For a summary of the conditions attaching to a typical claim for industrial buildings allowance, see **Chapter 6**.)

Below is a summary of the key conditions that must be met in order to secure a tax credit for expenditure on buildings used for R&D purposes.

- To be a 'qualifying building', at least 35% of the building must be used by the company for the purpose of carrying on R&D activities in Ireland or the EEA for at least four years.
- For expenditure to be regarded as 'relevant expenditure', it must have been incurred on the construction or 'refurbishment' of a 'qualifying building' that qualifies for industrial buildings allowance. Monies spent on the acquisition of rights in or over any land will not be regarded as 'relevant expenditure'.
- For the purposes of an R&D tax credit claim, 'refurbishment' is defined as any work of construction, reconstruction, repair or renewal, including the provision of utilities or heating facilities carried out in the course of repair or restoration, or maintenance in the nature of repair or restoration, of the building.
- Where the building has a dual use, then the amount of the eligible 'relevant expenditure' will be:

$$\text{Total relevant expenditure} \times \frac{\text{Square meterage of building used for R\&D purposes}}{\text{Square meterage of entire building}}$$

In determining the amount of the building used for R&D purposes, the company must use a 'just and reasonable' apportionment that can be supported.

- Where a company has incurred relevant expenditure that meets all of the conditions, it may claim the tax credit in the accounting period in which the expenditure is incurred.
- In the case of a newly constructed qualifying building, at least 35% of the building must be used for R&D purposes for at least four years, commencing on the date the building was first brought into use for the purposes of the trade (which is the date that the expenditure is 'incurred').
- In the case of the refurbishment of a qualifying building, assuming the conditions are met, the credit is generally available commencing from the date on which the refurbishment is completed (which is the date that the expenditure is 'incurred').[11]

In the following case study extract, we see that in addition to claiming an R&D tax credit for expenditure incurred on their R&D activities, the Neally Group also considered whether the building from which the Group operates could be eligible for R&D tax credits.

[11] Section 766A TCA 1997.

### Case Study: The Neally Group

The Neally Group's tax advisors had reviewed the proposed R&D project to create a stable silicone product that could be manipulated for use in the life sciences industry. They had concluded that, in their view, the new project constituted 'qualifying R&D activities' and that Neally Silicone Ltd was a 'qualifying company'. They had also given the company's financial controller advice and spreadsheet tools to identify and capture the eligible expenditure that would constitute the company's R&D tax credit claim. The tax advisors had also highlighted that, if the Neally Group were successful in securing a mooted Enterprise Ireland grant in respect of some of the eligible R&D expenditure, then the amount of the R&D tax credit claim would be reduced by the amount of this grant.

The next question was whether the 'refurbishment works' on the newly constructed mezzanine level would comprise 'relevant expenditure' so that an R&D tax credit could be claimed on the cost of some or all of these works. The company's financial controller had already assessed that these works would be eligible for the industrial buildings allowance. As all the other conditions for R&D tax credit had been met, the question of eligibility came down to the '35% test', i.e. whether the Neally Group would use at least 35% of the building for R&D activities for at least four years. The company's advisors recommended that the test be assessed on the basis of square meterage of the mezzanine level as a percentage of the entire square meterage of the building. As only 25% of the entire building's floor area was to be used for the R&D activities, it was concluded that there was no entitlement to R&D tax credit for the cost of building the mezzanine floor.

## 11.2 Surrender of a Company's R&D Tax Credit to 'Key Employees'

The previous section reviewed the conditions attaching to a company's claim for R&D tax credit for expenditure incurred on R&D activities and on the buildings that house those R&D activities. The use to which an R&D tax credit can be put by the company was also set out. We now look at an alternative use of a company's R&D tax credit, which is the surrender of the company's credit to one or more 'key employees'. Allowing key employees involved in the company's R&D activities to share in the tax relief and reduce their personal tax bills sounds like an excellent way to incentivise them. In practice, however, the conditions attaching to this surrender and the potential tax risk to the company can inhibit the use of this incentive/reward. In addition, given the fact that neither a company director nor a shareholder who has a 'material interest' in the company may avail of this tax credit, then this facility may not be available to many Irish SMEs, which typically have only a small pool of shareholders/directors/key employees.

The features/conditions of this surrender of tax credit include:

- The employee must perform at least 50% of their activities in the "conception or creation of new knowledge, products, processes, methods and systems".
- At least 50% of that employee's salary costs must be regarded as eligible expenditure.
- The employee must not be, or have been, a director of the company or be connected to a director of the company.
- Neither the employee nor a person connected to them may have a 'material interest' (at least 5% of the company's shares) in the company.
- The tax credit can be used to reduce income tax only; it will not reduce USC or PRSI liabilities.
- The employee's use of the tax credit is limited to an amount that reduces their effective rate of income tax to 23% in a given tax year. If the tax credit surrendered would reduce the effective rate below this level, then the 'excess' tax credit can be carried forward by the employee to future tax years.
- The amount of the R&D tax credit that can be surrendered to a key employee is capped at the company's CT liability calculated without taking into account the R&D tax credit. This means, of course, that the company must be tax-paying in order to be allowed to surrender the tax credit; a condition that results in many start-up businesses being unable to utilise this relief.
- In order to surrender the tax credit, the company completes the relevant sections of its CT return, noting the value of the R&D tax credit and the amount that it is surrendering to the key employee. The employee can use the tax credit in the tax year following the tax year in which the company surrendered the tax credit. The employee must file an income tax return for that tax year, claiming the credit, which will generate an income tax refund for them.[12]

## Case Study: The Neally Group

Danielle and Martin were conscious that their chemical engineer, Dirk, who was leading the 'silicone project' was key to the development of this new business line. They were anxious to ensure that he would not leave the Neally Group and initially proposed to give him shares in Neally Silicone Ltd. Dirk's response was that he was not interested in a minority shareholding as he did not see any real value for him in this. Danielle then suggested to Martin that if the

[12] Sections 766(2A) and (2B), and 472D TCA 1997.

company was eligible for an R&D tax credit claim that they could look at surrendering some of the company's R&D tax credit to Dirk. This could generate an income tax refund for him, which he would definitely regard as valuable!

Danielle was aware that if a Revenue audit were to find that the R&D tax credit surrendered to Dirk was unauthorised and 'deliberately false or overstated' then the company would suffer a clawback of the R&D tax credit, which could generate significant CT liabilities, interest and penalties. She was comfortable, however, that the company had secured proper advice from their tax advisors and that there was little risk in surrendering the tax credit to Dirk.

See further information on the clawback of a surrendered R&D tax credit in **Section 11.3.2** below.

## 11.3 Revenue Audit/Review of R&D Tax Credit Claims

A Revenue audit/review of an R&D tax credit claim may arise even though the claim has been processed, i.e. even though the company's CT liability has been reduced or it has received a cash refund of some or all of the tax credit. Although a claim has been processed, this does not mean that it has been accepted, and Revenue retain the right to audit/review the claim within the usual parameters set out in its *Code of Practice for Revenue Audit*, detailed in **Chapter 8**. Only when the Revenue audit/review has concluded can we say that the R&D tax credit claim has been 'accepted' by Revenue.

In **Chapter 8** we reviewed interventions from Revenue that do not comprise a full Revenue audit, including a 'desk review' (i.e. aspect query/assurance check). The significance of the fact that this type of intervention is not treated as a full Revenue audit is that the taxpayer retains an opportunity to make an 'unprompted qualifying disclosure', which can result in lower penalties if there are unpaid taxes. In the context of an R&D tax credit claim, Revenue often initiate a desk review of the company's R&D report, at which time the company still has the opportunity to make an unprompted qualifying disclosure. Depending on the outcome of this desk review, a full Revenue audit may follow.

There are two significant differences between audits of R&D tax credits and general Revenue audits:

1. the potential requirement for technical assessment of the activities to determine if they comprise qualifying R&D activities; and
2. the specific clawback of credit that may arise if the Revenue auditor determines that some, or all, of the claim for R&D tax credit does not stand up.

### *11.3.1 Technical Assessment of the Company's Claimed R&D Activities*

In **Section 11.1.4** above, we noted that one of the conditions that must be met in order for a company to be regarded as a qualifying company is that it must retain sufficient records of the expenditure that forms the basis for the tax credit claim. The 2015 Revenue Guidelines note that these records must meet both the science test (i.e. the activities are qualifying R&D activities) and the accounting test (i.e. the expenditure incurred on those activities is eligible expenditure).

The first focus of a Revenue auditor may be an assessment of the science test and this assessment sometimes requires the appointment of a technical expert who has specialised knowledge in the relevant field. This technical expert may be sourced from an Irish university or other third-level institution, or be an independent consultant. As there is a clear possibility for a conflict of interest, if, for example, the Revenue-nominated expert has a relationship with a business competitor of the company, the company has the right to appeal the appointment and to request an alternative appointment. The technical expert is subject to the same confidentiality obligations as a Revenue auditor.

The role of the technical expert is to report on whether, in their opinion, the claimed R&D activities of the company should be regarded as qualifying R&D activities under the terms of the tax legislation. The expert may conclude that all of the activities are qualifying, that none qualify or that the activities are a mixture of qualifying and non-qualifying. If the technical expert comes to a negative conclusion for the taxpayer, resulting in Revenue issuing a Notice(s) of Assessment for unpaid tax on the company, the company has the option to appeal to the Tax Appeals Commission. This could be a long and expensive process, resulting in the Tax Appeals Commissioner (who is not a technical expert) making a determination based on the evidence of two conflicting technical experts.

### *11.3.2 Clawback of Unauthorised R&D Tax Credit Claim*

Under previous rules, where an unauthorised R&D tax credit claim was surrendered to a key employee, then the employee was liable to repay the income tax refund secured by them as a result of the company's unauthorised claim. Since 1 January 2014, it is the company that is liable for the clawback.

In addition, new rules have been introduced which, in triggering a clawback of an unauthorised R&D tax credit claim, can result in CT liabilities that are higher than the original tax relief claimed. There are two possible situations:

1. In the case where a company claims an R&D tax credit and surrenders this credit to a key employee, if it is subsequently found that the claim is not authorised, then the company will be charged at the 25% non-trading corporation tax rate on an amount equal to four times the amount of the unauthorised tax credit.

CASE STUDY: NEALLY SILICONE LTD

For example, if Neally Silicone Ltd surrenders an unauthorised tax credit of €10,000, then the company would be liable for a corporation tax liability of €10,000 (i.e. 4 × €10,000 × 25%).

2. Where a company claims an R&D tax credit and surrenders it to a key employee and it is subsequently found that the claim is 'deliberately false or overstated' and that the claim is unauthorised, then the company will be charged at the 25% non-trading corporation tax rate on an amount equal to eight times the amount of the unauthorised tax credit.[13]

CASE STUDY: NEALLY SILICONE LTD

If Neally Silicone Ltd were to make an unauthorised, surrendered claim of €10,000, which was found to be 'deliberately false or overstated', then the company would have a corporation tax liability of €20,000 (i.e. 8 × €10,000 × 25%).

The usual schedule of penalties and interest, as set out in the *Code of Practice for Revenue Audit*, applies.

In **Chapter 8** we noted that in some (infrequent) situations, Revenue will not seek to levy penalties in an audit situation if they accept that they are dealing with a 'technical adjustment'. The audit of an R&D tax credit claim could give rise to just such a technical adjustment, where, for example, Revenue's technical expert and the claimant company's expert disagree on a specific scientific point.

## 11.4 The 'Knowledge Development Box'

As noted at the start of this chapter, this new tax regime operates to apply a lower corporation tax rate of 6.25% to profits that are derived from 'qualifying assets' and that are earned by an Irish company carrying on a 'specified trade'.[14] Like the R&D tax credit, the regime is only open to companies and not to sole traders/partnerships. The mainstream Knowledge Development Box (KDB) regime applies to profits earned in accounting periods commencing on or after 1 January 2016 and before 1 January 2021. At the time of writing, there is no commencement date for the expanded KDB regime for SMEs (see below).

[13] Section 766(7B) TCA 1997.

[14] Section 769G-R TCA 1997, as inserted by section 32 FA 2015.

### *11.4.1 What are 'Qualifying Assets'?*

The first point to highlight is that the definition of 'qualifying assets' is quite narrowly drawn, being, "intellectual property, other than marketing-related intellectual property, and which is the result of research and development activities".[15] The definition of 'intellectual property' specifically includes:

- computer programs, within the meaning of the Copyright and Related Rights Act 2000;
- inventions protected by qualifying patents; and
- inventions protected by supplementary protection certificates relating to protection for medicinal and plant protection products, and by plant breeders' rights.

There is a specific exclusion for "marketing-related intellectual property"; this includes "trademarks, brands, image rights and other intellectual property used to market goods and services".

This new Irish tax regime has been tailored to comply with a significant OECD project, which is focused on international tax planning strategies that involve moving profits into low-tax jurisdictions and erosion of the taxable profit base. This Base Erosion and Profit Shifting (BEPS) project is ongoing; reports on all of the topics covered by the project were issued throughout 2015 and the focus has now moved on to implementation of the various recommendations.[16] Irish patent legislation requires updating in order to incorporate elements of the OECD recommendations into the KDB patent certification process. At the time of writing (June 2016), the revised patent legislation had not been initiated.

The exclusion of marketing-related intellectual property and the limitation of the relevant intellectual property to patents, computer programs (subject to some restriction) and the niche areas relating to medicinal and plant supplies would appear to limit the use of the KDB regime quite significantly. Also, given the costs and length of time it takes to secure patent protection, the regime appears to be aimed at specific sectors within multinational business, such as the pharmaceutical industry. However, the regime may be of limited use to those multinational businesses if the majority of their Irish subsidiaries' R&D activities are outsourced to group companies based outside of Ireland/EU. As one of the requirements of the KDB regime is that the intellectual property, from which profits of the 'specified trade' are earned, is derived from R&D activities carried out in Ireland/EU, then where little or none of a multinational's R&D activities are carried on there, the KDB regime will be unavailable to that business.

An expanded KDB regime for SMEs has been announced, though no commencement date has been given for this expanded regime. The means by which the KDB regime would be opened up to the Irish

[15] Section 769G(1) TCA 1997.

[16] For more information on the BEPS project, see www.oecd.org/ctp/beps

SME sector is by relaxing the definition of 'qualifying assets' to include inventions that are not patented, but are certified by the Controller of Patents, Designs and Trade Marks as being "novel, non-obvious and useful".[17] This broadening of the definition applies only to SMEs that have the following characteristics:

- the company's (or the group's) turnover does not exceed €50 million in any 12-month accounting period; and
- the annual income deriving from the intellectual property is less than €7.5 million.

Again, existing Irish legislation does not include a certification process in respect of inventions that are "novel, non-obvious and useful", so new legislation will also be required before this aspect of the KDB regime can take effect.

### *11.4.2 Overview of the 'Knowledge Development Box' Regime*

As this is an entirely new tax regime, and certain enabling aspects require updated legislation that has not yet issued, we can only provide an overview here. Future editions of this book will, no doubt, expand on this area.

The regime applies to profits of a 'specified trade'; this includes the invention/creation of 'qualifying assets', the management/exploitation of this type of asset and the sale of goods/services that derive their value from this type of asset. Typically, the income that will generate the profits of the 'specified trade' will be royalty and licence-fee income generated from the use/exploitation of the 'qualifying asset', as well as any portion of the sales price of goods/services that is attributable to a qualifying asset.

The profits of the specified trade that will be subject to the lower 6.25% corporation tax rate are identified by applying a formula based on the qualifying expenditure on a qualifying asset. This means that the lower CT rate will be available only on a portion of the profits of the specified trade – this portion is calculated by reference to the amount of R&D activity underlying the qualifying asset that is carried on by an Irish company in Ireland/EU Member State. The formula is as follows:

$$\frac{\text{Qualifying expenditure on qualifying asset + uplift expenditure}}{\text{Overall expenditure on qualifying asset}} \times \text{Profits of 'specified trade'}$$

'Qualifying expenditure' means expenditure wholly and exclusively incurred by the company in carrying on R&D activities in Ireland/EU Member State, where such activities lead to the development, improvement or creation of the qualifying asset.

As group outsourcing costs and acquisition costs are excluded from the definition of qualifying expenditure, an 'uplift expenditure' amount is allowed to compensate for a portion of these costs. However, where a

[17] Section 769R(1) TCA 1997.

significant amount of the R&D activity underlying the qualifying asset is outsourced to a group company, this will significantly impact on the usefulness of this regime.

As we have seen, in order to access the KDB regime the qualifying company must undertake R&D activities. This means that the R&D tax credit regime and KDB regime are intrinsically linked, as illustrated in Figure 11.1 below.

FIGURE 11.1: INTERACTION OF THE R&D TAX CREDIT AND THE KDB

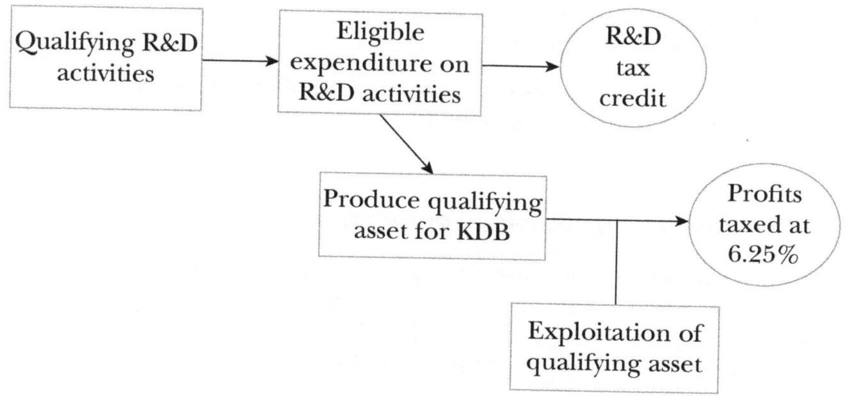


## CASE STUDY: THE NEALLY GROUP

The Neally Group was advised that the R&D activity being carried out by Dirk and his team met the requirements of the tax rules in relation to a claim for R&D tax credits on 'qualifying expenditure'. Once this research has been commercialised and the company begins to earn profits from sales of the silicone products that have been created as a direct result of the R&D activity, then company management can consider whether the company can use the KDB regime to apply the 6.25% CT rate to a portion of these profits. One of the key questions here will be whether the company has the means and/or the business strategy to apply for patent protection for the silicone stabilisation process they have developed. If not, then the company may nevertheless be in a position to utilise the KDB regime if it can satisfy the Controller of Patents, Designs and Trademarks that it has created an invention that is, 'novel, non-obvious and useful' *and* if the company remains within the definition of SME for the purposes of the SME KDB regime.

The fact that all of the R&D activities underlying the development of the silicone stabilisation process are carried out in Ireland may mean that the majority of the profits of the 'specified trade' (being the sale of products created as a result of the R&D activity) could be eligible for the 6.25% CT rate.

## 11.5 Tax Deductions for 'Scientific Research'

In **Chapter 6** we reviewed various types of capital allowance that may be allowed as a deduction in calculating a business's taxable profit or loss. Quite separate to the R&D tax credit regime set out above, there are tax deductions available to businesses that carry out 'scientific research', which is defined as "any activities in the fields of natural or applied science for the extension of knowledge".[18] This tax deduction can cover two types of expenditure incurred in carrying out scientific research:

- revenue expenditure; and
- non-revenue expenditure (i.e. capital).

***Note:*** these deductions/allowances are not available for businesses involved in exploring for specified minerals, or for petroleum exploration or extraction activities.

### *11.5.1 Deduction for Revenue Expenditure*

A 'person' (which in this case may refer to a sole trade, partnership or company) who either directly incurs revenue expenditure on scientific research *or* pays money to an Irish university or approved body to carry out scientific research will get a 100% tax deduction in respect of this expenditure.[19] This tax deduction is available even if the research is not related to the person's trade.

### *11.5.2 Deduction for Capital Expenditure*

Where a person incurs capital expenditure on scientific research and this expenditure relates to an existing or future trade, then a 100% capital allowance may be available.[20] Some of the relevant features of this allowance include:

- To secure the allowance, a specific claim must be made to the person's local Inspector of Taxes.
- As of 1 January 2016, the asset must be in use at the end of the period in which the expenditure is incurred, or in the case of pre-trading expenditure, at the end of the period in which the trade commenced.
- Revenue have confirmed that this 100% capital allowance is potentially available in respect of laboratories, as well as plant and machinery.[21]

We can see that the revenue deductions and capital allowances available for scientific research come with far fewer conditions than those attaching to a claim for a R&D tax credit. However, the types of taxpayer that may claim these deductions/allowances is limited (i.e. only those operating in the fields of natural or applied science) and the deductions/allowances themselves are less valuable.

[18] Section 763 TCA 1997.
[19] Section 764 TCA 1997.
[20] Section 765 TCA 1997, as amended by section 31 FA 2015.
[21] Revenue's, *Tax Briefing*, Issue 18 No. 2 (1995), Section 2.5.

# Appendix I: Categories of Activities that may Qualify for the R&D Tax Credit[22]

## "Natural Sciences

1. Mathematics and computer sciences, including mathematics and other allied fields, computer sciences and other allied subjects, software development.
2. Physical sciences including astronomy and space sciences, physics and other allied subjects.
3. Chemical sciences including chemistry and other allied subjects.
4. Earth and related environmental sciences including geology, geophysics, mineralogy, physical geography and other geosciences, meteorology and other atmospheric sciences including climatic research, oceanography, volcanology, paleoecology and other allied sciences.
5. Biological sciences including biology, botany, bacteriology, microbiology, zoology, entomology, genetics, biochemistry, biophysics and other allied sciences, excluding clinical and veterinary sciences.

## Engineering and Technology

1. Civil engineering including architecture engineering, building science and engineering, construction engineering, municipal and structural engineering and other allied subjects.
2. Electrical engineering, electronics including communication engineering and systems, computer engineering (hardware) and other allied subjects.
3. Other engineering sciences such as chemical, aeronautical and space, mechanical, metallurgical and materials engineering, and their specialised subdivisions; forest products; applied sciences such as geodesy and industrial chemistry; the science and technology of food production, specialised technologies of interdisciplinary fields, e.g. systems analysis, metallurgy, mining, textile technology and other allied subjects.

## Medical Sciences

1. Basic medicine including anatomy, cytology, physiology, genetics, pharmacy, pharmacology, toxicology, immunology and immunohematology, clinical chemistry, clinical microbiology, pathology.
2. Clinical medicine including anaesthesiology, paediatrics, obstetrics and gynaecology, internal medicine, surgery, dentistry, neurology, psychiatry, radiology, therapeutics, otorhinolaryngology and ophthalmology.
3. Health sciences including public health services, social medicine, hygiene, nursing, epidemiology.

[22] Excerpted from the 2015 Revenue Guidelines, p.46.

### Agricultural Science

1. Agriculture, forestry, fisheries and allied sciences including agronomy, animal husbandry, fisheries, forestry, horticulture and other allied subjects.
2. Veterinary medicine."

## Appendix II: Categories of Activity that are Not Research and Development Activities[23]

"(a) research in the social sciences (including economics, business management, and behavioural sciences), arts, or humanities;
(b) routine testing and analysis for purposes of quality or quantity control;
(c) alterations of a cosmetic or stylistic nature to existing products, services or processes whether or not these alterations represent some improvement;
(d) operational research such as management studies or efficiency surveys which are not wholly and exclusively undertaken for the purposes of a research and development activity;
(e) corrective action in connection with breakdowns during commercial production of a product;
(f) legal and administrative work in connection with patent applications, records and litigation and the sale or licensing of patents;
(g) activity, including design and construction engineering, relating to the construction, relocation, rearrangement or start up of facilities or equipment other than facilities or equipment which is to be used wholly and exclusively for the purposes of carrying on by the company of research and development activities;
(h) market research, market testing, market development, sales promotion or consumer surveys;
(i) prospecting, exploring or drilling for, or producing, minerals, petroleum or natural gas;
(j) the commercial and financial steps necessary for the marketing or the commercial production or distribution of a new or improved material, product, device, process, system or service;
(k) administration and general support services (such as transportation, storage, cleaning, repair, maintenance and security) which are not wholly and exclusively undertaken in connection with a research and development activity."

[23] Excerpted from the 2015 Revenue Guidelines, p.47.

# CHAPTER 12

# VAT AND PERSONAL TAX ISSUES ARISING FROM INTERNATIONAL SALES



Many Irish businesses start by supplying Irish customers only, while others have international customers from their commencement. Irrespective of when the supply to international customers starts, there are a variety of tax implications that arise from the internationalisation of an Irish business. In this chapter, we will review some of the most important VAT and personal tax implications of this internationalisation process. In **Chapter 13**, we will consider some of the issues that may arise for an Irish company that establishes a foreign presence, e.g. a foreign subsidiary company or foreign branch. Our focus in this chapter, however, will be on the Irish tax implications for an Irish business sending goods/services and staff abroad.

## 12.1 Value-added Tax: The International Perspective

In **Chapter 4** we focused on the VAT rules that generally apply when an Irish business makes all of its purchases and all of its supplies in Ireland, with a general overview of the relevant VAT rules where an Irish business purchases goods/services from another EU Member State or from outside of the EU.

In this chapter, we will look at the VAT implications generally arising where an Irish business sells goods/services outside of Ireland. Differing VAT rules apply depending on whether these supplies are made within the EU, outside the EU, to a VAT-registered business customer or to an unregistered private customer.

Note that what we will discuss below covers VAT rules applying to a business that is based in Ireland and that holds an Irish VAT registration number. We will see in **Chapter 13** that where an Irish business decides to expand their operations abroad, this so-called 'foreign presence' may take any of a number of forms, including a foreign subsidiary company, branch, permanent establishment, representative office or agency arrangement. These 'foreign presences' will attract their own local VAT rules, which are beyond the scope of this book. What is at issue here are the Irish VAT rules that generally apply where the business is *based* in Ireland and is supplying to customers located in other countries.

## 12.2 VAT Implications Arising on Intra-Community Supplies

In this section, we will review the Irish VAT implications arising where an Irish business sells 'goods/services' to customers that are based in other EU Member States. These supplies are called 'intra-Community supplies'.

### *12.2.1 Impact on Irish VAT Registration Thresholds*

Where an Irish business makes sales to customers based in other EU Member States, this will generally have no impact on the requirement for an *Irish* VAT registration and the turnover thresholds set out in **Chapter 4** will apply.

To recap on the general rules: when a business is supplying goods the turnover threshold is €75,000; when a business is supplying services the turnover threshold is €37,500. There are some exceptions to this general rule; for example, the supply of 'electronically supplied services' (e-services), which are reviewed at **Section 12.2.3.5** below, and sales of goods to non-business customers located in another EU Member State (so-called 'distance selling'), reviewed at **Section 12.2.3.3** below. For an Irish supplier of 'distance sales', the obligation to register for VAT in the EU Member State where the non-business customer is located will arise only if the distance-selling turnover threshold relevant to that country is breached. However, this option to avoid a foreign VAT registration presupposes that the Irish supplier is already registered for VAT in Ireland.

### 12.2.2 Requirement to File INTRASTAT and VIES Returns

#### 12.2.2.1 INTRASTAT Returns

In **Chapter 4**, we reviewed the requirement for an Irish business to file a monthly INTRASTAT return where it is in *receipt* of goods (not services) from EU Member States, the value of which exceeds €500,000 in a calendar year. The corollary of this is also true, as an Irish business that supplies goods (not services) to customers based in other EU Member States may also have to file monthly INTRASTAT returns. The difference for the Irish *supplier* of these goods is that the requirement to file monthly INTRASTAT returns only arises where the value of those supplies exceeds €635,000 in a calendar year. As we noted in **Chapter 4**, the requirement to file INTRASTAT returns does not displace the Irish business's obligation to include details of intra-Community sales in its regular Irish VAT return (Form VAT3 – Box E1).

In summary:

- for an Irish business whose intra-Community supplies of goods are valued at less than €635,000 in a calendar year, details of these supplies must be included in the Irish VAT3 return in Box E1; and
- where the value of an Irish business's intra-Community supplies exceeds €635,000 in a calendar year, details of these supplies must be included in monthly INTRASTAT returns and in the Irish VAT3 return.

#### 12.2.2.2 VIES Returns

VIES returns are another form of EU-wide VAT return that are required by European tax authorities to ensure that intra-Community supplies are correctly treated for VAT purposes and also for statistical purposes. Where an Irish business makes *any* intra-Community supplies of goods/services, details of these supplies must be provided in the form of monthly or quarterly VIES returns. For businesses that make intra-Community supplies with an ex-VAT value exceeding €50,000 a quarter, the filing obligation is monthly, though suppliers of services may request quarterly filing.

A business may file an annual VIES return if either of the following circumstances arise:

1. The business's intra-Community supplies do not exceed (or are not likely to exceed) €15,000 in a calendar year *and* the total business turnover of goods and related services will not exceed €200,000 in a calendar year *and* the supplies do not include new means of transport.
2. The business's intra-Community supplies do not exceed €15,000 in a calendar year *and* the total business turnover of goods and related services will not exceed €85,000 in a calendar year.

For more information on INTRASTAT and VIES returns, see Revenue's *VIES and INTRASTAT Traders Manual*.[1]

[1] Replacement 8, January 2016. See www.revenue.ie/en/customs/businesses/vies-intrastat.html (accessed June 2016).

### *12.2.3 VAT Treatment of Supplies to Customers Based in Another EU Member State*

In **Chapter 4** we reviewed the VAT rules that apply to intra-Community acquisitions made by an Irish business. We saw that these acquisitions are typically subject to a 0% rate of VAT by the supplier and that the Irish business must apply the 'reverse VAT charge' mechanism and self-charge VAT on the acquisition at the appropriate Irish VAT rate. The corollary of this typically applies where the Irish VAT-registered business is supplying goods or services to VAT-registered *business* customers based in other EU Member States, i.e. the Irish business charges VAT at the 0% rate, and the customer has the obligation to apply the reverse VAT charge mechanism at the local VAT rate. ***Note:*** different VAT rules apply to the supply of goods or services to *private* customers located in other EU Member States, as we will see below.

#### *12.2.3.1 Supply of Goods to EU Business Customers*

In relation to the intra-Community supply of goods, in order for the 0% rate of VAT to be applied by the Irish business, the following conditions must be met:

1. the EU business customer is registered for VAT in an EU Member State other than Ireland;
2. the Irish business retains commercial documentation showing the dispatch of the goods from Ireland and their destination;
3. VAT numbers of both the EU customer and the Irish business are recorded on the VAT invoice; and
4. the goods are actually transported to another EU Member State within three months of the date that the supply took place.

If any of the above conditions are not met, then the Irish business must charge Irish VAT, at the appropriate Irish VAT rate, on the supply as if it were a domestic supply within Ireland.[2]

The tax authorities in all EU Member States have come together to establish a centralised VAT number validation system, which businesses would be well advised to use as part of their standard procedures. If there is any doubt, the Irish business should charge Irish VAT on the supply as an adjustment can be made later if this turns out to have been unnecessary.

***Note:*** the reverse VAT charge mechanism may not be used in the case of the supply of new means of transport, distance sales and sales of excisable goods.

[2] Section 24(1) of the Value-Added Tax Consolidation Act 2010 (VATCA 2010) and regulation 29 of the Value-Added Tax Regulations 2010 (S.I. No. 639 of 2010) (the 'VAT Regulations 2010').

### *12.2.3.2 Supply of Services to EU Business Customers*

In general, where the services are being supplied to business customers based in other EU Member States, the 'place of supply' for VAT purposes, and therefore the place where VAT arises, is the country where the customer is located. The Irish business should secure details of the customer's VAT number and should not charge VAT on the supply. The EU business customer should 'reverse VAT charge' at the appropriate VAT rate in their country.[3] There are exceptions to this 'place of supply' rule, examples of which are set out in **Chapter 4, Section 4.6.1.3**.

The rules set out above in relation to intra-Community supplies of goods and services cover most transactions with *business* customers based in other EU Member States. When we refer to 'business customers', we mean entities that are in business and are registered for VAT in their home countries.

Another set of rules applies in relation to intra-Community supplies of goods or services to private non-VAT-registered individuals in other EU Member States.

### *12.2.3.3 'Distance Selling' (Supply of Goods to Non-business EU Customers)*

Where an Irish business supplies goods from Ireland to **private** individuals based in other EU Member States, then the 'distance selling' rules will apply.[4] These rules cover, for example, mail order sales and sales made by phone, fax or internet. In relation to the internet aspect, the 'distance selling' rules apply where the internet is used as a *method* of placing the order, as opposed to being the *means* by which a service is provided, i.e. the online delivery of 'electronically supplied services'. These latter supplies are discussed later in this chapter in **Section 12.2.3.5**.

Where the supplies are made by an Irish business that is not registered for VAT in the Member State in which the customer is based, then Irish VAT at the appropriate Irish rate must be applied to the supply. Once the 'distance-selling threshold' applicable to the country into which the Irish business is supplying is breached, then the Irish business is obliged to register for VAT in that Member State and charge VAT at the appropriate local rate on the supply. It is also open to the Irish business to register for VAT in that country even if the distance-selling threshold has not been breached.

Each EU Member State has discretion to choose a distance-selling threshold in the range €35,000 to €100,000. The thresholds for each Member

[3] Section 34 VATCA 2010.

[4] Section 30 VATCA 2010.

State are listed in Revenue's leaflet *Distance Sales in the EU*.[5] The thresholds for some of our main trading partners are as follows:

- United Kingdom: £70,000 (approx. €96,000);
- Belgium: €35,000;
- France: €35,000 (with effect from 1 January 2016);
- Germany: €100,000;
- Spain: €35,000.

### Case Study: Four Blue Ducks

Jim and Cathy expand their popular jam and preserves business and start selling these products online to private customers based in Germany and Belgium, which means that the business is obliged to monitor its turnover (on a calendar-year basis) to determine the correct VAT treatment on these sales. The turnover from these sales is:

| Calendar Year | German Turnover € | Belgian Turnover € |
|---|---|---|
| 2014 | 12,560 | 25,750 |
| 2015 | 58,255 | 41,000 |

Four Blue Ducks charge Irish VAT, at 23%, on the 2014 supplies to Germany and Belgium, and the 2015 supplies to Germany. In relation to the 2015 supplies to Belgian customers, once the €35,000 threshold is breached, the Irish business would be obliged to register for VAT in Belgium and, from that point on, charge Belgian VAT at the local rate for jam and preserves.

Where the Irish business is supplying excisable goods, e.g. alcohol, there is no distance-selling threshold and the Irish business will be obliged to register for VAT in any country into which it is making supplies to private customers.

Sales of new means of transport are excluded from the rules on distance selling; for these types of supplies, the private customer must always pay VAT in their own country, at the local VAT rates.

The value of the Irish business's distance sales must be included in Box E1 of the regular VAT3 return if the Irish business is registered for VAT in another EU Member State. If the Irish business is selling into another EU Member State and is not VAT-registered in that country, then the value

[5] See www.revenue.ie/en/tax/vat/leaflets/distance-sales-eu.html (accessed June 2016).

of the supplies should not be noted in Box E1 and the Irish VAT charges arising should be included in Box T1 of the VAT3 return, in the normal way.[6]

***Note:*** there may be changes on the horizon to the rules in relation to distance selling. As part of its May 2015 Digital Single Market Strategy for Europe, the European Commission proposed the introduction of a 'One Stop Shop' system (see **Section 12.2.3.5** below) to supplies of *goods* to private customers. This proposal, along with other proposals also aimed at simplifying VAT for cross-border e-commerce within the EU (especially for SMEs), was included in the European Commission's Action Plan on VAT, issued in April 2016.

### 12.2.3.4 *Supply of Services to Non-business EU Customers*

The general rule is that for a supply of services by an Irish business to private customers based in other EU Member States, the 'place of supply' for that service is Ireland, which means that the Irish business must charge VAT at the appropriate Irish VAT rate.

This general rule is displaced such that the 'place of supply' (and therefore, the country where VAT is charged) will differ in a number of instances, including:

- supply of services connected with immovable goods (i.e. property) – the place of supply (POS) is where the property is located. For example, if an Irish architect prepared designs for a UK private customer for a private home to be built on a site in Nottingham, then the Irish architect would be obliged to register for UK VAT and charge UK VAT on the supply;
- passenger transport services – POS is where transport takes place;
- transport of goods within the EU – POS is the place of departure;
- admission to cultural, artistic, sporting, scientific, educational and entertainment events – POS is where the event takes place;
- ancillary transport services or valuation/work on movable property – POS is where the services are physically carried out;
- restaurant and catering services – POS is where the services are carried out;
- restaurant and catering services for consumption on board trains, planes and ships – POS is the point of departure; and
- short-term hiring out of means of transport – POS is location where the transport is made available to the customer.

Where the POS is another EU Member State, then the Irish business will be obliged to register for VAT in that other Member State and charge VAT at the appropriate local rate on the supply.

[6] *Ibid.*

### *12.2.3.5 Supply of Electronically Supplied Services (E-services)*

We previously referred to 'electronically supplied services' in **Chapter 4** and noted that these services attract specific VAT rules. We have also noted that the use of a website or email to place/receive orders or to correspond with existing or potential customers does not constitute an electronically supplied service. Revenue's VAT leaflet on e-services and broadcasting defines an 'e-service' as

> "[one] that is delivered over the internet (or an electronic network which is reliant on the internet or similar network for its provision) and is heavily dependent on information technology for its supply – i.e. the service is essentially automated, involves minimal human intervention and in the absence of information technology does not have viability."[7]

The VAT rules define 'e-services' as including:

- website supply, web-hosting, distance maintenance of programmes and equipment;
- supply of software and updating of it;
- supply of images, text and information, and making databases available;
- supply of music, films and games (including games of chance and gambling events) and of political, cultural, sporting, scientific and entertainment broadcasts and events; and
- supply of distance teaching.[8]

We see below how the introduction of completely automated language courses changes the VAT treatment applicable to a portion of the business of Tigim Language Learning Ltd.

#### CASE STUDY: TIGIM LANGUAGE LEARNING LTD

Tigim Language Learning Ltd provides language teaching in various formats within a 'virtual classroom' environment. Some of its courses are supplied via tailored software that leads the student through automated modules, including tests and workbooks that are automatically marked without the need for human intervention. The student does not have contact with any individual teacher as they work through the modules. The company also supplies courses that involve interactive teaching between teacher and student over the internet. In order to avoid making expensive mistakes over the correct VAT treatment of its online courses, Tigim Language Learning Ltd has secured a ruling from Revenue that the purely automated courses are 'e-services', while the courses involving interaction between teacher and student are not.

[7] *Telecommunications, Broadcasting and Electronic (TBE) services (B2C) – New VAT Place of supply rules – 2015*, para 4.3 (available at www.revenue.ie/en/tax/vat/leaflets/place-supply-rules.html accessed June 2016).

[8] Section 2 VATCA 2010.

**Supply of E-services to EU Business Customers** The general rule in relation to place of supply (POS) of a service to business customers also applies to electronically supplied services, i.e. it is the place where the customer is established – the other EU Member State. Assuming the Irish business has the relevant VAT information for the business customer, the Irish business does not charge Irish VAT on the supply and the EU business customer applies the reverse VAT charge mechanism to charge VAT, at the relevant local VAT rate.

**Supply of E-services to EU Non-business Customers** Under the *usual* POS rules, the POS of services to a private EU customer will be the country in which the supplier is based, e.g. where an Irish business supplies services that are not e-services to an individual in Germany, the POS and, therefore, the VAT charge, will be Ireland/Irish. In an effort to reduce business distortion and possible unfair advantage where different EU businesses apply different VAT rates to the same supply, the POS of e-services to a private EU customer is now the country where the customer is located. The supplier is still obliged to charge VAT, but this will be at the appropriate local VAT rate of the country in which the customer is located. No turnover threshold will apply in this regard, which means that an Irish business supplying e-services to any private customers located in other EU Member States must register and charge VAT in each EU Member State, irrespective of the value of the supplies.[9]

With effect from 1 January 2015, an Irish business can choose to avail of the MOSS (Mini One Stop Shop) system. This allows the supplier to declare and pay the VAT due for e-services made to all private customers in other EU Member States in the country in which the supplier is based. This country is known as the Member State of Identification (MSI) and for an Irish business, the MSI will be Ireland.[10] MOSS returns are made on a calendar-quarter basis and include only the VAT information relevant to the supply of e-services to private consumers located within the EU (in the Member State of Consumption (MSC)) during the MOSS period.

### Case Study: Tigim Language Learning Ltd

Tigim Language Learning Ltd's online business has rapidly expanded and the company sells the courses regarded as e-services to private customers based in Germany, France, Italy and Belgium. From 1 January 2015, the company elects to operate the MOSS system in relation to the sales to these four EU Member States of Consumption. This means that the company must charge German VAT on the courses supplied to the

[9] For more information see Revenue's VAT leaflet, *Telecommunications, Broadcasting and Electronic (TBE) services (B2C) – New VAT Place of supply rules – 2015*. Available at www.revenue.ie/en/tax/vat/leaflets/place-supply-rules.html (accessed June 2016).

[10] Section 91A–F VATCA 2010.

German customers, French VAT on the courses supplied to French customers, etc., all of which can be returned and paid by Tigim Language Learning Ltd to the Irish Revenue via MOSS returns. As Tigim Language Learning Ltd is established in Ireland, Ireland is the company's MSI.

Note that, in relation to the supply of e-services, the obligation to register for VAT in the MSC where the private customer(s) is located – or alternatively to register for the MOSS system – will not override the turnover thresholds applicable to an Irish business making supplies in Ireland. This means that, for example, if the turnover from the Irish business's supplies of e-services to private customers based in Ireland is less than €37,500 in a 12-month period, then the Irish business would not be obliged to register for VAT in Ireland in relation to those supplies. The Irish business could, therefore, be registered for VAT in another EU Member State(s), or be registered for the MOSS system, but not be registered for VAT in Ireland.

While the (optional) MOSS system reduces the administrative burden by avoiding the need for a supplier of e-services to private customers located in other MSCs to register in all those other MSCs, this system does not relieve all of the administrative burden caused by changing the 'place of supply' of these services to the MSC where the customer is located. All local VAT rules will also apply to these services, including the local requirements in relation to VAT rates, and the currency and language of the invoice. These items vary from EU Member State to Member State.

The obligation to charge VAT, at the local rate of the MSC, and the opportunity to avail of the MOSS system, also applies to suppliers of broadcasting and telecommunications services. For more information, see Revenue's VAT leaflet on the MOSS system.[11]

## 12.3 VAT Treatment of the Supply of Goods/Services to Customers Outside the European Union

### *12.3.1 Goods*

VAT at the 0% rate applies to all exports of goods by an Irish business to customers, business or private, located outside of the EU. (***Note:*** some 'possessions' or 'territories' of various EU Member States are excluded from the definition of the EU for VAT purposes, e.g. the Channel Islands.[12])

[11] *The Mini One Stop Shop (MOSS): Special scheme for suppliers of Telecommunications, Broadcasting and e-Services to Consumers.* Available at www.revenue.ie/en/tax/vat/leaflets/mini-one-stop-shop.html (accessed June 2016).

[12] Further information is set out in Revenue's *Guide to VAT* under 'Export'. Available at www.revenue.ie/en/tax/vat/guide/exports.html (accessed June 2016).

The application of the 0% VAT rate also applies to supplies of goods to VAT-registered traders in Shannon Customs-Free Airport and Ringaskiddy Free Port.

The retail export scheme/tax-free shopping for tourists, which is referred to in **Appendix I** of **Chapter 4**, effectively constitutes an extension of this VAT treatment as it allows tourists who are normally resident outside of Ireland and the EU to avoid an Irish VAT charge on their purchases here. One of the scheme conditions is that the goods must be exported outside of Ireland and the EU within three months of purchase.

### *12.3.2 Services*

In general, no VAT is applied to the supply of services by an Irish business to non-EU business customers. The Irish business is obliged, however, to secure proof that the business customer is located outside of the EU and that the customer is a taxable person.

As a general rule, where an Irish business supplies services to non-EU private customers, then the default position is that the Irish business must charge VAT at the appropriate Irish VAT rate. This general rule is displaced where the service falls within a specified list of 'excepted services', including:

- services that are 'used and enjoyed' outside of the EU, e.g. hiring of movable goods;
- advertising services;
- the services of consultants, engineers, consultancy firms, lawyers, accountants and other similar services, as well as data processing and the provision of information;
- banking, financial and insurance transactions, including reinsurance;
- the supply of staff;
- telecommunications services;
- radio and television broadcasting services; and
- electronically supplied services.

If the Irish business is intending not to charge VAT on the basis that it is supplying one of the excepted services, then the business must secure proof that the private customer is located outside of the EU.

## 12.4 VAT Regime Applicable to the Purchase of Goods/Services by Certain Irish Businesses

In **Chapter 4**, **Section 4.6.3**, we briefly referred to a specific VAT authorisation – a VAT 56A authorisation – which allows *suppliers* to certain Irish businesses to zero-rate their supplies to that business.[13] The regime

[13] Section 56A VATCA 2010.

applies where the Irish business generates at least 75% of its turnover from the following supplies:

- intra-Community supplies of goods;
- export of goods outside EU; or
- supplies of certain contract work.

A business eligible for a VAT 56A authorisation should apply directly to their local Revenue district. While the regime anticipates the possible authorisation of a start-up business in the first year of trading, independent verification of the expectation of meeting the 75% turnover test in that first year will be required from a state agency, such as Enterprise Ireland, which supports Irish businesses trading outside of Ireland.

Where an Irish business secures a VAT 56A authorisation, it must provide a copy of this authorisation to its suppliers. This enables most supplies of goods and services to be made to the business at the zero rate of Irish VAT. There are a small number of exceptions to this rule; for example, an Irish business with a VAT 56A authorisation will continue to be charged VAT on the purchase/hire of any passenger vehicle, as well as on the supply of petrol.[14]

## 12.5 Income Tax and Payroll Tax Issues for Employees of an Irish Business who Spend Time Working Abroad

In the first section of this chapter we looked at some of the VAT implications arising when an Irish business makes supplies of goods/services to customers located outside of Ireland. In order to facilitate these foreign supplies, the Irish business may need to establish a presence in another country(ies) and we will review some of the different forms that this 'foreign presence' can take in **Chapter 13**.

We will now review the income tax and payroll tax (collectively, 'personal tax') issues arising when an employee of an Irish business travels abroad to carry out their 'Irish employment' duties. The first point to emphasise is that this section focuses on an employee of an Irish business, in other words, an employee employed under an 'Irish employment' who travels abroad. This should be distinguished from the situation where an Irish business establishes some form of presence in a foreign country, say a foreign subsidiary company, and that foreign company employs staff directly. An 'Irish employment' has the following characteristics:

- the employee has an employment contract that is subject to Irish law and jurisdiction;

[14] For further information, see Revenue's VAT leaflet on the VAT 56A authorisation, *Section 56 Zero Rating of Goods and Services*. Available at www.revenue.ie/en/tax/vat/leaflets/zero-rating.html (accessed June 2016).

- the employee's salary is paid into an Irish bank account; and
- the employer is based in Ireland.

As we have noted in **Chapter 5**, 'payroll taxes' refer to PAYE income tax, USC and PRSI, and an Irish employer is obliged to withhold payroll taxes from Irish employment income and pay these over to the Collector-General. Separate to this, an Irish tax-resident employee has their own income tax obligations. Generally, where an Irish tax-resident employee (who is not a proprietary director) has no other source of income, the withholding of payroll taxes by their employer will satisfy the employee's own income tax obligations and they will have no separate obligation to file an income tax return. In this case, the income tax obligations and the payroll tax obligations are generally in alignment.

We will see below, however, that where an Irish employee who has an Irish employment is sent abroad for periods exceeding about six months, differences arise between the employee's income tax obligations and the employer's payroll tax obligations.

### 12.5.1 Income Tax Rules and Payroll Tax Rules in Relation to Foreign Travel

An Irish tax-resident employee who travels abroad to carry out the duties of their employment for a few days, or even a few months, will generally remain a tax resident of Ireland and their employment income will continue to be subject to Irish payroll taxes in the usual way. This is usually the case as long as the period of foreign travel is less than six months in a particular tax year. Set out below are some specific tax reliefs and tax-free expenses that may be claimed by such travelling employees.

#### 12.5.1.1 Foreign Earnings Deduction

A specific income tax relief may be claimed by an Irish employee who undertakes foreign travel on behalf of their Irish employer where the travel is to one or more of a list of 28 'relevant states'.[15] As the list of countries has been expanded in successive Finance Acts, travel to recently added countries is the subject of income tax relief only in recent tax years. The 'relevant states' are:

- Brazil, Russia, India, China and South Africa (tax relief applies for tax years 2012 to 2017);
- Egypt, Algeria, Senegal, Tanzania, Kenya, Nigeria, Ghana and Congo (applies for tax years 2013 to 2017);
- Japan, Singapore, South Korea, Saudi Arabia, United Arab Emirates, Qatar, Bahrain, Indonesia, Vietnam, Thailand, Chile, Oman, Kuwait, Mexico and Malaysia (applies for tax years 2015 to 2017).

The tax relief is given by way of tax deduction (known as the 'foreign earnings deduction' (FED)), which will reduce the employee's taxable income

[15] Section 823A TCA 1997.

for a given tax year. The extent of the tax deduction can only be calculated after the travel for the year has been completed. This means that payroll taxes are deducted in the normal way throughout the year, as if the employee had not travelled abroad at all, and the employee must claim an income tax refund after the year has ended.

The FED deduction is calculated as follows:

$$\text{'Qualifying income'} \times \frac{\text{'Qualifying days'}}{\text{Number of days in tax year that the individual held the 'relevant employment'}}$$

The maximum tax deduction is capped at €35,000, which means that the maximum value of the tax relief is €14,000 (being €35,000 × 40%). ***Note:*** the tax deduction will reduce taxable income for income tax purposes only and will not reduce PRSI or USC liabilities.

From 1 January 2015, a 'qualifying day' must be one day of a trip of at least three days' duration. The individual must spend the substantial part of the day performing their employment duties and a travel day may be treated as a qualifying day for these purposes. (Before 2015, a qualifying day had to be one day of a trip of at least four days' duration and a travel day could not qualify). To secure this tax deduction, the employee is also required to spend a minimum number of qualifying days in one or more of the relevant states in either a tax year, or in a continuous period of 12 months crossing two tax years. For tax relief claims made before 1 January 2015, the minimum number of qualifying days was 60 days; from 1 January 2015, this minimum number is reduced to 40 days.

'Qualifying income' refers to wages, salaries and share-based remuneration, but does not include benefit-in-kind, expenses or pension contributions.

The FED tax deduction cannot be claimed where the employee is taking advantage of other tax reliefs, including:

- relief for key employees carrying on R&D activities (see **Chapter 11**);
- 'split-year residence' relief (see **Section 12.5.2.1** below);
- 'cross-border' relief (see **Section 12.5.1.2** below);
- Special Assignment Relief Programme (SARP) (see **Chapter 13**).

Also, the value of the FED deduction will be reduced where the employee is paying income tax both in Ireland and in another country, and relying on double taxation relief under a double tax agreement (DTA) between the two countries.[16]

The following case study extract involves an example of how an employee's travel days are assessed in determining whether a claim for FED arises, as well as a sample FED calculation.

[16] See **Chapter 13, Section 13.1.1** for commentary on DTA agreements. For more on the FED, see Revenue leaflet IT34, *Foreign Earnings Deduction*. Available at www.revenue.ie/en/tax/it/leaflets/it34.html (accessed June 2016).

### Case Study: Tigim Language Learning Ltd

Tigim Language Learning Ltd's online language teaching courses have taken off and Aoife, Sarah and Jamie are excited about developing new markets around the world. Their approach is to create strategic relationships with bricks-and-mortar language and business colleges based in other countries to promote Tigim Language Learning Ltd's online courses. For the next phase of expansion, they have decided to focus on the United Arab Emirates (UAE), especially Abu Dhabi, Dubai and Qatar. As head of business development, Jamie has the following travel to UAE and Qatar:

- 2014: 65 days, including eight travel days
- 2015: 45 days, including 10 travel days.

For 2014 and 2015, Jamie earns a salary of €40,000 each year.

His entitlement to FED deductions is:

- 2014: no FED deduction as Jamie has not travelled to a relevant state, as defined by the 2014 rules, and he also has not met the minimum '60 qualifying days' test in place for 2014 (travel days are excluded from pre-1 January 2015 FED calculations).
- 2015: as UAE and Qatar are treated as relevant states from 1 January 2015 and Jamie has met the minimum '40 qualifying days' test in place for 2015, Jamie will be entitled to an FED deduction calculated as:

$$€40{,}000 \times \frac{45}{365} = €4{,}931$$

This means that Jamie's taxable income for 2015 will be reduced to €35,069 (€40,000 – €4,931) and, on the basis that his marginal income tax rate is 40%, he will secure an estimated income tax refund of €1,972 after year end.

#### *12.5.1.2 'Cross-border Relief'*

For the sake of completeness, we mention here the tax relief known as 'cross-border relief' (also known as 'trans-border workers relief'). This is a tax relief that may be available to an Irish tax-resident individual who has a *foreign employment* in a country with which Ireland has a double tax agreement.[17] This tax relief is most often relied upon by tax residents of the Republic of Ireland who travel to Northern Ireland or elsewhere in the UK to work for a Northern Irish/UK employer. It is not discussed further here as the subject of this entire chapter is a business located in the Republic of Ireland that trades with foreign customers or sends employees abroad.

[17] Section 825A TCA 1997.

### 12.5.1.3 Travel Expenses and Subsistence Payments

In **Chapter 5** we reviewed the travel and subsistence allowances that may be paid to an employee on a tax-free basis where they are required to work at a location away from their 'normal place of work'. Details are set out in two Revenue leaflets: IT54 *Employees' Subsistence Expenses*[18] and IT51 *Employees' Motoring/Bicycle Expenses* (covering travel expenses).[19]

Essentially, all travel expenses associated with a return journey to another country may be treated as a 'business journey' and reimbursed on a tax-free basis on production of receipts. In relation to subsistence expenses, these may be reimbursed tax-free on the basis of either:

- actual expenses vouched with receipts; *or*
- flat-rate allowances based on a percentage of the schedule of Civil Service subsistence rates for a temporary period of absence from Ireland no longer than six months. ***Note:*** the applicable Civil Service rates are not the usual ones that apply to subsistence for assignments within Ireland; instead, there are specific rates for individual foreign countries and these can be secured from the employer's local Revenue office. These rates are subject to the following restrictions:

| Period of Assignment Abroad | Percentage of Subsistence Rate of Relevant Location |
|---|---|
| First month | 100% |
| Second and third month | 75% |
| Fourth, fifth and sixth month | 50% |

We now look at how travel and subsistence expenses are reimbursed for Jamie, who is travelling to the Persian Gulf on behalf of his company, Tigim Language Learning Ltd.

#### Case Study: Tigim Language Learning Ltd

We have seen above that Jamie has had a number of business trips to Abu Dhabi, Dubai and Qatar in 2014 and 2015. Jamie pays all of his travel, accommodation and meals expenses personally and is later reimbursed by Tigim Language Learning Ltd. His flight tickets, airport transfers and taxis are paid on the basis of vouched expenses, while Jamie claims the relevant overnight subsistence rates for each location, being 991 UAE dirhams for Abu Dhabi, 1,481 UAE dirhams for Dubai and 1,213 Qatari riyals for Qatar. These rates are reduced by reference to the table above once Jamie goes into his second month of foreign travel. If Jamie's actual accommodation and meals expenses

[18] Available at www.revenue.ie/en/tax/it/leaflets/it54.html (accessed June 2016).
[19] Available at www.revenue.ie/en/tax/it/leaflets/it51.html (accessed June 2016).

exceeded the overnight subsistence rates for these locations, he could have chosen to claim tax-free reimbursement of the actual costs, as long as he retained all relevant receipts.

### 12.5.2 Income Tax Rules and Payroll Tax Rules in Relation to Foreign Secondment

In **Section 12.5.1** above we looked at the FED income tax deduction that may be available where an Irish tax-resident employee travels abroad on behalf of their Irish employer and the payroll tax rules covering the tax-free payment/reimbursement of expenses on foreign trips. These two tax aspects of foreign travel may apply where an employee spends a relatively short time abroad, from a few days to a few months, and remains a tax resident of Ireland. Foreign secondment, on the other hand, refers to longer periods of assignment, generally six months or more, which, because of their longer duration, will likely impact on the tax residence status of the employee.

#### 12.5.2.1 Tax Residence and Exposure to Irish Income Tax and USC

Before setting out some income tax rules that apply to foreign secondments, we will look at the income tax concepts of 'tax residence', 'ordinary tax residence' and 'split-year residence'. These rules are set out in sections 819 to 822 TCA 1997.

To be treated as an Irish tax resident, an individual must meet either of the following tests:

- be resident in Ireland for at least 183 days in one tax year; *or*
- be resident in Ireland for at least 280 days over two consecutive tax years, with at least 30 days' residence in each tax year.

An individual who is in Ireland during any part of a day will be treated as present in the country for the purpose of calculating the 'days tests' noted above. An individual who has been tax resident in Ireland for three consecutive tax years would be treated as achieving 'ordinary tax residence' in the fourth year of tax residence. Likewise, where an individual leaves Ireland and loses 'tax residence' status, it would take three consecutive years of non-tax residence to lose 'ordinary tax residence' status.

EXAMPLE 12.1: LOSS OF IRISH ORDINARY TAX RESIDENCE STATUS

An Irish tax resident leaves Ireland at the beginning of 2013 and becomes non-tax resident in 2013. If that individual is non-tax resident for 2013, 2014 and 2015, he will lose 'ordinary tax residence' status in 2016.

An Irish tax-resident individual who is also an 'ordinary tax resident' of Ireland is subject to tax on their worldwide income, wherever it arises. When they lose Irish tax residence but retain 'ordinary tax residence' status, they will be taxable in Ireland on their worldwide income with the exception of:

- income of a trade/profession (i.e. a business), all of which is carried on outside of Ireland;
- employment income from an employment that is carried on outside of Ireland (except for 'incidental duties'); and
- other foreign income not exceeding a value of €3,810 in a tax year.

***Note:*** the above assumes that the individual is also Irish domiciled. 'Domicile' is a nebulous concept but, in essence, refers to the country to which an individual has the closest long-term ties.

Where an Irish individual is seconded abroad by their employer for a period of time that is long enough for them to lose their Irish tax-resident status, they will remain ordinarily tax resident in Ireland for three consecutive tax years. However, the employment income that they earn during that period of being non-Irish tax resident but an ordinary tax resident of Ireland will not be subject to Irish income tax, as long as the majority of their employment duties are carried on outside of Ireland.

Additionally, in relation to employment income only, a tax relief known as 'split-year residence relief' allows an employee who leaves Ireland to work abroad and who intends to be non-Irish tax resident for the following tax year to become non-Irish tax resident from the date of departure. This means that even though the individual may, in principle, be tax resident in Ireland in the year of departure (because they meet either the 183 days/280 days' test), they will be treated as non-Irish tax resident from the date of departure in relation to their employment income.

***Note:*** the rules in relation to tax residence and the exposure to Irish income tax also generally apply in relation to the exposure to USC.

Set out below is an example of how 'split-year residence relief' can remove an employee's foreign employment income from the Irish income tax net, despite the fact that the employee is Irish tax resident at the time.

### Case Study: The Neally Engineering Group

The Neally Engineering Group was looking to expand abroad and, because of Martin's previous experience working in Madrid, the group has been investigating that location. Once the directors decide to establish a Spanish operation, they ask one of their senior engineers, Hugh, to manage the setting-up of the new Spanish factory. Hugh continues to be employed by his Irish employer, Neally Engineering Ltd.

Hugh leaves Ireland on 12 April 2014 on an expected three-year secondment to Spain. Including some return trips to Ireland, he spends

190 days in Ireland in 2014 and 21 days in Ireland in 2015. Under the 'days tests' he would be treated as tax resident in Ireland for 2014 and non-tax resident for 2015. However, as he meets the conditions attaching to 'split-year residence relief' and solely for the purposes of taxing his employment income, Hugh will be treated as non-Irish tax resident from 12 April 2014 as opposed to from 1 January 2015. This means that, as a non-Irish tax resident who retains 'ordinary Irish tax residence' status, the employment income Hugh earns when working in Spain during 2014 will not be subject to Irish income tax or USC.

### *12.5.2.2 Obligation to Operate Payroll Taxes*

**PAYE Income Tax and USC** We noted earlier that, where an employee is sent abroad on secondment for periods of about six months or longer, differences can arise between the employee's income tax obligations and their employer's payroll tax obligations. Take Hugh in the Neally case study above, for instance. He has been posted to Spain by his Irish employer for a three-year secondment and may rely on split-year residence relief for 2014, which means that he will become non-Irish tax resident from 12 April 2014. As a result, no Irish income tax or USC liabilities should arise on the employment income he earns while working in Spain after this date. However, Hugh is employed by his Irish employer under an Irish employment, which means that for 2014 his employer is obliged to continue withholding payroll taxes on the salary Hugh earns while working in Spain. In other words, there is a mismatch between Hugh's income tax/USC position and Neally Engineering Ltd's obligations in relation to withholding payroll taxes.

One way of rectifying this is for Hugh to file an income tax return after the end of the 2014 tax year and claim a refund of the relevant payroll taxes. This means, however, that Hugh will suffer a serious time lag between the withholding of payroll taxes (April to December 2014) and their refund by Revenue (probably February 2015 at the earliest). Remember also that Hugh is likely to be paying some level of Spanish taxes on the employment income he earns while working in Spain, so his cash flow will be severely impacted.

An alternative method of dealing with this mismatch between income tax/USC rules and payroll tax rules is for the employer to secure a 'PAYE exclusion order' from Revenue on behalf of the employee. Securing this order allows the employer to pay employment income on a gross basis, i.e. there is no obligation to withhold PAYE income tax or USC. A PAYE exclusion order will only issue in respect of a tax year where the employee will be non-tax resident for that tax year and where the employee exercises the duties of their employment outside of Ireland.[20] 'Incidental duties' (being

[20] Sections 984(1) and 531AM(1)(a)(v)(III) TCA 1997.

duties that do not extend beyond 30 days in a tax year) that are exercised in Ireland are ignored for the purposes of this test.

As we noted above, non-tax residency may be achieved by failing either of the 'days tests' (183 days in one tax year or 280 days in two consecutive tax years) or by being eligible for split-year residence relief. Where the employee is entitled to split-year residence relief, it is usually possible to secure a PAYE exclusion order from the date of departure. Doing so would bring the income tax/USC rules and payroll tax rules back into alignment.

In Hugh's case, the PAYE exclusion order should take effect from 12 April 2014, meaning that his Irish employer, Neally Engineering Ltd, can stop withholding PAYE income tax and USC from Hugh's employment income from that date.

***Note:*** when Hugh ultimately returns to Ireland to resume his employment duties in Ireland, the PAYE exclusion order ceases and his employer must resume withholding PAYE income tax and USC on his employment income.[21]

We noted in **Chapter 5** that Irish company directors are subject to full payroll withholding taxes on their directorship income. Even where an Irish director works abroad for sufficient time to lose their Irish tax residency status, securing a PAYE exclusion order is difficult. The Revenue manual states that an exclusion order will only issue for a director who is not an Irish tax resident if that person's directorship income will fall outside of the charge to Irish tax under the terms of a relevant double taxation agreement. (See **Chapter 13, Section 13.1.1** for commentary on DTAs.)

**Travel, Subsistence and Relocation Expenses** At **Section 12.5.1.3** above, we reviewed the travel and subsistence expenses that may be reimbursed by an employer on a tax-free basis for shorter periods of foreign travel, i.e. those not exceeding six months. We noted that, in relation to subsistence expenses, there is a choice between claiming actual vouched expenses and flat-rate allowances that vary depending on the country to which the Irish employee is travelling.

For foreign assignments of more than six months' duration, tax-free flat-rate subsistence allowances are available on the following basis:

| **Period of Assignment Abroad** | **Allowable Subsistence for Relevant Location** |
|---|---|
| First month (to facilitate the employee obtaining self-catering accommodation) | Up to the overnight rate |
| Remainder of assignment | Up to cost of 'reasonable accommodation' plus 50% of the day rate (10 hours) for the location |

[21] For further information, see Revenue's *PAYE – Exclusion Orders Manual*, Part 42.04.01.

Where an employee is obliged to move house to take up employment at a new location, certain removal/relocation expenses associated with the move may be paid/reimbursed by the employer on a tax-free basis. These removal/relocation expenses are:
- auctioneers' and solicitors' fees, and stamp duty charges arising from moving house;
- removal of furniture and effects;
- storage charges;
- insurance of furniture and effects in transit or in storage;
- cleaning of stored furniture; and
- travelling expenses on removal.

Payment to reimburse some or all of the capital cost of acquiring or building accommodation, and any employer loans to facilitate this, will be subject to tax. The expenses must be supported by written receipts, the payment of the expenses must be properly controlled and the expenses must be reasonable in amount. Finally, it must be necessary to move house in the circumstances of the secondment.

For more information on the tax-free payment of these expenses, see Revenue's leaflet IT54 *Employees' Subsistence Expenses*[22] and Revenue's *Removal/Relocation Expenses*, Part 05.02.03.

### *12.5.3 PRSI (Social Security) Rules in Relation to Foreign Travel and Foreign Secondment*

The rules in relation to social security (PRSI) obligations for employees sent abroad are completely different and separate from the income tax rules and payroll tax rules discussed above in relation to income tax/PAYE income tax and USC. For an Irish employee working in Ireland, PRSI withholding obligations typically follow the PAYE income tax obligations and are collected through the PAYE system; in the case of employees on foreign secondment, however, the rules diverge.

First, we must note that the concept of tax residence is irrelevant to social security obligations and the basic rule is that an employee is insurable (i.e. subject to social security obligations) wherever they carry out their employment. In addition, Irish law requires that an employee who is normally insurable in Ireland will continue to be insurable in Ireland for the first 52 weeks after departure from this country. An employee travelling abroad for their Irish employer will often want to continue paying into the Irish social security system so as to maintain their entitlement to social welfare benefits in Ireland. In addition, the country to which the employee is seconded is likely to have its own social security obligations. Employers will look to avoid a double charge to social security, if possible.

[22] Available at www.revenue.ie/en/tax/it/leaflets/it54.html (accessed June 2016).

There are three possible approaches here:

1. The employee is seconded to a country within the European Economic Area (EEA). In this case, the employer should apply to the Department of Social Protection (DSP) to secure an A1 certificate, which will ensure that the employee is retained on the Irish social security system and that no social security obligations arise in the country to which the employee has been seconded. The employer continues to make social security contributions in Ireland.

### Case Study: Neally Engineering Ltd

We have seen that Hugh was sent on an expected three-year secondment to Spain from Ireland by Neally Engineering Ltd. As he intends to return to Ireland after this secondment, the company secures an A1 certificate from the Irish DSP. No Spanish social security contributions will be paid by Neally Engineering Ltd; instead, Irish social security contributions, based on a percentage of the salary Hugh earns while working in Spain, will be paid to the Irish DSP.

2. The employee is seconded to a country/region with which Ireland has a social security agreement: USA, Australia, New Zealand, Canada, Quebec, UK (covering the Isle of Man and the Channel Islands), South Korea and Japan. In this case, the DSP can issue a certificate of coverage which effectively achieves the same position as an A1 certificate.
3. The employee is seconded to a country other than those listed in 1 or 2 above. Where the employee wishes to stay within the Irish social security system beyond the first 52 weeks, then this position must be agreed with the DSP, which has discretion on this matter. If they agree to this request, the DSP will issue a certificate of coverage, but this is unlikely to prevent the authorities in the country of the secondment from imposing its own social security obligations on the employee. A double charge to social security payments may well result.

Where a PAYE exclusion order has been secured for an employee but the employee remains on the Irish PRSI system, the employer may pay these PRSI contributions through the PAYE system. More information on the application of the PRSI system to employees seconded abroad can be found on the website of the DSP.[23]

[23] See www.welfare.ie/en/Pages/Special-Collection-System.aspx (accessed June 2016).

# CHAPTER 13

# ESTABLISHING A FOREIGN PRESENCE



In the previous chapter, we looked at some Irish VAT and payroll tax implications where an Irish business supplies goods/services to foreign customers, and where employees of the Irish business travel abroad to carry out their employment duties.

Sending goods, services or employees abroad from an Irish base may work well when the Irish business is starting the process of internationalisation, but in the longer term, establishing some type of 'foreign presence' in one or more foreign countries may be the only way to really accelerate the development of the international business. This chapter looks at what form this foreign presence may take and the types of tax issues that may arise as a result of it.

The first point we should note is that the issues highlighted in this chapter are in no way an exhaustive list of all tax issues that will be encountered in relation to establishing a business presence in a foreign country. In addition, the tax knowledge set out in this book is limited to Irish tax law and practice only; where we refer to foreign taxes, we do so to illustrate a point with an example and not to provide a comprehensive review of that tax or other taxes in that country. As always, specific detailed advice tailored to the circumstances of the business should be sought.

## 13.1 Fundamental Concepts of International Taxation

Before considering the potential Irish tax implications of establishing a foreign presence, e.g. a foreign branch or subsidiary company, it is worth reviewing some fundamental ideas in international taxation that impact on the Irish business's foreign presence.

### *13.1.1 Double Taxation Agreements*

Double taxation agreements (DTAs) are bilateral (two-country) agreements that generally deal with three fundamental issues:

- the right of one/both countries to tax different classes of income where there is a cross-border aspect to that income, e.g. the income is sourced in one country and received in the other country;
- a mechanism to reduce or eliminate double taxation of this income, i.e. where both countries claim taxing rights in relation to the same income; and
- a mechanism for the exchange of tax information between the tax authorities of the two countries.

***Note:*** although one of the aims of a DTA is to reduce or eliminate double taxation on the same income, the rules for calculating double tax credits (one of the means by which double taxation is reduced or eliminated) are quite complicated. For our purposes, it is worth just noting that often the result of these calculations does not give a full credit for foreign tax paid, so some element of double taxation may still remain.

It is extremely important to note that a DTA does not in itself impose a taxation charge; instead the taxation charges are imposed by the domestic tax law and practice of the two countries that have signed the agreement and the DTA 'sits on top' of these domestic tax charges to deal with the fundamental issues noted above. This means that, when analysing the tax implications of a cross-border situation, the first step is to look at the domestic tax rules of the two countries that have signed the DTA and then to look to the relevant articles of the DTA.

***Note:*** the provisions of a DTA will apply to tax residents of one or both of the countries that have signed the DTA and will usually cover individuals, companies, businesses and any other taxable entities that are defined by the provisions of the specific DTA. Each DTA sets out a list of the tax heads of each country covered by the DTA; these typically include income tax, corporation tax (CT) and capital gains tax (CGT), though this list may be more limited or more expansive depending on the specific DTA. The DTAs will not cover VAT or other forms of sales tax.

Ireland's DTAs typically include an article in relation to the taxation of employment income and the allocation of taxing rights, depending on where the employee is tax resident and where the employment is exercised. Note that the possible application of tax relief under a DTA could impact on some of the income tax reliefs set out in **Chapter 12**. For example, when we reviewed the operation of the foreign earnings deduction (FED) in **Section 12.5.1.1**, we saw that the value of the FED would be reduced if double taxation relief was being claimed simultaneously under the terms of a DTA. Social security is not covered by DTAs – see **Chapter 12, Section 12.5.3**, which sets out the possible social security obligations of employees that are exercising their Irish employment outside of Ireland.

Most DTAs include what are known as 'tie-breaker' tests of tax residency, which will apply where an individual or other entity covered by the DTA is treated as a tax resident of both countries under the domestic tax rules of each country. These 'tie-breaker' tests will determine of which country the individual/other entity is ultimately a tax resident. For example, in the Ireland/UK DTA, the 'tie-breaker' test of tax residency for an individual must be assessed in the following order:

- the country in which the individual has a permanent home;
- if the individual has a permanent home in both countries, it is the country where their 'centre of vital interests' (personal and economic relationships) is located;
- if the location of the 'centre of vital interests' cannot be determined or the individual does not have a permanent home in either country, then it is the country where they have an 'habitual abode';
- if the individual has an 'habitual abode' in both countries or in neither of them, it is the country of which the individual is a national; and
- if the individual is a national of both countries or neither of them, then the tax authorities of the two countries must settle the issue "by mutual agreement".[1]

The 'tie-breaker' test of tax residency for a company under the Ireland/UK DTA comprises one test only: a company tax resident in both countries will ultimately be treated as tax resident in the country in which the 'effective management' of the company is located. In other DTAs (e.g. Ireland/USA), there is no corporate tie-breaker test of residency and the relevant article of the DTA states that the tax authorities of the two countries "shall endeavour by mutual agreement" to deem the company to be a tax resident of one country only.[2]

As of 30 June 2016, Ireland has operating DTAs with 70 countries. All of Ireland's DTAs, along with a description of the work ongoing in relation to negotiating new agreements, are listed on Revenue's website.[3]

[1] Article 4(2) Double Taxation Treaty between Ireland and United Kingdom.
[2] Article 4(4) Double Taxation Treaty between Ireland and USA (1997).
[3] See www.revenue.ie/en/practitioner/law/tax-treaties.html (accessed June 2016).

### 13.1.2 'Permanent Establishment' and Exposure to Foreign Taxes on Trading Profits

The concept of a permanent establishment (PE) comes from standard wording included in many of Ireland's DTAs and is of such significance to the question of when a business triggers an income tax/corporation tax exposure in another country that we will examine this issue separately.

Where an Irish business wishes to establish some type of foreign presence abroad, there are many forms that this can take, e.g. branch, subsidiary company, agency, distributorship arrangement, broker, permanent representative. When considering the most suitable form of foreign presence, the Irish business must understand the tax implications attaching to the different forms of this foreign presence so as not to find itself in a situation where an exposure to foreign tax has arisen inadvertently. An active decision to register a branch of the Irish business or a subsidiary company of an Irish company in a foreign country is one matter, one which will almost certainly trigger an exposure to foreign income tax or corporation tax on trading profits arising, as well as potential exposure to other tax heads. But what happens when the Irish business wishes to 'dip their toe' into the foreign market without much formality? Are there circumstances where even this might still trigger foreign taxes on trading profits? The straight answer to this is 'yes', if the foreign tax authorities believe that a PE of the Irish business has been created in that foreign country.

A definition of PE is usually included in Ireland's DTAs. For convenience, we will look at the definition at Article 5 of the Ireland/UK DTA, which defines a PE as "a fixed place of business in which the business of the enterprise [e.g. a sole trade, partnership or company] is wholly or partly carried on". PE will specifically include:

- a place of management, branch or office;
- a factory or workshop;
- a mine, oil well, quarry or other place of extraction of natural resources;
- an installation or structure used for the exploration of natural resources; and
- a construction site or installation project that lasts for more than six months.

Certain activities are not treated as creating a PE and these include: the use of facilities or maintenance of stock solely for the purpose of storage, display or delivery; and the maintenance of a fixed place of business solely for the purpose of purchasing goods or collecting information for the enterprise.

Article 5 goes on to note that, in general, where the business of the enterprise is carried on by a local independent agent or broker, then the enterprise will not be treated as having established a PE in that country. However, where someone other than an independent agent or broker (an employee of the enterprise, say) regularly exercises in Ireland/UK the authority to conclude contracts in the name of the enterprise, then that person is treated as having created a PE in that country. An exception to this arises where the individual's activities are limited to purchasing goods for the enterprise.

***Note:*** the tests of a PE noted above are specifically applicable to residents of Ireland or the UK who operate in the other country and are subject to the Ireland/UK DTA. Every country will have its own tax rules that determine when a PE has been established; in addition, the existence/absence of a DTA between Ireland and another country will also impact this analysis.

It is relatively straightforward to understand the 'PE test' at either end of the spectrum, i.e. having an office from which the business of the 'enterprise' is carried on will constitute a PE, while maintaining a goods storage facility in the other country or contracting an independent, local broker to generate sales will not. The difficulty is in the middle ground. An example of how an Irish business could inadvertently establish a foreign PE is a situation where the business sends, say, a sales employee to another country to explore the market for business development. In the early days there, the employee spends their time gathering information on the local market and making contacts. At some point, these contacts become potential customers and the employee then starts agreeing terms on behalf of their employer. If the employee is regarded as having 'concluded contracts' with the foreign customer (even if they have not signed a contract with that customer), then they will be treated as having triggered a PE for their employer in that country.

Once the enterprise is regarded as having established a foreign PE, then typically all trading profits attributable to that PE will be subject to taxes in the foreign country, using foreign tax rules and rates to calculate the tax liability.

In **Chapter 11, Section 11.4.1**, we briefly referred to an ongoing OECD project called the Base Erosion and Profit Shifting (BEPS) project, which is focused on international tax planning strategies that involve moving profits into low-tax jurisdictions and eroding the taxable profit base in high-tax jurisdictions.[4] One of the issues being considered is the artificial avoidance of creating a PE. As a result of the BEPS project, we can expect future changes to the definition of a PE in Ireland's DTAs, probably resulting in more businesses being found to have created a PE in Ireland/the other country.

We are highlighting here the possible tax implications where a business 'dips its toe' into a foreign market in a deliberately low-key/informal manner. This, of course, assumes that it is actually possible to do so. In many countries, however, local rules make it impossible to adopt an informal approach and the only way to do business in that country is in a formal manner, e.g. by registering a local company or by entering

[4] See www.oecd.org/ctp/beps-about.htm

into a partnership/joint venture with a locally owned and operated business. There may also be commercial considerations, such as the possibility that customers in that country will only do business with a local company.

## 13.2 Irish Corporation Tax Implications of Establishing a Foreign Presence

This topic is often referred to as the 'branch versus subsidiary' question, but it is broader than this. As we have seen above, the 'foreign presence' may take a number of different forms, but these can be broadly categorised into two categories:

(a) an incorporated company – this could be owned directly by Irish shareholders or be owned by an Irish company that is owned by Irish shareholders, in which case it will be a subsidiary company; or
(b) an unincorporated entity that is treated as a PE in the foreign country.

Although it is entirely possible for an Irish unincorporated business (sole trade or partnership) to establish a foreign presence, it is more likely that by the time of international expansion, the Irish business will be incorporated (i.e. it will be a company). For that reason, we will assume that the Irish business is an Irish company for the rest of this section. In the international context, note that the unincorporated entity ((b) above) includes a branch, but can also include any fixed place of business (as noted in Article 5 of the Ireland/UK DTA for example) and a PE that is established by virtue of an employee/dependent agent of the Irish business exercising the authority to conclude contracts on behalf of the Irish business in the foreign location. For ease of reference, however, we will use the terms 'subsidiary' and 'branch' here to describe categories (a) and (b) respectively.

The first key issue to note here is that, from an Irish tax perspective, a foreign company is a separate legal entity, while the foreign branch of an Irish company is not. This means that the financial results of the foreign branch will be included in the Irish company's financial results as if the activities of the foreign branch had taken place in Ireland. It also means that all assets and liabilities of the foreign branch will be included on the balance sheet of the Irish company and that, for Irish tax purposes, transactions between the Irish company and its foreign branch will likely carry no tax implications.

### *13.2.1 Implications of Establishing a Foreign Branch*

#### *13.2.1.1 Profits and Losses of the Branch*

Branch profits will generally be taxed both in Ireland and in the foreign country. Most of Ireland's DTAs provide that foreign tax on trading profits of the foreign branch of an Irish company will be allowed as a credit against the Irish corporation tax (CT) calculated on the same trading profits. An example of this is contained in Article 21(1) of the Ireland/UK DTA. Note that the Irish tax rules that provide for this tax credit specifically state that Irish tax rules in relation to calculating taxable income and deductible expenses should be applied to the foreign branch results to determine the branch's taxable trading profit.[5] This requirement for recalculation by reference to Irish tax rules, combined with the fact that the Irish CT rate of 12.5% for trading profits is usually lower than the corresponding rate in the foreign country, often results in the foreign tax *credit* (which is included in the Irish CT return and reduces the amount of the Irish CT liability) being lower than the actual foreign tax *charge*.

If the branch is located in a country with which Ireland does not have a DTA, then a unilateral form of double taxation relief may be available under Irish domestic tax rules. This means that where CT is charged by the foreign tax authorities on foreign branch profits, then the Irish company should be entitled to a credit against Irish CT for this foreign tax charge.[6] This foreign tax credit cannot exceed the Irish corporation tax liability.

Just as any profits of a foreign branch would be included in the Irish company's total profits and taxed in Ireland, so any losses arising in the foreign branch may be included in the Irish company's accounts and may reduce any profits arising in the Irish company. Alternatively, if the foreign tax rules allow the carry-forward of the branch losses for offset against future branch profits, then a decision may be made to use the foreign branch losses in the foreign country and not offset them, for tax purposes, in Ireland.

#### *13.2.1.2 Repatriation of Profits*

We noted above that, from an Irish tax perspective, a foreign branch is not a separate legal entity from the Irish company but is treated as a part of the Irish company. This means that repatriating profits to Ireland from a foreign branch will not generally trigger Irish tax implications. This does not automatically mean that this repatriation will carry no tax implications, however, as it may trigger tax implications in the foreign country in which the branch is located.

### *13.2.2 Implications of Establishing a Foreign Subsidiary Company*

#### *13.2.2.1 Profits and Losses of the Subsidiary Company*

Trading profits of a foreign subsidiary company will be subject to taxes on trading profits in the country in which the company is tax resident. Each country will have its own test of residency for companies and this must be

[5] Schedule 24, para 4(2A) of the Taxes Consolidation Act 1997 (TCA 1997).

[6] Schedule 24, para 9DA TCA 1997.

assessed. In Ireland, for example, a company incorporated on or after 1 January 2015 will be treated as Irish tax resident where:

- the company is Irish incorporated and no other country is claiming the company as a tax resident through the provisions of a DTA between Ireland and that country; or
- the company's '*central management and control*' is carried out in Ireland.[7]

'Central management and control' is generally located where the company's business decisions are made, board meetings and bank accounts are held, the company's accounts are prepared and examined, and the company's books and records are retained.

In the case of a foreign-incorporated subsidiary company of an Irish company, it is not unusual for the situation to arise whereby the tax authorities of that foreign country and the Irish tax authorities both claim that the foreign subsidiary company is a tax resident of their respective countries. Where there is a DTA between that foreign country and Ireland, the DTA will probably include a 'tie-breaker' clause in relation to tax residency. For example, in **Section 13.1.1** above we noted that, in the Ireland/UK DTA, the 'tie-breaker' clause in relation to the tax residency of a company looks at the place where the 'effective management' of the company is situated.

Where losses are incurred in a foreign subsidiary company, the opportunity to use these losses to reduce the Irish parent company's taxable profits is quite limited. This may be possible where the foreign company transferring the losses is resident in an EU Member State, or in a country with which Ireland has a DTA. One of the major conditions attaching to the use of this foreign loss by the Irish parent company is that there cannot be any way for the foreign subsidiary company to use these losses in that foreign country.[8]

### *13.2.2.2 Repatriation of Profits*

The profits of the foreign subsidiary company can be repatriated by way of a dividend paid to its Irish parent company. The receipt of a foreign dividend will typically be subject to tax in Ireland. There is also the issue of dividend withholding tax (DWT) to consider, as the tax rules of the foreign country may require that a percentage of the dividend be withheld by the foreign subsidiary company and paid over to the tax authorities in that country. It may be possible to reduce or eliminate this DWT obligation, depending on the terms of any DTA in place between Ireland and the country where the foreign subsidiary company is located. If DWT is withheld and paid to the foreign tax authorities, then the Irish parent company will have to determine if a credit for the foreign tax paid can be included in the Irish CT calculations.

[7] Section 23A TCA 1997.

[8] Sections 411 and 420 TCA 1997.

There is a further credit available under the terms of some of Ireland's DTAs that may allow a credit in Ireland for the tax paid by the foreign company on the trading profits from which it declared the dividend to its Irish parent company. This is known as 'relief for underlying tax'.

Set out in the case study extract below is a situation where an Irish business is obliged to register a formal foreign presence in a particular foreign country as the local people will only do business with a locally registered entity.

Case Study: Tigim Language Learning Ltd
(Choice of Foreign Presence)

As we have seen, Tigim Language Learning Ltd have moved their language courses online and are in serious 'business development' mode, with the UAE being amongst its first foreign target markets. Jamie, who is spearheading this expansion, aims to establish strategic relationships with 'bricks-and-mortar' language and business colleges to promote Tigim Language Learning Ltd's online courses. After a number of business trips to the UAE, Jamie has seen that in order to be taken more seriously, Tigim Language Learning Ltd will need to establish a local presence, with UAE nationals seen to be representing the business.

The possibility of incorporating a local limited liability company (LLC) was discounted immediately as Jamie understood that this would require that at least 51% of the company's shares be held by a UAE national. He was advised that the choices then were between a branch and a 'representative office', both of which require the appointment of a UAE service agent. As Tigim Language Learning Ltd was in the early stages of establishing relationships in the UAE, Jamie was wary of appointing a UAE national who would have discretion over Tigim Language Learning Ltd's UAE business activities. Jamie was advised, however, that under local laws, a 'representative office' is only permitted to promote its parent company's activities and is not permitted to undertake any income-earning activities. This would mean that the 'representative office' would not be treated as a PE in the UAE. For these reasons, Tigim Language Learning Ltd established a UAE representative office.

## 13.3 Foreign Tax Implications of Establishing a Foreign Presence

In **Section 13.1.2** above, we looked at when foreign taxes on trading profits (income tax or corporation tax) may arise, specifically focusing on the concept of a permanent establishment (PE) and noting that each country will have its own rules as to when a PE will be treated as having arisen. The domestic tax rules on this issue may then be impacted by any DTA in place between Ireland and that country.

Also of huge potential significance for a foreign presence are VAT and other similar sales-type taxes.

VAT is an EU-wide tax covering supplies of goods and services, and the importation of goods. It operates in all 28 EU Member States, as well as some non-EU Member States that choose to follow EU rules on VAT. The overarching VAT framework is set out in EU Directives, which are carried into the tax rules of each EU Member State by way of domestic legislation enacted in each State. In order to be clear on when a foreign presence in another country is obliged to register for VAT in that country and start applying VAT to their supplies, the Irish business should look at the domestic VAT rules of that foreign country.

In Ireland, for example, a foreign trader (i.e. a trader that is not established in Ireland) is generally obliged to register for VAT when it makes a supply of goods or services in Ireland.[9] In **Chapter 4** we reviewed the turnover thresholds that apply before an obligation to register for VAT arises; a foreign trader cannot benefit from any turnover threshold and must register for VAT as soon as the first supply is to be made.[10] Similar rules will apply where the Irish business's foreign presence is operating in any of the countries in which the EU VAT framework operates. Of course, where the foreign presence is operating in non-EU VAT countries, then an entirely different sales tax framework may apply. Take, for example, the US, where federal, state, city and county sales taxes may arise, depending on the location where the business is operating.

Payroll taxes are also potentially very significant where a foreign presence is established. Like taxes on profits, payroll taxes can also cause confusion and missed local obligations, with expensive consequences. Many people assume that if an individual is employed by the foreign presence, then local payroll tax obligations arise and, if not, then no local obligations will arise. In fact, it is really not that simple and the detailed circumstances of the employment must be reviewed. Examples of situations where there may be no direct employment relationship between the individual and the foreign presence, but where local payroll tax obligations can still arise, include:

- where the individual is employed directly by the Irish business but spends sufficient time in the foreign country, or in some other way meets the criteria to be regarded as a tax resident of that country; and
- where the individual is employed directly by the Irish business but the costs of that employment are re-charged to the foreign presence.

[9] Section 5(1) of the Value-Added Tax Consolidation Act 2010 (VATCA 2010).
[10] Section 6(3) VATCA 2010.

Local taxes on trading profits, VAT (or local sales tax) and payroll taxes are the most obvious examples of taxes that may be relevant to the foreign presence but they are not the only taxes to consider. The foreign presence may be subject to, say, local property taxes or water charges; it may also be subject to taxes that do not have an equivalent in Ireland. It would be impossible (and unwise) to attempt a comprehensive list of all the taxes that may impact on a foreign presence of an Irish business and the best advice, always, is to seek local and reliable tax advice.

## 13.4 Tax Treatment of Foreign Employees Coming to Ireland

In this section we will take the issue of payroll taxes further and look at the situation where the foreign presence employs an individual locally and then sends that person to work in the Irish business for a period of time. To clarify, in **Chapter 12, Section 12.5** we looked at payroll tax issues for employees of the Irish business who are posted abroad; in this section, we will look at issues arising for employees of the foreign presence that are posted to Ireland.

The detailed rules set out below relate to an employee with a 'foreign employment'. In **Chapter 12** we looked at the definition of 'Irish employment' and it is now worth noting the characteristics of a 'foreign employment':
- the employer (e.g. branch or company) is located in a foreign country;
- the employment contract is governed by foreign law; and
- the employment income is paid abroad.

### *13.4.1 Income Tax Rules and Payroll Tax Rules for Foreign Employees Travelling to Ireland*

As seen in **Chapter 12**, for foreign employees coming to Ireland we generally classify periods of less than six months' duration as 'travel', and periods of six months or more as 'secondment'.

Earlier in this chapter, we reviewed the purpose of double taxation agreements (DTAs) and in **Chapter 12, Section 12.5.2.1** we reviewed the concept of tax residence.

#### *13.4.1.1 Exposure to Irish Income Tax and USC*

If a foreign employee is coming from a country with which Ireland has a DTA, it is likely that the employment article of that DTA will exempt an employee who is tax resident in that foreign country from Irish income tax and USC on the employment income earned from a foreign employment where employment duties are carried out in Ireland. The conditions that must be met for the exemption to apply usually include:
- the foreign employee is not present in Ireland for more than 183 days in the tax year concerned (or in any 12-month period);
- the employment income is paid by, or on behalf of, a non-Irish resident employer (the foreign employer); *and*

- the cost of the employment income is not borne by a permanent establishment (PE) or fixed base of the foreign employer in Ireland.

Where the conditions of the relevant DTA are not met, or the employee is coming from a non-DTA country, Irish income tax and USC will apply to employment income earned while the employee is performing the duties of their foreign employment in Ireland.[11]

(***Remember:*** these are the *income tax* rules that apply to foreign employees travelling to Ireland to carry out their foreign employment duties in this country.)

#### *13.4.1.2 Obligation to Withhold PAYE Income Tax and USC*

As with an Irish employee working in an Irish employment who is sent abroad, the differing income tax and payroll tax rules are clearly highlighted where a foreign employee working in a foreign employment is sent to Ireland.

The general rule is that employment income earned while a foreign employee is carrying out their foreign employment duties in Ireland will be subject to Irish *payroll* taxes. This means that the foreign employer is obliged to register for payroll taxes in Ireland, withhold the appropriate PAYE income tax and USC, and pay these amounts to the Collector-General. ***Note:*** in certain circumstances, if a foreign employer does not fulfil its obligation to register for payroll taxes, then the Irish business where the foreign employee is physically working will become liable for the foreign employer's Irish payroll tax obligations.[12]

There are three specific exemptions to this general obligation on the foreign employer to register and withhold Irish payroll taxes:

1. Business visits of 30 working days or fewer to Ireland by tax residents of non-DTA countries.
2. Business visits of 60 working days or fewer to Ireland by tax residents of DTA countries – the conditions attaching to this exemption being:
   (a) the employee is tax resident in a DTA country and not tax resident in Ireland (tax residence is determined by Irish domestic rules, as set out in **Chapter 12, Section 12.5.2.1**);
   (b) there is a genuine foreign employment;
   (c) the employee is not paid by, or on behalf of, an Irish employer;
   (d) the cost of the employment is not borne by an Irish PE of the foreign employer; *and*
   (e) the duties of the foreign employment are performed in Ireland for 60 or fewer working days in a year of assessment (or any continuous period of 60 or fewer working days).

   In relation to the exemptions at 1 and 2 above, there is no requirement to apply to Revenue in order to avoid payroll tax obligations. As long as the conditions are met, then no payroll tax obligations will arise.

[11] Section 18(2) TCA 1997.
[12] Sections 985D and 985F TCA 1997.

In contrast, however, in order for the exemption at 3 below to apply, a significant amount of paperwork must be presented to Revenue and the foreign employer must actually register in Ireland for payroll tax purposes.

3. Visits of 183 days or less to Ireland by tax residents of DTA countries where the employment income is subject to payroll withholding taxes in the DTA country.

   The conditions attaching to this exemption include those set out at (a) to (d) in exemption 2 above, as well as the requirements that the foreign employee spend 183 days or fewer in Ireland in a year of assessment, and that the employee suffers payroll taxes in the foreign country on the employment income attributable to the performance of their foreign employment duties in Ireland. This exemption from Irish payroll tax obligations will only arise where the foreign employee also qualifies for exemption from Irish income tax under the employment article of the relevant DTA (noted above).

   ***Note:*** the application for exemption 3 must be made within 60 days of the employee starting to work in Ireland.

We can see that, in relation to employees coming from DTA countries, exemptions 2 and 3 above bring the income tax obligations and the payroll tax obligations back into alignment, i.e. a foreign employee who is exempt, under Irish domestic tax rules or the relevant DTA, from Irish income tax and USC will also be exempt from Irish payroll taxes.

We can see that it is extremely important to be clear from the outset on the length of the assignment to Ireland; if the employer does not withhold payroll taxes on the basis of expecting to meet one of the exemptions above, but the employee overstays, then the employer would be liable for payroll taxes on a backdated basis, with interest and penalties likely.

We can see that in the situation where no income tax obligations arise but there is no exemption from Irish PAYE income tax and USC, then the foreign employee may reclaim the PAYE income tax and USC withheld. This will require the submission of an Irish income tax return and will, inevitably, cause a significant cash-flow problem as the employee awaits their tax refund.

### *13.4.1.3 Travel Expenses and Subsistence Payments*

The rules in relation to the payment of tax-free travel and subsistence expenses to foreign employees who have been working for a foreign employer and who are sent to work in Ireland on a 'temporary assignment' are set out in Revenue's Statement of Practice IT/2/2007.[13]

In relation to travel expenses, the vouched cost of journeys to and from Ireland at the start and end of a 'temporary assignment' can be

[13] *Tax treatment of the reimbursement of Expenses of Travel and Subsistence to Office Holders and Employees* (SP IT/2/07 – Revised July 2015).

reimbursed tax-free. In addition, one vouched return trip per annum to the home location may be reimbursed on a tax-free basis; this covers a return trip for the foreign employee, and their spouse/civil partner and children, if they have accompanied the employee to Ireland. If the spouse/civil partner and children have remained in the home location, then the vouched cost of one return trip from that location to Ireland for them may be reimbursed on a tax-free basis.

There are a number of conditions that must be met in order for the foreign employee to be eligible for tax-free subsistence payments, including that the temporary assignment does not exceed 24 months. Where all of the conditions are met, tax-free subsistence payments for a period of *12 months* may be made by way of the higher of:

- vouched expenses; or
- flat-rate allowances.

The payment of vouched subsistence expenses is subject to the general rule that the expenses must not exceed the cost of "reasonable" accommodation and meals for the employee (and their spouse/civil partner and children, where relevant). While the possibility of a foreign employee living in hotel accommodation for up to a 12-month period is covered by the Statement of Practice, there is an expectation that rented accommodation will be secured within one month of arrival if the spouse/civil partner and children of the foreign employee have accompanied them to Ireland.

For the first two months of the assignment, the flat-rate subsistence allowances are based on the Civil Service rates as set out in Revenue's leaflet IT54 *Employees' Subsistence Expenses*, and after this period as follows:

| Period of Assignment | Allowable Tax-free Subsistence |
|---|---|
| First 14 nights of assignment | Up to the 'normal' Civil Service rate |
| Next 14 nights of assignment | Up to the 'reduced' Civil Service rate |
| Next 28 nights of assignment | Up to the 'detention' Civil Service rate |
| Remainder of assignment (to maximum of 12 months in total) | Vouched expenses, subject to a maximum of three nights' subsistence per week at the 'normal' Civil Service rate |

### *13.4.2 Income Tax Rules and Payroll Tax Rules for Foreign Employees Seconded to Ireland*

In general, those foreign employees sent to Ireland for periods of six months or more are treated as being on 'secondment' to Ireland, with differing tax consequences to those set out at **Section 13.4.1** above.

### 13.4.2.1 *Foreign Employees Seconded to Ireland becoming Subject to Irish Income Tax and USC*

In **Chapter 12, Section 12.5.2.1**, we set out the test for individual tax residence in Ireland. To recap, under Irish tax rules an individual will be treated as Irish tax resident where they meet either of the following tests (known as the 'days tests'):

- they are resident in Ireland for at least 183 days in one tax year (calendar year); *or*
- they are resident in Ireland for at least 280 days over two consecutive tax years, with at least 30 days' residence in each tax year.

This means that a foreign employee who is seconded to Ireland for a period of six months or more *may* become Irish tax resident in a given tax year, depending on their date of arrival in that tax year.

EXAMPLE 13.1: APPLYING THE DAYS TESTS TO ASSESS IRISH TAX RESIDENCY

If Sylvain is seconded from France to Ireland on 24 August 2014 for a period of six months to 28 February 2015 (189 days in total, of which 130 days are in tax year 2014), he will not meet the test of residency for 2014 under the 183 days test. Nor will he meet the test of residency for 2015, under either the 183 days test or the 280 days test. However, if the period of secondment ran from 24 March 2014 to 28 September 2014 (189 days in total, all of which are in tax year 2014), then Sylvain would be treated as Irish tax resident for 2014.

Under Irish tax rules, an Irish tax resident who is not 'ordinarily tax resident' in Ireland and does not have an Irish domicile will be subject to income tax and USC on all of the employment income earned from an employment carried out in Ireland *and* on any foreign-source income to the extent that it is remitted (brought into) to Ireland. (For an explanation of 'ordinary tax residence' and 'domicile', see **Chapter 12, Section 12.5.2.1**.) ***Note:*** the rules setting out when a 'remittance' of foreign income has occurred are complex and include some anti-tax avoidance elements.

The terms of the relevant DTA, if there is one, between Ireland and the country from which the foreign employee is arriving, may operate to take the foreign employee out of the Irish income tax and USC net.

Where a foreign employee who is arriving into Ireland to work has not been tax resident in Ireland during the previous tax year, and is expected to be tax resident in Ireland in the current tax year, then, under the 'split-year residence' rules, they will be treated as tax resident from the date of arrival into Ireland. This means that the employee will be subject to income tax and USC on employment income earned from an employment carried on in Ireland from the date of arrival.

### Case Study: Neally Engineering Ltd

In the previous chapter, we saw that Hugh, an employee of Neally Engineering Ltd, was seconded to Spain in April 2014 and tasked with opening a small engineering factory just outside Madrid. The premises had already been identified by Martin, so Hugh's focus in the first months of his secondment was to modify the premises to manufacture metal tools for the aviation industry (which are currently manufactured in Ireland), and to employ a suitably qualified workforce. As the ultimate plan is to transfer all of this metal tool production to the Spanish factory, Hugh decides that the senior Spanish technical/production engineer should spend time at the Irish factory. Marta is employed by a Spanish subsidiary company of Neally Engineering Ltd from 15 May 2014, with the intention that she will be seconded to Ireland for a 15-month period.

If Marta was seconded to Ireland on 15 November 2014 for a 15-month period to 15 February 2016, then, assuming that she was not Irish tax resident in 2013, she would be subject to the split-year residence rules and be treated as Irish tax resident from the date of arrival, i.e. from 15 November 2014.

(***Note:*** we saw the operation of the reverse of this 'split-year residence' concept, i.e. Irish tax resident leaving Ireland to work abroad, in **Chapter 12, Section 12.5.2.1**.)

#### *13.4.2.2 Payroll Tax Obligations for Foreign Employees Seconded to Ireland*

In relation to payroll tax obligations, we noted at **Section 13.4.1.2** above that unless a foreign employer can rely on one of three specific exemptions from payroll tax obligations, it will be obliged to register in Ireland and operate payroll withholding taxes on all employment income earned by foreign employees carrying out their duties in Ireland. We saw that no exemption from Irish payroll taxes will be available where an employee spends more than 183 days in Ireland during a tax year (or a 12-month period), which means that employees seconded to Ireland for six months or more will be subject to Irish PAYE income tax and USC.

### Case Study: The Neally Engineering Group's Spanish Subsidiary Company

In Marta's case, as she is employed by the Spanish subsidiary of the Neally Engineering Group, under a Spanish contract of employment, that Spanish subsidiary would be obliged to register for payroll taxes in Ireland and deduct PAYE income tax and USC from the employment income Marta earns while working in Ireland.

### *13.4.2.3 Special Assignee Relief Programme (SARP)*

This is a potentially valuable income tax relief available to higher-earning foreign employees, who are seconded to Ireland by a foreign employer, who spend at least 12 consecutive months working in Ireland and who become tax resident in Ireland.[14] The incoming foreign employee must perform the duties of their employment for a 'relevant employer' (or its associated company) in Ireland. A 'relevant employer' means a company that is incorporated and tax resident in a country/jurisdiction with which Ireland has a DTA or a tax information exchange agreement (TIEA).

The first step in assessing whether or not an employee is eligible for SARP is to determine if their 'relevant income' is greater than €75,000. In this context, 'relevant income' refers to basic salary, *excluding* benefits, bonuses, commissions, etc. If this is the case, then relief is given by way of a deduction for income tax purposes (but not USC or PRSI) of the following:

(Employment income – €75,000) × 30%

In general, 'employment income' *includes* salary, benefits, bonuses, commissions, etc. that the employee earns from exercising their 'relevant employment' in Ireland, though some items are excluded. Tax relief is available for a maximum of five consecutive tax years to a relevant employee who is first assigned to work in Ireland in any of the tax years 2012 to 2017.

EXAMPLE 13.2: YEAR OF ARRIVAL IN IRELAND AND DURATION OF A SARP CLAIM

If an individual arrives in Ireland during 2015 and meets all of the relevant conditions for that year and four subsequent tax years, then they can claim the tax relief for tax years 2015 to 2019.

There are a number of conditions that must be met in order for the relief to apply, some of which have been amended significantly by Finance Act 2014, with the majority of the amended conditions applying to new arrivals during tax years 2015, 2016 and 2017. Some of the more important conditions include the following:[14]

[14] Section 825C TCA 1997.

| Condition | Year of arrival in Ireland to start relevant employment: 2012, 2013, 2014 | Year of arrival in Ireland to start relevant employment: 2015, 2016, 2017 |
|---|---|---|
| Period of employment with relevant employer prior to arrival in Ireland | 12 months | Six months |
| Performance of duties for at least 12 consecutive months | From date of first becoming tax resident in Ireland | From date of first arrival in Ireland |
| Application of tax relief | Available for tax year in which tax resident in Ireland and not tax resident elsewhere | Available for tax year in which tax resident in Ireland |
| First entitlement to relief | First tax year in which tax resident in Ireland and not tax resident elsewhere | First tax year in which tax resident in Ireland |
| Cap on relevant income | €500,000 for tax years 2012 to 2014 but removed, for 2012 to 2014 arrivals, in respect of tax years 2015 *et seq.* | None |

We can see that the €500,000 cap on relevant income applies to tax years 2012 to 2014 but does not apply to *either*:

- the tax relief available in tax years 2015 to 2018 for a relevant employee who arrived in tax years 2012, 2013 or 2014; *or*
- a relevant employee who arrived in tax years 2015, 2016 or 2017.

***Note:*** there are strict reporting requirements for the employers of foreign employees who are eligible for SARP tax relief. Also, it is possible for the employer to secure confirmation of the SARP deduction and code this into the employee's regular payroll tax calculations. This avoids the necessity for the employee to wait until after the end of the tax year before securing an income tax refund; however, an obligation to file an income tax return for that year will still arise.

An employee who is eligible for the SARP tax deduction will not be eligible for other tax reliefs, including the foreign earnings deduction and cross-border relief (set out in **Chapter 12, Sections 12.5.1.1** and **12.5.1.2**) and the R&D relief for key employees (set out in **Chapter 11, Section 11.2**). Also, where an employee is eligible for double taxation relief, this will reduce/eliminate the tax relief available under SARP. For further information on the operation of the SARP tax relief, see the *Revenue Operational Manual,* Part 34.00.10, Special Assignee Relief Programme (SARP), available on Revenue's website.

### Case Study: The Neally Engineering Group's Spanish Subsidiary Company

The Neally Engineering Group takes advice on the tax implications of Marta's secondment and discovers that if she is seconded to Ireland before the end of 2014, she will never be eligible for SARP relief. This is because she would be classified as a '2014 arrival', and therefore be subject to the condition that she must have worked for the Spanish company for at least 12 months before arrival into Ireland. Instead, Marta is seconded to Ireland from 1 January 2015 and is treated as a '2015 arrival', which means that the minimum pre-arrival employment period in Spain is reduced to six months. As Marta meets this condition and all other conditions attaching to SARP relief, she will be eligible for this tax relief.

Marta's 'relevant income' and total employment income for 2015 is €120,000, so she is entitled to the following SARP tax deduction for 2015:

$$(€120,000 - €75,000) \times 30\% = €13,500$$

This translates into an estimated tax saving of €5,400 (i.e. €13,500 × 40%, the marginal income tax rate for 2015).

### *13.4.2.4 Travel Expenses and Subsistence Payments*

The general rules in relation to the tax-free payment of travel and subsistence expenses for foreign employees seconded to Ireland on a temporary assignment not exceeding 24 months are set out at **Section 13.4.1.3** above.

For those employees who are entitled to SARP relief in a given tax year, there is a specific entitlement to payment/reimbursement of tax-free expenses as follows:

- The reasonable costs associated with one return trip from Ireland for the foreign employee (and their spouse/civil partner and children, where relevant) to any one of three different countries with which the foreign employee may have a connection. This return trip must occur during the tax year in which SARP relief is available to the foreign employee.
- The cost of primary/secondary school fees in Ireland, to a maximum of €5,000 per annum, for each child of the foreign employee or their spouse/civil partner.[15]

[15] Section 825C(6) TCA 1997.

### *13.4.3 PRSI (Social Security) Rules in Relation to Travel and Secondment by Foreign Employees into Ireland*

In **Chapter 12, Section 12.5.3** we looked at Irish PRSI obligations for Irish employees being seconded abroad and noted that the concept of tax residence is irrelevant in this regard. The reverse of this is also generally true, i.e. Irish social security obligations may arise for the foreign employee seconded to Ireland purely by virtue of the fact that they carry out employment duties in Ireland.

Also set out in **Chapter 12** were three possible approaches in relation to Irish PRSI obligations and these apply in the opposite direction also, i.e. where the employee is being seconded to Ireland. In brief, the approaches are:

1. The employee is seconded from any country within the European Economic Area (EEA). The production of a Form A1 from the social security authorities of any EEA Member State will eliminate any Irish PRSI obligations for the foreign employee.

CASE STUDY: THE NEALLY ENGINEERING GROUP'S SPANISH SUBSIDIARY COMPANY

Marta was sent on an expected 15-month secondment to Ireland from Spain. As she intends to return to Spain after this secondment, the Spanish subsidiary of the Neally Engineering Group (which remains her employer) secures an A1 certificate from the Spanish social security authorities. This ensures that the Spanish subsidiary is not obliged to deduct Irish social security contributions from the salary Marta earns while working in Ireland, but the company remains responsible to the Spanish authorities for Marta's continuing Spanish social security obligations.

2. The employee is seconded from a country/region with which Ireland has a social security agreement, being: USA, Australia, New Zealand, Canada, Quebec, UK (covering the Isle of Man and the Channel Islands), South Korea and Japan. Again, Irish PRSI obligations may be avoided if a certificate of coverage from the social security authorities of any of these countries/regions is secured.
3. If the employee is seconded from a country other than those listed at 1 or 2 above, then the foreign employer will have Irish social security obligations to the Irish authorities. It is likely that social security obligations will also arise in that foreign country.

# INDEX